Remaking the Middle East

Edited by
Paul J. White and William S. Logan

BERG
Oxford • New York

First published in 1997 by
Berg
Editorial offices:
150 Cowley Road, Oxford, OX4 1JJ, UK
70 Washington Square South, New York, NY 10012, USA

© Paul J. White and William S. Logan 1997

Berg is an imprint of Oxford International Publishers Ltd.

Library of Congress Cataloging-in-Publication Data

Remaking the Middle East / edited by Paul J. White and William S.
Logan. -- English ed.
      p. cm. --(Nationalism and internationalism, ISSN 1360-93351)
   Includes bibliographical references (p.) and index.
   ISBN 1-85973-163-5 (alk. paper). -- ISBN 1-85973-168-6 (pbk. :
alk. paper)
      1. Middle East--Politics and government--1979-   I. White, Paul J.
II. Logan, William Stewart, 1942- .   III. Series.
DS63.1.R463 1997
956.9405´4--DC21   96-46379
                                                                          CIP

British Library Cataloguing-in-Publication Data

A catalogue record for this book is available from the British Library.

ISBN 1 85973 163 5 (Cloth)
      1 85973 168 6 (Paper)

Typeset by JS Typesetting, Wellingborough, Northants.
Printed in the United Kingdom by WBC Book Manufacturers, Bridgend, Mid Glamorgan.

Contents

Contents

Acknowledgement

The editors and authors warmly appreciate the support of the Deakin University Faculty of Arts Research Committee which helped make this publication possible.

Notes on Contributors

Shahram Akbarzadeh was born in Mash'had, a northern city of Iran, in 1964 and arrived in Australia in 1984. He completed his BA at Swinburne Institute of Technology (1989) and his MSocSc (Russian and East European Studies) at the University of Birmingham (1991), and is currently working on the role of Islam in the politics of the three republics of Tajikistan, Turkmenistan and Uzbekistan in the aftermath of the Soviet collapse for his Ph.D. thesis at La Trobe University. He visited this region in 1992. Some of the material for his article was collected during that visit. Among his publications are short entries on 'Kazakhstan', 'Kyrgyzstan', 'Tajikistan', 'Turkmenistan' and 'Uzbekistan' in *The SBS World Guide* (1994), and 'Another Trouble Spot: Tajikistan', *Arena* (Feb.–Mar. 1994).

David Beirman attained his Ph.D. from the University of New South Wales in 1990 for his thesis entitled *Impact of the Arab–Israeli Conflict 1967–1989 on Jewish Communities in Sydney, London, New York, the Making of Australian, British and U.S. Foreign Policy in the Middle East and Media Coverage of the Arab–Israeli Conflict*. He is a management consultant and the Director of the Israel Tourism Office (Australia). He has been a frequent commentator on the Arab–Israeli conflict and the peace process in the Australian media. He also lectures in postgraduate research methods at the University of Technology, Sydney.

Daryl Champion was a student of Jewish, Islamic and Christian history and culture for nearly ten years, privately and at the University of Sydney, before concentrating on the contemporary politics of the Middle East at Macquarie University, Sydney. He is now studying for a Ph.D., specialising in Middle East politics, at the Centre for Middle Eastern and Central Asian Studies at the Australian National University, Canberra.

Fiona Hill is a graduate of the erstwhile Middle Eastern Department at the University of Melbourne. She has taught Islamic and Middle Eastern Studies there and at Deakin University, and now lectures at Melbourne in 'Arab Society and Civilisation' for the Department of Arabic and Islamic Studies. Fiona is an Associate in Anthropology at the University of Melbourne, and tutors in Anthropology and Sociology at La Trobe University.

Michael Humphrey is a senior Lecturer in the School of Sociology at the University of New South Wales. He is a long-standing member of the Australasian Middle East Studies Association. He has published extensively on the themes of Lebanese immigrants, Islamic politics and labour migration in the Middle East. His publications include *Islam, Multiculturalism and Transnationalism: from the Lebanese Diaspora*, I. B. Tauris, 1995 (forthcoming) and he is currently writing books on 'Ethnicity and Globalisation' and 'Civil War in the City'.

Nabila Jaber obtained her Ph.D. in Sociology from the Southern Illinois University at Carbondale, Illinois, USA. Her doctoral work focused on women, development and 'modernisation' in the Middle East. She currently teaches in the Feminist Studies Department at the University of Canterbury, in Christchurch, New Zealand. She has published articles on women and Islam, gender and pay equity, and feminism and the politics of difference. She is currently working on two themes: feminism, nationalism and post-colonialism, and gender and war.

Maroun Kisirwani is Associate Professor of Public Administration at the American University of Beirut. He has been chairperson of the Department of Political Studies and Public Administration, adviser to Ministers of Administrative Reform in Lebanon and consultant to the Minister of Foreign Affairs. His publications include: *Patron–Client Politics and Bureaucratic Corruption: the Case of Lebanon* (1974); *Assessing the Impact of the Civil War on the Lebanese Administration* (co-authored with William Parle — 1978); *Foreign Interference as a Variable in the Religious Animosity in Lebanon* (1980) and *Lebanon in the Wake of the Gulf War* (1992).

William S. Logan is Professor of Geography and Director of Research in the Faculty of Arts at Deakin University, Melbourne, and formerly President of the Australasian Middle Eastern Studies Association. He was instrumental in establishing the Arabic and Middle East programmes at Deakin as well as exchange agreements between

Deakin and universities in Israel, Jordan, Turkey and the West Bank. He is a member of the Editorial Board of the *Journal of Arabic and Middle Eastern Studies.*

Larbi Sadiki is a member of the Cairo-based Arab Human Rights Organisation. He is a Maghrebi research scholar based at the Political Science Department, Australian National University, where he is a Ph.D. candidate. He is working on the process of 'Arab Democratisation and Political Islam'. Over the past three years he has done extensive fieldwork looking at the major Islamist movements in the Arab world. He also tutors politics and the Middle East studies courses at the ANU.

Jeremy Salt, a graduate of the University of Melbourne, has taught at universities in Australia and Turkey. He has written on the politics and recent history of the Middle East for a number of scholarly journals, including *Middle Eastern Studies, Journal of Palestine Studies, International Journal of Turkish Studies* and *JAIMES (Journal of Arabic, Islamic and Middle Eastern Studies).* His book, *Imperialism, Evangelism and the Ottoman Armenians: 1878–1896* was published in 1993 by Frank Cass.

Pam Stavropoulos lectures in Politics at Macquarie University. Her research interests include anthropological perspectives on International Relations, political theory and gender issues, and the politics of cross-cultural comparison.

Adam Tarock was Tehran correspondent for *The Guardian* and *The Times* of London, covering Iranian and Persian Gulf political developments in the 1960s. He has contributed to both Australian and overseas academic journals specialising in Middle East politics. He has also taught international relations at the Council for Adult Education in Melbourne. He is currently teaching politics at the University of Melbourne.

Derek Verrall attained his Ph.D. from the Department of International Relations at Deakin University in 1978 for a thesis 'The Development of the Soviet Navy Since World War II'. He currently teaches 'Introduction to Politics' and 'International Conflict Management' at Deakin University in the School of Australian Studies. His research interests are in the area of contemporary Russian Foreign Policy, with special emphasis on relations with former republics of the USSR.

Paul J. White is a member of the Centre for the Study of Asian and Middle Eastern Studies at Deakin University, where he is also part of the Editorial Board of the *Journal of Arabic and Middle Eastern Studies*. He has served as a committee member of the Australasian Middle East Studies Association and organised its Fifteenth Annual Conference in 1996. He is currently completing his Ph.D. in Political Science (Middle East Politics). His Ph.D. thesis concerns the political development of Kurdish nationalism in Turkey. He visited a Kurdish guerilla training camp in Lebanon in 1992, as part of fieldwork for this thesis. He has taught various Middle East Politics courses at Deakin University and the Royal Melbourne Institute of Technology, and also tutored in the same field at the University of Melbourne.

Introduction

William S. Logan and Paul J. White

The 1990s have emerged as a period of great change in the Middle East. Certainly, on the surface at least, there is the appearance of a new Middle East taking shape. These changes relate to moves towards peace and a greater stability than the region has known for generations. Economic progress is being made and some countries in the region are experiencing reconstruction following lengthy periods of international and civil war.

This is the optimistic view; deeper down, some analysts see simply more of the same – *plus ça change* . . .. Because of long-standing antipathies between countries in the region as well as contradictions in the current processes of international political readjustment, many of the changes, they argue, may be doomed to failure. Some of the analysts holding this view would also stress that worsening social conflict could still be on the agenda in the period ahead. Others would assert that additional vexed problems such as gender relations are no closer to resolution as a result of recent changes.

New hopes for peace, stability and reconstruction and political, economic and religious tensions, sometimes lingering from the past and sometimes newly emerging – these are the issues addressed by the thirteen authors in this volume. All the contributions bear on the central theme of change and obstacles and resistance to change in the Middle East as it nears the third millennium. Coming from differing disciplinary contexts, the papers defy convenient compartmentalisation, their themes mutually intertwining and overlapping. To a large extent they all also challenge stereotypes about the Middle East, showing the complexity of the underlying political, economic and social forces in the region, the major countries within it, their foreign policy problems and the major issues of nationalism, religion and gender relations confronting them. Pam Stavropoulos's discussion of Islam reflects the general approach of authors in this book to the

Middle East as a whole, as well as to the particular aspects of the Middle East that they tackle. Put shortly, this is that the Middle East, like Islam, 'subsumes considerable complexity and diversity, and cannot be reduced to any single essence or position. At the same time, it evokes and is identified with a number of themes, some of which are potentially contradictory'.

The Peace Process

For decades, particularly in the Cold War days, it was the Palestinian–Israeli conflict which seemed the critical barrier to re-establishing peace and stability in the Middle East. This struggle between two peoples over the same patch of the Middle East was certainly the most explosive element in the region's and, frequently, the world's political constitution, with the potential to flow over into conflict involving the major world powers. As well as Arab–Israeli wars fought out within the immediate area of the two main antagonists in 1948, 1967 and 1973, the United States's involvement on the Israeli side, the possession of nuclear capability by Israel, and the launching of Scud missiles on Tel Aviv by Iraq during the Gulf War have threatened peace on a much wider geographical scale.

A resolution of the Arab–Israel conflict thus evoked the greatest hope for a new Middle East that emerged at the start of the 1990s. Peace, many thought, would ultimately allow the establishment of sensible economic links – perhaps even an economic union after the European Community model – and prosperity would flow to all parties. But the promise of the Oslo and Madrid peace meetings has dwindled: the handing back of powers to the Palestinian authorities has been slower than expected, and the promises of massive international financial aid to Arafat's administration have not been delivered. On the other hand, elections for a representative Palestinian assembly have finally been held, the Palestinian national assembly has been convened, and Palestinian authorities control a range of administrative functions, including education and police, in the Gaza Strip and much of the Occupied West Bank. Jerusalem – claimed by three great world religions – remains a major stumbling-block, with both the major (Labor and Likud) parties in Israel adamant that the city is indivisible and should remain in Israeli hands. Continued confiscations of Arab lands around the city by the Israeli authorities – and in the West Bank and Gaza following the Likud Party's return to power – could well undo the progress so far made towards reaching a lasting peace. It also has to be asked whether the creation of an economic community would once again give the upper hand to Israel in its relations with its Arab neighbours.

David Beirman and Jeremy Salt take very different views on the Israel–Palestine conflict. Beirman believes that this nationalist conflict can be settled by enacting the sequence: ceasefire/peace treaty–economic development/territorial concessions – provided the United States continues to act as 'guarantor of the peace process'.

He sees both the Israeli government and the PLO as sincerely wanting the peace deal to continue, but believes that this opportunity to resolve the conflict only came about when the PLO finally signalled its 'acceptance of UN Resolutions 242 and 338 as the appropriate framework for peace', and indicated it was willing to 'renounce terrorism'. The Palestine National Council's further renunciation in April 1996 of the thirty-two-year-old call in the PLO Charter for Israel's destruction helps cement the orderly process of reconciliation foreseen by Beirman.

According to Beirman, another vital element was the collapse of the USSR and thus of the Cold War – previously 'the most significant element guiding United States Middle East policy from 1945 to 1990'. It was this historic event, he argues, that compelled the PLO to improve relations with the United States, allowing the latter eventually 'to oppose Israel openly on certain key policies', thus further encouraging a more conciliatory PLO. The United States has remained actively involved following the signing of the PLO–Israel Accord, by trying to draw other Arab states (especially Syria) into the peace process. Without discounting the ability of extremists inside Palestine/Israel to do considerable mischief (especially the Islamist Hamas), Beirman believes firmly that the future of the process now depends above all on whether the United States will remain resolute and actively involved, using its tremendous strength as a pressure for and 'guarantor of the peace process'.

While Beirman's focus is mostly towards an outside player in the Palestine–Israel conflict, Jeremy Salt's is directed at showing how the Arabs (including the Palestinians) themselves see the events since the emergence of the 'Palestinian problem' in 1948. For large numbers of Arabs, he explains, Israel's establishment that year represented nothing less than '*al-Nakba* – the disaster' of Palestinian dispossession from their homeland. Nor is he any more optimistic regarding the peace agreement between the PLO and Israel, predicting that its only results will be to 'enable Arab governments to unburden themselves of the vexatious "Palestinian problem"', and to allow Israel to flood the West Bank with settlers, while entering lucrative Arab markets for the first time.

Salt then discusses European colonial domination and the Arab nationalist search for alternative identities to those imposed by the colonisers. The Arab states that eventually emerged were stunted societies, soon locked in an unequal battle for full independence with the developed West. The Arabs were humiliated and their social and economic difficulties exacerbated.

The heyday of Arab nationalism after the Second World War brought 'radical' Arab states (principally Egypt) directly into conflict not only with Britain, France and the United States, but also with the resource-rich countries of the Gulf. The withdrawal of Britain and France left the United States and the USSR as the key external players in the region. The collapse of the USSR made it possible for the United States to assert a hegemonic role unparalleled in the modern history of the region. Playing on the fears of conservative Gulf States and the desperate economic needs of poorer countries such as Egypt, the United States has been able to establish a network of dependent states in the region. On frequent occasions these states have shown themselves incapable of taking collective action to defend even the clearest Arab interest, in Salt's estimation.

Unemployment, economic disparities and the inability to accommodate political change have created a rising tide of popular unrest throughout the region. Looking at the ramifications, Salt asks whether in combination all the issues impinging on their lives 'are taking away from the Arabs as people the right to define themselves, control their own territory and resources and determine their future'.

Locating the Palestinian question in the general context of Arab politics, Salt views the 1993 agreement between the PLO leadership and the government of Israel as an imposed treaty devoid of any basis in the internationally acknowledged rights of the Palestinians. Far from preparing to withdraw from the territories seized in 1967, the West Bank in particular, Israel has used the treaty to entrench its military, strategic and settler presence there. Palestinian opposition is now widespread, not just in the ten 'rejectionist' groups based in Damascus, but in the mainstream.

Peace – a real peace – remains a possibility, but only provided Israel withdraws from the territories taken in 1967 and acknowledges Palestinian claims to Jerusalem as part of a historical accommodation with the Palestinian people. This, unfortunately, does not appear to be likely, given the pace of Israeli settlement on the West Bank and around Jerusalem. The Palestinians are despondent, but 'Palestine' as an issue is unlikely to disappear among Arabs in general. Given Israel's nuclear weaponry, and the inevitable pressure on Arab governments to develop a nuclear capacity of their own, the failure to reach a durable settlement has frightening implications. As Salt concludes, 'the historic choices are now in the hands of the Israeli people and their government'.

Daryl Champion complements the contributions by Beirman and Salt. His chapter takes up the vexed question of religious fundamentalism – not Islamic, but Jewish, probing whether this phenomenon poses a threat to Israel's security. Jewish fundamentalists have been in the forefront of the Israeli opposition to the PLO–Israel Accord, with the February 1994 Hebron Massacre and the November 1995 slaying of Prime Minister Yitzhak Rabin being two of the most shocking manifestations of the radical Jewish opposition to Israeli–Palestinian reconciliation so far witnessed. Exploring the origins and principal factions of Jewish fundamentalism, the author traces the emergence of such groups as the Gush Emunim in the 1970s, who campaign for a Jewish *Eretz Yisrael* (Greater Israel), involving the consolidation of Israeli control over the Occupied Territories and, in some cases, the conquest of other Arab lands. This perspective, of course, if implemented, would spell the end of prospects for regional peace, which would endanger Israel's security. Champion also argues that Jewish fundamentalism is destabilising Israel on the domestic front, as it cannot but unsettle a country founded as the culmination of a secular ideology.

What could have been described as an Israeli social paradox – symbolised by the September 1993 Washington Accord and the Hebron Massacre – characterised most of 1994 and 1995. 'Paradox', however, may now be seen as an ambiguous term for the process of polarisation that culminated in the 1996 elections for the fourteenth Knesset. This process was discernible many years ago, but its results are now entrenched and are openly admitted by Israelis across the spectrum of society and politics. Whatever threat to Israel's security Gush Emunim and similar groupings represented in the past is only likely to become further cemented with the electoral victory of the broadly goal-sympathetic – if not ideologically-sympathetic – Likud-dominated bloc. The immediate risk of civil clashes between the state and these groupings has been reduced, but the new paradox is one that will see the seeds of future and more serious disturbance send down deeper roots while, despite ideological cleavage, an outward appearance of relative calm between Israelis prevails.

With the new political environment in Israel, under Prime Minister Benjamin Netanyahu, the more extremist Jewish fundamentalist elements have become emboldened; whether – or how much – tangible support is received from the new government remains to be seen. It is possible that actions conceived during the Rabin–Peres era that were calculated to thwart peace initiatives and prevent the relinquishing of Israeli-controlled territory may proceed less in desperation than in new-found hope and justification. Thus, during the period immediately ahead, internal social strains may yet be played out. The extremist minorities of Jewish fundamentalism, Champion demonstrates, have the potential to bring down the state of Israel from within. Clearly, Rabin's assassination and the subsequent political turmoil and social division in Israel fit this thesis, although civil crisis has no doubt been averted for the time being. But a postponement of the inevitable confrontation between divergent Israeli destinies is only likely to make that confrontation more destructive when it does occur. In the meantime, it is also clear that the peace process as witnessed in the region is not going to continue as it has to date.

While Islamic fundamentalism is seen negatively by the non-Islamic world, and receives particularly hostile treatment in the Western media as a whole, Daryl Champion's chapter on Israeli Jewish fundamentalism provides an interesting and necessary counterbalance. In the case of the most significant 'remaking' of the Middle East, the Israel–PLO deal, it can be seen that there are compelling reasons why some observers would argue that very little has really changed for the most numerous players in these real-life dramas – the ordinary people on the ground. Similar conclusions can arguably also be drawn for the other countries and regional groupings discussed in this book. In some instances, it has even been contended, the basic problems remain, only these now become deeper and more threatening to social stability.

The Post-Cold War Environment

In the post-Cold War world, the United States' role as power-broker in the Middle East has emerged as super-eminent, reshaping, among other things, the nature of opposition to its protégé, Israel. The realignment of Saudi Arabia and the Gulf States with the United States – and hence, indirectly, with Israel – during the Gulf War seems to be holding. This was a key change in Middle Eastern political orientations and international relations, in line with the United States' self-perception as the guardian of the New Order in a post-Communist world. It undermined Arab solidarity in the fight against Iraq's Saddam Hussein – the primary objective; but its other major effect was to split these wealthy regimes away from supporting the Arab states opposed to Israel. In the case of the Palestinians, Yasser Arafat's apparent support for President Hussein did not help win friends in the United States, or anywhere else for that matter.

Introduction

The PLO was not alone in being caught out by the rapid pace of post-Cold War political developments. The collapse of the Soviet Union in the late 1980s left the various Central Asian republics to fend for themselves politically and economically. They are being wooed by both Turkey and Iran, but the Russians, having come to a new realisation of the imperial nature of their state, have not given up their efforts to keep the Central Asian republics within Moscow's orbit. Oil and gas resources make the republics particularly attractive. The inclination of the republics appears to be to realign themselves with the Middle East, making a major extension to the traditional notion of the region and justifying the inclusion in this volume of chapters dealing with them. The revival of Islamic cultural identity may give strength to such a realignment, but regimes tend also to stir up narrower nationalist feelings that engender instability and often belligerence towards neighbouring states.

The collapse of the Soviet Union and international Communism caught politicians and political commentators alike by surprise. No longer was Soviet power a countervailing force in the Middle East, as Beirman has indicated. The Soviet collapse has clearly had a major geopolitical impact on the Middle East itself, especially by encouraging competing Middle Eastern states – Turkey and Iran – to extend their influence over the territories once part of the Soviet Union. The role of Islam in this refiguring of political alignments and, indeed, the extension of the notion of 'Middle East' to cover neighbouring ex-Soviet territories has been crucial.

Shahram Akbarzadeh dissects the complex experiences of three important Islamic Central Asian republics – Tajikistan, Turkmenistan and Uzbekistan – in the wake of the Soviet Union's collapse. Popular resistance to the Soviet Communist Party's attempts to smother Islam in these three republics had ultimately proved successful. In fact, Akbarzadeh indicates, Islam seems to be the key to this remarkable turn of events. Surprisingly, however, the leaders of the new, allegedly Muslim, states are no other than their previous Communist Party rulers.

In examining how Islam – or what posed as Islam – was mobilised for political ends in these states, Akbarzadeh explains that Moscow was both a source of power and a source of conflict for the Central Asian élites prior to the Soviet collapse. Before this collapse, nationalist opposition to Moscow was tied to arguments for protecting Islamic traditions. When the Soviet empire's disintegration occurred, the native Central Asian élites 'returned to supposedly traditional modes of government'. The predominant feature of this was the instrumental use of Islamic images: 'Linking the present (often authoritarian) politics with traditions that are presented as indigenous has been largely successful in circumventing socio-political instability.'

The author argues that the prevalence of Islamic images results from the post-Soviet regimes in Central Asia searching for acceptable identities for these newly independent states – states in which culture is 'unimaginable without Islamic traditions'. In reality, he argues, it is not simply Islamic traditions that are being revived by élites desperate for new legitimacy, but a fusion of native 'pagan cultural traditions' and politically stunted Islam.

Akbarzadeh shows how (except for Tajikistan's rulers), the old native élites in Central Asia were able to survive the immediate post-USSR period undamaged. The exception seems to prove the rule, however; the Tajik élite's difficulties sprang from its initial hesitation to embrace Islamic symbols at the onset of the Soviet break-up. Thus, despite the Soviet leaders' promises to eradicate religion, it appears that religion was still able to march boldly in through the front door the moment that the Russian system collapsed. The more that Central Asia politically and culturally renovates itself, it could therefore be argued, the more it reverts to previously dominant political and cultural forms, as in the Middle East. Indeed, as Akbarzadeh shows, Islam was already beginning to have an effect before the Soviet system fell completely. What was really at work here was not so much religious as national fervour: 'the durability of culture, not in spite of, but especially because of, external pressure'.

Derek Verrall extends the discussion of the search for national identity in Central Asia to introduce the aspect of economic development in these states. Verrall echoes Akbarzadeh's view that events have proved that religion had not been eradicated in Central Asia, as the Soviet Union's leaders had formerly boasted. Verrall shows, however, that Moscow's granting of a form of nationhood to the Central Asian states – 'while insisting on the supremacy of the central state and proclaiming the aim of transcending national separateness and ethnic identity' within the old Soviet Union – 'resulted in an inherently unstable dualism'. This perceived dualism soon broke down with the USSR's demise.

The post-Soviet independent Central Asian states were ethnically heterogeneous, however. Pockets of irredentist peoples in each of these Soviet republics were left uncatered for as the maps were redrawn, creating potential territorial disputes. Earlier, in the 1920s, the modernisation of the Central Asian states had been achieved at great human cost. More recently, what Verrall terms a 'creeping Russification' alarmed the Central Asians, becoming a serious issue in the region following the USSR's collapse, as did the lower status of ethnic minorities in the newly independent states. Civil disturbances resulted.

Verrall argues that the Central Asian states' economic development was distorted, keeping them both backward economically and dependent upon Russia. Now members of the new Commonwealth of Independent States (CIS), the Central Asian states face the daunting challenges of building links with Moscow and neighbouring countries on a non-dependent, equitable basis, and of achieving real economic growth. While some progress has been made, real problems remain in achieving these goals. At the same time, however, there is an inadequate basis for the Central Asian states to turn away from Russia – however unsatisfactory the relationship with the latter – in favour of a 'Central Asian Commonwealth'. Nor does joining an organisation of economic co-operation with Iran, Pakistan or Turkey seem likely. The distortions introduced into the Central Asian states' economies during the previous long period of Soviet domination seem to compel continued close economic ties with the new CIS. Increased ties with the industrialised West are being attempted, but these, Verrall argues, are also a source of serious conflict between Moscow and the Central Asian states.

Like Akbarzadeh, Verrall shows how the search for national identity in Central Asia has involved an adaptation of Islam and led to conflict with Moscow, adding that the focus of the conflict soon shifted to 'a series of increasingly violent incidents', in which ethnic minorities in the region were attacked and even massacred. The economic problems cited earlier, plus the complex internal problems in each state of ethnic and national identity, the reader must conclude, pose daunting tasks for the future fortunes of Central Asia.

The foreign policy of Iran, competitor with Turkey for influence over the Central Asian states, is discussed by Adam Tarock, particularly concentrating on the period since the 1990–91 Gulf War. Tarock maintains that, far from being a secure, expansive regional power, Iran feels threatened by its neighbours, not to mention the West, particularly the United States. In reality, he argues, Iran's foreign policy responses are not expansionist, but merely calculated to defend its own immediate interests. Thus, Iran stood on the same side as the United States against Saddam Hussein in the Gulf War, and has followed a concerted policy of winning the trust and economic co-operation of the Western-inclined Arab Gulf states and the six newly independent Central Asian states.

Iran's friendly gestures towards these states have brought it very limited economic or political returns, however, although some very modest breakthroughs have been made with the smaller Gulf sheikhdoms and the Central Asian republics. The strong United States military presence continues in the region, and the Gulf sheikhdoms remain willingly under the American eagle's protective wing. Meanwhile, Egypt and Israel have been urging the United States since the Gulf War to deal with the remaining regional threat, Iran, now that Saddam has been weakened. The threat to Iran from the United States must be said to be increasing – yet Iran has so far been unsuccessful in convincing even the Gulf State rulers to form a security alliance with it. Unconvinced that Saddam Hussein's might has been totally broken, the Gulf States remain cautiously wedded to a protective military alliance with the United States, and are unlikely to go against America in any serious way.

The Iranians must also be concerned that the break-up of the Soviet empire has not brought relief from another external threat, but has simply multiplied the threats to its interests. The Central Asian states that emerged from the old USSR have attracted some of the Islamic Republic's potent traditional rivals, such as Turkey and Saudi Arabia. Even more worryingly, the United States – already being urged to teach stern military lessons to the Iranians – now has its hands free of its former global rival, the former Soviet Union.

Iran under Prime Minister Rafsanjani shows signs of seeking a *rapprochement* with the West – Europe, Canada and even Australia and New Zealand, if perhaps not yet the United States. It is still seen as the cradle of aggressive Islamic fundamentalism and as encouraging international terrorism. How much of this is real, and how much is this image the result of America's need to find a new bogeyman now that the threat of international communism has evaporated? And how much of Iran's responses to the changes continues to be dictated by the perceived need by its power élite to divert public attention towards external opponents, in order to mollify opposition among the country's poorer classes who were the backbone of the 1979 'Islamic Revolution'?

Iran's recent actions to end its isolation have yet to bear rich fruit, and Tarock argues that such rewards are unlikely to be plucked by the Islamic Republic while the United States remains in a condition of deepening hostility. This problem, above all others, must be overcome by the Iranians, or else economic chaos could threaten 'the very survival of the regime' by the year 2000. Clearly, the United States believes that economic pressure will cause the Iranian system to implode – as the Soviet system did. United States military action is possible against Iran, should this approach fail. Iran is obviously faced with a complex and menacing future; it remains to be seen whether armed conflict can be avoided.

Nationalism and Democratisation

Development problems throughout the Middle East have thrown social and political movements into flux. Movements favouring nationalism, democratisation, secularisation, or a turn to political Islam have all come up against serious obstacles. In stark contrast to the Palestinians, therefore, the Kurds have yet to obtain any degree of ethnic autonomy within the states that contain them – Turkey, Iraq, Iran, Syria and the new Republic of Armenia. For a time, in the immediate aftermath of the Gulf War, they caught the sympathetic attention of the international media. The world learnt, to its surprise, that the Kurds are one of the most populous – indeed, perhaps the largest – ethnic group to remain without its own state. Hopes glimmered that a new Middle Eastern state was a possibility. Following the recent disastrous conflicts with the Iraqi and, more recently, the Turkish armies, this prospect has disappeared over the horizon once again.

Paul White's chapter examines the clash between Turkish and Kurdish nationalisms in Turkey. White shows that both these nationalisms have failed, leaving open the possibility of a full-blooded civil war between the two communities. On the Kurdish side, the principal Kurdish nationalist movement, the Kurdistan Workers Party (PKK) launched a bloody guerilla insurgency in 1984. Over a decade later, the only result is more than 15,000 civilians, guerillas and security forces dead, many thousands more wounded or maimed, and still more forced out of their homes in the disputed region. The war has even spread across the border into Iraq's Kurdish region – the supposed 'Kurdish Safe Haven' – as the Turkish military displays determination to purge PKK bases and civilian supporters.

The various phases of this violent intra-nationalist conflict are outlined – including the missed opportunities for a peaceful settlement between the warring political forces. Arguably, unlike Northern Ireland or Israel/Palestine, where it is usually asserted that peace processes are now in action, the war between the PKK and the Turkish state appears obstinately to elude a political settlement. Despite the urgings of opposition MPs in Turkey's parliament, the PKK's attempts to organise a ceasefire, and its willingness to drop the cherished demand of an independent state, Ankara remains adamant that it will never negotiate with 'PKK terrorists'.

The explanation seems to be that the army – which has staged *coups d'état* in 1960, 1971 and 1980 – is not as distant from the centre of power as is often asserted by mainstream Turkish politicians. White argues that the top echelons of the military have merged with industry and business leaders, to 'become a very central part of the political apparatus of the state, as well as remaining its physical guardians' and giving it 'considerable autonomy from the rest of the ruling political apparatus'. Both sides in this conflict are aware that a political settlement must eventually be concluded, White claims, since neither can definitively destroy the other. In the meantime, however, the fighting continues, with civilian Kurds and Turks continuing to pay a very high price.

Larbi Sadiki argues that several Arab countries appear set on a more felicitous course. Sadiki's chapter surveys trends towards democratisation in Algeria and Egypt. His study is set against the background of a perceived general trend towards democratisation in a dozen Arab countries. The article concentrates especially on progress made by Algeria and Egypt towards more 'pluralist politics' and upon the factors which tend to inhibit this progress. In both countries, the author argues, what appear to be democratic reforms are more accurately understood as top-down partial liberalisations, which change nothing fundamental in the established power structure.

Turning then to current tension between violent secular nationalism and political Islam, he concludes that 'the spiral of violence and counter-violence exemplifies the uncertainties and contradictions inherent in Algeria's and Egypt's liberalisations'. Further, while far-reaching economic liberalisation has continued in both countries, both of them also experience 'continued political centralisation' coupled with rising political repression.

Sadiki discusses the political dilemma posed by the exclusion of radical political Islam from the legal political framework of Algeria and Egypt:

> The secularisation quandary has created a kind of Catch-22 situation. On the one hand, no secularisation, and for that matter, real democratisation, can be achieved if polity is Islamised. This is argued to cause tensions as between irreconcilable notions of popular and divine sovereignty. On the other hand, if secularisation is to be about democratisation it cannot be so if it excludes an important segment – Islamists – of the civil society from political participation and contestation.

Arguing that it seems impossible to prevent the politicisation of Islam in these two countries, Sadiki predicts that both Algeria and Egypt will be compelled to allow the Islamists entry to the legal political process. Neither physical repression nor attempts at state co-optation of the Islamists will persuade the latter to cease their drive towards political power. The secular nationalists will have to open the door to political Islam, or themselves risk delegitimisation.

In reaching this conclusion, Sadiki notes how the 'hysteria' of the various secular Arab regimes over the Islamists has become internationalised: 'There is a new Arab inter-dependence, with a concerted effort to combat Islamism. The effort has been scapegoatist, with Iran and Sudan being linked to Islamist violence, a linkage that is yet to be substantiated.'

In a more general chapter, 'Dichotomy and Complementarity: Tenets of Islam and their Interrelationship', Pam Stavropoulos explores diverse approaches within Islam to issues that have become central to our troubled turn-of-the-century world – nationalism compared with internationalism, and 'modernity' contrasted with 'tradition'. This approach enables her to show that both dissonance and complementarity exist within Islam on these vital issues – while affirming that a core 'Islamic ideal' nevertheless still remains intact.

In Stavropoulos's analysis, a certain dynamic ambivalence is typical of rich and complex phenomena such as Islam. Thus apparently counterposed terms such as 'nationalism' and 'internationalism' do not necessarily confront each other antagonistically. Similarly, reality is frequently more complex than the usual complacent opposition of 'modernity' and 'tradition' suggests. Otherwise, how can one explain occurrences such as the use of modern electronics to bring to the Muslim faithful the amplified *Qur'an*?

Few readers can legitimately question this author's stress on the richness and complexity of Islam – especially modern Islam – and her warning against placing Islamic debates about 'modernity' and 'tradition' within a Western framework and without reference to the dynamics and impetus of Islam's evolution. Stavropoulos does not deny that tensions exist within Islam, between the concepts under examination; indeed, her article illuminates many of these contradictions. Her point is simply that the concepts themselves are multi-dimensional within Islam and that the existing tensions are not easily or simplistically resolved. Dichotomies in Islam, she contends, can neither be glossed over nor uni-dimensionally opposed: 'The more one rebels against seeming contradiction, the more one becomes enmeshed in it.' At the same time, she suggests that Islam's 'long history of adaptation and accommodation' might even suggest that it is able to contain these tensions, through synthesising a 'middle way'. Such synthesis will not develop easily but, she asserts, a road leading to it must be found.

Civil War and Reconstruction

The recent history of this region is one marked by a sorry cycle of crisis, war and physical and spiritual reconstruction, prior to a new onset of violence. The Lebanese Civil War, the Iran–Iraq War, the Gulf War are merely the most obvious examples in this destructive pattern. Contributions by Michael Humphrey and Maroun Kisirwani examine this phenomenon from different angles. Michael Humphrey's chapter, 'Civil War, Community and State in the Middle East', provides a context for the discussion by Maroun Kisirwani of the process of reconstruction in Lebanon following its long and disastrous civil war. In particular, Humphrey examines a sensitive issue too often ignored in Western academic discourse – the political significance and social impact of violence in civil wars. He asserts that 'the violence of civil wars is as integral to the rearrangement of people/state relations in the contemporary world as it has been to the history of nation-state formation'.

After showing how civil wars are variously interconnected with states outside the territory where the wars are raging, he discusses the methods used by governments to discredit insurgent oppositions. Whatever method is used, he suggests, a degree of destabilisation in governmental authority seems inevitable.

Humphrey examines alternative explanations of the savagery of civil conflicts. This leads him to question whether any counterweights to unrestrained political violence exist in 'peripheral states'. Examining civil wars as wars between unintegrated communities, Humphrey sees this phenomenon as both the most common cause of civil conflict and its bloodiest variant. Developed Western states have no reason for smugness in this interpretation, however, since the author sees these wars resulting from the failed logic of colonisation (which involved using social and cultural divisions to divide and conquer) and decolonisation (which left the former colony with the unenviable task of forming a coherent and mutually beneficial whole out of colonialism's divisive legacy).

Humphrey squarely confronts what is arguably the most chilling aspect of civil war violence – the ritualised acceptance by the warring communities of a frightening, even unrelenting level of violence, torture and killing. This is the 'space of death', in which 'death itself can act as the basis of a discourse on the amoral and anarchic'. It is therefore hardly surprising that massacres are so prevalent in civil wars, from ex-Yugoslavia to Rwanda. Once again, hopes are being dashed (in these cases the hopes for national security and freedom) upon the rocky shores of contemporary political realities. This could arguably have been the case in the Middle East, where the conflicts in Israel/ Palestine, Turkey/Kurdistan may appear as bloodily intractable as ever.

The apparently increasing number of such bloody civil wars is likely to result in more outside states seeking to intervene in them, giving the need to impose order as their rationale. The examples used by the author to illustrate and demonstrate his arguments are several, including several Middle Eastern states. Humphrey points out that the Kurds are an example of the extreme difficulty in creating new states through 'self-determination' struggles. The Kurdish nationalists' use of outside intervention – especially from members of the Kurdish diaspora – is also cited as an important lever in their conflict with the Turkish state. Humphrey's observation that a country beset with civil war faces threats to its territorial sovereignty, not to mention 'its monopoly over the use of violence', is an apt one, and one that applies to a number of states. Such states become vulnerable to outside intervention, and frequently find themselves becoming the 'site of many proxy wars conducted by a variety of states through their support for local surrogates'.

The chapter by Maroun Kisirwani turns the book's focus away from the actualities of civil strife and warfare to post-war reconstruction in a key Middle Eastern country. The author tackles the difficult task of the rehabilitation and reconstruction of Lebanon, following the 1975–89 civil war in that country. He examines progress made in rebuilding the country's political, administrative and economic system, and the obstacles which these efforts have encountered. This examination is based on scrutiny of Lebanon's unique political system, and an estimation of the Lebanese state's viability – including the capacity of its bureaucrats to implement reconstruction.

Kisirwani makes the magnitude of the reconstruction and rehabilitation necessary quite clear. Commenting upon what he terms the 'permanent pathologies of the bureaucracy', however, he doubts the eventual success of this project: 'Unless political harmony is reached among communal groups and national consensus is developed, and unless the bureaucracy itself is rehabilitated and fortified against political interference and sectarian cleavages, the reconstruction of Lebanon will remain an unattainable objective far beyond Horizon 2000.'

If Lebanon is rebuilding its social structures, economic framework and physical infrastructure, including its strife-torn cities, following the cessation of its civil war, are the social cracks merely plastered over waiting to reappear as a result of interference from one or more of its neighbours? This ties back into the earlier discussion of the Middle East peace negotiations, not only between Israel and the Palestinians but also between Israel and Syria. However, even if the Golan is returned to Syria and Syria ceases using Lebanon as an advance base for its hostilities against Israel, there is still the Iranian influence at work among some anti-Israel groups in Lebanon. Until Israel withdraws from its self-declared security zone in southern Lebanon, as required by UN Resolution 425, the motivation for continued strikes against the Israeli occupying forces and, indeed, Israel itself, will remain. Inter-ethnic frictions between Lebanon's religious groups may also erupt over what might seem to outsiders to be minor issues.

Islam and Gender Relations

Islam's teachings on the role of women in society have long been the subject of fascination in the West. The final two essays in this collection address pertinent aspects of this question. The chapter by Nabila Jaber echoes and extends some aspects of the discussion in Pam Stavropoulos's contribution. Yet, while the Stavropoulos chapter examines approaches within Islam to nationalism compared with internationalism, and 'modernity' contrasted with 'tradition', Jaber's chapter discusses and contrasts the twin themes of nationhood and gender equality, investigating how women's identity is reconstructed in the discourses of nationalism and Islam.

According to Jaber, Arab Muslim women (like most women in the world) are fundamentally placed in a subordinate, secondary position. Already subjugated by male sexual 'rights' and paternal privileges, as these form the foundation of Islamic *Shari'ah* law, it therefore follows that the project of Arab nationalism must 'also construct patriarchal supremacy' so as not to disavow, while implicitly affirming, the legitimacy of such a repressive framework. While the notions of a state based on Islamic law and one founded on secular national concepts are normally thought of as opposites, Jaber points out that, in both concepts, 'the positioning of women as a specific group is held crucial in maintaining the linkage between the two. In one community women's nationality is regulated by the *'umma*, through the *Shari'ah* law; in the other it is constructed as a "state" agent, following specific secular doctrines, associated with civil laws'.

The modern nation-state exalts the nation-state and nationalism as of overriding importance. Nationalism engulfs and subsumes all other identities (including women's), elevating the state 'as the sole legitimate force and protector of citizens' rights'. Islam is already clearly constructed as 'an exclusively male domain'. The Islamist scheme of an Islamic nation-state, while obviously different from a secular state, provides no liberation for women from patriarchal forms, since 'women are positioned in a relationship of dependency and subordination to men's will' in even the most 'modernist' discourse within Islam.

While nationalist movements in the developing world generally have, by contrast, 'created a space for women from which to speak and organise a multiplicity of women's interests', Jaber argues that the achievement of national independence in the Arab world has proved to be limited, particularly for women. It has already been noted above how Stavropoulos asserts that a certain dynamic ambivalence is typical of complex phenomena, allowing apparently contradictory designations such as 'nationalism' and 'internationalism' to co-exist harmoniously. For Jaber, nationalism and Islam both seem antagonistic to the interests of women as autonomous subjects, as both wish to relegate women to the sphere of domesticity (even when taking on their designated roles in the public arena). Whether anchored in secularism or merged with Islam, nationalist discourses 'remain fundamentally sexist and discriminatory and provide women with little opportunity to challenge their subordination to patriarchal institutions'.

Fiona Hill's chapter utilises the dual themes of gender and tradition to examine the status of Syrian women. Once again, a feminist problematic is employed to investigate relevant nationalist and Islamist ideologies. The author's argument 'that the cultural, political, and religious codes of the region create points of intersection, and of tension, for all women' echoes some of Jaber's concerns – although in a divergent manner, and with a different specific focus.

Hill examines the agendas of 'espoused ideologies of religious conservatives and modernists, of nationalists and of socialists in the region' and questions whether these advance Middle East women's rights. The answer seems basically negative, for she concludes that a tension exists 'between formulations of Arab feminism in Western/imperialist and Third World/Marxist paradigms'. Rather than propose that Arab women oppose these paradigms, however, she points to the over-arching 'paradigm of patriarchy in the Arab world, which displays so many points of convergence with orientalist/imperialist epistemology in its conscious and politically effective fixing of difference between the sexes'.

For Hill patriarchy today is the outcome of not only colonialism, but also 'the indigenous domains'. She stresses that this patriarchal 'intersection' of colonial and indigenous chauvinisms is played out 'on the body of women'; the Arab woman therefore often suffers physical repression, and even physical violence, in addition to the traditional woman's burden of not being assessed for who she is, but only by what the man who accompanies her is.

In Syria, official women's bureaux are often seen by many women as self-serving bureaucracies of little practical use to women in general. Focusing on Syria once again, Hill suggests that women's 'rights' in this 'patriarchal' society are defined with respect to 'their place in a family, and in a co-local, and often confessional, community, rather than in terms of their position as citizens of the state'. Yet, precisely because Syria is a patriarchal society in the author's view, 'it is questionable whether Syrian women can fully define their rights in their own communities, let alone feel the impact of state policy in their daily lives'. If this is so, the reader might conclude, here is another important Middle East country where resistance to change is proving stubborn.

With the exception of the contributions by Tarock and White, the chapters in this book were originally presented as papers at the 1993 Conference of the Australasian and Middle East Studies Association, held at Deakin University, Melbourne. All papers have been substantially updated and reworked for publication. The views expressed in them are those of the authors, and are offered as part of an on-going scholarly debate about the past, present and future character of the Middle Eastern region.

– 1 –

Civil War, Community and State in the Middle East

Michael Humphrey

The fascination with civil war in the modern world derives from its popular representation as something abnormal, something discontinuous with the world of 'peaceful' nation-states. The sight of 'communities' brutally murdering each other, motivated, apparently, by ancient enmities and unconstrained by their states, suggests both a breakdown of order and a reversion to the barbaric, the uncivilised. International news reporting, through its concentration on the sensational and violent, reinforces this perception by witnessing trouble spots as remote and alien, evoking responses like: 'What a mess we have here!'; 'How could it be like this!'; 'How could people do this to each other?'; 'The best thing to do is stand back and let them finish among themselves.' The medium of television, in particular, acts as a mirror in which we witness the inverse image of our ordered worlds – chaos. The Middle East is a region that has long been treated as the mirror of our ordered world.

This paper explores the meta-narrative implicit in the 'coverage' of civil wars and the discourse on violence and identity by participants. It argues that the discourse on civil wars is both an indication of the contemporary crisis of the nation-state in many parts of the Middle East, and in the South more generally, and a window on the changing relationship between the global and local.

The focus is on the politics of fear and the construction of political cleavages, reinforced by the re-writing of history as communal, through violence. The subject is that of massacre, its political significance in civil wars, its social impact, and its importance in the international discourse on intervention. The argument presented here is that the violence of civil wars is as integral to the rearrangement of people–state relations in the contemporary world as it has been to the history of nation-state formation.

Michael Humphrey

War, State-Making and Un-Making

Civil wars, by definition, take place within the boundaries of states, in contrast to wars between states. The fact that since 1945 most wars have been civil wars is a measure of the global ascendancy of the nation-state as the standard political unit and the fixity of territorial boundaries within the inter-state system. The same holds for the Middle East. Sectarian violence in Lebanon, Kurdish autonomist and secessionist movements in Iraq and Turkey, the Black September repression of PLO fighters in Jordan, the Islamist struggle against the state in Algeria and Egypt, the Iranian revolution and even the *intifada* in the Occupied Territories are all cases of war between the state and segments of the population rather than with other states. Even the wars between the Arab states, the Palestinians and the Israelis and the war between Iran and Iraq have their origins in political contests over the control of the state – civil war – and the politics of intervention in support of one side or another.

Civil wars are about the crisis of the nation-state and its perceived failure to recognise the collective interests and rights of a particular section of the population *vis-à-vis* the state and the dominant cultural group. State power is seen to have been seriously eroded by economic crisis and lack of political legitimacy. This makes the central political issue in civil wars the role of state power and its capture by a particular group or segment of society to the disadvantage of others. Thus, although civil wars are generally seen to be, and represented as, conflicts between proto-national groupings (tribal, religious or ethnic), the underlying issue is control of the state apparatus and the social integration of the population in a national community.

Most civil wars have been about capturing the existing state rather than creating a new and separate state. The task of creating a new state through national self-determination and succession has become very difficult, because states police not only their own boundaries but those of their neighbours as well. Hence the Kurdish national aspirations to create their own state in the post-Gulf War uprising had few prospects of success because they were opposed by both Saddam's regime and the Turkish state. The idea that a Kurdish state contiguous to its own could gain greater autonomy or independence was seen as a potential threat to Turkey's territorial boundaries.

Consequently the Turkish military, with the tacit (if not explicit) agreement of the Iraqi government, has frequently crossed the border to pursue its 'enemies' into Iraq. Only in the former Soviet bloc has the possibility of the formation of new states re-emerged, with the collapse of Soviet state power in regions as yet unincorporated into the global economy.

The political challenge to the state has been expressed in ethnic and religious discourses. The representation as ethnic or religious signals a challenge to the legacy of the postcolonial national secular states that have inherited power in the Middle East. The struggle over historicity in civil wars is an integral part of the politics of mobilisation and control of the course of events – how they are to be understood, explained and deployed.

In contemporary civil wars the trajectory of the discourse about the conflict has been from the national to the communal. Even during the Lebanese civil war Lebanese historians resisted defining the conflict as communal and the product of the history of intercommunal relations (Beydoun, 1993: 59–60). The Israeli invasion of 1982 was the turning-point when groups changed their attitude to the unity of the state. Before that the conflict had been seen as a product of either class conflict or the weaknesses of the Lebanese political system.

The weakness of the state invites intervention, a dimension of civil war that contradicts the nomenclature of the conflict as 'civil'. Civil wars invariably involve the intervention of other states (Buheiry, 1989: 137). This intervention, invited by one party or other, is a necessary part of the process of maintaining the struggle in the absence of state resources and a collapsed economy. In many cases intervention comes from other (bordering) states; it also comes in the form of support from diaspora communities, in some cases formed over generations through out-migration and in others the product of exile. Recent Kurdish demonstrations and occupations of Turkish consulates in Europe against Turkish Government policy on Kurdish rights are just one example of expatriate/exile communities' role in sustaining internal conflicts at home through political and financial support from abroad.

Where the state remains powerful and is able to repress part or all of its own population a different taxonomy of violence applies. Instead of the language of ethnic rights or the recognition of national aspirations for greater autonomy or even secession, the state de-legitimises its opponents, by defining them as being outside normal politics – separatists, urban guerrillas or terrorists. State repression is presented as legitimate and in the interests of national security – counter-insurgency or merely law enforcement.

In civil wars the weakening of state power is expressed in the break-down and territorial fragmentation of national society. Social space and communal living is redefined by new physical boundaries – green lines, no-man's lands – across regions, towns and cities. Contiguous living is shattered and social interaction contracts to intimates and

familiars. The state loses territorial sovereignty, its monopoly over the
use of violence, and opens itself up to intervention, especially from
neighbouring states who seek political advantage or act to protect
themselves from the chaos spilling over into their own territories –
for example in the form of refugees or mobilisation of a contiguous
ethnic group in a neighbouring state.

One of the principal strategies in civil war to reorder social space
is the use of violence against communities. Massacres of defenceless
civilian populations are hallmarks of the radical breakdown in state
power and national society. The violence shatters national society
along fault lines that are seen as pre-existing the nation-state. These
cleavages are often represented as the source of violence rather than
as a way of constructing and ordering the fragmentation of national
society.

The taxonomy of the conflict as 'civil war' also suggests the primary
causes of the breakdown of order are societal rather than political. This
very Durkheimian construction assumes violence is irrational and the
antithesis of order, reinforcing the idea that a 'tragic chasm separates
violence from non-violence' (Rule, 1988: 174). The re-establishment
of order through state repression is thus seen as legitimate because
it provides the basis for reconstituting normal social processes. The
dreams of ethnic purity, now popularly described as ethnic cleansing,
as the basis for a moral community and social harmony, are also
premised on this value integration approach.

An alternative view of civil war is that, far from being an abnormal
or irrational event, it should be understood as the outcome of normal
social processes. Tilly insists on the purposive and rational character
of civil violence, which he regards as being 'oriented to achieving
authentic and enduring ends of those involved' (Rule, 1988: 170). In
contrast to the value integration approach, which sees violent action
arising from states of moral weakness or failed legitimacy, Tilly argues
that civil violence is the product of collective interest, and highly
continuous with other kinds of social action. It is not whole societies
that convulse as if in an 'epileptic fit', but only fragments of them,
mobilised for collective ends. Collective violence grows out of collective actions – strikes, demonstrations, festivals, meetings – that are
based on co-ordination, communication and solidarity that extends
beyond the moment of the event. In other words, collective action
grows out of previously mobilised forms of solidarity.

For Tilly, collective violence is shaped by normative and historical
characteristics that are closely associated with the growth of the nation-
state. He distinguishes three types of collective violence:

1. *primitive violence*: occurs in autonomous communities prior to the growth of the state, and includes feuding.
2. *reactionary violence*: is the product of the encroachment of national political and economic control over previously autonomous groups, and may include food riots, machine-breaking, peasant occupations of land, and community resistance to conscription.
3. *modern violence*: takes the form of struggles for control of the state rather than reaction to it. New systems of alliances and oppositions emerge in complex and shifting patterns.

In this schema, state violence, like civil violence, is instrumental: 'war makes states' (Tilly, 1985: 170). States offer protection, extract rent and, in the process, enhance war-making capacities. The formation of nation-states in Europe involved states in:

1. *war-making*: eliminating or neutralising their own rivals outside the territories in which they had clear and continuous priority as wielders of force.
2. *state-making*: eliminating or neutralising their rivals inside those territories.
3. *protection*: eliminating or neutralising the enemies of their clients.
4. *extraction*: acquiring the means of carrying out the first three activities – war-making, state-making and protection (Tilly, 1985: 181).

In Europe, however, a corollary to the development of state power and war-making was the constraints imposed by states' own populations. Internal struggles against great regional lords and the taxation of peasant villages shaped the state in particular ways. Military power was gradually subordinated to civilian control, the economy to bureaucratic regulation, and individuals gained the right to address their wronged interests to parliament and petition. Mann presents a similar argument about the realisation of citizenship rights through war (Mann, 1987).

However, the European model, in which external war-making went hand-in-hand with constraints on state power in the form of citizenship rights, was not 'available for export' to the post colonial states. European states built up their war-making capacities after long struggles with subject populations and through the selective protection of different classes. Agreements on protection constrained the rulers themselves, making them vulnerable to courts, to assemblies, to withdrawals of credit, services and expertise.

No such counterweight to state military power developed in postcolonial states, especially in the Middle East. The military was developed as a central institution of colonial power to pacify subject populations, unconstrained by internal struggles between the 'rulers and ruled'. Decolonised states were born into an established inter-state system, with boundaries delimited by neighbouring and/or dominant core states. No other institutions rivalled the military, and their capacity to seize power was great. Thus, despite the importance of war-making in the formation of European states, they 'almost never experienced the great disproportion between military organisation and all other forms of organisation that seems the fate of client states throughout the contemporary world' (Tilly, 1990: 186).

In the Middle East war has been conducted by states overwhelmingly against their own populations. In terms of Tilly's classifications, armed force was used to eliminate or neutralise rivals inside the state, rather than against outside enemies/states. The consolidation of state power and the integration of diverse populations was achieved by pacification. These states were formed through coercion-intensive strategies, and inherited the colonial instruments of social control, which ranged from legal instruments (martial law, detention without trial) to aerial bombing and dispossession.

War-making in the Middle East has been equally central to state-making, but rather than forging closer links between the state and people it has led to states' becoming more dependent externally on the political and military guarantees of state support or intervention. As states have become more enmeshed in the inter-state system, the need to be responsive to their populations has diminished (Halliday, 1987). War-making between Middle Eastern states has also been an integral part of state-making. War against a neighbouring state has been central to disciplining the domestic population, as well as to consolidating inter-state alliances. The former 'confrontation' states against Israel, and even Israel itself, have used war-making as a centrepiece in the organisation and mobilisation of their societies and the consolidation of their states through external alliance and support. Iraq's adventurous (and widely internationally supported) war against Iran in the 1980s was launched with similar aims in mind – to consolidate control over the domestic population (especially the Shi'ite and Kurdish populations) and reinforce state regional power through strategic alliances to get the necessary finance and weapons to pursue the conflict.

Civil wars, then, have most frequently occurred in weak states where state coercive power, guaranteed by external states, has been central in forging state–people relations. In these states citizenship, the basis of social membership in the modern nation-state, was organised around a minimalist strategy, which limited social rights, resisted political rights, and employed the strategy of divide and rule. The state chose to 'negotiate with the more moderate sections of excluded groups, then repress the rest; play off incorporated interest groups and classes against each other; and preserve a vital element of arbitrary regime discretion' (Mann, 1987: 197). The failure of the Middle East to create national societies in which citizenship meant equal (formal) rights has resulted in conflicts that are expressed in anti-national terms – ethnic or religious. In other words, the minimalist citizenship has generated a politics based on exclusionary practices defined by cultural identities.

Civil Wars as 'Community' Wars

If war-making has been an integral part of state-making in European state-formation and in the Middle East, how has this shaped the very cultural identities that are regarded as the essential causes of civil wars? If civil wars are seen as arising out of competing claims of particular religious, linguistic, and territorial groups for autonomy or for control of the existing state, how do we understand the relationship between these identities existing within the boundaries of the nation-state and their pre-state forms?

In the Middle East and the South more generally, cultural pluralism has been seen as the major obstacle to national integration. Historically, however, national integration of plural societies from a strong state centre is but one strategy in managing cultural diversity. In fact, the idea that cultural homogenisation across extensive geographical areas was a feasible political strategy – the project of the nation-state – is only a recent phenomenon. Imperial management of cultural pluralism has been the historical societal norm. Under imperial systems – for example the Austro-Hungarians, or the Ottoman Turks – cultural pluralism was the basis of social integration. Society was conceived of as constituted by discrete communities that stood in a hierarchical relationship to the centre. In the Ottoman system this was formalised in the *millet* system, which conferred varying degrees of autonomy and privilege on minority religious communities.

The colonial state enclosed precolonial cultural groupings within new boundaries, actually forging a plural colonial society. Whatever the precolonial relationships existing between these cultural group-ings, the colonial state changed the relationship of culture and power, placing 'tribes', 'ethnic groups', 'urban quarters' and 'religious communities' in a new social and political order. In the Middle East the new state boundaries enclosed culturally plural societies and placed new élites in power, often on an explicitly sectarian or tribal basis. Cyprus provides an early example of the way new national identities were formed and incorporated in colonial structures. The British in Cyprus constituted Greek and Turkish as communal identities within a new colonial administrative structure. In 1882 they created a Legislative Assembly in which they relied upon Turkish Cypriot deputies to pass legislation, thereby helping to institutionalise these communal divisions. Some colonial officials at the time perceived the dangers of this policy: 'The system is also bad because it relies for its efficiency upon keeping alive the racial hostilities between the two sections of the population' (Lozios, 1988: 643). British use of Turkish constabulary to hunt for EOKA (the Greek Cypriot underground nationalist party) members in the 1950s to quash intercommunal violence only exacerbated the communal divisions. The process of colonial pacification itself forged particular identities, and also specialised functions (for example martial, administrative), for groups according to their spatial, social and economic positions in the colonial order. It also shaped the subsequent post-national cleavages that saw Cyprus divided.

Colonialism employed social and cultural divisions to regulate unintegrated populations within imposed political boundaries. A common cleavage that was often exploited was the urban–rural one, tribes used against the cities and townsmen and peasants used against frontier tribes. These identities, while built upon precolonial social ties, were formed in relation to the colonial order and the roles and status groups were given in it. The colonial regulation of cultural pluralism was coercive and punitive – it was often referred to as 'pacification'. Violence, in the form of deportation, land expulsions, destruction of villages and massacres, etched in the collective memories of uncooperative/resisting communities identities sculptured by the colonial state.

In decolonisation, the legacies of the colonial policy on 'minorities' themselves often became the focus of nationalist politics. Mapped upon colonial cultural divisions were differential allocations of citizenship rights in the new state. Lebanon is the emblematic example here. Differences in citizenship rights – greater protection and support by the state to particular groups over others – reflected the relative political influence of cultural groups in the state. This in turn served to reinforce cultural identity as the basis for differential social membership in the new state and to undermine the effectiveness of nationalist (egalitarian) ideology as the basis for incorporation. But this was not without a wider political purpose. The practice of restricting citizenship rights was a ruling class strategy aimed at deflecting social class movements into 'conflicts that were less defined, more limited and complex, sometimes more orderly, sometimes more erratic' (Mann, 1987: 190). Instead of individuals, 'groups and classes were integrated as organisations into the state, rather than into rule-governed marketplaces. The state could alter the rules by dissolving parliament, restricting civil liberties and selecting new targets for repression' (Mann, 1987: 197).

Historically, cultural pluralism and identity have been closely linked to strategies of state power, whether that be imperial, colonial or national. The 'imagined' community of tribe, of minority, or of sect, was shaped by the exigencies of power and the overarching ideologies of social membership, which helped forge the very modern notion of cultural identity as 'community'. The emergence of the nation-state not only created a new form of membership but created the possibility of all 'communities' imagining themselves to be nations and pursuing the political goal of self-determination – in the words of Khalil Gibran 'pity the nation divided into fragments, each fragment deeming (*imagining*) itself a nation' (Gibran, 1934). As Walid Jumblatt, the Druze clan leader, once responded to the question 'What is a Lebanese?': 'A Lebanese has not been invented yet!' Here he meant that there were only minorities in Lebanon, not a national community. There have been limitations to this process, however. The United Nations (UN) certified only the winners in the formation of the interstate system. As a corollary to making people with states, the UN has also created the category of 'stateless' person – those who lost out in different international and national forums in not being recognised as having the right to self-determination. In the Middle East this has had particularly traumatic consequences for the Palestinians, who are still trying to realise statehood.

Nationalism handed down from the centre has always been problematic, because the violence implicit in its realisation reinforces the cultural identities it seeks to deny. The construction of national myths, an imagined community, national language and institutions are all part of the cultural standardisation of populations. Those unable to be incorporated were the potential object of 'denationalisation' through repression, extermination or expulsion.

Michael Humphrey

Social Death, Social Birth

The contemporary experience of national breakdown has seen the imagining of a national community, constituted as a subset of the former one. The latter, however, rather than being simply a repressed form of pre-national community, is in fact integral to it. Community identity (in the sense of ethnicity) is formed, and informed by, the process of nation-state-formation. Contemporary civil wars are one possible outcome of the pluralism of cultural autonomy in which the massacre of innocents becomes a strategy of separation in the name of the new community. Massacres are part of a process of destruction and creation – 'ethnic cleansing' is about the death of one community and the creation of a more restricted and 'purified' one.

'Ethnic cleansing', the idea that through cultural homogeneity the moral community (and nation) can be realised, is more than just an instrumental action. It is also a consummatory rite exercising the creation of community by massacre. There are two sides to violence: one is physical destruction, the other metaphysical desecration. Violent acts in African societies, for example, are as likely to be 'followed by purification as much as direct retribution' (Parkin, 1986: 206).

Massacre, collective killing, is simultaneously an act of destruction and of creation. Massacre rids the 'community' of the eternal contamination of the 'Other', and uses the 'space of death' to exclude other constructions of the 'social' or other possible political action. The retreat to the communal surrenders the possibility of other solutions. This violence is deployed to redefine the social and the moral community in order to make other mobilisations and conceptions almost impossible. What this suggests is that massacre and death form an integral part of the discourse on the death and birth of the new 'community'.

Violence and murder can be seen as central themes in the formation of the 'social', as well as threatening the very destruction of the social. Writing on the relationship between violence and religion Burket, Girard and Smith (1987), for example, see violence as endemic in human society, and the practice of ritual sacrifice as a mode of controlled killing. Ritual, they argue, substitutes for a prior event which involves an interpretation of the act of killing. The prior event that all ritual killings rationalise, and represent, is a collective murder, an act of mob violence. 'Sacrifice' becomes a term that can be used to refer to the complex phenomenon of the collective killing of a human victim, its mythic rationalisation, and its ritualisation. The elements of this ritual mechanism, they argue, include mimetic desire, sacrifice, the surrogate-victim mechanism and sacrificial crisis.

Killing is at the centre of social formation because it generates a solution that makes social life possible and able to be resumed. Murder is endemic and provokes additional murders, in cycles of retaliation. A 'final killing ' is needed to bring the cycle to an end; this is achieved by finding a surrogate victim. The selection is spontaneous and arbitrary, but the victim must be recognisable as a surrogate victim – to be vulnerable, unable to retaliate, without champions to continue the cycle of death, and believed unanimously by the group to be at fault.

Burket, Girard and Smith (1987) find the origins of violence in 'mimetic desire'. Desire is usually seen as being focused on desirable objects with inherent value; but in reality, the value of the desired object derives from the fact that someone else desires it. While desire is learned by imitation, it shifts its focus from desire for the object to desire to be like the Other. But the imitator misrecognises his/her desire as the value of the object, but finds that the closer she/he comes to its acquisition the greater becomes the hostility of and rejection by the one imitated. This creates a 'double bind' in the relationship; veneration and rejection, mimesis and difference, are therefore experienced together in a tension which they call the 'monstrous double'.

The violence that is the outcome of rivalry can bring the breakdown of ritual, but it can also bring into play that which generates religion and culture in the first place. It is 'generative' of collective violence that can transform the 'monstrous double' as saviour. It does this by erasing all memories of rivalry and rejection, allowing only the benefits of the sacrificial death to be remembered. Only by retaining a fictional or mythic account of the event can the community avoid the truth about itself, which would destroy it. The mythic account casts the victim as saviour and the event of his death as sacrifice. Rituals of sacrifice are instituted to substitute for the real thing. The circle closes. 'The paradox of the mimetic cycle is that men can almost never share peacefully an object they all desire, but they can always share an enemy they all hate because they can join together in destroying him, and then no lingering hostilities remain, at least for a while' (Burket, Girard and Smith, 1987: 128).

If killing can be ritualised and made integral to the integrity of the moral community, death itself can act as the basis of a discourse on the amoral and anarchic. The 'space of death' as, Tausigg puts it, can be constitutive of order through terror. Order and chaos are symbiotic: 'that great steaming morass of chaos that lies on the underside of order and without which order could not exist' (Tausigg, 1987: 4).

The 'space of death' is not a void, but a site for the cultural elaboration of fear, in which meaning and consciousness are created. Both sides involved in the struggle believe themselves to be dealing in great passions and deeds. 'We victims and victimisers, we're part of the same humanity, colleagues in the same endeavour to prove the existence of ideologies, feelings, heroic deeds, religions , obsessions. And the rest of humanity, the great majority, what are they engaged in?' (Tausigg, 1987: 4). The addictiveness of Beirut to its inhabitants during the civil war caused events to take on an epic quality. Many people felt compelled to remain, and many of those who had fled returned, in spite of the danger, because they felt their lives were meaningless outside the city metamorphosed by war. They wanted to be part of this consuming event. And perhaps the reasons for the popular fascination with these events also lie in the apparent importance of the upheavals and the passions with which they appear to be fought.

The 'space of death' is where 'the social imagination has populated its metamorphosing images of evil and the underworld' (Tausigg, 1987: 5). It is where evil resides, the thing one needs protection against. The culture of terror is nourished in the silence and myth of this space. Politically it is where fears are elaborated, crowding out other possible meanings, and used to control communities.

The culture of terror creates 'the need for a hated object and the simultaneous fear of that object' (Tausigg, 1987: 9). In the process, boundaries are defined and victim and victimiser are terrorised alike. The Others are the source of evil, they must be destroyed; they must be destroyed or they will destroy you; you are safe only with us. This is written upon the bodies of the Others through their death and mutilation. In this economy of power there are no excesses!

Massacre in Civil War

Massacre is the centrepiece of violence in civil wars, because massacre, more than any other act, defines these wars as communal, through the isolating impact of acts of collective killing. Every civil war has its massacres, which define the meaning of the struggle by writing it upon the bodies of the victims. A brief list includes for the Palestinians Deir Yassin, Tal al-Zaatar and Sabra and Chatila; for the Iraqi Kurds Anfal and Halabja; for the Iraqi Assyrians Sumayl; for the Bosnian Muslims Srebrenica, Prijedor and Sarajevo.

The memory of massacre creates history, identity and the focus for future mobilisations. The political significance of massacres is that they continue as a defining moment beyond the event, and become part of historical collective memory, a reference point in the past. Or, as in the collapsing Yugoslavia, repressed events are invoked to mobilise and define new struggles. Victims of earlier massacres are exhumed, made heroes, and reburied (Lincoln, 1985: 241). The political significance of 'massacre' is, as a collective act, its ability to define conflicts as communal, precluding other cross-cutting constructions. For the participants, victimisers and victims alike, massacre is an act of social destruction and creation. It is an act of solidarity and protection through terror. Massacres shape communal identities (for example sectarian, tribal, city quarter) out of social cleavages, or even loose categories, who then imagine themselves as separate. In this sense, massacres engender through fear the 'imagining' of community the modern state has achieved by the standardisation of culture through popular culture. The historicity they invoke merely reinforces cleavages increasingly etched in collective memory through fear. Civil wars have an unstoppable quality. Peace cannot be achieved by simply stopping the war (Beydoun, 1993: 181).

In Cyprus, intercommunal killing reinforced communal identity by its collective and cyclical character. Militia violence is hard to stop, because it works through fear and because its victims are its traditional enemies. By massacring your enemies you have dispensed with the need for reciprocity, or the need to negotiate an end to the killing, since there is no possible response in this excess. For the nationalist in a civil war there is a 'totalising doctrine of collective passive solidarity' which allows all members of the enemy group to be viewed as dangerously active. 'If they are fertile women they will reproduce and nurture children who will grow into fighting men, or reproducers in turn. Older men and women are givers of advice and succour, and children are simply potential adults. To the reflective nationalist there can be neither non-combatants nor innocents' (Lozios, 1988: 650).

The desecration and destruction of cultural symbols that mark off community distinctiveness are also targeted in order to eradicate the memory of the 'Others' and their living connection with social space. Graveyards are destroyed, gravestones uprooted, monuments disfigured and place-names changed.

In the politics of violence the act of murder is also culturally recognised as a strategy of personal empowerment. In the Beirut politics of '*qabadaya*' (urban strong men) Johnson (1986) notes how the ability to murder with impunity enhanced an individual's reputation, respect and power. In North Lebanon Gilsenan (1988) notes the instrumental character of individual and collective violence in creating history and shaping identity. Lords on occasion resorted to the collective beating of *fellahin* (peasants) from a large village. 'That's how he is: brutal, excessive, do anything and take on the whole lot of them if he feels like it, a thug, but he knows two thousand lines of classical Arab poetry mind you' (Gilsenan, 1988: 29). Collective killings are justified historically by drawing upon the heroes of past encounters.

These memories are, however, very selective. Lozios comments on the kind of nationalist history Greek Cypriot militiamen put forward to justify their massacres of innocents. What is stressed are Turkish 'conquest, subjugation and humiliation of Greeks, their forced conversions, experiences of rape, torture, martyrdom for their religion, their subsequent rebellion, and successful liberation struggle' (Lozios, 1988: 642). The *devshirme*, an Ottoman levy on the children of Christian families for Janissary military service, is recalled as an example of cultural genocide. Ignored in such accounts are the long peaceful periods in which the culturally plural Ottoman world experienced voluntary conversion, intermarriage, ethnic accommodation and syncretism.

Nationalist histories in the Middle East are littered with memories of massacre. Between 1821 and 1922 Greeks fought wars against their Turkish and Slav neighbours almost every decade. They were marked off by massacres of whole villages, islands and towns on both sides. During the 1919 Greek-Turkish war both sides employed 'organised atrocities' against unarmed civilians as part of official war policy to achieve expulsions (Lozios, 1988: 643–4).

State involvement in massacres points to the broader nationalist project of which they are a part – the state also becomes a metaphor of silence through the use of violence. But the use of military repression and massacre of civilian populations by postcolonial nation-states can also be understood as continuous with colonial government – ordered centres and disordered frontiers. Colonial rule frequently employed massacre to subjugate populations in territorial boundaries that they had determined. The postcolonial nationalists sought to impose cultural hegemony on top of these colonial constructions, often resorting to the same colonial military strategies to do so. The remnants of coercive colonial administrative legislation linger in the codes of many decolonised states.

The heritage of European colonial policies of repression and massacre practised in the Middle East (notably massacre and aerial bombing of rebellious frontiers) were also brought home to Europe. In the Spanish civil war terror was the strategic centrepiece of employing colonial Moroccan tribal troops. The brutal *Moro* (Moor) conjured up in colonial policy and discourse was employed against the Republicans to terrorise them. During the civil war the *Moros* became strongly associated with 'disembowellings, decapitations and mutilations – the severing of ears, nose, testicles, etc.' in the minds of the Spanish people (de Madariaga, 1992: 88). These practices, often condoned by Spanish officers, actually dated back to Spanish colonial wars in Melilla in 1893. The logic was that of terror: 'the more numerous the misdeeds and savage acts committed by Moroccan troops, the less would be the courage of Spanish soldiers facing them' (de Madariaga, 1992: 87). The policy exploited orientalist constructions of the 'savage' *Moro*, with the consequence that all acts of cruelty during the Spanish civil war were regularly attributed to Moroccans, since, it was believed, only they were capable of such savagery.

Another colonial military technique brought home to Europe in the Spanish civil war was massacre through aerial bombardment of civilian populations. The bombing and massacre at Guernica in 1937 was not a fascist initiative so much as the adoption of techniques of British colonial military administration developed in the 1920s and 1930s in Iraq and on the North West Frontier (Heiberg, 1989: 88). The RAF was deployed on these imperial frontiers to 'hammer' Kurdish and Pashtun tribes who resisted colonial rule. It was considered a cost-effective strategy that would minimise British casualties and thereby hostile public opinion towards these campaigns.

The colonial policy of ethnic or tribal recruitment for shock troops on occasion became the focus of 'anti-imperialist' and 'nationalist' repression and massacre. In Iraq, for example, the massacre of members of the Assyrian community by the Iraqi army in 1933 was popularly seen as a nationalist assertion against a fifth column – a community who had sought patronage and protection as a minority within the British mandate. It is estimated that some 3,000 Assyrians were rounded up and massacred by the Iraqi army because of an alleged revolt.

The Assyrian community were a refugee population from Turkey who had been recognised as a *millet* in the Ottoman system and came to regard their relationship to the colonial state under the British mandate in similar terms. They wanted to be granted *millet* status within the new Iraq. The resentment towards them derived from their activities in the Iraq Levies, a special colonial military unit, which had become entirely Assyrian in 1928 (al-Khalil, 1989: 169).

Among Iraqis, the Assyrian massacre was seen as a nationalist and anti-imperialist act. As al-Khalil points out, the modern institution of the army was seen to have resolved, by force, the issue of minority claims in the new nation-state. The British formulation of the problem as a 'minority' one was seen as 'a foreign invention designed to undermine the country's capacity for nationhood'. The massacre was therefore not regarded as regressing to old confessional feuds, but a modern act of nation-building and a 'progressive measure' (al-Khalil, 1989: 171). Even this version was subsequently rewritten in the *Encyclopaedia of Modern Iraq*. No longer were there massacres, simply a surprise Assyrian attack against the unsuspecting Iraqi army. In fact, both the colonial reconstitution of the social order in the new state and the massacre underwrote the social cleavages, which have remained a constant focus of state repression.

In Iraq there is a long history of state victimisation of minority communities and the delineation of power through massacre. Makiya, in a very evocative book, explores the meaning of state violence on peoples' lives and emphasises the role of state terror in eclipsing reason and forging collective identity. He formulates state policy as being constructed around cruelty and silence. An Iraqi Kurd who had witnessed the massacre of his village (Guptapa) by aerial gas bombardment commented that the experience was very difficult to communicate – 'cruelty of this kind is a threat to reason . . . cruelty silences' (Makiya, 1993: 210).

At the same time the social impact of state violence reinforces the very identities it has sought to deny, and even eradicate. 'If you attack someone for being a Kurd or a Shi'ite, the natural response is to assert that one is the very thing one is attacked for being' (Makiya, 1993: 211). On the same basis, Kurdish nationalism is stronger and more assertive than ever as a result of state repression experienced as the repression of an Arab state. Politically, none of these 'labels' is going to solve the problems of the state and its repression. For Makiya the lesson to be drawn for Iraqis is to recognise the collective pain they have shared, albeit as victims for being from particular ethnic or religious groups. He says 'the real existential question for them is no longer Saddam, it is how to build for themselves a future in conditions where everyone – Arab and Kurd, Shi'a and Sunni – has to confirm different varieties of the same legacy of searing pain' (Makiya, 1993: 211).

The use of terror and violence is articulated in intensely culturally specific and intimate ways. There is no abstract violence, or even a universal content of violence. Violence is 'conditioned by the symbolic meaning of actions – meaning which is implicit to the actors and not always apparent to observers' (Corbin, 1986: 47). Violence is written upon a cultural landscape that underlines its ferocity and significance. Thus violence that penetrates the house is more terrifying than that which happens in the street, and in Arab culture this is experienced through the humiliation of dishonour. The desecration of the house, especially the women of the family, by sexual or physical violence is the most humiliating act of social and individual degradation. In Iraq, the state officially sanctioned violence against the 'house' as an instrument of repression. The policy of social humiliation and enforced silence was conducted by state employees whose official vocational description included 'violation of women's honour': 'Rape as an act of conquest and subjugation of whole societies, involving deliberate national humiliation as a means of suppression and social control, has often accompanied warfare and social breakdown' (Makiya, 1993: 294).

In the Lebanese civil war, similar acts of violence against the women of other men's families were culturally understood as the absolute defeat and humiliation of one's opponents. Social contraction and arbitrary violence reduced the conflict, in many individuals' eyes, to a matter of the protection of the 'house' and 'family honour'. The massacre of Palestinian women, children and old men at Sabra and Chatila in Beirut was an act of this sort executed by a victorious militia. With the PLO militias removed, the vulnerability of the Palestinian camps was absolute, except for the promises of safety secured as part of the terms for military withdrawal. The rightist Christian militias were deployed, under the eyes of the Israeli Defence Forces, to take revenge for the death of Bechir Gemayel and demonstrate to all Palestinians remaining in Lebanon that they had no future there.

The point about state use of terror and massacre is that it represented continuity in the practices of integrating culturally diverse societies around political centres that remain tied to external state backing for their support and even survival, when these national societies fractured along ethnic or religious lines in civil war.

Interventions

If massacre forges communal identities in its victims and victimisers, it draws a line between order and chaos globally. As one observer of the Bosnian civil war recently observed:

> Yugoslavia has another message for Europe. European optimism over integration through national communities yielding to market forces is being severely strained by Bosnia and the siege of Sarajevo. The 'barbarian' and ethnic purity have been resurrected. The European Community implicitly believes that its border lies somewhere in Catholic Europe, before the Balkans. There are the borders of civilisation and the land beyond, the land of ethnic cleansing, rape, and barbarians (Hutton, 1993).

This discourse on disorder implies the need to order, to intervene in either direct or indirect ways.

The international discourse on intervention in civil wars – to bring a conflict to an end – focuses on order and massacre. The first choice for intervention is the provision of weapons and financial support to embattled states. Western support for the Algerian and Egyptian regimes against militant Islamic oppositions are cases in point. In other cases intervention is couched in humanitarian terms. In Somalia and Bosnia intervention was discussed in terms of international obligations (through the vehicle of the UN), to prevent further slaughter of innocents and the suffering of displaced and starving people. Extending the meaning of human rights a little further, intervention has sanctioned the creation of 'safe havens' and 'no-fly zones' in Iraq and Bosnia, to protect the Kurds from the Iraqi military and the Muslims from the Serbs and Croats.

The discourse on intervention also subscribes to the definition of massacre as internal and communal. Order is constituted by the inter-state system and guaranteed by it. But this conceals the political economy of war, which necessitates the means to be able to wage war. If, as Tilly suggests, the cost of making war by states was itself an impetus to state-making, then in civil wars the cost of war-making has been an impetus to secure outside support. Intervention is a condition of civil war that the international discourse on massacre generally obscures.

The transformation of massacre into a discourse on human rights reinforces the focus of the state, since it is the state where 'human rights' are enforced. If the state is unable or unwilling to implement a legal order then this can only be achieved by external intervention, which itself is aimed at re-establishing state order.

As was the case in Cyprus, Lebanon, and more recently in Bosnia, intervention has aimed at drawing lines between communal groups. It has sought to confirm the outcome of the fighting in territorial terms. In practice intervention has meant long-term occupation and *de facto* partition in the case of Cyprus. In the case of Lebanon it has meant, after several different attempts by the Syrians, Israelis and Western multinational forces, the organisation of the state under Syrian tutelage, leaving unresolved the question of sectarianism, except in terms of modified balances. The fragments of communities distributed like a patchwork quilt across Bosnia produced by the Dayton Peace Accord are another version of the 'safe haven' in which populations, unable to realise a share of state power, are left outside it, long-term dependent and virtually denationalised.

The solution of the 'safe haven' is a political confirmation of national crisis and fragmentation in postcolonial states. What we are seeing emerge in the context of civil wars is the dependent 'ethnic community', too small to defend itself or achieve statehood. The dependence of 'ethnic communities' creates internationalised communities supported through diaspora communities and by states they have successfully solicited as allies and backers. The role of the UN as witness to massacre and provider of humanitarian aid is about the globalisation of ethnic dependencies on core states.

Safe havens, the localisation of conflicts that are seen as either too difficult or too expensive to intervene in, are also about keeping disorder at a distance, quarantining the impact of civil war and ethnic fragmentation. The relationship between states and people shaped by this strategy is the globalisation of the dependency, not of states, but of parts of states. It confirms ethnicity as the basis for 'peoplehood', but not statehood. What we are witnessing is a new kind of imperialism in which segments of states, detached from their former nation-state, become dependent on the core states.

Conclusion

Contemporary civil wars have assumed the character of 'communal' wars, highlighting the crisis of the nation-state in the Third World. The politics of massacre have recast the histories of national societies into those of long-standing communal conflicts. The project of nationalism is replaced by 'communalism' as the basis of peoplehood and statehood. The empowerment of people is imagined to lie in 'community', national or religious, at a time when national space is becoming increasingly intruded upon by global forces.

In pursuing 'ethnic nationalism' these movements are not merely seeking separation, but the reordering of their relationship with states. Abandoning their experience of one state they are seeking to establish political and economic ties with the core states in the inter-state system. The violence of civil wars is about divorce and remarriage in a new client relationship with more powerful states, often geographically removed. The Islamic movements against the state in Algeria and Egypt can also be understood in this way. By establishing support at the local level, a cleavage is driven between the secular (nationalists) and the religious, as sectors that identify with and support the state in the first case and those that oppose it in the second. The rejection of the national secular state in Algeria and Egypt is not in fact the rejection of the state so much as its transformation and political reorientation.

These movements are reinforced by another dimension of globalisation, the formation of ethnic identities amongst immigrant diasporas in the developed world. Globalisation of the labour market has generated ethnic pluralism in the core states. These immigrant identities are the basis for mobilisation and organisation of support for national ethnic movements back home. Not only states 'intervene'; expatriate and exile communities are also agents of intervention.

Intervention is no more than the confirmation of this process of fragmentation and the ascendancy of communalism created by the politics of contemporary civil war. Localism is being reinforced by this process. In some cases states may emerge, but in others 'ethnic nationalisms' will remain in limbo, trapped in their new dependency.

In political terms this amounts to a kind of neo-colonial ordering nationally and transnationally, in which the assertion of the 'local' in communally restricted terms is contingent upon globalisation – the linking, subordination and clientship of regional entities (sub-national as well as new states) to the core politics and economy. It can be understood as a dimension of 'peripheralisation', which is also taking place in the core. In the Middle East this is exemplified in the fracturing of the Palestinians into national secularists and religious pan-nationalists, the Kurds into secessionists and accommodationists, the Shi'ites into sectarian autonomists and separatists.

The tragedy of contemporary civil wars is not only the suffering and destruction they have brought but that the politics of massacre are socially and globally bankrupt. They offer no hope for wider social integration in the context of globalisation, only fragmented dependencies.

References

Beydoun, Ahmad (1993). *Le Liban: itinéraires dans une guerre civile*. Paris and Amman: Karthala-CERMOC.

Buheiry, Marwan (1989). *The Formation and Perception of the Modern Arab World*. Princeton: The Darwin Press.

Burket, W., Girard, R. and Smith, J. (1987). *Violent Origins: Ritual Formation and Cultural Formations*. Stanford: Stanford University Press.

Corbin, John (1986). 'Insurrections in Spain', in David Riches (ed.), *The Anthropology of Violence*, pp. 204–24. Oxford: Basil Blackwell.

De Madariaga, Maria Rosa (1992). 'The intervention of Moroccan troops in the Spanish civil war: a reconsideration'. *European Historical Quarterly*, 22: 67–97.

Gibran, Khalil (1934). *The Garden of the Prophet*. London: Heinemann.

Gilsenan, Michael (1988). 'Domination as social practice: patrimonialism in North Lebanon: arbitrary power, desecration, and the aesthetics of violence'. *Critique of Anthropology*, 6 (1): 17–37.

Halliday, Fred (1987). 'State and society in international relations'. *Millenium*, 16 (2): 215–29.

Heiberg, M. (1989). *Making of the Basque Nation*. Cambridge: Cambridge University Press.

Hutton, W. (1993). *Guardian Weekly*, 7 February.

Johnson, Michael (1986). *Class and Client in Beirut: The Sunni Muslim Community and the Lebanese State 1840–1985*. London: Ithaca.

al-Khalil, Samir (1989). *Republic of Fear: The Inside Story of Saddam's Iraq*. New York: Pantheon Books.

Lincoln, Vease B. (1985). 'Revolutionary exhumations in Spain, July 1936'. *Comparative Studies in Society and History*, 27: 241–60.

Lozios, Peter (1988). 'Intercommunal killing in Cyprus'. *Man*, 23 (4): 639–53.

Makiya, Kanan (1993). *Cruelty and Silence: War, Tyranny, Uprising and the Arab World*. London: Jonathon Cape.

Mann, M. (1987). 'Ruling class strategies and citizenship'. *Sociology*, 21: 339–54.

Parkin, David (1986). 'Violence and will', in David Riches (ed.), *The Anthropology of Violence*, pp. 204–24. Oxford: Basil Blackwell.

Rule, James (1988). *Theories of Civil Violence*. Berkeley: University of California Press.

Tausigg, Michael (1987). *Shamanism: A Study in Colonialism and Terror and the Wild Man and Healing*. Chicago: University of Chicago Press.

Tilly, Charles (1985). 'War-making and state-making as organised crime', in P. Evans, D. Rueschemeyer and T. Skocpol (eds), *Bringing the State Back In*. Cambridge: Cambridge University Press.

—— (1990). *Coercion, Capital, and European States, AD 990–1990*. Oxford: Basil Blackwell.

– 2 –

Dichotomy and Complementarity: Tenets of Islam and their Interrelationship

Pam Stavropoulos

[I]t is certain that everybody will continue to use 'Islam' as a shorthand expression, and thus the important thing is always to ask: whose Islam? and when?

James P. Piscatori (1984: 8)

The term 'Islam' subsumes considerable complexity and diversity, and cannot be reduced to any single essence or position. At the same time, it evokes and is identified with a number of themes, some of which are potentially contradictory. This paper addresses contrasting orient-ations within Islam toward nationalism and internationalism, and 'modernity' and 'tradition' respectively. With reference to the tensions within and between these orientations, it will be argued that there exists dissonance within contemporary Islamic thought which is not easily, if at all, resolvable. Yet it will also be argued that degrees of complementarity co-exist with such antagonism, and that these pose significant challenges to the ways in which Islam is conceptualised.

It is over a decade since Ernest Gellner (1981: 99) described the diversity of Muslim civilisation as 'a well-established fact', and declared a need 'to re-assert the thesis of homogeneity, not so much as a thesis, but as a problem'. While ambivalent about certain aspects of Gellner's analysis, this insight seems to me to retain suggestiveness and rele-vance. How, within the diversity that is Islam, does 'homogeneity' operate? To what extent are the tensions within Islamic thought, both latent and explicit, addressed and/or transcended? A focus on differing orientations within Islam allows consideration of such questions, and the dimensions of nationalism/internationalism and 'tradition'/'modernity' raise issues that are as crucial as they are contested. While exploration of either of these seeming dichotomies (which we know from the outset we will want to challenge) taxes the boundaries of a single chapter, the addressing of both is deliberate. This is because there are intriguing parallels – as well as divergences – among them, which it may be rewarding to delineate. That many issues touched on will not be analysed or described in sufficient detail will be offset, at least to some extent, by the additional dimension this dual focus allows.

In making these preliminary comments, I want to add a cautionary note regarding questions of nexus, overlap and interrelationship. And despite, or because of, my ambivalence about Gellner, I am drawn to quote from him again. In *Muslim Society* (1981: 70) he said '[s]ome-times one has the feeling that a stress on, almost an intoxication with, the idea that concepts and conduct are mutually intertwined in a complex and subtle manner, as indeed they are, acts as a substitute for theory'. While I'm not sure that it is 'theory' I am trying to write, the point he makes seems salutary. Though by no means confident that I will manage to avoid this pitfall, I hope that subsequent and inevitable references to 'intertwining', 'paradox' and 'subtlety' do not become overworked, or at least that they clarify rather than compound the complexity I want to address.

In Search of Commonality: Themes of Islam

At the same time as contending that language 'is never a neutral medium', Albert Hourani (1984: 228) isolates some of the 'common themes' that Islam evokes:

> [W]herever the political language of Islam is used it brings with it certain attitudes and tendencies: a heightened sense of the difference between Muslims and non-Muslims; a certain alienation from Western power, a suspicion of imported ideas; an increased respect for the great ritual observances of the faith . . . a tendency to hold on to what is left of the *Shari'ah* . . . and an emphasis on certain symbolic acts.

Similarly, while taking care to note the 'divergent experiences' and expressions of Islam, John Esposito (1984: 155–6) elaborates '[c]ommon themes in Islamic politics and socio-political thought' which both echo, and present slightly different perspectives on, the above.

It is not possible here to canvas the many readings of Islam that have been advanced. But neither is it necessary. Even at this point one can glimpse the problematic nature of some of the facets of thought connoted by the label of 'Islam'. In the context of this chapter, references to 'alienation from Western power' and 'suspicion of imported ideas' are immediately suggestive, since both nationalism and modernism are regarded by many as Western imports (Sardar, 1979: 59; Smith, 1986: 144). This takes us to the heart of the tension that contemporary Muslims and Islamic thinkers must both live with and to some extent accommodate. Nor is such tension the sole province of *contemporary* Muslims. As Esposito (1984: 29) has observed, '[w]hatever the belief concerning the unity of religion and politics, the historical experience of the community often contradicted the ideal'. Tension and contradiction might themselves be viewed as themes of Islam; indeed, in Esposito's view (1984: 30) 'the symbol of Muslim unity and identity was preserved' through 'a legal accommodation'. It is important, however, to note his corresponding contention (1984: 31) that despite being 'often circumvented', the Islamic ideal 'remained intact and authoritative': 'For the believer, the Islamic character of Muslim history and political life was not belied by the disparities of history.'

These points are important, I think, for several reasons. Throughout his analysis, Esposito stresses the dynamism and creativity of Islam's development; a dynamism that did not preclude, but was even predicated upon, 'selective borrowing' from the civilisations with which it came into contact. Indeed, Esposito frequently implies that despite ambivalence within Islam about the syncretic nature of Sufism, this is a characteristic that Islam has always shared and manifested (Esposito, 1984: 296). The fictive, mythical aspects of Islamic (as perhaps of all) thought are now much emphasised; especially in the postmodern age we are suspicious of 'pure' forms and 'fixed' essences, as of 'golden ages' characterised by 'unity' and 'harmony' (which could only exist, to the extent that they can exist at all, because of suppression of difference). But this does not mean that Islam's relationship to the past is illusory, or that such 'syncretism' as was (always?) apparent erodes the sense in which we can speak of particularly and peculiarly *Islamic* thought.[1]

Though not elaborated explicitly by Esposito, this point is powerful and transparent in the work of Jacques Berque. In attempting to account for the strength and meaning 'Arabism' possesses for its followers, Berque (1983: 46) defines Arabism 'as a myth, sustained by a culture and sharpened by historical events'. Yet in a crucial corollary, he adds that '*[t]his should in no way be taken as meaning that it is fiction. The fact that it alternately serves or transcends harsh reality does not mean that it lacks the latter. In this battle for the future, for renewal, and at the same time for survival, it is based upon a still living heritage*'

(Berque, 1983: 47; emphasis added). Interestingly and evocatively, Berque (1983: 48) speaks of the perennial attempts 'to ensnare the Arabs in reality', which is why 'the revolt against facts, especially "accomplished facts"' is one of the hallmarks of Arabism. The point is also applicable to Islam, and if this entails tension and contradiction, it also suggests powerful challenges to the 'real' and 'ideal' dichotomy, which, even as it is increasingly criticised, maintains resilience and must be constantly renegotiated.

Nationalism and Internationalism: the One and the Many

In his contribution to the dauntingly dense literature on nationalism, Nigel Harris (1990: 2) speaks of the simplifications that

> allow us to escape the vast and growing area of ambiguity – for that 'Japanese car' is assembled in the United States by Mexican and Korean workers, from parts made in twenty other countries, by a corporation whose parent is registered in Tokyo but owned by a consortium of companies registered in five other countries, and the general-manager is a German.

Implicit in this illustration of the ambiguity of nationalism is, already, the ambiguity of the relationship between nationalism and what is widely (if erroneously) regarded as its polar opposite – internationalism. The quotation suggests that the two dimensions cannot be counterposed; a point which has obvious implications for any study of nationalism in the context of Islam.

How can we begin to apprehend the concept and 'reality' of nationalism? For Harris (1990: 3) it is 'not just a chameleon, but a different creature altogether in different contexts and times'. Indeed, it even seems to encapsulate obfuscation, for 'the national is often a concept used deliberately to conceal conflict over the issues, to force one kind of unity around an existing status quo'. It is partly for this reason that many critics prefer to study what Heywood (1992: 150) calls 'a range of nationalisms', rather than 'to pretend that nationalism is a single or coherent political phenomenon'. I cannot address the many questions that recur within the burgeoning literature on nationalism, the broad themes of which are in any case familiar. Is nationalism 'natural' or 'constructed'; primordial or 'invented'? Is it modern or pre-modern? Élite or mass? Positive or negative? While the most interesting work attempts to challenge, and thus break down, the very formulation of such questions (with their presumed binary oppositions) the continued necessity for such challenges is itself interesting. And while

it is now usual to stress the *modern* nature of nationalism (and, corres-
pondingly, to contest its 'naturalness'), such readings are themselves problematic.[2] Even when conceding its inherent elusiveness,
however, few writers dispute the potency of nationalism, and even its
primacy.[3]

One dimension of the debate that is especially relevant in the context of a focus on Islam concerns what are widely considered to be
the *Western* origins of the nationalist phenomenon. Anthony Smith
(1986: 144) has expressed this reading succinctly – 'Historically, the
nation and nationalism were Western concepts and Western formations'; 'The Western experience has exerted a powerful, indeed the
leading influence on our conception of the unit we call the "nation"'
(Smith, 1991: 9). Such readings do not need (though inevitably in
some accounts they are implied) to rest on notions of 'superiority'
(indeed, in the vehement critiques of nationalism, the opposite is also
implied). Rather, the *preconditions* for the emergence of nationalism
(Smith (1991: 59–61) speak of a 'triple revolution' – economic,
administrative and cultural) are seen to have occurred first in the West.
In such readings, the nature and character of European imperialist
expansion – particularly during the last quarter of the nineteenth
century – and the corresponding phenomenon of colonialism 'forced
all to be nationalist in response' (Harris, 1990: 22).

This implication of nationalism in the non-European world as in
a broad and fundamental sense 'derivative' requires, however, some
important qualification. Firstly, that description cannot be *confined
to* the non-European world, as even within Europe the 'Western'
conception of nation both predated other kinds, and in many ways
predominated. As Knutsen (1992: 164–5) elaborates, '[t]he ideals of
the Enlightenment were forced upon the peoples of eastern and
central Europe by the soldiers of Napoleon'. This led to both a reaction against them, and a different conception of nation with which to
combat what was alien.[4] Thus the contention that 'nationalism' in
Africa, Asia and the Middle East was precipitated, and in an important
sense *formulated* by a technologically dominant 'West' has some parallel
in the fact that even within Europe, Western conceptions of the
nation were initially defining.

A second qualification to the reading of 'non-Western' nationalism/s
as 'derivative' is suggested by the above comments. This is that in
the act and process of responding, a new conception of 'nation' and
'nationalism' can be forged, which in its very distinctiveness, poses a
challenge to the type against which it reacts. Once crystallised, it can
manifest an impetus and dynamic of its own, so that it cannot be
depicted adequately as 'derivative' or 'reactionary'. Indeed, it might

even be characterised as initiatory: to have in some ways superseded the model that initially served as its catalyst. It is not surprising that exponents of nationalism in different parts of the world resent and reject the suggestion, however implicit, that their conceptions are the product of Western contact and/or impact, and, most gallingly, of colonialism. For the many who have experienced colonial occupation and influence, it is the crucible in which their nationalism was forged that accounts for Smith's contention (1991: 9) that Western exper-ience has left its imprint on non-Western conceptions 'even when the latter diverged from their norms'. As Sardar (1979: 61) notes, '[n]ationalism that has arisen from confrontation with a colonial occupying power and that of a country that has never experienced colonialism are distinctly different'. (In the context of the Middle East, the 'distinctiveness' of Iranian nationalism is significant in this regard.)

A third qualification that needs to be noted relates – somewhat ironically in the light of the above – to the *limits* of too sharp a deline-ation between 'Western' and 'non-Western' nationalist conceptions. We are all familiar with such typologies, their binary reductions and simplifications, and their incipient and outright racism (see Arnason, 1990). Thus, while attempting to preserve the 'distinctive' elements that have informed 'rival' conceptions of the nation, Smith (1986: 149) emphasises as well the common features they share, the merging of some of their emphases, and what he calls the 'uneasy confluence of a more recent "civic" and a more ancient "genealogical" model of social and cultural organisation'. To the extent that there exists a 'dualism' at the heart of the concept of the 'nation', it is a dualism and 'inherent instability' (Smith, 1986: 149) that all nations share and with which all must contend, notwithstanding the diversity of respective 'national' experiences.

The above points provide more than an orientation to what has become one of the most confronting and urgent topics of the late twentieth century. For if 'nationalism' (its origins, manifestations, evolution and relationship to internationalism) is problematic in *any* context, how much more problematic is it likely to be in the context of Islam, which in a fundamental, and some would say overriding, sense is hostile to the very notion of 'nation'? As Piscatori (1984: 319) notes, '[i]t is undeniably true that Islamic political theory places substantial emphasis on the idea of world-wide community'. Countless critics have explicated '[t]he ideal of Islamic universalism' (Perry, 1992: 105) and the many issues and questions this entails. As Enayat (1982: 112) has noted, in the context of nationalism, 'the basic contradiction [is] between nationalism as a time-bound set of principles related to the qualities and needs of a particular group of human beings, and

Islam as an eternal, universalist message, drawing no distinction between its adherents except on the criteria of their piety'.

In the view of some (such as Rosenthal, 1965: 3) it is 'inevitable' that 'political nationalism [should have] diverted and diluted the consciousness of belonging to the *''umma*, the universal Islamic community of believers'. While this contention is itself problematic (as will be discussed, there are orientations that not only see nationalism as *compatible* with Islam, but as *necessary* to it) the latent tension within a system of thought and body of belief that is both formally opposed to nationalism, and forced to accommodate it, cannot be denied. What is interesting (though it should not be surprising) is the diversity of view within and regarding Islam on the extent to which nationalism and internationalism are antagonistic and/or compatible. Here the full spectrum of attitudes is apparent – from uncompromising rejection of the possibility of co-existence, to the perceived necessity of it, and intermediate positions between the two.

The contention that Islam and nationalism are antithetical, and that there is fundamental and irrevocable antagonism between them, is conveyed starkly in Sardar's (1979: 64) assertion that the term 'Islamic nationalism' is 'self-contradictory and absurd'. Not only is there tension between the two in this reading, but the tension is such that Islam 'cannot be integrated' with nationalism. Enayat, too (1982: 115) has spoken of the extent to which 'the particularistic and often contradictory demands of individual Arab states can take precedence over the unifying ideals of Islam' (a situation which applies 'with particular force' to the non-Arab varieties of nationalism among Muslims – such as in Turkey and Iran – where 'nationalism has no intrinsic link with Islam, and even sometimes implies its total negation'). Such perspectives have their respected adherents, and are, at one level, unexceptionable.

Yet the very ubiquity of the nation is intrinsically problematic, and partly accounts for the existence of alternative views. While advancing the surely incontestable claim that 'nationalism and the nation-state have become a powerful presence on the modern Muslim landscape', Piscatori (1984: 323) goes so far as to say (and this, conversely, would seem to be much more problematic) that 'the overwhelming modern intellectual consensus among Muslims is that Islam and nationalism can co-exist, even as it is thought that Islamic unity is ultimately desirable'. (The extent to which one can speak of 'modern intellectual consensus among Muslims' – let alone an 'overwhelming' one – seems to me to be dubious. In any case, views that dissent from any 'majority' would still, and even especially, retain significance.) Piscatori's conception can also lead to the view that the 'nation' is not just a necessary evil, but necessary *per se*. Hourani (1984: 228–9) has expressed this position forcefully – '*To be effective*, Islam needs to be combined with two other languages: that of nationalism, with its appeal to the unity, strength and honour of the nation, however defined, and that of social justice.'

It is interesting to note the extent to which this contemporary view implicitly draws on the dramatic contention of Rashid Rida (disciple of Jamal al-Din al-Afghani, who is widely regarded as 'the Father of Muslim nationalism') – 'The Muslims consider in fact that their religion does not really exist unless an independent and strong Islamic State is established which could apply the laws of Islam and defend it against any foreign opposition and the domination' (*sic*: quoted in Esposito, 1984: 65). Such views would also seem to bear out Gellner's (1981: 179) point concerning both the pervasiveness – and to this extent, *ipso facto* acceptance – of the modern state, and the degree to which it can be viewed by Muslims 'in a simply instrumental manner' (Gellner, 1981: 68).

At another level, however (and here is where the labyrinthine complexity becomes apparent) the latter reading is itself problematic. The extent to which the state can be 'simply' viewed or used at *any* level is highly questionable. Moreover, and as Enayat (1982) has insightfully and persuasively argued, the attempt to marry or reconcile 'Islam' and 'nation' is intrinsically problematic. Particularly interesting and revealing in this context is his reference to those Arab writers who 'try at first to prove that there is no contradiction between Islam and Arab nationalism', only to 'end up confirming the Arabic identity of Islam' (Enayat, 1982: 112). The more determined the attempt to reconcile such dilemmas (this reading suggests) the more deeply one can become enmeshed in them – 'In defining its relationship with Islam, Arab nationalism thus often ends where it started: with the glorification of Arabism as a commanding value in Islam' (Enayat, 1982: 114). Here it is also interesting to note that some Muslims – extremely problematically I would have thought – emphasise the Arabic identity of Islam quite unselfconsciously.[5]

To highlight the implicit, and one might want to argue, *irrevocable* tension and contradiction between Islam and nationalism is not, however, to deny that 'a case for a more Islamically acceptable nationalism can be made' (Esposito, 1984: 294). Pertinent in this context is Esposito's suggestive intimation (1984: 295) that '[m]odern liberal nationalism is objectionable more for its Western secular origin and orientations than for its organisation of Muslims in modern states'. Confirmation of this point, and of its intellectual antecedents, can be found in the debate between Muslim divine Sheikh-ul-Hind Maulana

Husayn Ahmad Madani and poet-philosopher Muhammad Iqbal, who, as Zakaria (1988: 5) points out, 'disagreed on what constituted a nation in Islam'. As Zakaria (1988: 6) elaborates, not long before his death Iqbal conveyed his belief that the disagreement was unnecessary, since his objection was to 'the non-ethical approach of the West to the problem of nationalism, and not the concept of a composite nation as elucidated by Madani'.

While the extent to which the two can be delineated is again problematic, the notion of 'composite' nationalism is, I think, suggestive. It is also one Zakaria (1988: 241) goes on to elaborate with reference to the context of Bangladesh ('Though most Bangladeshis are deeply religious, their attachment to the Bengali language and culture is equally deep'). Drawing on the work of Peter Bertocci, he contends that the failure of Pakistan's rulers to appreciate the strength of this allegiance was 'a major reason for Bangladesh's separation from Pakistan' (Zakaria, 1988: 241). Some of these issues would seem to be encapsulated in Zakaria's reading (1988: 229) of Maududi and Pakistan – 'he had earlier opposed the creation of Pakistan on the ground that territorial nationalism and Islam could not go together; however, since Pakistan had been created, he wanted to make it a model Islamic state'.

There are many areas and levels of complexity in relation to these points that I cannot explore here. One of the most fundamental, however, would also seem to be one of the most elusive – disagreement as to what constitutes a nation in Islam. Hourani's (1984: 228; emphasis added) contention that for Islam to be effective it needs to be combined with nationalism and an appeal to the nation '*however defined*' is emblematic and revealing here. Esposito (1984: 295) sees 'the general climate today' to be 'one that seeks to reformulate or reconstruct the nation-state rather than to reject it; to make it compatible with Islam'. The process involved, he says, is 'one of Islamisation' – which takes me beyond the parameters of this chapter, but which both evokes and compounds the multiple dilemmas I have signposted. The recurring theme of unease concerning the secular dimension and identity of nationalism is also an appropriate point at which to consider the overlapping and intersecting orientations within Islam toward the equally problematic conceptions of 'tradition' and 'modernity'.

'Traditional' Modernism and 'Modern' Tradition

Just as the relationship between nationalism and internationalism is less clear-cut than may initially appear (the case of the 'Japanese' car), so distinctions between 'modernity' and 'tradition' seem increasingly difficult to maintain. As Esposito (1984: 271) remarks: 'the technological tools of modernisation have often served to reinforce traditional belief and practice as religious leaders who initially opposed modernisation now use radio, television, audio and videotapes to preach and disseminate, to educate and to proselytise . . .'.

(The point was made eloquently in a recent documentary addressing the resurgence of Egyptian fundamentalism, which told of schoolchildren who 'ride on a German-made bus, on streets paved with foreign aid, and use Japanese electronics to bring them the amplified *Qur'an*'.) While such anomalous situations do not render comparison between the dimensions of 'modernity' and 'tradition' illegitimate (any attempt to conflate them would be at least as problematic) they certainly circumscribe the extent to which such dimensions can be counterposed.

The value-laden nature of concepts such as 'modernity', 'tradition' and 'development' is a further complicating factor, although one which is now widely recognised and challenged. This point is especially pertinent in the present context, for in the taxonomy of Western indices and criteria, Islam was long equated with cultural 'backwardness' and stagnation, and seen to represent the very antithesis of 'progress'. Such perspectives were particularly apparent in post-war debates on 'modernisation' and 'development', but as Kiernan (1986), Said (1978) and others have shown, they have a long and sorry antecedence. Contemporary developments and history have, of course, seen a revising of many of these static and Eurocentric assumptions, and it is significant that developments within the Islamic world have strikingly highlighted the need for such revision. As Esposito (1984: 271) and others have remarked, 'The resurgence of Islam has challenged many of the presuppositions and expectations of development theory.'

The challenges modernity poses to Islam – and which Islam poses to what are widely considered to be 'Western' conceptions of development – are scarcely separable from those of nationalism. This is because the role of the West (and of 'Westernisation') is intimately related to both,[6] and a source of considerable and continuing ambivalence. This is not to imply the centrality of 'Westernisation' to modernisation, when the nexus between the two is increasingly questioned, and when Islam is one of the most insistent challengers.

Nor is it to imply that in the often anguished debates surrounding issues subsumed by the term 'modernisation', Islam is simply *reacting* to Western contact and influence (which, though incontestably important, was as much a catalyst for *internal* fissures and divisions as an agent of novel ideas and influences: see Esposito, 1984: 32).

This qualification (which parallels that made previously in relation to nationalism) is important, because situating Islamic debates about 'modernity' and 'tradition' within a *Western* framework and parameters – without reference to the dynamics and impetus of Islam's evolution – is both to underestimate the sources of Muslim ambivalence, and to compound the difficulty of attempts to dissect these. In this context, a distinction needs to be made between *pre-modern Islamic revivalism* ('which addressed the internal weakness of Muslim society') and *Islamic modernism* ('which responded to the challenge of Western colonialism'; Esposito, 1984: 32). Such an approach also avoids what Piscatori (1984: 318–19) has referred to as 'preoccupying comparisons' with the West, which both implicitly rest on assumptions of antagonism (thus denying 'a long history of accommodation between them') and perhaps even more importantly, 'overstate the degree of coherence of each'. Exclusive focus on the tensions between an amorphous 'Islam' and equally amorphous 'West', and between 'modernity' and 'tradition' (one critic [Gusfield, 1971: 15] describes these categories as 'misplaced polarities') is thus insensitive to both the tensions *within* these dimensions, and the dynamics of their interplay.

Consideration of the problematic nature of 'tradition' within Islam throws such dilemmas into sharp relief. As Esposito (1984: 273) notes, '[a] key factor in the discussion of political modernisation is the status and hold of tradition, the authority of the past, in Islam'. Yet as Perry (1992: 100) points out, the very notion of 'tradition' is misleading in the sense that 'any society has diverse traditions that it can draw on, some of which – particularly the ideals of the remote past – are often congruent with modernity'. In the context of Islam, the pertinence of this contention is borne out by the number of regimes which, having attained power, combine quests for national development and modernisation with appeals to Islam. Hourani (1984: 229) has discussed how, with the notable exception of Iran, regimes in the Islamic world try to claim legitimacy in terms 'of development, of a concerted national effort, directed and led by government, in order to create a modern society, one which is directly administered, literate and predominantly urban and industrial'. To the extent that such regimes appeal to Islam for justification, they will mean by it '*an Islam which is compatible with modern development and which can even be said to demand it*' (Hourani, 1984: 229–30; emphasis added). Moreover, such a version of Islam is not only 'particularly suited to the needs of a "modernising" society' (an echo of Gellner's [1981: 170] point concerning the extent to which the discipline of Islam can be not only *compatible* with modernisation, but 'positively favourable' to it), but has antecedents which date back to the nineteenth century.

Esposito (1984: 43) has elaborated how, by the late nineteenth and early twentieth centuries, Islamic movements 'seeking to bridge the gap between tradition and modernity' had developed. They did this by presenting an Islamic rationale for modern social, political and legal change. The problems and complexities suggested by this 'traditional' case for modernisation are as elusive as they are numerous. In contrast to their 'secular counterparts' (who 'simply looked to the West') Islamic reformers 'attempted to establish a continuity between their Islamic heritage and modern change' (Esposito, 1984: 56). In so doing, they 'planted the seeds for the acceptance of change'; a struggle, Esposito says, 'that has continued'. Thus one of the many legacies of nineteenth-century Muslim modernism has been 'espousal of an assimilative and creative process for reinterpretation [which] fostered a transformation in the meaning of traditional beliefs and institutions' (Esposito, 1984: 57).

Nor can the complexity of the phenomenon of 'traditional reform' be dated only to the nineteenth century. As Esposito (1984: 273) goes on to develop his argument, during the early centuries of Islam 'the very meaning of tradition was redefined and standardised' (a process, he says, that 'obscured the complex, dynamic historical development of Islamic tradition with its inclusion of non-Islamic sources'). Thus 'the significant role' of personal judgement and local customary law was either 'officially overlooked or forgotten', or relegated to marginal status – 'No wonder that Islamic tradition became fixed and sacrosanct for many', and that 'any substantive addition or change' was viewed as heresy (Esposito, 1984: 274–5). Gellner's reference (1981: 112) to the relationship between 'ideological excess' and 'organisational weakness' is pertinent here.

The anomalous nature of 'tradition' within Islam means that those who lay claim to it must do so in a cultural context that has been both coloured and altered by modernisation and reform. In his study of conservative thought, Covell (1986) has discussed the ambivalent relationship between conservatism and liberalism, and the extent to which conservatives are implicated in the views they seek to challenge. To the extent that they must operate within a climate that has been radically and irrevocably transformed by liberalism, they are obliged to appeal to liberal ideas in the very act of challenging them (Covell, 1986: xi). And to the extent that no situation or ideology is static, they are themselves influenced by, and are even in some senses the product of, the very orientation they criticise. It scarcely needs to be said that the problems this poses for Muslim 'traditionalists' and 'reformers' alike (there are of course many varieties of each) are formidable, and that they are certainly not confined to the realms of esoteric discourse. The need to reject any dichotomy between 'modernity' and 'tradition' (and between 'traditionalist' and 'reformer') is qualified, however, by the corresponding need to reject any simple dissolution of the genuine differences they subsume. To attempt to dissolve such differences is to deny implicitly the significance, and even existence, of the often vehement debates within Islam about the nature of their interrelationship. Esposito (1984: 275) notes that '[t]he compatibility of Islam and modernity itself is not the issue', since most Muslims 'would acknowledge the traditional place and acceptability of Islamic renewal and reform'. Yet in simultaneously noting their disagreement as to 'the direction, method, and the extent of the changes required', he implicitly concedes not only the *possibility*, but the *inevitability* of dissension, which can be as bitter as it is laden with urgent practical implications.

In the view of African writer Ali Mazrui (1990: 244) 'Islam is the only major culture to rebel against the West', and its challenge 'is born of concern for cultural authenticity' (Mazrui, 1990: 26). But it does not diminish the scope or significance of this challenge to confront the extent to which it is problematic. Indeed, it can be argued that engagement with the many dilemmas it raises is a prerequisite for its viability. V. S. Naipaul (1981: 168–78) has elaborated the symbiotic relationship between Islam and the West, and Ruth McVey (1984: 212) the tension between Western influence and legacy, and religious norms and values (a tension, she says, that 'compounds the nationalists' problem', and that takes us back to misgivings about the nature of secularisation). McVey (1984: 225) also speaks of '[t]he cultural alienation' of ruling élites from Muslim populations, and the dependence on non-Muslim foreign and domestic allies, which renders 'the credible adoption of piety a very awkward proposition'.

In these contexts, Esposito's (1984: 50) reference to 'the diffuse and at times inconsistent nature of the modernist legacy', and the notion of societal 'bifurcation', seem apposite. Dissension within the *'umma* cannot (and could never) be attributed solely to external sources, and Islam unquestionably challenges long-held assumptions about the nature of 'modernisation' and 'development'. But Wang Gungwu's (1988: 3) contention that 'Westernisation as a necessary condition of modernisation has [now] been rejected' is perhaps a little unequivocal in its skating over the enduring and undeniable tensions between

Pam Stavropoulos

(which is not to deny the tensions within) these dimensions. Having challenged the artificiality and illegitimacy of dichotomies, the very resilience of these comes back to challenge in turn.

Distance and Proximity

Consideration of the relationship between dichotomy and complementarity in Islam evokes Enayat's (1982: 112) reading of those Arab writers who, in attempting to sustain the universalism (internationalism) of Islam, end in confirming its Arab identity. The more one rebels against seeming contradiction, the more one becomes enmeshed in it. Yet Islam has a long history of adaptation and accommodation; its identification with equilibrium and 'the middle way' may even suggest that it is particularly well-equipped to contain the tensions I have highlighted.[7] To what extent is this possibility persuasive?

While the *potential* for synthesis of diversity and antagonism is clearly present in Islam, the obstacles to actualisation of such synthesis are equally (and arguably more) apparent. Esposito (1984: 153) has referred to 'a general consensus' regarding Muslim failure to achieve 'a viable political and social synthesis that is both modern and true to their history and values'. The point has been made even more strongly by other writers (for instance Sardar, 1979: 43–5). In the light of the dilemmas that have been noted, such readings are at one level unsurprising. Yet they are also inadequate if they imply the attainability of a 'synthesis' that, even if envisaged, could scarcely be implemented. There is also a sense in which reference to 'synthesis' can deflect attention from consideration of other possibilities and strategies, which, though unable to reconcile opposites, and themselves problematic, clearly need to be addressed.

What, more specifically, can be said of the contrasting orientations that have been addressed, which, though 'dualistic' at one level, seem to be inextricably related at another? That there exist striking parallels between contrasting orientations toward 'nationalism' and 'internationalism' and 'modernity' and 'tradition' is clear. These are both interesting on their own terms, and suggestive of links that are not always explicated as clearly as they need to be. The existence of competition between and within these orientations would also seem to be apparent. Quoting Fazlur Rahman's observation with respect to pan-Islamism and nationalism in the work and life of Afghani ('Actual influence has been in both directions of pan-Islamism and nationalism, sometimes in conflict with one another') Esposito (1984:

52) suggests that this reading 'is true of the Islamic modernist legacy in general'; and it is difficult to dispute this. What is less clear is the implications of these dual orientations and conflicting legacies, or how to develop them further. Is it even possible to do so? In a recent work, Étienne Balibar and Immanuel Wallerstein (1991: 29) speak of the symbiotic relationship between 'presumed opposites', and of the 'seeming paradox' that the major challenge to particularistic doctrines is universal belief, while the major challenge to universalism is particularism ('We assume that the proponents of each set of beliefs are in opposite camps. Only occasionally do we allow ourselves to notice . . . that most of us . . . find it perfectly possible to pursue both doctrines simultaneously'). The closer one looks, 'the more one observes that these two ideologies, universalism and particularism, exist and define themselves in function of each other, to the point that they begin to seem like two sides of the same coin' (Balibar and Wallerstein, 1991: 29).

Because of its monotheism and fundamentalism (characteristics which are not, of course, peculiar to Islam) it has been relatively easy for critics to highlight the tensions within Islam at the expense of its complementarities. Yet, as consideration of the dimensions of 'nationalism' and 'internationalism' and 'tradition' and 'modernity' indicates, superficial oppositions obscure more complex relationships. To this extent, it is illegitimate to focus on dissonance within Islam in the absence of corresponding emphasis on the tensions within these related categories.

There is now a burgeoning literature that addresses the problematics of homogeneity in the face of Islamic diversity (see, for example, Sivan 1985; Nasr 1987; Boularès 1990; Ahmed 1992). Much of this literature is detailed and sophisticated; Ahmed's study of Islam and post-modernism (a focus that facilitates consideration of juxtaposition and ambivalence) is particularly suggestive. My purpose in this chapter has not been to comment on the merits or otherwise of particular accounts, but rather to highlight the limits of approaches that detach questions of Islamic 'contradictions' from the extra-Islamic tensions they both mirror and challenge.

Notes

1. See Enayat's (1982: 111) reference to issues 'which are immanent in Islamic culture, however much the rhythm and the ascent of each phase of the discussions may have been determined by developments in the contacts between Muslims and the outside world'. In this reading, '[d]espite the occasional venturings of some Muslim thinkers into unfamiliar grounds . . . the basic questions they reviewed remained close to the original sources of Islamic law and ethics'.

2. How, for example, can a comparatively recent 'invention' (to use Kedourie's famous description) account for nationalism's pervasiveness and deep-rootedness? For detailed consideration of such questions, see Anthony D. Smith (1991).

3. This is notwithstanding trends toward 'globalisation', which, while seeming to challenge nationalism at some levels, even reinforce it at others (see Smith, 1991: 143–77).

4. As against the 'Western' emphasis on territory, sovereignty and institutions, 'Romanticism and nationalism became intertwined concepts for anti-Western views' – 'In self-defence, German theorists searched for the distinctive qualities of their Volksgeist . . . It was said to possess greater spiritual depth – more music – than the materialist or cerebral Western imports' (Knutsen, 1992: 164–5; emphasis added).

5. See Rana Kabbani's comments (1989: 33–4) concerning the 'indivisibility' of the Qur'an 'from the language in which it was communicated', and her expressed sympathy for non-Arabic speaking Muslims for whom the Qur'an 'remains . . . a silent text', and whose 'attempts to analyse it can hardly amount to much' (!).

6. See Esposito (1984: 45, 46, 57, 151); Gellner (1981: 58); and Zakaria (1988: 169). Esposito's (1984: 46) contention that 'the process of modernisation was . . . accompanied by the emergence of nationalist sentiments' is illustrative.

7. See, for example, Gellner's (1981: 15, 68) comments concerning the extent to which seeming opposites can be synthesised 'in one and the same language and set of symbols', and his consideration of the degree to which Islam can 'escape th[e] fork' of development dilemmas and 'have it both ways'.

References

Ahmed, Akbar S. (1992). *Postmodernism and Islam: Predicament and Promise*. London: Routledge.

Arnason, Johann P. (1990). 'Nationalism, globalization and modernity'. *Theory, Culture and Society*, 7 (2–3): 207–36.

Balibar, Étienne and Wallerstein, Immanuel (1991). *Race, Nation, Class: Ambiguous Identities*. London: Verso.

Berque, Jacques (1983). *Arab Rebirth: Pain and Ecstasy*. London: Al Saqi Books.

Boularès, Habib (1990). *Islam: the Fear and the Hope*. London: Zed.

Covell, Charles (1986). *The Redefinition of Conservatism: Politics and Doctrine*. London: Macmillan.

Enayat, Hamid (1982). *Modern Islamic Political Thought: The Response of the Shi'i and Sunni Muslims to the Twentieth Century*. London: Macmillan.

Esposito, John (1984). *Islam and Politics*. New York: Syracuse University Press.

Gellner, Ernest (1981). *Muslim Society*. Cambridge: Cambridge University Press.

Gungwu, Wang (1988). 'Trade and cultural values: Australia and the four dragons'. *Asian Studies of Australia Review*, 11 (3): 1–10.

Gusfield, J. R. (1971). 'Tradition and modernity: misplaced polarities in the study of social change', in J. Finkle and R. Gable (eds), *Political Development and Social Change*. New York: John Wiley.

Harris, Nigel (1990). *National Liberation*. London: Penguin.

Heywood, Andrew (1992). *Political Ideologies*. London: Macmillan.

Hourani, Albert (1984). 'Conclusion', in J. Piscatori (ed.), *Islam in the Political Process*. Cambridge: Cambridge University Press.

Kabbani, Rana (1989). *Letter to Christendom*. London: Virago.

Kiernan, V. G. (1986). *The Lords of Humankind: European Attitudes Towards the Outside World in the Imperial Age*. New York: Columbia University Press.

Knutsen, Torbjørn L. (1992). *A History of International Relations Theory*, 1st edn. Manchester: Manchester University Press.

McVey, Ruth (1984). 'Faith as the outsider: Islam in Indonesian politics', in James P. Piscatori (ed.), *Islam in the Political Process*. Cambridge: Cambridge University Press.

Mazrui, Ali (1990). *Cultural Forces in World Politics*. London: James Currey.

Naipaul, V. S. (1981). *Among the Believers: An Islamic Journey*. New York: Knopf.

Nasr, Seyyed Hossein (1987). *Traditional Islam in the Modern World*. London: Routledge.

Perry, Glen (1992). 'The Islamic world: Egypt and Iran', in George Moyser (ed.), *Politics and Religion in the Modern World*. London: Routledge.

Piscatori, James P. (ed.) (1984). *Islam in the Political Process*. Cambridge: Cambridge University Press.

Rosenthal, Erwin I. (1965). *Islam in the Modern National State.* Cambridge: Cambridge University Press.

Said, Edward (1978). *Orientalism.* London: Routledge & Kegan Paul.

Sardar, Ziauddin (1979). *The Future of Muslim Civilisation.* London: Croom Helm.

Sivan, Emmanuel (1985) *Radical Islam, Medieval Theology and Modern Politics.* New Haven: Yale University Press.

Smith, Anthony D. (1986). *The Ethnic Origins of Nations.* Oxford: Blackwell.

—— (1991). *National Identity.* London: Penguin.

Zakaria, Rafiq (1988). *The Struggle within Islam: the Conflict between Religion and Politics.* London: Penguin.

– 3 –

The Impasse of Liberalising Arab Authoritarianism: The Cases of Algeria and Egypt[1]

Larbi Sadiki

The Arab world seems to be precariously perched on a precipice of democratisation. The flurry of electoral politics that has either happened, or is in the offing, is both unprecedented and impressive. In the mid-1970s Egypt, widely considered as the trail-blazer of Arab democratisation, kick-started the process of political reform. Since the mid-1980s, at least a dozen Arab countries have held pluralist elections. These elections are not always open, free and fair. They have taken place in countries with differing sources and levels of income, social stratification and organisational social structure, patterns of urbanisation and industrialisation; differing degrees of militarisation of the polity, coercive authority, legitimacy; differing ethnic composit- ions, forms of state–society relations, degrees of state interventionism in the economy; differing strengths of civil society, and differences in the role of political Islam.

The torrent of Arab electoral activities (Table 3.1) in the 1980s and 1990s seems to signal that transition to democracy, or at least away from authoritarianism, is under way. On their own, elections – an important democratic institution and an integral component of democratic development – are not adequate criteria for determining the extent of transition. The 'trickle-down' effect of the elections, while being the most far-reaching since the Arab intelligentsia cried out for new thinking and democratisation in the 1960s, remains very modest. The 'trickle-down' remains modest in the sense that neither decentralisation of power, nor significant broadening of participation, have occurred.

Hence the focus of this chapter. It looks at Algeria's and Egypt's experimentation with pluralist politics and the factors that inhibit a

Table 3.1. The Most Recent Arab Elections (January 1996)

Algeria	December 1991	Multi-party parliamentary elections (first round)
	November 1995	Presidential Election
Egypt	November 1995	Multi-party elections for People's Assembly
Iraq	April 1990	Parliamentary elections
	October 1995	Presidential referendum
Iraqi Kurdistan	May 1992	First free elections for legislature
Jordan	November 1993	Multi-party parliamentary elections
Kuwait	October 1996	Pluralist parliamentary elections
Lebanon	Aug.–Sept. 1992	Three-phase National Assembly elections
Mauritania	January 1992	Multi-party presidential elections
Morocco	June 1993	Multi-party Legislative Assembly elections
Sudan	April 1986	Multi-party Legislative Assembly elections
Syria	May 1990	People's Council elections
Tunisia	March 1994	Multi-party National Assembly elections
Yemen	April 1993	Yemen's first multi-party parliamentary elections

sustainable movement towards more participatory politics. The rise of Islamic movements, identified here as a problem in both countries, warrants closer comparative analysis of their experiments. The chapter argues that:

• Algeria's and Egypt's democratic experiments are quintessential forms of political liberalisation as against democratisation (O'Donnell and Schmitter, 1986: 6–14; Przeworski, 1988: 61; Huntington, 1991: 9). For both countries' democratic initiatives consist of controlled liberalisation, that is, liberalisation from the top that is designed to ease pressure from below engendered by acute socio-economic malaise. Despite partial openings in the authoritarian political structure, the institution of greater civil and political liberties, and procedural minimums (universal adult suffrage, elections, parties. . .), power is still wielded unilaterally from the top down in virtually the same absolutist fashion by the same power cliques. Accordingly, their political liberalisations qualify as classic cases of tutelary democracy or liberalised authoritarianism. Both remain subject to the vicissitudes of Arab domestic politics, to the whims of rulers and, hence, to either retrogression (Egypt) or total retraction (Algeria). The process of economic liberalisation is occurring without parallel political democratisation.

* Despite greater contestation/competitiveness and participation/ inclusiveness – the two dimensions of Dahl's polyarchy by which he means democracy (Dahl, 1972: Ch. 1) – at no stage has the alternating of power between the incumbents and the sets of potential rulers in either country's opposition been seriously considered (Sadiki, 1992: 1–50).

* The present tension between secular nationalism and political Islam (hereafter Islamism) and the spiral of violence and counter-violence exemplify the uncertainties and contradictions inherent in Algeria's and Egypt's liberalisations. Islamism is assumed to originate, *inter alia*, in the history of economic liberalisation and political authoritarianism in the two states.

The First Liberation: Independence, Statism and Authoritarianism

By dint of her population size (60 million), her geography, her eclectic and rich past civilisations, her dynamic role as exporter of arts and culture to all Arab countries, her past and present politico-strategic weight, Egypt has always been the undisputed 'mother' of the Arab nation. Algeria is to the Maghreb what Egypt is to the whole Arab world. With more than 25 million people, Algeria is the third most populous Arab country. In surface area (2,381,741 square kilometres) she is second only to Sudan. And if Egypt's 1952 Free Officers Revolution (or July Revolution) was to set an example to be replicated later in Iraq, Syria and Libya, Algeria's liberation revolution, which culminated in independence in 1962, continues to be the pride of all Arabs.

Both revolutions inaugurated a new era of indigenous rule. The July Revolution marked both the beginning of the rule of Egypt by Egyptians and the end of centuries of Ottoman–Mamluk rule and from 1882 British rule. Algeria's revolution terminated 132 years of French colonialism, which was preceded by the reign of the Deys, the officer-rulers of Ottoman–Mamluk background. In their revolutions, the new and inexperienced indigenous ruling élites had a solid basis of legitimacy. The post-independence national-secular order stressed state control, according state/élite/centre primacy over society/

masses/periphery, and promoting national unity over the slightest forms of pluralism. These statist and integrativist (Owen, 1992: 38) tendencies had deep repercussions on the nature of both polity and economy.

Politically, the newly-found sovereignty meant not only control over vast and European-demarcated territories, but also monopoly over the 'legitimate use of force' and law-making. From day one, self-rule was asserted through the developing of the instruments – police, army, security apparatus – of exercising that monopoly. This monopoly was instrumental in expanding financial, legal and administrative control. It also entailed monopoly over value-assignment and over all moral and political 'wisdom'. The new élites' clamour for development and modernisation proceeded on the assumption that they alone knew best what was best for their peoples and how to achieve it best.

The state's bureaucratic-authoritarian structure gradually increased. Public space, with its attendant autonomous organisation, expression and mobilisation, gradually decreased. Power was essentially a zero-sum game instead of a positive-sum game (Hyden, 1992: 12–14), that is, wielded from the top down, unfettered and benefiting mostly the power-holders, with little or no reciprocity and accountability in state–society relations. Autocracy as opposed to democracy was to take hold. Nasser's Egypt banned all pre-revolution political parties like the conservative Wafd. Pre-independence Algeria had no experimentation with constitutional-representative politics. The national liberation movement, however, produced many political tendencies – assimilationist, traditionalist, and populist-nationalist (Entelis, 1980: 40) – and a number of parties and movements of both the left and right, like the Algerian Communist Party (PCA) and the Front de Libération Nationale (FLN). The centrifugal forces within and without the FLN that united to defeat the French advanced their own claims for power after independence. These claims ranged from those of the disenchanted Berbers from the Aures and Kabyle regions to those of the provincial leaders of individual *wilayas* (*vilayets*). Leading nationalist leaders like Hajj Messali and Mohammed Boudiaf (the late president) were banned from the FLN in 1962. In the same year the PCA was banned, while dissidents amongst students and the Union Générale des Travailleurs Algériens (UGTA) were either silenced or co-opted by the FLN. Colonel Houari Boumediene, who ousted the first president Ahmed Ben Bella in the 1965 coup, further consolidated state power.

No meaningful electoral or representative politics were present in either polity, despite local elections and mono-candidate and single-party presidential elections of the 99.9 per cent genre. Nasser's 30

March 1968 (Owen, 1992: 269–70) corrective initiative raised for the first time the notion of political liberalisation, most notably inside his own ruling Arab Socialist Union (ASU). Boumediene's own rectification initiative went a little further (Entelis, 1980: 94–101). It began with two referenda in 1976. The first approved the National Charter, which, while it opened up debate and criticism of widespread mismanagement and corruption, also affirmed the FLN's pre-eminence as the sole repository of popular will. The second referendum had people endorse a new constitution providing for the restoration of the country's Assemblée Populaire Nationale (APN), suspended since July 1965. In the February 1977 legislative elections, only the second since 1962, nearly three-quarters of all voters elected 261 deputies from some 783 FLN candidates.

Single-man/single-party rule through coercion and social tradition was the standardising characterisation of both polities. Both had recourse, in the shape of the military and *mukhabarat* (security apparatus) bureaucracy, to coercion. And in the conservative Islamic establishment they had a reliable ally, whose complacency or occasional *fatwas* (religio-legal counsels) served as a kind of indirect *bay'ah* (oath of allegiance) on behalf of the populace. Accordingly, with such routinised politics, participation was to be mobilised, not autonomous. Furthermore, motives of participation were deferential among the masses, particularistic amongst the state's clients and bourgeois interests, and only rarely civic.

Economically, the parallels with politics were striking. With the same statist and integrativist zeal, both countries' economies were indigenised. Nationalisation was at the core of economic indigenisation. This was achieved at a faster pace in Egypt. In Algeria, the nationalisation of the oil and gas industries had to wait until the early 1970s. Economic control and expansion were epitomised by state-led planning (Owen, 1992: 35–42), funding and managing of education, health, housing, industry, agriculture and trade. This accorded the state independent and vast economic resources that reinforced political authority.

Huge financial outlays from the nationalised resources were channelled to emancipate the masses from poverty and illiteracy. Education and health were free for all. Nasser's land reforms of 1952 and 1962 gave one-seventh (Owen, 1992: 36) of Egypt's expropriated cultivated land to landless *fellahs* (peasants). In Algeria, huge tracts of millions of hectares expropriated from either fleeing French *colons* or absentee landowners were distributed to landless farmers. This kind of welfarism served to shore up support for the new regimes amongst the impoverished masses and to cement the rulers' legitimacy. It created political patronage and engendered a deferential political culture. The bulk of the masses with no previous familiarity with politics were even further depoliticised (Entelis, 1980: 93).

Industrialisation was at the core of both countries' ambitious plans to develop and modernise. It emphasised both import substitution and export promotion (Mansour, 1992: 92–113). The enthusiasm to industrialise so quickly spawned unforeseen problems: drying up of foreign currency reserves, indebtedness, dependence, pollution, rural exodus, and neglect of agriculture. Under the banner of socialism, the state-led economies alienated the old bourgeoisie, only to create and cater for a new bourgeoisie – the military and technocratic bureaucracies. The consumer goods that the state-owned industry produced reflected the predilections of the new bourgeoisie: the private car and the TV set (Mansour, 1992: 92–113). The all-pervasive and interventionist role of the state in the economy hindered the emergence of rival sources of economic power that might act as a bulwark against state power. Public subsidisation of food and social services delayed demands for political participation – the principle of 'no taxation, no representation'. Depoliticisation and deference were further made possible by the use of powerful idioms, such as 'development', 'growth' and, in Nasser's case, *dimuqratiyyat al-khobz* (the democracy of bread) (Ahmad Shalabi, pers. comm., 30 March 1992).

The Route to Liberalisation: Economic *Malaise*

Neither brand of socialism in Algeria and Egypt was godless; and neither was about class struggle (Moench, 1987: 60). Both, however, were authoritarian and economically inefficient. Egypt's military setbacks against Israel further delegitimised Nasser's Arab Socialism. The ditching of socialism in Egypt in the late 1970s (the constitution still refers to Egypt as a democratic, socialist system) and, more so, that in Algeria in the 1980s were conceived in a milieu of economic *malaise*: soaring foreign debt, high unemployment, housing crises and heightened social polarisation between rich and poor. The state welfarist inducements that in the 1960s and early 1970s served to depoliticise the masses became in the 1980s too broadly outstretched, or totally unaffordable owing to bigger populations. Egypt's high military expenditure and Algeria's dwindling revenues from oil rents, which decreased by more than one-third between 1984 and 1986, from 45 to 28 billion dollars (Farsoun, 1988: 155–75), were intolerable burdens on both countries' economies. The limitation or unaffordability of state welfarism and economic *malaise* produced the twin opposite effects: politicisation of both *khobzists* (bread-seekers) and *hittists* (the unemployed, who were usually young and educated) on the one hand, and de-legitimisation of the rulers on the other.

For the educated jobless in both countries, where unemployment still ranges between 20 to 30 per cent of the active workforce, dis-illusionment with the regimes was vented in the bread riots of 1977 in Egypt and 1988 in Algeria. These riots were a kind of *intifada* in defiance of the status quo (Duran, 1989: 403–21). These bread riots also constituted some kind of indirect and spontaneous elections in countries where no pluralist politics existed. The bread rioters' anger amounted to votes of no confidence against the incumbent regimes. The rioters – *khobzists, hittists* – rioted to express the widespread feelings, amongst the hitherto anonymous masses, of ungratefulness towards their regimes, which still based their legitimacy on past achievements of little value to the rioters' present struggle for *khobz* (bread). The gap widened between the masses' rising expectations and their regimes' ability to satiate them.

Accordingly, Chadli's 'de-Boumedienisation' and Sadat's 'de-Nasserisation' were preliminary tinkerings with liberalisation, especially economic (Entelis, 1988: 47–64), and, hence, initial attempts at ditching socialism. With regard to ditching socialism Sadat's *infitah* ('open door') policy was a pace-setter in the Arab world (Hosseinzadeh, 1988: 299–317). *Dimuqratiyyat al-khobz* gave way to *al-dimuqratiyya al-siyasiyya* (political democracy). *Khobz*, the powerful idiom of the past, ceded to the idiom of the present: the vote. In immediate post-independence the vote was denied to the Arab masses in return for *khobz*. In the 1980s the regimes failed to deliver *khobz*; and when the masses took to the streets demanding *khobz* they were given the vote.

Dicing with Democracy: Tensions and Contradictions

Egypt is unquestionably the Arab world's pace-setter. Egypt, however, does not always set the best example. This is at least true with regard to democratic stirrings. If Egypt is the Arab world's democratic pace-setter, Algeria is its democratic example-setter, or at least was between 1989 and 1991. The significance of their democratic openings lies in their effect upon their combined population of eighty-five million. Their crossing of the democracy threshold in the future would effectively democratise 40 per cent of all Arabs. The implications of that happening would be far-reaching: a spill-over effect or, at least, a demonstration effect in the rest of the Arab world. Their present dicing with democracy has, however, thus far been fraught with tensions and contradictions.

What are these tensions and contradictions and their roots? The personalised nature of Arab politics made democratic initiatives inherently tentative or retractable, especially when the rules, the procedures and the ends of the democratic game clashed with the rulers' interests. Further, nowhere in the Arab world has democratisation been a matter of choice. Compelled by the *diktats* of economic stagnation, dubious legitimacy, pressure from below and new atmospherics, rulers set to rescue their regimes by giving them a gloss of liberalism. This personalisation has made the creature (democracy) depend on and bear the imprints of the creator (ruler).

In Egypt, Sadat created 'his' democracy and chose 'his' opposition. Emboldened by the gains of the October 1973 Arab–Israeli war, Sadat launched a quasi-'New Deal' with his *infitah al-iqtisadi* (open economy). While political *infitah* was secondary to economic *infitah*, Sadat activated Nasser's 1968 proposal for 'democratising' the ASU. Sadat's initiatives were designed, *inter alia*, to shake off Nasser's ghost – his popularity – as well as to establish Sadat's persona on his own merits and with his own new-found historical legitimacy – winning the Ramadan War.

The initial democratisation process began as an internal ASU affair. Acting on Sayyid Mar'ai's presidential committee's recommendation, three *manabir* (platforms), as against parties, representing the ASU's left, right and centre, gained the right for expression, organisation and mobilisation. This was a kind of change within continuity. Veteran Free Officer Khalid Muhi al-Din emerged as leader of the leftist tendency, al-Tajammu' al-Watani al-Taqaddumi al-Wahdawi (National Progressive Unionist Coalition). Another, Mustafa Kamal Murad, became leader of the rightist tendency, al-Ahrar (Liberal). The main centrist platform, Hezb Misr (Egypt Party) was led by the then Prime Minister, Mamduh Salim. The latter's victory in Sadat's first elections of November 1976 was decisive, winning 280 seats in the Majlis al-Sha'ab (People's Assembly). Independents won forty-eight, al-Ahrar twelve and al-Tajammu' only two. The Parties Law of June 1977 marked the re-emergence of political parties in Egypt after a twenty-five-year ban. The June 1979 elections signalled the return of party politics after an absence of nearly three decades (Moench, 1987: 60–3; Makram-Ebeid, 1989: 423–36; Owen, 1992: 273–7).

Sadat's democracy was inherently self-serving. His democracy neither stopped rule by decree and draconian practices under continued emergency rule, nor allowed for genuine opposition and an unfettered press. Following the January 1977 bread riots, Sadat retrogressed to non-liberal practices. For instance, striking, inciting disorder and anti-government protest and formation of political organisations outside the three legalised parties all carried punishment by hard labour for life.

Secure with his own 'manufactured' non-influential opposition, Sadat had no desire to widen political contestation. In 1978 he had the non-autonomous Majlis al-Sha'ab adopt a law to that effect. That law set a minimum number of twenty members for parties' entry into the Majlis. This exclusionary law was a blow to the Muslim Brothers and the New Wafd. Furthermore, when the leftist al-Tajammu' sharpened its anti-Sadat criticism and grew increasingly autonomous, Sadat took punitive action: al-Tajammu' and its mouthpiece *al-Ahali* were banned. Likewise, the anti-Camp David agreement stance by some fifteen members of the Majlis precipitated its dissolution by Sadat and new elections in 1979.

In July 1979, at Sadat's behest, the old ruling Arab Socialist Party (which for a brief period was the Egypt Party) became the National Democratic Party (NDP), which is still the ruling party in Egypt. Sadat sold the change of name as the actual creation of a new party – his own. In the change, the adjective 'socialist' was dropped, and the populist word 'democratic' was substituted. Again, Sadat looked for and found his own official opposition: Hezb al-'Amal al-Ishtiraki (the Socialist Labour Party) was legalised in September 1978. Sadat assigned Ibrahim Shukry to lead it, and even fielded candidates from his own NDP to run on al-'Amal's tickets in the June 1979 elections. That they did, only to defect back to the NDP after the elections. Al-Amal failed to live up to Sadat's democratic standards. It grew increasingly uncompromising, with a taste for autonomous politics and for passing independent judgements that were unfavourable to Sadat, Camp David and his economic *infitah* (Moench, 1987: 62–3). With the 1981 crackdown on official and unofficial opposition, Sadat's open door was shut (Auda, 1991: 70–8).

The press and civil society fared better under President Mubarak. Egypt's press is probably the most diverse and the freest in the Arab world. Egypt's civil society has also grown in numbers and in autonomy. With at least five legalised parties and periodic elections, contestation has been evidently higher under Mubarak. Although reluctantly, the government legalised the New Wafd in January 1984. The regime also adopted an ambiguous approach *vis-à-vis* the country's Islamists: suppression of extremists and electoral accommodation of moderates, who can enter parliament only through other legalised parties' tickets. In the May 1984 elections the New Wafd–Muslim

Brotherhood alliance gained 15 per cent of the total vote, winning 59 seats in the new increased 450-seat Majlis. Again, in the 1987 April elections the al-'Amal–al-Ahrar–Brotherhood alliance won 60 seats, 37 of which went to Islamists, who displaced the New Wafd (35 seats) as the leading opposition group in the Majlis.

Nonetheless, alternance of power is still far off in Mubarak's democracy. This is made possible not only through rigged ballots, but also through electoral systems continuously favouring the ruling party. Mubarak's 8 per cent threshold condition for representation in the assembly is only a variation of Sadat's twenty-member minimum quota. Parties with real electoral potential have to battle through courts for legalisation – the Nasserites and the Brotherhood. Yet Hezb al-'Umma (the Nation Party), with a mediocre power base, has been legalised (Moench, 1987: 63).

Algeria's short-lived experiment with pluralist politics appealed to the imagination of democratically-minded Arabs and aroused fear amongst non-democratic regimes, especially in the Maghreb (Morocco and Tunisia). Like Egypt, economic liberalisation was at the core of Chadli's *islah* ('reform') and *infitah* ('openness'). In the late 1970s and early 1980s, when ordinary Egyptians started feeling the full pinch of Sadat's *infitah*, which favoured the already rich and created *nouveaux riches*, Chadli embarked on his own *infitah*. Between 1980 and 1991 Chadli practically inverted all the politico-economic pillars that held up Algeria's system and shaped its authoritarian-bureaucratic polity. His *infitah* de-Boumedienised, partly de-nationalised, de-ideologised, de-centralised, and in the process de-legitimised, Algeria's ruling élites.

Three phases in Chadli's *infitah* have been identified (Entelis, 1992: 17–20). The first phase (1980–7) of economic restructuring met with little success, owing to contrived (bureaucratic resistance, lack of funding and political resolve) and fortuitous factors (dramatic collapse in oil prices in the 1980s and a drop in OPEC quotas). This phase's targets (domestic investments in agriculture, in light industry instead of heavy industry and in consumer goods; privatisation, encouragement of private investment in industry and manufacturing, and reorganisation of the giant *sociétés nationales* into smaller and efficient enterprises) (MacDonald, 1989: 47; Mansour, 1992, 104–13) were tackled more aggressively in the second phase, which began in 1987 with the FLN-dominated APN legislating for privatisation and managerial autonomy. Emphasis shifted from central planning to market forces. International Monetary Fund and World Bank-instigated austerity measures targeted lowering subsidies for 'strategic' consumer staples (bread, tea, sugar, cooking oil, kerosene, semolina, flour), lifting of price controls and increasing taxes.

Chadli's *infitah*-reduced hydrocarbon sales, accounting for 95 per cent of total exports ($45 billion in 1984 as against $28 billion in 1986), burdensome foreign debt ($23 billion in 1988), and high unemployment (more than doubled from 11 per cent in 1984 to 25 per cent in 1988) served as detonators of social discontent and political instability. Disaffection was widespread in the lead-up to the 1988 October social unrest. Sectoral interests in the trade union movement (UGTA) caused unrest to peak over enterprise restructuring. Thus disputes such as that over new pay scales and economic streamlining in the Rouiba heavy vehicles assembly plant spawned rolling stoppages (Mortimer, 1990: 163–4). The youth, unemployment's fodder, were as disaffected. Many marginal groups, who were hit hardest not only by high prices but also by water rationing, took refuge in Bab el-Oued or al-Qobba, where Islamists provided charity and welfare support systems. It was against this backdrop that the riots erupted, only to be brutally repressed by the Armée Populaire de Libération (APL), leaving more than 500 dead (the official figure was about 150).[2]

Thus the third phase began with the promise of democracy from the de-legitimised FLN and, indirectly, the APL. Despite the July 1987 legalisation of the country's human rights league and the legislative clearance for more open associational activities, Chadli's political *islah* developed clarity of purpose and direction only after the bloody bread riots. The reforms were the most far-reaching anywhere in the Arab world. They amounted to launching not only a 'second republic' but also a second revolution in Algeria's post-independence political development.

What are the markers of Algeria's short-lived second revolution (of democratisation) between October 1988 and December 1991? The brutality with which the bread riots were suppressed only sharpened Algerians' resolve for change. The feeling was that there was no place in the Algeria of the 1990s for repression, which belonged in colonial, not in Arab, Muslim and independent Algeria. That resolve was translated into the wide popular endorsement of Chadli's reforms in two referenda. In the first, 3 November 1988, 83.1 per cent of eligible voters approved, with a more than 92 per cent yes-vote, constitutional reforms investing power in the government of the day, not the president (who historically had also been FLN Secretary-General and Defence Minister) and adopting the principle of government accountability to the APN. In the second, 23 February 1989, despite a lower turnout of 79 per cent of voters, a 73.4 per cent yes-vote approved a new constitution that laid the foundation for a market economy and a multi-party system. It de-ideologised the system, with the dropping of references to socialism. It defined state–society relations. The breaking up of the historical FLN–state alliance was completed. It enshrined the classic civil liberties, and provided, with qualifications, for the formation of 'associations of a political nature'. A follow-up to this provision was the 5 July 1989 law that cleared the way for political parties' formation and hence for Algeria's first experimentation ever with party politics. This law further marginalised the FLN, which in its November 1988 Congress had adopted a ban on the formation of political parties.

Despite bitterness over the regime's heavy-handed approach to the riots, most Algerians still identified Chadli, a former colonel, as a reformer. His single candidacy for a third presidential term was endorsed with 81 per cent of the total vote on 22 December 1988. Chadli weeded out the die-hards like his FLN deputy, Mohammed Messaadia, and a number of military commanders in the APL. In a system where appointment, not election, rigidified the incumbents' hold on power, Chadli's purges introduced badly needed new blood to boost the reform effort. The system was in such a state of flux that Chadli had three prime ministers between November 1988 and September 1989. This latter date marked the entry of Mouloud Hamrouche and the exit of Kasdi Marbah, who ten months earlier had replaced 'Abd al-Hamid Brahimi. Hamrouche's Government was noted for younger, unknown and mostly non-military ministers. In June 1990 Sid-Ahmed Ghozali became the fourth prime minister in less then two years. Chadli resigned as Secretary-General of the FLN. He then relieved himself of the post of Defence Minister in the July 1990 government reshuffle, thus ending the tradition Boumediene began in 1965. This was a boost to both the integrity and the credibility of the democratisation process.

The spontaneous mass participation and the gains from the bread riots inculcated the idea that Algerians could stand up to the state and earn freedom from authoritarianism, just as their forebears did against colonialism. The state recognised the limits of repression, and offered concessions in the form of wider participation. Furthermore, expansion of public space produced a kind of snowballing effect, with Algerians growing ever more accustomed to participatory politics. Mobilisation and scrambling for power was universal. The FLN, fighting for survival, held two special congresses in November 1988 and 1989. The pace of change was too fast for the APL, which declared on 3 March 1989 its retreat from politics, in accordance with the provision in the February 1989 constitution in which it is assigned the role of defending the country. The APL also declared its intention to end its involvement in the FLN's central committee. The Algerians' new-found citizenship rights were exercised without delay. Between

February 1989 and December 1991 the country witnessed more labour strikes and demonstrations than in its entire 29 years of independence. According to one account, strikes averaged 250 per month in 1989 (Dillman, 1992: 31). Women marched for and against Islamists, and Berbers marched for cultural and language rights. In April and May 1989 Algerians of all political colours protested against soaring prices and corruption. On 20 April 1990 the Front Islamique du Salut (FIS) marched in Algiers to press the government to hold Parliamentary elections. Secularist parties counter-marched in May to protest against the politicisation of Islam.

The February 1989 constitution institutionalised not only multi-partyism but also, indirectly, the democratic notion of contestation. The previously all-pervasive state had to be more responsive to a more assertive society. The long-serving FLN no longer monopolised politics. Competing with it were, beside the FIS, the Parti Socialiste Démocratique (PSD), historic leader Ahmad Ait's Front des Forces Socialistes (FFS), Ben Bella's Mouvement pour la Démocratie en Algérie (MDA) and the Berber Rassemblement pour la Culture et la Démocratie (RCD). At least another twenty minor legalised parties existed in the new political playing-field. Contestation revolutionised the information industry. Following the 1989 constitutional reforms the state's press monopoly was ended. The turning-point was Hamrouche's abolition of the Information Ministry – source of all wisdom since independence. The March 1990 Information Law provided for private ownership of electronic media.

Open, free and fair contestation climaxed twice during Algeria's democratic spring between the February 1989 new constitution and the December 1991 APN first-round elections. In the first, the Arab world's most reputable elections were held on 12 June 1990. Although provincial elections for the country's Assemblées Populaires de Wilaya (APW) and council elections for the Assemblées Populaires Communales (APC) were always held periodically, they were FLN-dominated and were noted for low turnout. The 1990 elections, while boycotted by the FFS and MDA, and with only 65 per cent of the eligible voters taking part, were still a boon to the cultivation of a democratic tradition. They were significant in three ways. They were pluralist. They were a break with the familiar Arab government practice of rigging the vote. The FLN suffered a decisive loss, but accepted the outcome, with the Interior Ministry announcing the results without delay. With more than 55 per cent of the votes cast, the FIS won 32 of the 48 APWs and 853 of the country's 1,539 APCs. The FLN, with nearly 32 per cent of the votes, won fourteen *wilayas*.

The RCD took the APW of the town of Tizi Ouzou, with the remaining *wilaya* going to independents.

Again in December 1991, the second climax of free contestation, the FIS won a landslide first-round victory in the APN elections. The Islamists won 188 out of the contested 430 APN seats, and were certain to gain a majority in the second round in January 1992. There were 231 seats contested in the first round. By winning 188, the FIS was only 27 seats short of a majority (Hermida, 1992: 13–17; Maghraoui, 1992: 20–6). Then came the anticlimax: in January 1992 the APL and FLN usurped control, forcing Chadli's resignation, cancelling the election results and the second round, dissolving the APN, imposing a state of siege, and replacing the presidency with a High Council of State (HCS) in which General Khaled Nezzar was the most influential figure (Addi, 1992: 36–8; Kaidi, 1992: 7–8; Pautard, 1992: 10–11; Yahmed, 1992: 9; Yared, 1992: 5–7.). Thus, Algeria's democratisation was derailed, and her gradual edging towards a praetorian system began.

Again the die-hards' self-interest was given primacy over the voters' choice – a choice that former Premier Bilaid 'Abdessalam once pedantically and chauvinistically described as the wrong choice (*Reuter Australasian Briefing*, 22 June 1993). The view among the coup leaders was that, for the FIS, democracy was just a means to win office and then revert to a theocratic dictatorship. But, if Algerians were to be ruled by dictators, secular or religious, they might as well be ruled by their elected dictators.

Decentralisation, one goal of democratisation, is pursued more religiously with regard to economy than to polity. Maintenance of, or reversion to, political centralisation is the norm. This contradiction is a fixture of recent Arab liberalisation.

Economic liberalisation in both Algeria and Egypt preceded political liberalisation. Liberalisation in both countries, especially in Algeria, caused limited state shrinkage in economic management. Sadat's *infitah* sought to charter that path. Mubarak's more timid *infitah* freed exchange rates in October 1991 and later on liberalised pricing policy on cotton and labour relations. Mubarak intends to privatise some state-owned enterprises, singling out medium- and small-sized industries for sale. Privatisation has gained momentum with the creation in 1992 of 27 holding companies in charge of 85 per cent of the country's manufacturing assets. A Capital Markets Authority is assigned to improve the Alexandria- and Cairo-based stock exchanges, which will be instrumental for privatisation.

In Algeria, notorious for guarding its economic sovereignty (Mansour, 1992: 105; Pfeifer, 1992: 103) from what Boumediene always decried as the developed world's predatory trade practices, Chadli initiated many liberalising policies. Of these, the most far-reaching was the December 1991 Hydrocarbons Law, giving oil exploration licences to fifteen Western companies. Since the coup of January 1992, 'Abdessalam, who was Premier until late 1993, followed a two-track economic policy. 'Abdessalam, who in the 1970s oversaw Boumediene's discredited industrialisation, sought to balance austerity – restrictions on imports and public expenditure – with continued opening up of the hydrocarbons industry for foreign investment, but under stricter conditions. In fact he signalled the adoption of a 'war economy' to extricate Algeria from her economic mire.

In spite of these economic decentralising tendencies, both Algeria and Egypt witness today continued political centralisation. In Algeria the APN, APWs and APCs remain suspended, and retrogression to the pre-1988 practices of press censorship and restrictions on asso-ciational and political life has caused society to shrink and state to rebound. In March 1992 the FIS was banned and its main leaders 'Abbas Madani and 'Ali Ben Hadj were sentenced to ten years' imprisonment on the charges of conspiring against state security and national economy. The rebounding of the state and political central-isation are evidenced by:

- the return between 1992 and 1994 of old-guard figures like 'Ali Kafi, the guerilla and FLN veteran who replaced the assassinated Boudiaf as head of the HCS, and 'Abdessalam;
- resurrection of the old FLN–APL alliance and rule by decree;
- re-emergence of the FLN and the old FLN political discourse on national unity. 'Abdessalam's address in June 1993 to the FLN-sponsored organisation of Martyrs' Sons Conference is instructive. He not only made Algeria's rebuilding incumbent on 'the unity of nationalists', but also defined nationalists as those 'who once belonged to the historic National Liberation Front (FLN)' urging Algerians to return to it (*Reuter Australasian Briefing*, 22 June 1993);
- return to centrally-controlled debate on the content, pace, partici-pants and conditions of future political transition. This has been evident in three rounds of national dialogue begun on 25 May 1993. Its corollary was an HCS-drafted blueprint, setting a two- to three-year transition period beginning at the end of 1993 when the HCS quits, making way for a new presidential body. The blueprint asserts commitment to a Muslim and democratic state, and to a free econ-omy. The blueprint also makes mention of transitional bodies, the legalities and modalities for restoration of political parties' and associations' activities, and future modification of electoral and

information codes (*Reuter Australasian Briefing*, 23 June 1993). Up to the end of 1996 the only step taken in this direction has been the November 1995 presidential election, which, as predicted, confirmed the incumbent, General Liamine Zeroual. Associational life is almost non-existent, and oppositional activities are largely proscribed.

In Egypt the 'centrality' of the centre has been a fixture of political life since the Pharaohs' times. Despite freer political debate and limited administrative deconcentration, no genuine delegation or devolution have taken place at the regional government level. The centre still retains its omnipresent decision-making power. Party legalisation must be cleared by the semi-governmental Political Parties Committee (PPC). It keeps on rejecting the application for legalisation by the Muslim Brotherhood, potentially the most formidable opposition to the ruling NDP. Nor is it easy for secular parties to obtain legalisation. In May 1993 al-Mustaqbal ('The Future'), a staunchly anti-Islamist party, got its application rejected because the founders' signatures had not been legally certified. The founders were colleagues of secularist journalist, Farag Foda, who had been assassinated by Islamists in July 1992. Although the PPC is supposedly semi-governmental, its neutrality has been recently doubted by the Cairo-based Arab Human Rights Organisation (AHRO). A majority of the PPC's board is made up of NDP members, including the Consultative Council president and the Ministers for the Interior and Justice.

The December 1992 amendments to the Parties Law (no. 401 of 1977) by the Majlis were described by AHRO as running counter to democratisation. The amendments banned all activities by political parties until their legalisation was cleared by the PPC. The amendments also restricted or made illegal contacts by existing legalised parties with Arab and foreign parties. The AHRO questioned the manner and the speed with which the Majlis ratified the amendments on 16 December 1992. The amendments proposal was drawn up by a meeting of government ministers on 13 December. The next day the Constitutional and Legislative Committee was called on to convene to study the proposal impromptu. This committee's inconclusiveness over the proposal prompted its passing to the Political Parties Affairs Committee to draft new laws embodying the proposed amendments. The amendments were rubber-stamped by the 454-member Majlis. Only 90 members were present, of whom 76 voted in favour of the new laws (AHRO, 1993: 2–3).

Political parties are also restrained by electoral laws favouring the NDP, electoral irregularities that include early closure of voting booths, harassment of opposition campaigners, under-developed voter-registers, and the NDP's use of the votes of the dead. The May 1984, April 1987 and the November 1990 elections were called earlier than their due dates (by up to two years). The Supreme Court held unconstitutional the 1984 and 1987 People's Assembly elections on account of the exclusion of independents. The November 1990 elections produced the least representative Majlis, owing to the boycott by al-'Amal, the Brotherhood, the New Wafd, and al-Ahrar. These last two, however, had members standing as independents, gaining respectively fourteen and one seats. Al-Tajammu' did not boycott the election, winning six seats. Voter turnout is low in national elections, and is higher in rural than in urban electorates. Although voting is compulsory, in the 1984 election, for instance, 80 per cent of urban electors abstained from voting despite punitive measures. Such low turnout is attributed to voters' apathy owing to their knowledge that elections change nothing in Egypt, and to Islamists, who simply boycott the system they regard as illegitimate (Moench, 1987: 49). This has not changed in the most recent Majlis elections of November 1995. They too took place against the backdrop of a climate that was not conducive to free and fair contestation and participation: anti-Islamist crackdown; electoral irregularities; harassment of opposition candidates; violence; and limited or no electronic media access for genuine independent and opposition candidates. The 71 per cent of the votes (330 seats) that went to the ruling party must not be taken as a reliable gauge either of the NDP's actual power base or of its electoral performance. Although 114 seats were taken by so called *mustaqillun* (independents), at least half of them will be occupied by deputies who are regime clients.

The 17 February 1993 law on professional syndicates and unions has been cause for concern within civil society. The law, brought about to curb what its legislators call 'minority dictatorship' aims to 'widen democratic participation'. The law, entitled 'safeguards of the professional syndicates' and unions' democracy', is widely recognised as a mechanism to frustrate future Islamist take-overs of syndicates and unions. The law comes after the September 1992 Bar Association elections, when Islamists, with less than 10 per cent of the total vote, beat liberals and leftists to gain control of the country's prestigious and powerful Lawyers' Syndicate. The law makes future syndicates' and unions' elections conditional on 50 per cent voting participation of the membership. Failing that, the government will have the discretion to make appointments to fill the seats for the syndicates' and unions' executive committees (Mattoon, 1992: 16–18; Mattoon, 1993: 36–7). This law has alarmed the Egyptian Human Rights Organisation

(EHRO) which fears 'life tenure as a mode of selection for union directorates' will result from government intervention (EHRO, 1993a). Islamist scholar Fahmi Huwaydi has criticised the new law as hypocritical, pointing out how the current Majlis has been voted in by only 10 per cent of all voters, and how voter turnout for local councils ranges between 5 and 6 per cent (Huwaydi, 1993: 139–45).

While secularists maintain exclusionary policies *vis-à-vis* Islamists on the basis that separation between religion and state is a democratisation prerequisite, they continue either to employ Islamic idioms for legitimation or to meddle in religious affairs.

The question of secularisation in the Arab world is a complex one for at least two obvious reasons. First, the ruling secularists administer political realms whose constitutions declare Islam to be the state religion. The constitutions of the secular states of the West do not generally do anything like this. (The preamble of the Irish constitution accords Catholicism an official status. Those of Australia and the United States make clear the importance of Christianity, but do not stipulate anywhere that it is the official religion.) From this perspective, most Arab countries have never been secular, even if they were ruled by secularists. Second, while contestable, the overwhelming view is that separation of religion and politics is alien to Islam, which has no Church.

The complexity of these questions manifests itself in the present impasse of democratisation in both Algeria and Egypt. In both countries the Islamists are powerful, despite systematic repression. The Muslim Brotherhood is tolerated but not legalised in Egypt. In Algeria the powerful FIS was disbanded in March 1992. Egypt's Parties Law of 1977 bans the formation of sectarian (religious) parties. The rulers fear not only the wide following legalised Islamist parties will be able to muster, but also that the formation of Islamist parties will trigger similar demands from the country's 10 per cent Coptic population. In Algeria, the Parties Law of 2 July 1989 disallows religious parties. The view is that Islam should not be monopolised for political ends.

The secularisation quandary has created a kind of Catch-22 situation. On the one hand, no secularisation, and for that matter, real democratisation, can be achieved if polity is Islamised. This is argued to cause tensions as between irreconcilable notions of popular and divine sovereignty. On the other hand, if secularisation is to be about democratisation it cannot be so if it excludes an important segment – Islamists – of the civil society from political participation and contestation.

Most important, however, is the continued meddling in religion or its use by secularists for political ends – legitimation. Is not this the secularists' very basis for objection to mixing religion with politics? Algeria's revolution was founded on Islamic grounds, uniting Berber and Arab against the infidel French *colons*. The holy war for liberation by the *mujahideen* (holy warriors) cost the lives of more than one million *shahids* (martyrs). From the outset of independence not only were the *mujahideen* revered by the state, but they also, in their turn, built and controlled the hegemonic state. Both al-'Amir 'Abd al-Qadir and al-Sheikh Ibn Badis, who resisted French colonialism through the operation of Islamic *'asabiyya* (group feeling), are still national and historical heroes. In the same vein, secularist Nasser inspired awe in the Arab masses, not only through pan-Arabist discourse, but also through messages of liberating the occupied *Filistin al-muqaddasa* ('holy Palestine'). Sadat, the vodka drinker, was *al-rais al-mu'min* ('the pious president'). During his rule, the adoption of *Shari'ah* (Islamic Law) as the basis of Egyptian law was one of a number of constitutional amendments introduced in April 1980.

Politicisation of the mosque seems to be inevitable. While arguing for *imams* (prayer leaders) to be non-partisan, the regimes in both Algeria and Egypt have been appointing their own *imams*, those who could be relied upon to support the rulers' own version of Islam. To stop anti-tourist violence, which costs Egypt millions of dollars in hard currency earnings, the government had its appointed grand *mufti*, al-Sheikh Sayyid Tan Tawi, the country's most senior jurisprudent, assert that tourism was *halal* (permitted) in Islam and not *haram* (forbidden), as some Islamists contended (Mattoon, 1993: 36). In May 1993, the highest Saudi religious authority, al-Sheikh 'Abd-al 'Aziz Bin Baz, ruled that the killing of non-believers (tourists) was *haram* (*Reuter Australasian Briefing*, 22 May 1993).

In Egypt, Islamist hysteria prompted introduction of stricter control measures on mosques. Amongst these were plans to: bring all of Egypt's more than 100,000 mosques under the *al-Awqaf* (religious endowments) Ministry's control; to make mandatory prior government approval of Friday sermons in state-controlled mosques; and to impose restrictions on the building of private community mosques (Mattoon, 1993: 36). The regime has begun a systematic and large-scale crackdown campaign on Islamists, including the moderate Muslim Brethren (MB), since 1994. Leading MB members who are active in the professional unions and syndicates, the only arena of free and fair contestation and participation in Egypt until 1995, have been arrested. Of those jailed, Isam al-Iryan, the youngest to have ever entered parliament in the 1987 elections, told this author in an interview that 'excessive coercion is the sign of a decaying regime with no confidence in its ability to shore up its legitimacy via legitimate means' (Isam al-Iryan, pers. comm., 6 April 1994, Cairo).

Even when rulers prefer Islam to be relegated to a personal religious experience, interference seems to be unavoidable. Algeria has adopted the Tunisian formula of rendering *hijab* (Islamic head-dress) and beards illegal in the public service. President Mubarak is reported to have described veiled women as *tentes ambulantes* (moving or walking tents). At a time when Western secularists are planning to conquer space, their Arab counterparts are concerned with beards and veils.

The bifurcated approach to religion and politics is as evident in Algeria. Systematic repression continues to eradicate the FIS threat in conjunction with co-optation of Islamists and the use of Islam. Islamists were, for instance, included in Boudiaf's cabinet soon after the coup. Non-threatening Islamist parties like Ennahda and Hamas were included in the state-sponsored May–June national dialogue. The HCS-drawn blueprint for transition to democracy and free economy emphasised Islam as intrinsic to Algeria's identity, and proposed the setting-up of a Higher Islamic Council.

While notions of Western secularisation and democratisation are based on respect for the rules and procedures of citizenship and on human rights, the opposite is more or less true of similar Arab processes. The attendant corollary is violence and counter-violence.

The atrophy of democratisation in Algeria and its retrogressive nature in Egypt have led both polities to an impasse where the rationality of participation and free and fair contestation has ceded to the irrationality of exclusion and bloody violence (Sadiki, 1993: 9). For the rulers, violence is the state's legitimate prerogative to eradicate anti-democratic forces. For the targets, Islamists, state violence has gone beyond that mandate. Islamists regard state violence as being executed, not by democrats, but by anti-Islam and anti-democracy rulers. Stripped of the political means for empowerment, many Islamists feel justified in resorting to *jihad* (holy struggle or war). The suppression of Algeria's Islamists' certain victory in the polls and the subsequent state violence against the FIS have created a bad precedent. That precedent has strengthened the hands of radical Islamists, for whom Arab rulers have never been serious about democracy, so that *jihad* remains their only option for empowerment. Although anti-state violence by Islamists is nothing new in Egypt, the FIS débâcle in Algeria fanned it further.

The pattern of anti-Islamist state violence in Algeria has been focused on the FIS. Since the imposition of the state of siege in February 1992 at least nine thousand of its members have been detained in

Sahara camps. The crackdown targeted the remaining leadership and active followers. The party's headquarters and its newspapers were closed down. The gendarmerie, the security apparatus and the army have combined forces to combat Islamist armed resistance, and aircraft have been used to comb the mountainous region for hideouts. Hundreds of resisters have been killed, and almost 450 death sentences were handed down by special courts to arrested Islamists between February 1992 and December 1995. The casualty toll among the government forces continues to rise. At least 30,000 Algerians have lost their lives since the beginning of the democracy débâcle in early 1992.

Anti-state Islamist resistance is daily routine in Algeria. For Islamists their anti-state *jihad* has pre-independence resonance. Resistance is by *mujahideen*, including army deserters, organised in ten various groups (Tezgharit, 1993: 50–4). Their main tactic is hit and run. Their targets are state symbols, as in the Algiers international airport bombing of August 1992; government leaders, legal, military and security personnel, with already one failed attempt to kill General Nezzar; and establishment intellectuals and journalists like Djilali Liabes, El-Hadi Flici, Tahar Djaout, and Mahfoudh Boucebsi. The recent presidential election has not served as a harbinger of either social peace or polyarchal politics, the two major electoral promises of General Zeroual. The impasse lingers on (Ghezali, 1996: 1; 12). State violence and Islamist counter-violence in Egypt pre-dated the 1952 revolution. Nasser dealt with the Muslim Brotherhood with an iron fist. Sadat followed suit, especially in the last two years of his rule. That legacy survives with Mubarak.

Under the emergency rule, still in force since 1967 except between 15 May 1980 and 1 October 1981 when Sadat was assassinated, the security forces have emergency powers, which no doubt have been abused. Such abuses are well documented by both Amnesty International and AHRO. Torture, for instance, remains widely used. The Amnesty October 1991 report 'Egypt: Ten Years of Torture' confirms this. Hostage-taking of children by security forces has been used to pressure suspects to surrender. Incommunicado detention and mass arrests of Islamists since the second Gulf War have been systematic. As if emergency powers were not enough, a new anti-terrorism law was introduced in July 1992. Under this law, terrorist acts are punishable by death and possession of material that can be construed as condoning terrorism is a crime. It is feared that the new law will further strengthen police powers. Military, not civilian, courts have been trying Islamists. While the voting age is eighteen, fifteen-year-olds can be tried by state security courts. Three interior Ministers (Zaki Badr, 'Abd al-Halim Mousa and Hassan al-Alfy) between 1990 and 1995 failed to reverse the spiral of violence.

In Egypt, the anti-state violence campaign was sustained and intensified in the early 1990s. The deployment of foreign troops, accompanied by Egyptian soldiers, in the Gulf and the subsequent anti-Iraq war galvanised Islamists into armed anti-state action. Almost nine years after Sadat's assassination, the Majlis speaker Rifa'at al-Mahjoub was gunned down. In March 1993 an attempt to assassinate Information Minister Safwat al-Sharif failed. What makes the state more vulnerable is the multiplicity of Islamist groups operating in Egypt. At least five known groups have been blamed for various acts of anti-state violence. The al-Jihad of al-Sheikh 'Umar 'Abdal-Rahman has been connected with both Sadat's and Mahjoub's slayings. Al-Jihad al-Islami al-Jedid ('New Islamic Jihad'), an offshoot of al-Jihad, is also known for carrying out acts of anti-state violence. The same goes for al-Takfir wa al-Hijra ('Denunciation and Holy Flight') and al-Najoun Min al-Nar ('Survivors from Hell'). The fifth group, al-Jama'a al-Islamiya ('Islamic Group'), has been connected with recent attacks on the tourist industry, Copts, security and military personnel, intellectuals and journalists. Many professionals even in the armed forces sympathise with and covertly support these groups (Jabr, 1993: 18–20).

The slaying by extremists of nearly 20 tourists in the first half of 1996 is yet another sign that the security forces' war against Islamist guerillas is not the right solution to Egypt's political impasse. The idea of a wide-ranging and unconditional dialogue between the regime and all oppositional forces, which has widespread support within the country's fledgling civil society and intelligentsia, is perhaps the one realistic option left to the regime if it is to avoid slipping further down the slippery slope of violence and counter-violence (Sadiki, 1995: 249–66).

More than a dozen people have been killed in a bombing campaign in Central Cairo (the Tahrir Square El-Nil coffee-shop in February and the car bomb nearly a mile away in May 1993). Clashes between security forces and Islamists have intensified, as in Imbaba, north of Cairo, in early 1993, with the EHRO criticising the brutality of both the police and the armed Islamists (EHRO, 1993b). Similar clashes happened in al-Fayoum and upper Egypt, a bedrock of radical Islamism, in Asyut (especially Dairut) and Aswan. More than a hundred lives have been lost in such clashes since 1992. Dozens of Islamist suspects have been sentenced to death, and a few have already been hanged. Thousands have been jailed (Sid-Ahmed, 1993: 18).

Hysteria over the Islamist threat is being internationalised. The hysteria over Islam's return as an international menace has been helped by Arab regimes. In Tunisia Ben 'Ali coined the term 'fundamentalists' internationale', a dramatisation equating Islamism with the old communist threat. There is a new interdependence of Arab regimes, with a concerted effort to combat Islamism. The effort has been scapegoatist, with Iran and Sudan being linked to Islamist violence, a linkage that has yet to be substantiated. Since May 1993 Egypt has cut fax and direct-dial telephone links with both countries, in addition to Afghanistan, Pakistan and Iraq. The aim is to weaken the Islamist 'internationale' network. Algeria and Egypt have pressured the Gulf states to stop unofficial funds to Islamists via Islamic banks. There is an international campaign for the extradition of Islamist leaders or for banning their political activities, especially in Europe. Pakistan has already handed over a number of Arab 'Afghan' *mujahideen* to Egypt. In June 1993, Germany temporarily arrested the main FIS spokesman in Europe, Rabah Kebir, who headed the party's political committee before the ban of March 1992, and Oussama Madani, the imprisoned FIS leader's son. Both were wanted in Algeria, where they were sentenced to death *in absentia*. In June also, Morocco arrested 'Abd al-Haq Layada, the Armed Islamic Movements' leader. Egypt is still seeking al-Sheikh 'Abdal-Rahman's extradition from the United States. Egyptian authorities have linked him with the Islamic Group's anti-state violence.

The political discourse has also caught up with the upward spiral of violence and counter-violence. In both Algeria and Egypt the epithet describing Islamists active in anti-state violence is *irhabi* ('terrorist'), a term that once, for Arabs, described Israel's Stern and Hagana. What were once *al-usuliyin* (fundamentalists), and then *al-islamiyyin* (Islamists) are now *al-irhabiyyin* (terrorists). The term *'al-islamiyyin'* has taken on a pejorative meaning. Active movements seeking empowerment have adopted it as a more positive and assertive appellation for self-description. This term is growing in both popularity and negativity, as the label 'terrorist' is increasingly used to describe the rising number of Islamists engaged in violence. Reference to Islam has also been dichotomised: moderate and extremist 'Islams'.

The strategy has changed too. Electoral politics and political struggle as forms of *al-jihad al-akbar* (greater *jihad*) are giving way in Algeria to *al-jihad al-asghar* (lesser *jihad* – holy war). In Egypt, groups excluded from politics are visibly engaged in lesser *jihad*, and, without the Muslim Brotherhood's legalisation, things could get worse. In Lebanon, Hezballah has withdrawn from anti-state/anti-society holy war except against Israel and has engaged in greater *jihad* in domestic politics. Hamas has done the same in Occupied Palestine.

Concluding Remarks

The near death of the 'providential' state has spelt danger for state hegemony in low- and middle-income Arab states. Algeria's politics have come nearly full circle: from bureaucratic-authoritarianism through to a unique democratisation experiment and then reversal. Egypt's sustained electoral politics is an approximation *par excellence* to liberalised authoritarianism. The state in both countries has shown remarkable resilience by rebounding from shrinkage. Society's expansion has occurred with increasing habituation to electoral politics and principles of citizenship. Low economic performance and state violence are possible causal linkages for the unsustainability of democratic gains and state re-expansion after retreat. Liberalised authoritarianism's exclusion of Islamists accounts for current violence and counter-violence and the retreat of *al-jihad al-akbar* (ballot) and the expansion of *al-jihad al-asghar* (bullet). To purge the stain of their illegitimacy, in the future, regimes will have no choice but to co-rule with Islamists.

The impasse of democracy in Algeria and Egypt does not bode well for democratising the Arab world. This is not either to attach the label 'exceptionalism' to the Arab world's democratic stirrings or to say that the notion of an Arab democracy is an 'oxymoron'. Democracy has become the parrot cry of debates and discourses on Arab governance, in line with trends in other regions. And the problems of political monolithism, statism, bureaucratism, authoritarianism and transition to democracy are not specific to the Arab world. Successful democratic transitions in either country – Egypt for most of the Arab world and Algeria for the Maghreb – could present Arabs with demonstration effects and models to emulate. Egypt, in particular, is in a position to provide that model. Its anti-monarchy and socialist revolution in the 1950s was replicated in many Arab countries. On the surface, the present toying with democracy in many Arab countries seems to be an improvement on past authoritarian practices. In practice, however, as the Algerian and Egyptian cases show, toying with democracy has been, as is widely recognised, a mechanism for clinging to power, not sharing it. Reforms are pre-emptive: being controlled from above, they hinder the growth of civil society and of any rival sites of self-expression and mobilisation. Formidable forces and leaderships are either co-opted or excluded. Nor have these reforms put a stop to widespread human rights violations. Is it not paradoxical that Egypt is at once one of the leading Arab democratisers and one of the worst violaters of human rights anywhere in the Arab world? In fact, this is true of a small league of Arab democratisers, such as Algeria, Tunisia and Morocco. Jordan fares better than all three. Arab experiments up to the present confirm the conclusion of this chapter, that the routes of Arab transition to democratic rule are taken via 'undemocratic means'. With the kind of democracy rulers in Algiers or Cairo have in mind, that is, one which lends itself to a 'voluntaristic' interpretation of democratic government, the democratic breakthrough awaited by millions of Arabs is not yet in the offing. This verdict, however, is not the last word on Arab democracy.

Notes

1. An earlier abridged version of this chapter appeared in the February 1994 *Current Affairs Bulletin*, 70 (8). This article has benefited from interviews the author had with the Algerian Islamist opposition (FIS): and the Muslim Brotherhood and the Neo-Wafd party in Egypt.
2. The official figure (150) understates the number of those killed. Both Algerian sources – human rights activists – and Arab ones, such as the Arab Human Rights Organisation, estimate the number to be close to 500.

References

Addi, Lahouari (1992). 'Algeria's democracy between the Islamists and the "elite".' *Middle East Report*, 22 (2): 36–8.

Auda, Gehad (1991). 'Egypt's uneasy party politics'. *Journal of Democracy*, 2 (2): 70–8.

Dahl, Robert A. (1972). *Polyarchy: Participation and Opposition*. New Haven: Yale University Press.

Dillman, Bradford (1992). 'Transition to Democracy in Algeria'. in John P. Entelis and Phillip C. Naylor, *State and Society in Algeria*. Boulder, Colorado: Westview Press.

Duran, Khalid (1989). 'The Second Battle of Algiers'. *Orbis*, 33 (3): 403–21.

Entelis, John P. (1980). *Comparative Politics of North Africa: Algeria, Morocco and*

Tunisia. Syracuse, New York: Syracuse University Press.

—— (1988). 'Algeria under Chadli: liberalisation without democratisation or, perestroika, yes; glasnost, no!' *Middle East Insight*, 6 (3): 47–64.

—— (1992). 'Introduction: state and society in transition', in John P. Entelis and Phillip C. Naylor, *State and Society in Algeria*. Boulder, Colorado: Westview Press.

Farsoun, Samih K. (1988). 'Oil, state, and social structure'. *Arab Studies Quarterly*, 10 (2): 155–75.

Ghezali, Salima (1996). 'Fausse éclaircie en Algérie' ['False dawn in Algeria']. *Le Monde Diplomatique*, 1: 12 (February).

Hermida, Alfred (1992). 'Algeria: democracy derailed'. *Africa Report*, 37 (2): 13–17.

Hosseinzadeh, Esmail (1988). 'How Egyptian state capitalism diverted to market capitalism'. *Arab Studies Quarterly*, 10 (3): 299–317.

Huntington, Samuel P. (1991). *The Third Wave: Democratization in the Late Twentieth Century*. Norman: University of Oklahoma Press.

Huwaydi, Fahmi (1993). *'Ijhadh al-Hulm al-Dimuqrati fi Misr'* ['Abortion of the democratic dream in Egypt']. *Qira 'at Siyasiyya*, 3 (2): 139–45.

Hyden, Goran (1992). 'Governance and study of politics', in Goran Hyden and Michael Bratton, *Governance and Politics in Africa*. Boulder, Colorado: Lynne Rienner.

Jabr, Karam (1993). *'Al-Murashihoun lil-Ightiyal fi Misr'* ['Candidates for Assassination in Egypt']. *Al-Kifah al-Arabi*, 20 (770): 18–20.

Kaidi, Hamza (1992). *'Comment l'armeé fait de la politique malgré elle'* ['How the army makes politics in spite of itself']. *Jeune Afrique*, 16–23 January: 7–8.

Macdonald, Scott B. (1989). 'The Middle East's new economic wave'. *Middle East Insight*, 6 (6): 47.

Maghraoui, Abdessalem (1992). 'Problems of transition to democracy: Algeria's short-lived experiment with electoral politics'. *Middle East Insight*, 8 (6): 20–6.

Makram-Ebeid, Mona (1989). 'Political opposition in Egypt: myth or reality'. *Middle East Journal*, 43 (3): 423–36.

Mansour, Fawzi (1992). *The Arab World: Nation, State and Democracy*. London: Zed Books.

Mattoon, Scott (1992). 'Islam by profession'. *The Middle East*, 218: 16–18.

—— (1993). 'A sense of foreboding'. *The Middle East*, 219: 36–7.

Moench, Richard U. (1987). 'The May 1984 elections in Egypt and the question of Egypt stability', in Linda L. Layne, *Elections in the Middle East: Implications of Recent Trends*. Boulder, Colorado: Westview Press.

Mortimer, Robert A. (1990). 'Algeria after the explosion'. *Current History*, 89 (546): 163–4.

O'Donnell, Guillermo and Schmitter, Philippe C. (1986). *Transitions from Authoritarian Rule: Prospects for Democracy*. Baltimore: Johns Hopkins University Press.

Owen, Roger (1992). *State, Power and Politics in the Making of the Modern Middle East*. London: Routledge.

Pfeifer, Karen (1992). 'Economic liberalisation in the 1980s: Algeria in comparative perspective', in John P. Entelis and Phillip C. Naylor, *State and Society in Algeria*. Boulder, Colorado: Westview Press.

Pautard, André (1992). *'Algérie: le plan des généraux'* ['Algeria: the junta's agenda']. *L'Express*, 2115 (January): 10–11.

Przeworski, Adam (1988). 'Democracy as a contingent outcome of conflicts', in Jon Elster and Rune Slagstad, *Constitutionalism and Democracy*. Cambridge: Cambridge University Press.

Sadiki, Larbi (1992). *Progression and Retrogression of Arab Democratisation*. East Jerusalem: PASSIA.

—— (1993). 'Islamists Fight the Secular State'. *Canberra Times*, 9 (13 August).

—— (1995). 'Guided Democracy in Algeria and Egypt'. *Australian Journal of International Affairs*, 49 (2) (November): 249–66.

Sid-Ahmed, Mohamed (1993). *'Impasse en Égypte'* ['Stalemate in Egypt']. *Le Monde*, 1 (9 June): 18.

Tezgharit, Outhman (1993). *'Askar Jabhat al-Inqadh'* ['The FIS soldiers']. *Al-Majallah*, 692 (May): 50–4.

Yahmed, Bechir (1992). *'Chadli était la malchance de l'Algérie'* ['Chadli was Algeria's misfortune']. *Jeune Afrique*, 1619 (January): 9.

Yared, Marc (1992). *'A la tête de l'Algérie: deux généraux et deux civils'* ['Leading Algeria: two generals and two civilians']. *Jeune Afrique*, 1619 (January): 5–7.

Primary Sources

AHRO (1993). *'Al-Ta'dilat 'ala Qanun al-Ahzab al-Siyasiyya Khutwa fi al-Ittijah al-Mu'akis'* ['Amendments to the political parties law: a step antithetical to pluralism']. In *Background Briefing*, 60/61 (February–March).

EHRO (1993a). *Onslaught on Union Freedoms and the Right to Organise*. EHRO Press Release (21 February). Cairo: EHRO.

—— (1993b). *'Imbaba: Sura Mukathafa li-Attadahwur al-Mutazayid Li-Halati Huquq al-Insan wa li-Ihtiram al-Qanun fi Misr'* ['Imbaba: a vivid image of Egypt's increasing deterioriation of human rights and respect for the law']. EHRO Special Report (20 March). Cairo: EHRO.

Reuter Australasian Briefing (22 May 1993). 'Top Muslim Theologian Opposes Murder of Foreigners.' *Reuters News Textline*.

—— (22 June 1993). 'Algeria: PM says there will be no Dialogue with Destructive Forces.' *Reuters News Textline*.

—— (23 June 1993). 'Algeria: High State Council Issues Document on National Dialogue.' *Reuters News Textline*.

– 4 –

The Rehabilitation and Reconstruction of Lebanon

Maroun Kisirwani

The fierce fighting that engulfed Lebanon for fifteen years, starting from 1975, left deep scars in some of its institutions and crippled others. Of a total population of three million, over 150,000 were killed, 300,000 were displaced, and approximately half a million emigrated. As the war intensified, society was increasingly dismantled and divided on confessional grounds, as were its social, political, administrative and military institutions. The prosperity that the country had known before the war was destroyed, and its infrastructure was devastated. The physical destruction of residential and industrial areas was immense.

After fifteen years of continuous destruction of human and material resources, the country was ready for any reasonable settlement to end the prolonged blood bath and a socially, economically and politically crippling war. A political accord known as the T'aif Agreement was finally drawn up in 1989, by Lebanese politicians, in the Saudi city of T'aif, under Saudi patronage, with the blessing of the United States and with Syrian approval (*The Economist*, 20 October 1990).

To a war-weary population desperate to end its prolonged misery and the appalling destruction of its country, the T'aif Agreement certainly appeared as a great relief and an important and necessary step towards reuniting the country and rehabilitating and reconstructing its institutions (Salibi, 1988: 3). Yet the agreement which is credited for ending the war and introducing accommodating changes to the political system has left behind serious socio-economic problems and a political maze with which the country continues to struggle. The unsettled problems have led to genuine disappointment among major Christian groups, and consequently to their withdrawal from political affairs. The Gulf War of 1990, which drained the Gulf states financially, forced these states to default on their financial commitment of

US$2,000 million for the rehabilitation and reconstruction of the Lebanon. Thus, after approximately seven years since the signing of T'aif Agreement, the country remains politically precarious, and its reconstruction continues to stagger.

The aim of this chapter is to investigate the efforts that the Lebanese state has been exerting towards the rehabilitation and reconstruction of its political, administrative and economic system, and the restraints it has encountered in the process. Although the three systems – the political, the administrative and the economic – are interrelated and interdependent, each will be treated separately. What will be examined, firstly, is the dynamics of the current political system and their impact on the establishment of a permanently viable state. Next, an attempt is made to assess the scope and intensity of the economic destruction caused by the war, and the financing required for economic recovery. Third, the paper investigates the post-war capabilities of the bureaucracy, which is primarily responsible for the implementation of the rehabilitation and reconstruction scheme.

The Quest for a Viable Political Structure

Modern Lebanon was established in 1920 under the tutelage of France, the mandatory power over Lebanon and Syria, following the defeat of Turkey in the First World War. Prior to this period, and for approximately four centuries, the Lebanese political system, which functioned under Ottoman tutelage, had known various structures with varying degrees of semi-autonomous status, depending on the military power of the local prince or governor and his relationship with the Ottoman authorities.

The semi-autonomous status of the Lebanese province came to an end in 1915, when the region was placed under direct Ottoman rule during the First World War. It remained in this position until 1918, when Syria and Lebanon were occupied by the Allies (Longring, 1958: 65). On 25 April 1920 the Allied Supreme Council granted France a mandate over Syria and Lebanon, and on 31 August of the same year the French High Commissioner declared the establishment of Greater Lebanon. The territory of the old province of Lebanon was extended to its present boundaries by adding the coastal regions of Beirut, Sidon, Tyre and Tripoli, as well as the Bekaa Valley (Longring, 1958: 376).

Since its inception in 1920, the modern state of Lebanon faced internal confessional conflicts as well as regional claims by parts of its territory, both of which have constituted factors contributing to the country's political instability and military confrontations. Both the

Lebanese Muslims and Syria opposed the establishment of Greater Lebanon from the very start. The Muslims questioned the legitimacy of the new state and their own citizenship in it, and demanded the return to Syria of the annexed regions, which were largely Muslim in population. Syria claimed that the annexed territories were Syrian territories that had remained under effective Syrian control. The Maronites, who were the largest Christian community, declined to accept any changes, affirming that the boundaries of the new geopolitical unit constituted the natural frontiers of Lebanon (Naamani, 1982: 65).

The categorically opposing views of the religious communities and the Syrian rejection of the new frontiers of Lebanon led to an exchange of serious accusations, which kept the country in a state of frequent confrontations and turmoil. The Muslims accused the Maronites of pursuing policies that aimed at isolating Lebanon from Syria and the Arab hinterland, and on one occasion consequently submitted a written memorandum to the French High Commission calling for unity with Syria. Also, a delegation of Muslim notables visited Damascus, pleading with the Syrian authorities to incorporate into the Syrian constitution an article laying claim to the Muslim districts of Lebanon. Although the Mandatory power subdued the Muslim requests and dissolved the Syrian constitutional assembly that issued a constitution including articles claiming Lebanese territory, the dispute over the question of the territorial integrity of Lebanon and the legitimacy of the Lebanese state as established remained far from settled (Lenezowski, 1952: 233).

While ideological conflicts and opposing political outlooks persisted among the communal groups during the Mandate period, the first conciliatory breakthrough in communal relationships came with independence in 1943, when a power-sharing political arrangement, known as the National Pact, was reached between Christians and Muslims. The Pact sought an end to the Sunni-Muslim demand for unity with Syria, or any Arab state, in exchange for the Maronite Christians' relinquishing French protection. The National Pact had the positive aim of putting an end to the conflicting communal outlooks by recognising the full and complete independence of Lebanon from both East and West, affirming its national identity as part of the Arab World, and denying any concession or privileged position for any foreign state.

The pact provided the newly independent state with a period of relative stability and prosperity, but was often ignored before the 1958 civil war by both Christians and Muslims. The pact collapsed completely with the beginning of the 1975 turbulence (Salem, 1991: 76).

As the war intensified, the state was divided into warring camps, with the majority of Christians on one side and the Muslim and Palestinian groups on the other. Each group sought, and actually received, political, financial and military support from foreign nations. The causes of the tragic developments that pervaded Lebanon for fifteen years are as varied and numerous as the hundreds of scholars and statesmen who tried to unfold the riddles and make sense out of a chaotic situation that involved local, regional and international players simultaneously, albeit pursuing different objectives. Each group involved in the conflict, directly or by proxy, had its own objectives, and history alone may uncover the real causes of the Lebanese war. In the midst of confusing interpretations of the causes of Lebanon's war one fact seems certain; namely, that communal tensions have been, and remain, easy targets for manipulation by local and foreign forces alike to achieve their respective personal objectives at the expense of the general interest of Lebanon as a nation-state. During the last phases of the war, the Muslim demand for a more equitable power-sharing arrangement resurfaced, with the claim that the National Pact of 1943 had become obsolete and inequitable. The T'aif Agreement was the culmination of several earlier endeavours to bring a cessation to hostilities through a new power-sharing arrangement. The often-expressed assumption that the T'aif Agreement had established a viable political settlement remains questionable; and, consequently, political rehabilitation remains precarious.

Pitfalls of the T'aif Agreement

Though the T'aif Agreement put an end to the war, it failed to end political conflicts and meet the aspirations of all communal groups. Paul Salem (1991) provides a balance sheet of the main points of the agreement, along with the major arguments surrounding them. Salem's account (Salem, 1991: 77–8) of the fundamental changes dealing with internal political reform includes the following:

a. Executive authority was shifted from the Maronite President of the Republic to the Council of Ministers, thus rendering the government one of collegiate decision-making, and stripping the president of most of his executive powers by reducing him 'to a largely ceremonial figure who reigns but does not rule'.
b. The Sunni post of Prime Minister became the central position in the affairs of government, since the holder of this post 'controls the agenda of the Council of Ministers and oversees the daily

operations of the state bureaucracy'. In addition, his appointment and dismissal is no longer under the control of the Maronite President, as was the case before. The Prime Minister can now be removed only by a decision of the parliament.

c. The Shi'ite post of speaker of Parliament was also strengthened 'by extending its term to four years and centrally involving the speaker in designating a Prime Minister'.

d. Equality of representation between Christians and Muslims was established, replacing the old formula, which gave the Christians a representational edge over Muslims.

e. The abolition of political confessionalism is, according to the T'aif Agreement, a fundamental national goal, along with the establishment of universal social and economic justice.

The internal political reforms introduced by the T'aif Agreement into the Lebanese Constitution represent a new start in inter-confessional relationships in Lebanon – a start that is not without its inherent dangers and serious threats to the revival of the state and, consequently, to the rehabilitation and reconstruction process that is now under way. Among the dangers that have already become apparent in the new political structure, two appear to be the most significant. Firstly, there is a growing complaint among the Christians that the state, according to the new Constitution that stripped the Maronite President of his executive powers, is currently dominated by a Sunni Prime Minister and a Shi'ite Speaker of Parliament, to the disadvantage of the Christians in general. This complaint represents the opposite extreme to the old Muslim complaint that the state, under the National Pact of 1943, was dominated by a Maronite President to the disadvantage of other groups (Salem, 1991: 77–8). If the Muslims' dissatisfaction with the old political formula had deprived the state of stability, national identity and national consensus for several decades, then the Christian dissatisfaction with the new political framework is likely to lead to similar paralysis and political instability within Lebanon, unless remedial measures are introduced to provide a fair and equitable power-sharing structure.

Secondly, the majority of Christians boycotted the first parliamentary elections under the new constitution, in protest against the reluctance of the Syrian forces to withdraw from western parts of Lebanon within two years of the enactment of the political reforms, as ordained in the T'aif Agreement. This reluctance to withdraw and redeploy in the Bekaa Valley, in addition to the absence of any commitment, as yet, to a full Syrian withdrawal from the country, intensified the fears of the Christians of permanent Syrian domination;

and, consequently, they had doubts about the guaranteeing of free and democratic elections. Yet, the elections were held, and Christians were elected to occupy the parliamentary seats allotted to them. Real representation of the Christian community, however, was absent, since most of the recognised leaders either boycotted the elections or remained outside the country.

In concluding this part of the chapter on the political structure since the T'aif Agreement and its impact on the rehabilitation and reconstruction process, one may venture the opinion that as long as a majority of the Christians, including those who supported T'aif, continue to express genuine frustration with the new system, feeling that the agreement was negotiated under duress and that its implementation was skewed to suppress them, political rehabilitation as a process of reviving the state through the reconstitution of a unified political culture and a national identity is not likely to be achieved in the near future.

Economic Collapse

The Lebanese economy has traditionally been marked by liberalism and a *laissez-faire* economy – a trait that to some extent accounts for the prosperity that Lebanon had experienced prior to the war. A further partial explanation for the former economic prosperity of Lebanon, other than its *laissez-faire* system, is that it could be attributed to the effects of various overall political and economic developments in the region. The occupation of Palestine in 1948, the closure of the Suez Canal in 1967, the nationalisation and socialisation of economies in several Arab countries and the oil boom of 1973 have all contributed to the economic development of Lebanon, though to varying degrees (LCPS, 1992: 26).

These developments led to the transfer of human and material resources to Lebanon, and this, in turn, transformed the country into the banking, education, hospitalisation and tourism centre of the Middle East. Lebanon's success during this period of favourable circumstances, however, was also attributable to a number of skills and traits that the country and its people have provided. Paramount among these skills are its *laissez-faire* economic system, its entrepreneurial spirit, an educated labour force exposed to both Arab and Western culture, the absence of currency exchange controls, a well-developed banking sector and good transport and telecommunications facilities. These facilities, along with regional developments, attracted many

Western firms to Beirut, which served as their base for regional and international trade and services (International Bechtel, 1992 (42): 1).

The per capita GDP in 1973 amounted to US$940, a figure surpassed in the region only by some of the oil states, Cyprus and Israel. The sectoral composition of the GDP in this period revealed that the bulk of the economic activities (58 per cent) were in trade and non-financial services, such as transport, rents, health and education services (Table 4.1).

While economists agree that Lebanon's economy was growing in the pre-war period at an average compound rate of 6.8 per cent, raising per capita real national income at a yearly average of 4.3 per cent, they differ in their interpretation of this remarkable growth and its social and political repercussions. One view asserts that the economic growth 'did not come from any coherent development strategy carried out by the public sector, nor were the fruits of this growth evenly distributed among the different categories of the population' (Awad, 1991: 82). The high dependence, according to this view, on the service sector, the absence of a dynamic role for the public sector and a well-designed developmental policy 'led to socio-economic imbalances and strains which contributed to the breakdown of the socio-political order and the outbreak of civil strife' (Awad, 1991: 85). While the country's economy was growing, it was not developing, according to this view, because the benefits of growth were heavily concentrated in one sector – the tertiary sector, and especially trade. Table 4.2 shows per capita income in Lebanon by economic sector

Table 4.1. Sectoral Composition of GDP, 1973

Sector	Percentage		Percentage
Agriculture	9.3		
Industry	14.4		
Construction	4.4		
Utilities	2.0		
Trade (Including Hotels/Restaurants)	31.7		
Non-Financial Services	27.1	*of which*:	
		Transport	7.2
		Rents	8.6
		Others (health, education, etc.)	11.3
Financial Services	4.0		
Public Administration	7.1		

Source: International Bechtel, 1992 (42): 2.

in 1970. Regardless of the imbalance in the distribution of income clearly shown in Table 4.2, the pre-war Lebanese economy was managing well until the Israeli invasion in 1982 and the events of 1984, which constituted a major turning-point (al-Khalil, 1992: 85).

The pre-war growth of the Lebanese economy was, therefore, steady and relatively healthy. It was the war that wrecked its foundations. The massive destruction of the country's infrastructure, following the Israeli invasion in 1982; the huge damage inflicted on agriculture, industry, and the service sector; the loss and impairment of human resources; all these had detrimental effects on the Lebanese economy (al-Khalil, 1992: 85). As the war intensified, not only was Lebanon cut off from the rest of the world, but also the destruction of its human and material resources was immense, and its infrastructure was crippled (LCPS, 1992: 27).

The heaviest blow to the economy, however, came with the beginning of 1984, when the army was split, the state lost control of the capital and other areas of the country to the militias, and lawlessness began to prevail. The economy was then completely exhausted, as the public revenues were cut off, the GNP continually contracting and the public sector expenditures steady. The state was forced to finance its budget through deficit financing, mainly by printing money and borrowing from the private sector. By the early 1990s, the state had accumulated a public debt of over US$4,000 million, which contributed to the devaluation of the Lebanese pound from US$1.00 = LP 3.00 in 1975 , to US$1.00 = LP 2,750 in October 1992. This economic plunge was accompanied by skyrocketing inflation of over 500 per cent, excessive destruction of residential and industrial areas, industrial stagnation, and phenomenal devastation of electricity and telecommunication infrastructures (LCPS, 1992: 30).

In brief, the economic consequences of the war could be grouped into three broad areas. First, the destruction of productive facilities and infrastructures. Second, indirect damages caused by the failure

Table 4.2. Per Capita Income by Sector in 1970

Sector	Per Capita Income $	Per Capita Increase as of % of GDP	Sector as % of Population
Agriculture	175	9.1	175
Industry	503	18.1	503
Services	1,256	72.8	1,256

Source: adapted from Awad, 1991: 14.

to renew capital assets and to develop human resources. Third, the migration overseas of hundreds of thousands of the educated élite and of skilled manpower, which resulted in a great loss to the country (International Bechtel, 1992 (42): 2).

The National Reconstruction Programme

On 8 June 1991 the first step in an arduous journey for the rehabilitation, reconstruction and development of Lebanon began. The Lebanese government, represented by the Council of Development and Reconstruction (CDR), and the Hariri Foundation entered into an agreement with International Bechtel Incorporated and Dar Al-Handasah Consultants for providing consulting services for 'Recovery Planning for the Reconstruction and Development of Lebanon' (International Bechtel, 1992 (42): 3).

Bechtel and Dar Al-Handasah prepared extensive reports and working papers covering all aspects and strategies pertaining to the reconstruction process, culminating in a grand plan labelled *Horizon 2000 for Reconstruction and Development*. Some of the proposed strategies, whose foundations would be laid during the course of the reconstruction programme, would come into effect around the year 2003 and beyond. The long-term aims of these strategies were to maximise income growth, minimise income distribution disparities, and increase social cohesion.

Lebanon's recovery programme, according to the Bechtel and Dar Al-Handasah study, presents an opportunity to recreate and reposition the nation advantageously for the future. The reconstruction period affords Lebanon the chance to engage in thinking about the future and pro-active planning (International Bechtel, 1992 (42): 1). The six strategies that are intended for implementation by the private sector, operating within a free market, concentrate on the development of tourism, agriculture, niche industries, higher education, Lebanon's geographic and cultural position as the 'bridge' between Europe and Arabia, and the development of 'consultancy and knowledge-based service industries'. All the strategies, however, presume the success of the reconstruction programme and look beyond its initial economic growth (International Bechtel, 1992 (42): 1). The question, however, remains: what are the chances for the success of the rehabilitation and reconstruction programme?

A pivotal role in preparing the plan *Horizon 2000 for the Reconstruction and Development of Lebanon* was entrusted to the CDR. In co-operation with Bechtel and Dar Al-Handasah and a number of local and foreign firms, the Horizon 2000 plan was finalised and submitted by the CDR to the Council of Ministers in February 1993, with a total cost of US$10,995 million (at current fixed prices reaching US$12,900 million over a ten-year period). Table 4.3 shows the estimated cost per sector.

Financing the Programme

The Bechtel and Dar al-Handasah study has recommended a number of fiscal and monetary measures for the Lebanese government to introduce for financing the Horizon 2000 plan, and concluded by identifying three major financing sources. First is the surplus from the Lebanese national budget that is expected to be achieved by the beginning of 1996. Secondly, internal borrowing through treasury bills 'could be used to cover unfinanced local costs' (International Bechtel, 1993 (37): 1). Thirdly, foreign financing would be obtained from various donors and financial institutions; this would consist of funds provided either on an outright grant basis, or concessional loans, or a mix of grants and loans (Bashir, 1994 (42): 67).

In terms of expenditure stages and financing sources, the plan recognises the following three periods. First, the rehabilitation period

Table 4.3. Lebanon's Ten-Year Reconstruction Programme 1992–2003

Sector	Cost (Million US$)
Electricity	1,800
Health	825
Waste Management	180
Communications	620
Transport	2,845
Water	415
Education	1,135
Social Welfare	600
Agriculture	585
Industry	350
Fuel Oil	70
Services	300
Public Buildings	170
Management	150
Housing	950
Total	10,995

Source: Republic of Lebanon, 1992.

(1993–5), which is expected to cost US$2,700 million in current prices, the money to be secured from internal borrowing (13 per cent), grants (21 per cent), and external borrowing (66 per cent). Second, the reconstruction period (1996–8), which is expected to cost US$4,000 million in current prices, the money to be secured from national budget surplus (38 per cent), external grants (10 per cent) and external borrowing (52 per cent). Third, the development period (1999–2003), which is expected to cost US$6,200 million in current prices, the money to be secured from national budget surplus (65 per cent), external borrowing (31 per cent), and external grants (4 per cent). The figures that have been quoted above, used when the plan was submitted to the Council of Ministers in February 1993, are already being reconsidered, and CDR sources were, by November, 1993, estimating that the total cost would reach US$17,700 million in current prices, and that the rehabilitation phase was expected to cost US$3,200 million, instead of the US$2,700 million estimated earlier (Bashir, 1994 (42): 68).

This ambitious scheme for financing Lebanon's reconstruction requirements rests on a number of long-range political, administrative, economic and monetary assumptions that are, to say the least, precarious. Among the strategies recommended for maximising external assistance is that Lebanon should assure donors that the security situation in the country has improved enough to allow the implementation of assistance programmes, and that its debt service to the donor countries will be paid on time (International Bechtel, 1993: 37: i). Lebanon is in no position to extend such a 'warranty' while its political security is subject to regional and international developments beyond its control. Likewise, the government confidence that the financial requirements for implementing the *Horizon 2000* plan would be secured is not substantiated by the funds that have been externally committed, in contrast to those that have materialised internally. The T'aif Agreement provided, seven years ago, for the creation of an International Fund for the assistance of Lebanon, during which the signatories pledged to pay over US$2,000 million as initial capital. Yet hardly US$300 million has been paid so far. Finally, the implementation of such an ambitious plan, even if the political and economic variables were favourable, would still depend on the existence of a public bureaucracy capable of coping with such a task.

Bureaucratic Disintegration and Revitalisation

Lebanon's bureaucracy has been shaped both by indigenous cultural and political traditions and by the long history of Ottoman and, later, French domination. Despite strong French influence on formal structures, however, the Lebanese bureaucracy, in practice, is quite different from the French, as might be expected, considering the great differences between the two societies. French society is modern, and its institutions possess a common cultural tradition and national identity. Lebanon is a transitional society, with many traditional elements. It is relatively undifferentiated in its social institutions, encompasses a number of different and often conflicting cultural traditions, and possesses a much weaker sense of national identity.

Informally, the Lebanese bureaucracy is built on the principle of sectarianism. This stems from the National Pact of 1943, which allocated political and governmental positions among Lebanon's different religious groups. The principle of sectarian representation is also found in the composition of parliament, the army and the bureaucracy, and encompasses seventeen officially recognised sects.

The Lebanese bureaucracy also differs from the 'ideal type'[1] in two common practices of great political importance: the granting of favourable treatment by bureaucrats on the basis of political loyalty, family influence, class or sect; and the charging of a cash gratuity by officials for government services (Kisirwani and Parle, 1987: 1–2). These forms of bureaucratic pathology are of great significance in a conflict-prone society, where these practices have helped to make bureaucratic performance a continuing political issue. Most Lebanese view these practices as corrupt and undesirable, yet despite the pre-war reform efforts of over three decades, they have persisted (Kisirwani, 1992: 32). Corruption, sectarianism and subservience to political influence are, by themselves, formidable obstacles that would undermine the effective and efficient performance of the daily routine work of the bureaucracy. With the additional pathologies and the dismantling of the bureaucracy, along with the increased responsibilities, of the post-war era, the role of the bureaucracy in the rehabilitation and reconstruction process is critical.

The civil war period severely impaired the ability of the Lebanese bureaucracy to function, but by no means destroyed it (Kisirwani, 1992: 29–42). Generally speaking, the major functions of a public bureaucracy are the provision of infrastructure, the production and delivery of public services, and the maintenance of social order. The most visible impact of the conflict over the civil war years was the inability of the bureaucracy to maintain order and to provide security.

The conflict rendered the army and the courts unable to function.

Among the most serious effects of the war that dominated Lebanon were the erosion of hierarchical authority, increased problems of co-ordination among and between administrative units, considerable loss of personnel, the inability of the oversight agencies to perform their functions, the loss of much of the professional workforce and a decline in employee professionalism and career attachments, and an increase in the prevalence of economic corruption and the use of political and personal influence (Kisirwani, 1992: 33).

The foundations of the bureaucracy were destroyed, and its machinery was dismantled. Yet its destruction does not appear to have been a major goal of any of the contending factions. For the most part, the governmental bureaucracy was permitted to operate, albeit in limited way, in areas under the armed control of the different factions. This led to some bizarre incidents. For example, on several occasions in Beirut, temporary ceasefires were called during the fighting so that government workers could enter the contested area to repair damaged power and telephone lines, or to cash their wages at the end of each month.

This does not imply that the combatants always acted neutrally with respect to the bureaucracy. The Lebanese factions did exert considerable influence on the activities of the bureaucracy in areas that they controlled until 1990; but they stopped short of dismantling it. The most serious challenge to the bureaucracy occurred in East Beirut and the Shuf Mountains. In these districts, the factional organisations collected 'taxes' and provided some types of services, such as street cleaning, rubbish collection and food distribution. But these efforts seemed to have been supplementary and temporary in nature, not permanent replacements for governmental activity. In 1977, when a settlement of the conflict seemed imminent, the militias in all districts indicated a willingness to restore to the central government certain collective functions they had assumed and to dissolve some local government structures they had established. In 1989, they allowed the government to establish control over the ports that they had built or controlled. By 1990, the Lebanese government had succeeded in re-establishing its administrative control over most of the country in accordance with the settlement reached at T'aif.

During the more intense years of the conflict, the government leadership found itself unable to enforce decisions by the bureaucracy and unable to guarantee the personal safety of officials who made unpopular but correct decisions. Ultimately it was even unable to enforce its own rules of conduct against officials with political connections. Consequently, in these areas of activity, the political leadership eventually gave up, perceiving no action to be possible. Bureaucratic forms were maintained: most employees continued to report for work; salaries continued to be paid; committees met; paperwork was maintained. Confrontation with the political groups and their armed wings was by and large avoided. In less controversial areas, the bureaucracy continued to function, but suffered difficulties arising from lack of co-ordination.

Generally, the government attempted to take advantage of periods of relative calm, perceiving them as opportunities to reassert its authority. During these periods, also, high-level political and administrative leaders would make public statements announcing the restoration of normal activities. During these periods, also, administrative rulings or circulars would be issued to government employees. These directives would exhort employees to return to their jobs on a regular basis, and also inform them that various rules of conduct that might have been overlooked as a result of the conflict were now reinstated and were not to be ignored. In short, efforts could be made on these occasions to promote the notion of an impending return to normalcy. On the whole, however, these efforts met with only limited success. In fact, the bureaucracy guaranteed its survival during those difficult periods by tacitly abandoning many of its formal rules for the sake of expediency. For example, employees were allowed to transfer to safer government offices closer to their residence, often on their own initiative. Even government officials who were out of the country remained on the employment rolls and continued to receive salaries and salary rises. Almost no one was fired or forced to resign.

Even the practice of condoning widespread economic and political corruption had a functional aspect. Although it had badly tarnished the image of the bureaucracy, it kept employees on the job. The small salaries paid to lower-level officials might not have provided the necessary economic incentive for many to remain with the civil service. Only at higher levels were some officials provided with the incentive of potentially accumulating substantial wealth if they stayed in their jobs. Otherwise, bureaucrats imposed a gratuity as a kind of personal tax on any public transaction.

Another area where the bureaucracy tended to ignore the formal rules was in the way that it responded to the pressures brought to bear upon it by political groups and organisations seeking favoured treatment. Requests for such special treatment were sometimes based on family, friendship, or political ties. But, they were often accompanied by threats against individuals and their families – threats that were perfectly credible. When such threats came from more than one group, the result was frequently bureaucratic paralysis. When caught in a political cross-fire, doing nothing was sometimes the most prudent course of action. In large measure, this was simply reflective of one of the realities of Lebanese life. The government could not enforce the laws, nor could it provide security to officials whose decisions made them unpopular with one political group or another. It is difficult to blame individual bureaucrats for giving in to this sort of pressure.

In terms of bureaucratic behaviour, note must be taken of the choices and incentives that individual bureaucrats had to face in the circumstances of the civil war. By and large, the dynamics of the situation converged to promote traditional rather than formal bureaucratic values.

The government's inability to enforce the regulations governing employees' conduct was one aspect of the situation. The lack of security in the country was another. The general need to accumulate funds as a possible source of security, should the situation deteriorate, enhanced the importance of economic incentives, and perhaps the tendency towards economic corruption. In addition, the need for political influence in order to maintain one's position or to advance in the bureaucracy became increasingly important.

Finally, in a country where political assassinations and kidnappings became regular occurrences, the need to avoid antagonising any of the armed factions was very real in a personal sense. Given these inducements, it is easy to understand the non-professional behaviour of many officials. There were also many officials who deplored what they regarded as the poor performance of the bureaucrats and the bureaucracy, but who felt helpless, frustrated and unable to act.[2]

Although the bureaucracy has survived despite considerable damage and lasting scars, it has succumbed further to economic corruption, favouritism and political intervention in the face of the pressures generated by the intensity of the conflict. The most serious problems that the bureaucracy encountered during the war and that are still felt at present, though in various degrees of intensity, are the following:

a. Paralysis of the central control agencies; the Civil Service Board, the Central Inspection Board, the Disciplinary Council and the Bureau of Accounts.
b. 'Institutionalisation' of bribery and extortion. Civil servants in certain administrative units 'priced' public transactions, and would not process any transaction unless the price – a personal tax – was paid. The revenues were shared among employees in a ratio corresponding to their ranks.

c. Understaffing. The vacancies that have accrued over the war years in the top administrative positions have deprived the bureaucracy of executives and planners. Up to few months ago, vacancies amounted to 48 per cent of grade one positions (these were filled recently), 60 per cent of grade two positions, and 62 per cent of grade three positions.

d. Overstaffing. Vacancies in lower positions (grades four and five) have reached 62 per cent, but this was over-compensated for by ministers appointing thousands of unqualified daily workers and contractors in total disregard of their qualifications. The bureaucracy is swollen now with appointees of this type, whose numbers exceed twenty thousand.

e. Collapse of hierarchical authority and loss of bureaucratic credibility.

As a result of the emergence of new values and behaviour patterns and the new political-military élites of the militias, the structure of bureaucratic authority collapsed. And, as a consequence of this phenomenon and of the epidemic spread of economic corruption and political favouritism, bureaucracy lost whatever credibility it had had (Kisirwani, 1993). To free the bureaucracy of these pathologies – or at least to curb them – is an elephantine task in Lebanon. Administrative reform has been an eternal theme for both governments and people. Governments have resorted to it with varied motivations, one of which has been to obtain credibility. The public has always aspired to a reformed administration that provides services efficiently and effectively and ensures equitable treatment. Both governments and the public in Lebanon have lost their bids so far.

After approximately seven years of relative peace and security, it appears that the efforts of Lebanese governments to reform the administration have lacked the political will, determination and perseverance that are the basic requirements for achieving reform. Despite the assistance that has been provided by the World Bank, the United Nations Development Programme and the United States Agency for International Development, there is no indication yet of any improvement in the performance of the Lebanese bureaucracy. Considering the gigantic task of rehabilitation and reconstruction, and the combined old and war-generated pathologies of the administration, the bureaucracy is not ready yet to undertake such an operation.

In concluding this chapter, and in view of the preceding account of the post-war political maze, economic destruction and precarious assumptions regarding the availability of funds, along with the permanent pathologies of the bureaucracy, one is justified in doubting the prospects for success of the reconstruction programme. Unless political harmony is reached among communal groups and national consensus is developed, and unless the bureaucracy itself is rehabilitated and fortified against political interference and sectarian cleavages, the reconstruction of Lebanon will remain an unattainable objective far beyond Horizon 2000.

Notes

1. The designation 'ideal type' refers to the common practices among Lebanese bureaucrats of granting favours to citizens on a basis other than merit, and the charging of cash gratuities. These practices are bureaucratic pathologies that defy rationality, impersonality and professionalism – which constitute the pivotal characteristics of Max Weber's formulation of an 'ideal type' bureaucracy.
2. A number of civil servants, including the Director-General of the Ministry of Finance, were assassinated.

References

al-Khalil, Yusif (1992). 'Economic developments in Lebanon since 1982'. *The Beirut Review*, 3.

Awad, Fuad (1991). 'The economics of coincidence and disasters in Lebanon'. *The Beirut Review*, 2.

Bashir, Iskandar (1994). *Development in Lebanon – in Arabic*. Beirut: Dar-Al-Ilm-Lil-Malayeen.

International Bechtel (International Bechtel Inc. and Dar-Al-Handasah) (1992). *Recovery Planning for the Reconstruction and Development of Lebanon*. Beirut: reports prepared for the Council for Development and Reconstruction, 42 and 39.

—— (1993). *Recovery Planning for the Reconstruction and Development of Lebanon*. Beirut: reports prepared for the Council for Development and Reconstruction, 37.

Kisirwani, Maroun (1992). 'The Lebanese bureaucracy under stress. How did it survive?'. *The Beirut Review*, 4.

—— (1993). *Strategies for Administrative Reform*. Paper submitted at a Washington, D.C. workshop on the reconstruction of Lebanon. AID and Chemonics International.

Kisirwani, Maroun and Parle, W. (1987). 'Assessing the impact of the post civil war period on the Lebanese bureaucracy. A view from inside'. *Journal of Asian and African Studies*, 22.

LCPS (Lebanese Center for Policy Studies) (1992). *Postwar Institutional Development in Lebanon*. Beirut: report prepared for America Mideast Educational and Training Services.

Lenezowski, George (1952). *The Middle East in World Affairs*. New York: Ithaca.

Longring, Stephen (1958). *Syria and Lebanon Under French Mandate*. London: Oxford University Press.

Naamani, Bassam (1982). Confessionalism in Lebanon, 1970–76. The Interplay of Domestic, Regional and International Politics. Columbia University Ph.D. dissertation.

Republic of Lebanon (1992). *The Year 2000 Plan*. Beirut: Republic of Lebanon.

Salem, Paul (1991). 'Two years of living dangerously. General Awn and Lebanon's second republic'. *The Beirut Review*, 1. 1.

Salibi, Kamal (1988). A House of Many Mansions. London: I. B. Tauris.

— 5 —

Islam Revisited: Wo(man)hood, Nationhood, and the Legitimating Crisis of Gender Equality

Nabila Jaber

In recent developments of political and cultural revivalism,[1] the discourse of 'identity politics' has merged with claims of nationalism and political state formation. Cultural authenticity and the 'rediscovery' of the history of peoples have become a central theme of global politics. These discourses have been articulated in both mainstream and feminist political and social theories (J. N. Anderson, 1983; Pateman, 1988; Yuval-Davis and Anthias, 1989). At the centre of this recent feminist debate, including Arab feminist contributions, is the subject of constituted women in nation-states. The arguments concerning women cover a wide spectrum, ranging from the representation of women in political discourses, and conceptions of citizenship, human rights and equality, to concerns with liberalising and/or constraining social policies that serve to legitimate gender inequality or reproduce (unequal) specific-gender identity. The political project of the state is thus placed at the centre of feminist analyses.

In Arab feminist discourses,[2] the analysis of the state and gender equality is concerned with the way in which gender identity and the constructed dichotomies of public and private worlds are reproduced in the discourses of the nation-state and nationalism (Badran and Cooke, 1990; Toubia, 1988). This 'discovery' of inherent sexism in the discourses of nations and identities is not confined to the Arab and/or Muslim worlds. In the Western tradition of feminist thought, it is argued that the maintenance of the separation between private and public (Phillips, 1991; Pateman, 1988) contradicts the assumptions of gender equality, the ideology of liberal individualism and the associated claims of citizenship rights.

However, unlike the Western tradition, Arab feminism, including Third World feminism, as a body of literature is concerned with nationalism and emancipation. The discourse(s) situate(s) the subject Woman in a postcolonial condition. In doing so, it both disrupts the constructs of 'modernity' and 'traditionalism' in colonial discourses, and at the same time critically analyses (male) discourses of national independence and development in terms of their implications concerning gender (in)equality and citizenship (Hatem, 1993; Badran, 1993; Helie-Lucas, 1990).

This chapter is concerned with the institutional legitimacy of women's citizenship in both domestic and public arenas in the Arab world. In particular, my aim is to explore the construct 'Woman' as a national subject, by focusing on the discursive productions of Arab nationalism and Islam. The analysis critically examines and problematises the way in which women's identity is reconstructed in the discourse(s) of nationalism and Islam. The construction of gendered national subjects is illustrated through an analysis of Arab nationalism, Islam, and the project of 'imagining' nations.

Defining the Problematic

Islam, as a religion and a practice, claims to constitute a historical continuity in the Arab world. The position of women within this common (patriarchal) Islamic tradition is constituted through the Islamic Law of the *Shari'ah*, which is derived from *Qura'nic* injunctions, and the *Hadith* (deeds and sayings of the prophet). Under the *Sharia'h* law, legislation dealing with the constitution of the family, including marriage, divorce and inheritance, and the duty of the wife *vis-à-vis* the husband, invariably positions women within an exclusively male terrain. The historical positioning is complicated by more recent discourses of Arab nationalism.

Discourses of Arab nationalism are situated in secular modernism – and in being so, are legitimated by 'emancipatory' civil laws – as well as in cultural traditionalism rooted in the ideology of Islam and legitimated by the *Shari'ah*. Each discourse is said to represent a specific social space, territorially divided and identified as public and domestic. I will argue, however, that the separation between these social spaces or locales, as represented in their corresponding legitimating discourses, is both the basis for reproducing gender inequalities and, paradoxically, a resource for what I will term a crisis of identity.

Between the project of modern aspirations and the continued Islamic cultural affirmation, I argue that the identity of Muslim women[3] manifests itself in what Kristeva (1980) terms a 'splitting subjectivity'.[4] On the one hand, the female subject is discursively positioned in the nationalist discourse to be men's equal in the public domain, when and if she earns a 'transcendental' subjectivity beyond her connectedness to her assumed natural feminine characteristics. On the other, she is constructed as an embodied subject whose identity is enshrined in motherhood and the family, the realm of the domestic and the personal. This 'splitting subjectivity' of Muslim women is thus situated in two constructed (male) discourses, each of which corresponds to a specific legitimating order. These two different sets of orders are represented in the institutionalisation of the *Shari'ah* law, prescribing the familial and the personal status code, and the emancipatory secular (civil) laws in the public sphere. In practice, the state legislation and the religious norms of the *Shari'ah* concerning women are in contradiction as much as they are in agreement. In both discourses women are positioned through the law of, to borrow Pateman's (1988) term, 'the sexual contract', or, put another way, in 'the law of male-sex rights' (Rich, 1980).

In *The Sexual Contract*, Pateman critically highlights the unspoken sexism inherent in social contract theory,[5] whose enactment in Western countries was only made possible by subjecting the female citizen to a 'sexual contract'. In Pateman's argument, patriarchy, instituted as a 'paternal contract', is fundamentally based on the 'conjugal contract', under which men as men exercise their sexual 'rights' over women. In the Arab/Muslim world, the subjection of women to men's sexual 'rights' as well as paternal privileges constitutes the foundation of the Islamic Law. It is in this context that discourses of nationalism, what Benedict Anderson (1983) calls 'imagined communities', also construct patriarchal supremacy.

Imagined Communities

In his book, *Imagined Communities* (1983), Benedict Anderson provides critical insights into the way in which communities are socially constructed by drawing on and at the same time problematising the boundary between reality and fiction. Imagined community, to Anderson, is a story about 'a dream possessing all institutional force and affect of the real', leading to practices that endlessly redefine the reconstructed boundaries between reality and illusion. In actualising the specific project of their dream, 'communities', according to Anderson, 'are to be distinguished not by their falsity/genuineness, but by the style in which they are imagined' (B. Anderson, 1983: 15).

In the Arab world, two dominant competing discourses of imagined communities can be located: the discourse of Islam as an *"umma'* that is regulated by the law of the sacred, and the discourse of the nation-state as a secular modern form of community. While each community is said to be in tension with the other, the positioning of women as a specific group is held crucial in maintaining the linkage between the two. In one community women's nationality is regulated by the *'umma*, through the *Shari'ah* Law; in the other it is constructed as a '"state" agent', following specific secular doctrines, associated with civil laws. The paradox of this positioning within the two communities is that the discursive woman subject comes to embody difference as much as sameness. In the following section the questions of how women are positioned between these two imagined communities and how woman's identity is shaped through a system of difference in nationalist discourses are discussed.

Nationalism and Nation-States: The Case of the Arab World

Nationalism in the modern world is intimately linked with the 'birth' of the modern nation-state where the state is identified with the nation and the two are collapsed into one. 'Nation-ness', according to Benedict Anderson (1983: 12) 'is the most universally legitimate value in the political life of our time'. As a model of 'political legitimacy', nationalism could be defined, as Radhakrihan (1992: 78) puts it, as 'an overarching umbrella that subsumes other and different political temporalities'. As a result, other identities – for example, religious, ethnic, or political – may carry political weight and appeal to national values, but their allegiance, it is claimed, is to be first and foremost to the state, which is often positioned as the sole legitimate force and protector of citizens' rights.

This homogenising force of nationalism has been recently challenged and redefined in non-fixed terms. For example, *Woman–Nation–State* (Yuval-Davis and Anthias, 1989: 4) problematises the conceptualisation of the nation-state as 'a unitary entity'. In their argument 'national processes can extend beyond the boundary of the state and vice versa'. Similarly, Bhabha (1990) has argued that the definition of modern nationhood is problematic, for 'no single term adequately defines the multiple difference dividing one nation from another or from itself'. This can be seen, for instance, in the current 'national liberation struggles' claimed by Islamists who reside in more than one Arab or Muslim state. In practice, then, the political allegiance assumed by the state is held in tension with other forms of collective allegiance. This is particularly so when the state fails to fulfil its claims of protection.

In addition to the state project of political allegiance, the project of nation-building also constitutes a legitimising narrative in the discourse of the modern nation-state. Nation-building is a story about national development and/or modernisation, a process of social change that penetrates the spheres of the economy, politics and culture, each of which assumes a crucial place in the making of national trans-formation. For example, industrialisation and technology are seen as necessary elements in developing the economy, and bureaucratisation and secularisation (separation between the state and religion) are held to furnish a rational approach to organising institutional arrangements, including the institution of the family and that of education (Turner, 1990). It should be emphasised that the project of national trans-formation in this context always holds promises of a possibility of a 'better future', such as an improved standard of living and independent political sovereignty.

In the Arab world, the formation of nation-states has been a twentieth-century phenomenon. Independent nation-states were established in the two decades following the Second World War. They were constituted through nationalist struggles and national independence movements against Western colonialism. For example, for Nasser, in Egypt, the project of nation-building constituted both a crucial step toward economic development and political sovereignty and an end to colonial domination. Significantly, however, in express-ing his opposition to Western influence, Nasser called for an Arab solidarity among newly emergent Arab nation-states on the grounds of shared commonality in religion, culture and (Arabic) language (Abdel Kader, 1987). In this case, Islam as a part of Arab identity constituted one element within the discourse of Arab nationalism.[6] This was to be true in all Arab countries (with the exception of Leb-anon), where Islam constituted an overarching umbrella for defining cultural boundaries and solidifying religious values (J. N. Anderson, 1976).

Whether modelled on principles of capitalism or socialism, nation-states in Arab countries (with few exceptions) have come to constitute 'corporate identities' (Lewis 1981:12), combining both religious and secular authorities and power (see, for example, Erturk, 1991). The outcome of this authorial duality is manifested in the structure of only partially secularised legal institutions. The secular (state) authority took on the political and economic projects, modernising the nation. As a result, modern secular legislation was carried out in virtually all institutional arrangements. The crucial exception was the institution of the family. In this area of gender relations religious authority retained power. The Law of the sacred or, *Shari'ah*, was thus retained in personal and family matters: 'The matters pertaining to personal status are however still regulated by *Shari'ah* Law which is administered by separate *Shari'ah* courts; and as such religion has still a great deal to do in governing the legal status of women' (Parveen, 1975: 195). It is, therefore, in the sphere of the family (culture) that Islamic religious allegiance takes precedence over the state, and in doing so claims continuity with an Islamic/cultural heritage concerning (traditional) gender relations.

As a result Arab nationalism 'speaks' through a dual discourse, situated in both the sacred and the profane. The sacred serves to stress historical continuity, or more accurately cultural 'heritage', while the secular promotes economic and political change. The significance of this dual discourse is that it constitutes itself as an oppositional force to cultural Westernisation (Coulson, 1978; Esposito, 1980).

In the following section I critically analyse the working of this dual discourse in relation both to women and to the way in which it has been utilised as a resource throughout nationalist struggles in the Arab world. In doing so, I briefly discuss the nature of legal reforms introduced and their implications for women.

Legal Reforms: the Secular and the Sacred

The transformation of the Muslim religio-political system in the Arab Middle East was a consequence of external control initiated by Western colonialism in the nineteenth century (J. N. Anderson, 1976). As a result, the *Shari'ah* law was replaced by secular law in its hold on penal, constitutional, and commercial laws. In the sphere of the family, however, the *Shari'ah* was successfully maintained.

After national independence was achieved in Arab countries, legal reforms were introduced in response to new demands associated with projects of development and modernisation. These reforms constituted the national ideology of the newly emerging nation-states, such as Egypt, Syria, Jordan, Tunisia, Morocco, Algeria, and Libya. However, the outcome of these reforms was to promote a further polarisation of the legal system: secular reforms in civil relations between the state and its citizens contrasted with the hold of the Muslim clergy and the *Shari'ah* Law over the sphere of the family and personal status. It should be noted that a similar approach was followed in many non-Arab Muslim nation-states, for example, Iran, Pakistan and Malaysia. However, in Turkey, under the rule of Atatürk (1920–38), the approach to modernisation involved a process of secular legal reform aimed at emancipating women from traditionalism by replacing the *Shari'ah* Law with civil codes (Coulson, 1978; Kandiyoti, 1991).[7]

On the question of social equality, for example, Arab governments, following the Egyptian model under President Nasser in the 1960s, introduced a set of civil laws that promoted women as citizens in terms of their rights to education, paid work, and political participation. Such initiatives were justified on the grounds of women's rights and were also linked to the potential contribution of women to social and economic development. However, it was not until 1962 that gender equality was explicitly recognised in the Egyptian National Charter: 'Woman must be regarded as equal to man and she must therefore shed the remaining shackles that impede her free movement, so that she may play a constructive and profoundly important part in shaping the life of the country' (Abdel Kader, 1987: 109). Currently, the secular civil laws that are administered in Arab nation-states advocate 'near' equality with men on issues pertaining to public activities, such as the right to vote and to be elected to national public offices, equal access to education and occupations, and equal pay for equal work.

Against these secular social policies of Arab states, Islamic reform movements were initiated in the late 1950s and adopted in various forms in most Arab countries. These reform movements addressed changes to the *Shari'ah* law regulating gender relations and gender-specific tasks and duties. The concern of the movements was to improve the situation of oppressive gender relations in the sphere of the family in the face of mounting men's abuses of their unconditional privileges and control over women's daily lives. In addition, state pressure combined with women's organised activities, in Egypt, Tunisia and Algeria, led the religious establishment to introduce a set of reforms in the *Shari'ah*. However, the changes were (and still are) minimal in terms of women's emancipation from patriarchal control, since differential inheritance, custody of children, obedience, punishment and discipline, and male guardianship have remained under the control of men. Women, whether as wives, daughters, sisters, or simply as kin, remain as subordinates with little power over their own movements (Mernissi, 1975; Coulson, 1978).

Most significantly, the reforms established a *Shari'ah* court as a legal authority, in contrast to the previous practice of following moral authority, to enforce claims to 'fairness' of treatment on the part of women primarily in relation to issues of divorce by repudiation and polygamy. Again, the concern was not to remove a man's exclusive privileges, but rather to restrict his total freedom and the potential of abuse that this freedom provided. For example, in Syria, Jordan, Iraq, Algeria and Morocco, a man's access to polygamous marriage has been subjected to scrutiny under the observance of the court, and if any failure of equal treatment between co-wives is feared, the court has the power to withdraw the permission for polygamous marriage (J. N. Anderson, 1976).

In practice, equal treatment has mainly been judged by crude measurements such as the financial capacity to provide or men's wealth (al-Nowaihi, 1979). By contrast, in South Yemen and Sudan, polygamous marriage has been more restricted, and permitted only on certain specific grounds; for example, if the wife is barren or afflicted with an incurable disease (J. N. Anderson, 1976). Women here can then be easily dismissed or become useless when their performatory 'role' fails to multiply the Islamic community and strengthen men's paternal power. In Tunisia, however, alone among Arab countries, the changes in the Personal Status Code in 1956, under the influence of President Bourguiba, were substantial. In this case polygamy was out-lawed, marriage and divorce were made a civil matter, adoption was made legal, improvements were made in women's inheritance rights, and women's rights to choose to work outside the home were conceded (Tessler *et al.*, 1978; Dwyer, 1991). (Note that many studies have shown that the status of Tunisian women in terms of educational achievement and paid employment is far more advanced than in most Arab countries.)

In general then, these reforms of Islam were very limited, given that they were administered by 'modern' Muslim jurisprudence, which claimed the right to reinterpret the religious family laws in order to meet women's social needs (Coulson, 1978; Esposito, 1982). Moreover, the *Shari'ah* law in the majority of Arab countries (except Tunisia and Egypt) remains and is still applied by the *kadi* system. This means that it remains as a separate legal authority apart from state laws and policies. In doing so it retains its power. As Unger (1976: 65) argues, when 'the sacred law is viewed as an expression of the true and right order of things and placed beyond government's reach', the sacred law inevitably 'provides a framework of legitimacy for social arrangements'.

Ironically, the result of these Islamic reforms was to privilege a discourse of the 'family' in which (traditional) gender relations remain inscribed in a patriarchal system of domination. This is readily apparent in the codification of rules of the personal status laws and the family. Youssef (1976), for example, powerfully depicts the nature of those legal inequalities in the conjugal 'contract' as codified in the *Shari'ah* that have gained primacy in subjecting women to a condition of patriarchal power and control. This has meant that, under the *Shari'ah*, the Muslim woman

> has had to adjust her behaviour to a religious and legal endorsement of patriarchy and polygamy; to the unilateral power of her husband in divorce; to the granting of custody rights to the father of minor children in the event of divorce; to the husband's right to restrict a rebellious wife to the conjugal home; to unequal rights of female inheritance; and to the unequal weight given a woman's legal testimony in court (Youssef, 1976: 204).

In deconstructing the above statements, it could be seen that the legitimacy of patriarchy is inscribed at two levels: the paternal 'contract', under which the father secures his dominance over minor kin, including women, who are always constructed as minor, and the conjugal 'contract', which privileges men's sexual rights as men over women (see, for example, Pateman, 1988). The *Shari'ah*, then, not only provides men with exclusive sexual rights, but also sanctions their paternal contract with the power to dominate and control all other aspects of familial life.

In addition, the *Shari'ah* provides for the patrilineal male to be legally, morally and economically responsible for his female kin. For example, the protection of women's chastity, upon which men's honour rests, can involve the mechanisms of veiling and seclusion.[8] These practices, therefore, remain a powerful means of controlling freedom of movement on the part of women, and they remain sensitive and critical controls in their effect on the position of women in the public domain.

Patriarchal gender arrangements inevitably come into conflict over the issue of women exercising their public rights, as advanced in (secular) state legal provisions. This is particularly so when women's rights to obtain work or to pursue education or other public activities are made, according to the enforcement of the *Shari'ah*, conditional; that is, dependent on men's official permission. In reality, however, owing to social and economic demand, education and paid work for women have become accepted, if not tolerated, by men as a means of improving the family's standard of living. In the sphere of paid work, for example, this has given rise to work areas segregated between the genders. These changes should not, however, be exaggerated; for, in comparison with the situation in other developing countries, women's share of the total labour force in Arab countries is among the lowest (below 10 per cent), and less than 20 per cent of all working-age women are engaged in paid work outside the agricultural sector (Youssef, 1976; Jaber, 1987).

The outcome of this legal polarisation implies two modes of being, which are likened to the (illusionary) separation between domestic and public spheres. This polarisation translates, I argue, into an identity crisis for women. On the one hand, women are rendered subordinate to 'private' or family patriarchy, following the practice of the *Shari'ah*; on the other, women are supposedly endowed with democratic or civil rights to contribute towards development and social progress. In resolving the ensuing tension and contradiction imposed on women, Hatem's study (1993), for example, suggests that the apparent contradiction between these two sets of legal provisions (state laws and religious order) has little bearing on the reality of women's lives, since women, in both discourses, are effectively relegated to the margins of the struggle for real equality and freedom. In pointing to the ineffectiveness of the state emancipatory discourse, Hatem locates the problem in the 'remaining forms of existing inequality' in the sphere of the family. In Hatem's (1993: 40) words,

> The modernist-liberal discourse which stressed the public liberty of women coexisted with personal forms of subordination in the family and/or new public forms that developed in the socio-economic arenas where women were located. It adopted concepts legitimising male leadership in the family, the work place, and the political system . . . It also showed how the emphasis on women's obedience to men within the family influenced the definition of the public positions they were expected to fill in the public arena.

The position of women (of all socio-economic groups) is, therefore, to be located as much in their limited access to the public sphere as in their constructed 'otherness' in the domestic domain. In reality, what this amounts to is that the emancipatory civil reforms for introducing gender equality have been rendered subordinate to those of the *Shari'ah*. With regard to the women's question, then, state nationalism, along with its accompanying project of national development, has accommodated itself to the sacred foundations of 'cultural heritage', the *Shari'ah*.

Defining the Boundary: The *'Umma* and Nation-State

Historically, Islam, as a religio-political system, has been conceived of as a community constructed through both religion and kinship ties. In the logic of Islam, an Islamic community is not necessarily limited to a specific territorial representation, as this is conceived in the ideology of the Western nation-state. According to Benedict Anderson (1983), this ideology means that the nation and the state are identified as a one unifying entity, necessarily characterised by a geographical boundary. By contrast, Islam ideally makes its claim to reconstruct an encompassing community, referred to as an *'umma*, that transcends all social forms of boundary instituted by states. Thus to be a Muslim, especially from the point of view of Islamist groups, implies a particular cosmic vision of the world, with a specific organisation of institutions based on religious ideology.

The construction of a Muslim identity in the logic of a Muslim theocracy, therefore, extends beyond the boundary of the state. As one religious thinker puts it:

> Islam does not provide a foundation for the state. Of course there is a tie in Islam between religion and politics, but our basic texts do not call for the state. That is why I believe that Islamic society must be basically a non-state society, where civil society must attain real power in order not to be absorbed by the state (cited in Dwyer, 1991: 216).

This imagining is also based on a reality in the (pre-colonial) traditional Muslim Middle East, which was structured upon the notion of the sacred nature of 'government'. Religion legitimised the social, economic and political structures, and the state of the *'umma* was at the same time a social and a religious group (Vesey-Fitzgerald, 1955). Significantly, according to various socio-historical accounts, it is also the case that the practices of the so-called *'umma*, as far back as the seventh century AD, after the death of the prophet Muhammad, were explicitly misogynistic toward women (Mernissi, 1975, 1991; Sabbah, 1984). Drawing on current interpretations of the narratives of Muslim theologians concerning the women's question would provide a necessary step towards understanding the ambiguity of this complex.

To be a woman in this constructed Muslim community (*'umma*), conveys a multiplicity of meanings, ranging from a woman-centred family to a subject with social equality. Historically, two dominant competing discourses emerged in Muslim theology, representing two schools of thought: traditional-conservative, which follows the *Sunna*, meaning tradition and consensus, and liberal-modernist, which adopts an interpretative approach or *Ijtihad* to reconstruct a modern Islam in accordance with the spirit of the time (J. N. Anderson, 1976; Stowasser, 1993). According to traditional Islam, the construct woman is identified with paradoxical qualities, signifying vulnerability and power. Her vulnerability is represented in being weak and emotional, which justifies her half-weighted testimony compared to that of man, as well as her exclusion from participation in politics or decision-making. Power, on the other hand, a much loaded concept, is attributed to Muslim woman precisely because of her embodied 'nature' that situates her at the centre of the family and connects with the feminine qualities, those of a nurturer and (community) carer. As this view is argued by a Muslim scholar:

> The Prophet said about the women that 'they were created from a crooked rib; the most crooked part is its highest portion' . . . The 'crookedness' in the Hadith does not imply any corruption or imperfection in woman's nature, because it is this crookedness of hers that enables her to perform her task, which is to deal with children who need strong compassion and sympathy, not rationality (cited in Stowasser, 1993: 16).

In this version of traditional Islam, the notion of equality between the sexes is not considered an issue, since each sex is assigned to perform specific gendered duties and tasks.

> Gender inequality or extreme patriarchy is justified in the discourse of conservative Islam by adhering to 'tradition' and to what is claimed as the literal meaning of the sacred text. In this interpretation, any interference or man-made legal restriction on men's power to (freely) use their 'God given' privileges is considered unlawful (Coulson, 1978).

In contrast to the conservative discourse of womanhood, in the modernist tradition women are constructed on equal terms with men in terms of both religious responsibility and social duties toward developing and maintaining the Islamic community. For example, Khalaf Allah, with the publication of his influential works,[9] represents, according to Stowasser (1993: 12), 'an important voice in contemporary Islamic modernism'. Muslim women, he argues, like their predecessors during the Prophet's lifetime (seventh century AD), are endowed with full rights to participate equally with men in public life, including economic and political activities. Women are then positioned as men's 'intellectual equals'. Hence, in the language of modernist Islam, the concept of gender equality in public life is positively acknowledged.

However, concerning the equality of women in the sphere of the family, the dominant narrative of Muslim modernists invariably depicts the male figure as the head (parallel to the assumption: 'no man, no family') in his capacity as a provider and a protector. For the modernist, Khalaf Allah, such differential positioning between the sexes does not imply the assumption of men's superiority over women, as in mainstream, traditional Islam (see, for example, Stowasser, 1993: 12–14). However, the arguments against claims of men's supremacy in the modernist discourse remain unsound and shaky when women's rights to public participation, while not denied, are seen primarily as an extension of women's 'duties', as against men's responsibility for the maintenance of the family. Given that the institution of the (patriarchal) family constitutes the cornerstone of Islam, the conceptualisation of equality, therefore, is inseparable from the family as an index of social progress.[10] Progress, an ambiguous term, is also associated with the idea of 'public interest' and, consequently, has less to do with individual/personal achievement than with societal progress (Stowasser, 1993).

Most importantly, what remains unsaid in this modernist discourse, however, is the fact that, under the *Shari'ah* law, women are positioned in a relationship of dependency and subordination to men's will, as these configurations are clearly stated regardless of uses and abuses of the Law of God. For example, on the question of men's privileges over women in the family, the modernists, as previously mentioned, articulate a discourse that seeks to delimit men's ultimate privileges with regard to polygamy and repudiation, but not to remove, for instance, child custody and paternal rights or females' half-share of male inheritance. Nonetheless, these restrictions on men's power in the *Shari'ah* are 'progressive' when compared to conservative narratives (including those of the fundamentalists) as represented by the religious establishment – al-Azhar in Egypt, for instance.

Between the two discourses of conservative and modernist Islam, the differing positionings of women in the imagined *'umma* continue to be a divisive and conflicting issue, not only for male theologians but equally for women, who are also divided on the issue of domesticity and inclusiveness in redefining the project of their imagined community (see, for example, Zuhur, 1992).

In modern times, to be a Muslim is, according to Mernissi (1991: 20–1), 'to belong to a theocratic state, to follow a family code of laws, a code of public rights' – all of which constitute a national identity. At the same time, given that Islamic practices never cease to manifest themselves in re-producing gender hierarchy across virtually all Arab/ Muslim nations, I supplement Mernissi's observation with the argument that women are represented as having a transnational identity in this constructed community.

Nabila Jaber

Repositioning Gender in the Discourse of Crisis

With the recent rise of religious (referred to as Islamist) movements across the Middle East, the imagined community of Islam as an *'umma* has taken a renewed interest in repositioning itself against the secular model of Arab nation-states. In the process of weaving a discourse that represents their religious cosmic vision, I argue that Islamists, like secular nationalists, have also positioned women as boundary-markers.

It could be argued that in periods of national crisis, resistance movements are often predicated upon the re-construction of women's identities (Kandiyoti, 1991; Tucker, 1993). Articulated in a discourse of 'public interest', the redefinition of gender roles is often justified, and hence legitimated, on the grounds of managing or serving national interests. This phenomenon could be observed in both periods of national crisis in the Arab world. It is central to the current cultural/political movements, often referred to as 'Islamist' and, ambiguously, as 'nationalist', and similarly was central during the earlier national independence movements from Western colonialism.

The establishment of Islam as an identity in the Arab Middle East is heightened with the current Islamist movements. In the quest for identity, the dominant discourse of Arab experience, from precolonial time to the present, constantly shifts positions. As Dwyer argues: 'In the 1950s, identity tended to be articulated in terms of the struggle to be free of colonialism and to establish (or re-establish) the nation; in the 1960s and 1970s people sought national identities in terms of capitalist or socialist options; from the mid 1970s on, the religious dimension has become increasingly significant' (Dwyer, 1991: 214).

The new religious significance attached to the formation of national identity has been argued in the context of mounting economic and political crises, coupled with repressive government control, mass poverty, social disintegration and cultural alienation (El-Guindi, 1981; Abdel Kader, 1987). The rise of Islamist movements during the mid-1970s, an offshoot of the Muslim Brotherhood, could also be situated in, as Dwyer (1991: 215) puts it, 'the current residue of historical problems: neo-colonial structures and international dependency', which constitute a fertile ground on which to reclaim the 'imagined community' of the Muslim *'umma*. Again, in searching for this Islamic vision, the religious narratives highlight the 'ills of "modern" Western society', including its materialist culture and social fragmentation (Dwyer, 1991). In opposition to the West, they place their constructed image of the *'umma*, as the 'good' integrated society. In so far as the project for rebuilding the *'umma* has manifested itself, there appears to be little tolerance for political pluralism in defining its female members.

Islamists' claims to 'liberation' struggles from Westernisation and neo-colonialism situate woman as nurturer, and a maintainer of community boundary, as against man, the provider, the protector, and the guardian. This is exemplified by the widespread movement calling for the return to wearing the *hijab* (veil) as an expression of 'authentic' Islam, as well as for the valorisation of the ideology of family-woman. The current sweeping veil hysteria enforced by Islamists in many parts of the Muslim world is another indication of positioning women as a marker of identity, bearing the burden of safeguarding a threatened (nationalist) identity. For example, in Algeria, the enforcement of the veil that has caused the killing, not to mention harassment, of many unveiled women is an instance of how the self-defined 'resistance' movement, as Tucker (1993: x) puts it, 'made the wearing of the veil synonymous with patriotism'. In addition, in articulating anti-imperialist and anti-colonial rhetorics, Islamist movements convey arguments concerning the 'loss of national identity' and by implication loss of 'moral standards', often associated with loose control over women (Afshar, 1989).

Parallel to the so-called Islamist resistance movements, nationalist independence movements from Western colonialism have also exhib-ited a specific, quasi-secular, pattern in redefining gender positionings. In the discourse of national 'progress' and social development, women constituted a particular place in the project of national transformation. As previously mentioned, women, in their respective countries, were constructed as national subjects and, consequently, gained a social recognition of their potential labour power in contributing to the assumed developing economy. In privileging both work outside the home and secular education, women's progressive roles become embodied in the figure of an active economic agent of society and an educated mother and nurturer of the community. At times of national crisis, then, nationalism in the Arab world has come to express itself in two distinct but necessarily gendered ways. For the female subjects, the emphasis is placed on 'cultural' nationalism, privileging a discourse rooted in morality and (Islamic) cultural consciousness. For the male national subjects, nationalism assumes a political discourse (political nationalism) concerned with the specific socio-political formation of statehood. The following examples provide an understanding of how nationalist state discourses conveniently resituate women as men's Other in restructuring priorities for safeguarding 'public interest'.

In Egypt, for instance, the need for productive women's labour at one point in history – the 1960s (as this was represented in the project for socio-economic development) – led to the reconstruction of women's identity as an active economic agent for the state. At other times, during the 1970s, when faced with high (male) unemployment, working women outside the home were being held responsible for producing 'delinquent' children, and, subsequently, a draft law was debated in parliament calling for educated women to give up their jobs (Abdel Kader, 1987). Similarly, in Tunisia, a country in which the reforms of the Personal Status Code (1956), under the influence of Bourguiba, were considered as 'a sweeping attack' on women's traditional lives, the state implemented cultural programmes in the 1960s that led to a rapid increase in women's education and professionalisation. However, during the rise of economic hardship combined with political crisis in the 1970s, the cultural reforms met with 'reactivation of tradition' as expressed in Bourguiba's public speech warning 'that too much reform' in the status of women will lead to 'a loosening of our morals' (cited in Tessler *et al.*, 1978: 145). Likewise, in Algeria, after national independence in 1962, the state agenda for women's emancipation from traditional repressive life reconstituted them as economic agents by granting them the right to work outside the home irrespective of men's permission or authority. With the rise of unemployment and economic deprivation coupled with political unrest, the ideology of women's emancipation became identified, as Helie-Lucas (1990: 107) puts it, with 'specific' (religious) 'socialism', as against secular or 'scientific socialism'. In other words, the emancipation of Algerian women could only be achieved by retaining, according to the Algerian National Charter (1976), 'the ethical code deeply held by the people' (cited in Minces, 1978: 169).

The commonality shared by these nationalist state discourses highlights notions of morality and community ethics whose burden of proof is unquestionably identified with women, since it is women who are expected to safeguard a threatened identity. It can be argued, therefore, that at times of national development, women are constructed as signifiers, and during national crisis as solidifiers, of cultural hegemony. In other words, the identification of women with culture and tradition represents the very discourse of religious ideology, which retains a privileged space in the construction of gender identity. On the basis of the above observations, therefore, it can be concluded that, in the name of nationalism and liberation struggles, the women's question becomes merely an extension to securing a system of, to borrow Mosse's (1985) term, 'male–male arrangements', signifying a male-dominated public world.

Women's Liberation and National Liberation

Nationalism, for women, has been crucial in the history of struggle and resistance against colonialism; but it must also be recognised that nationalist movements have also created a space for women from which to speak and organise a multiplicity of women's interests. In her book, *Feminism and Nationalism in the Third World* (1986), Jayawardena, for example, documents how the emergence of women's liberation movements in what is known as the 'Third World' has been necessarily linked to the rise of nationalist independence movements against Western colonisation. 'Third World feminism', as Jayawardena puts it, 'was acted out against a background of nationalist struggles aimed at achieving political independence, asserting a national identity, and modernising society' (Jayawardena, 1986: 3).

Nonetheless, it could be argued that the achievement of national independence in the Arab world (as in many other Muslim countries) has proved to be limited for women. National independence, in other words, has effectively failed to remove cultural and sexual barriers that constitute gender oppression. In various modes of knowledge production, such as testimonial accounts and sociological studies, there is ample evidence that women continue to be defined as men's other and are often subjected to and controlled by (unequal) patriarchal relations (see, for example, Badran and Cooke, 1990; Dwyer, 1991; Mernissi, 1991; Tucker, 1993).

For Arab women, the subject of nationalism and the place of national/cultural identity have been problematised, for both constructs have an ambivalent affinity with feminism. In anti-colonial struggles, women's concerns were sacrificed to the cause of national liberation (Jayawardena, 1986). Yet after independence, and the ensuing national crisis, male discourses contested women's political and civic rights, with an attempt to reconsign them to their formerly domestic roles. This move is repeatedly portrayed in the Arab Middle East, particularly in the case of the Egyptian Feminist Union, in the 1920s, and the Algerian Women's National Liberation Front, during the 1950s.[11] It is also the case that, owing to men's deep-seated moral insecurity, which continues to be nourished by existing Islamic practices (see Jaber, 1995), women then had little choice but to negotiate around discourses that appealed to national values so as to register their claims. In doing so, their social and familial concerns were articulated in a discourse that accentuated women's potential contribution to the making of 'good' society, following the tradition of Muslim modernist interpretations of Islam and women.

Currently, Arab feminist movements, which originate predominantly from an educated middle class with a secular approach, convey a new challenge to patriarchal institutions. Exemplified in current independent women's social organisations, such as the Arab Women's Solidarity Association (AWSA), the Tunisian Women's Federation, and the Arab Women's Studies Association (al-Raida), the debates are concerned with deconstructing discourses of sexual politics against prevailing nationalist paradigms. In this tradition, not only have women sought to disrupt the existing legitimacy of women's legal subordination under the *Shari'ah*, the realm of private patriarchy, but they have equally questioned their second-class citizenship under the secular public patriarchy. For these women, therefore, (male) discourses of nationalism, whether born out of secular ideology or rooted in religious (Islamic) texts, remain practically discriminatory and fundamentally sexist.

Furthermore, in her comprehensive coverage of the proliferation of women's associations in the Arab world, Hatem (1993: 29) makes an interesting point, arguing that these women's voices express 'a desire for new types of change that are at once post-Islamist and postmodernist'; this move, to Hatem, far from representing a 'total break from Islam' suggests, in my view, at best a women's standpoint of knowledge production that highlights the materiality of women's lived experiences and their associated personal, sexual and social problems.

Increasingly, women's discourses, I would argue, are shifting to issues concerned with feminist political consciousness and the notion of women's citizenship rights articulated in a discourse of civil society.[12] For these women, the struggle for greater freedom has become, as Dwyer (1991: 217) puts it, a 'double battle' manifested at both levels, a public discourse of civil society and its association with the notion of democracy, and a psychological battle 'taking place in their inner world too'. It is with this understanding that feminist (secular) movements in the Middle East wage their battle on two fronts: confronting new forms of restrictions on women's previously obtained rights, and mobilising for social change in seeking to remove old barriers toward their personhood. Paradoxically, though, against the claims of (Western) modernism, the ideological struggle for women's equality remains fundamentally rooted in a humanist/modernist discourse, inclusive of both genders.

As part of a global move, feminism in the Arab world remains crucial in creating a women's platform on which to stand and a voice from which to speak. The widespread success of this movement, however, is yet to be seen – awaiting the endorsement of the majority of Arab and/or Muslim women.

Notes

1. The question of political and cultural revivalism has been an issue of global concern, raised and manipulated by local politics against the Western notion of a linear model of societal development. In the Western world, the debate has mainly rested in the framework of postmodernism, confronting national cultures in terms of practices of exclusion and racism. In developing countries the debate is situated in the context of postcolonial struggles, questioning the meaning and effectiveness of national political independence when neo-colonial dependency is retained in economic and political relations.

2. Feminism in the Arab World is concerned with women's rights and equality, based on the ideology of democracy and human rights and in opposition to the system of exclusion of women as citizens with equal rights. This stance is best represented by the Arab Women Solidarity Association (AWSA), presided over by the renowned Egyptian feminist Nawal al-Saadawi (see, for example, N. Toubia (1988) and N. al-Saadawi (1988)). The major concern of this movement is to bring about the consciousness of gender exploitation, as manifested in local cultures as well as in regional political control. While it could be argued that feminism has been mainly the concern of educated professional women (and men), there has recently been an increasing interest from the general public, partly owing to expanding modes of knowledge production, such as magazines, conferences and specific cultural events.

3. The concept of gender identity here does not necessarily imply a unitary category, in the sense that all women share the same material conditions and social interests. While it remains true that women's oppression varies with a set of modes of differentiation – class, region, ethnicity, and education – the fact remains that the ideal construct of Womanhood constitutes a system of oppositional difference in the discourse of patriarchy.

4. The concept of splitting subjectivity does not necessarily mean that, in practice, a total separation or divorce exists between women's subjectivity in the private or domestic sphere and the public sphere. The subject, according to Kristeva, is always in the making and hence 'a subject in process', effecting while being affected by change and experience.

5. A growing body of Western feminist scholarship is concerned with unfolding the myth of gender equality based on the ideology of human liberalism. For example, Carole Pateman, in her insightful study of *The Sexual Contract* (1988), seeks to unfold the sexism

inherent in the philosophical principles of Social Contract theories advanced during the Enlightenment period. For Pateman, women's inclusion in civil contractual relations in the name of equal citizenship rights fails to undo the sexualisation of women and its associated ideology of gender-based sexual hierarchy.

6. The identification of Islam with Arab nationalism gained public appeal under the leadership of Nasser (1950s), who argued for an Arab unity and solidarity among the newly emergent Arab nation-states. However, I would like also to emphasise that Arab nationalism was, and still is, a concern for Arab Christians.

7. It should be noted that Turkey was the first (1920s) Muslim nation-building state to undertake the project of national development, with a commitment to complete secularisation following the Western secular model. However, according to Erturk's (1991) study, legal change by itself has proved limited in inducing radical change and transformation of consciousness and identity on the part of women (and men) residing in both rural and urban areas.

8. Some scholars have maintained that the *Qur'an* prescribes the total confinement and complete segregation of women. Other scholars have argued that the *Qur'anic* verses merely lay down certain restrictions as to dress, speech and movement to preserve women's chastity. However, the confinement of women, followed by such restrictive measures on their behaviour within and outside the domestic sphere, has been largely reinforced. Consequently, the legitimation of such oppressive practices in modern times has constituted a source of permanent social control over women that leaves little if any independence (Sabbah, 1984; Mernissi, 1991).

9. According to Barbara Stowasser (1993), Muhammad Ahmad Khalaf Allah's is the voice of a Muslim modernist thinker who advances the notion of women's rights in Islam in Egypt today. He is the editor of an important journal entitled *Al-Yaqza Al-'Arabiyya*, and the author of two influential books written in Arabic – *The Koran and the Problems of Our Contemporary Life* (1967) and *Studies in Islamic Systems and Legislations* (1977).

10. Islamic understanding of the term 'progress' refers to completion and not violation of (traditional) ascribed sex roles, translated into men's duties and women's obligations (see, for example, Mernissi, 1991).

11. For a detailed analysis of these movements, see for example, Helie-Lucas (1990); Badran (1993).

12. See for example al-Saadawi (1988), Toubia (1988) and Hatem (1993) among others. It is also noteworthy that – as women in

organised political activities draw on their experiences both inside 'nationalist' movements and in the daily exercise of inequality in the domestic scene – the discourses of gender equality have come to embody both concerns: the political and the domestic. While the political resides in the issue of citizenship, civil rights and democracy, the domestic searches for a 'new' meaning of the concept gender equity within the family. For example, against mainstream Islam, a number of 'Muslim' feminists (and male) scholars have recently challenged the validity of patriarchal interpretations of Islam and women. See, for instance, Nawal al-Sadawi (1988) and particularly Fatima Mernissi's (1991) controversial book on the use and abuse of Islamic Law on women: *Women and Islam: a Theological and Historical Enquiry.*

References

Abdel Kader, Soha (1987). *Egyptian Women in a Changing Society, 1899–1987.* Boulder, Colorado: Lagneia Rainier Publishers.

Afshar, Haleh (1989). 'Women and reproduction in Iran', in N. Yuval Davis and F. Anthias (eds), *Women–Nation–State*, pp. 110–25. New York: St Martin's Press.

al-Nowaihi, Mohammed (1979). 'Changing the law on personal status within a liberal interpretation of the Sharia', in C. Nelson and K. Koch (eds), *Law and Social Change in Contemporary Egypt*, Vol. II.

al-Saadawi, Nawal (1988). 'The political challenge facing Arab women at the end of the twentieth century', in Nahid Toubia (ed.), *Women of the Arab World*, pp. 8–26. London: Zed Press.

Anderson, Benedict (1983). *Imagined Communities: Reflections on the Origin and Spread of Nationalism.* London: Verso Editions.

Anderson, J. Norman (1976). *Law Reform in the Muslim World.* London: Athlone Press.

Badran, Margot (1993). 'Independent women: more than a century of feminism in Egypt', in J. Tucker (ed.), *Arab Women*, pp. 129–48. Bloomington: Indiana University Press.

—— and Cooke, Miriam (1990). *Opening the Gates: A Century of Arab Feminist Writing.* Bloomington: Indiana University Press.

Bhabha, Homi K. (ed.) (1990). *Nation and Narration.* New York: Routledge.

Coulson, Noel (1978). *A History of Islamic Law.* Edinburgh: Edinburgh University Press.

Dwyer, Kelvin (1991). *Arab Voices: The Human Rights Debate in the Middle East.* Berkeley: University of California Press.

El-Guindi, Fadwa (1981). 'Veiling infitah with Muslim ethic: Egypt's contemporary Islamic movement'. *Social Problems*, 28 (4): 465–85.

Erturk, Yakin (1991). 'Convergence and divergence in the status of Moslem women: the cases of Turkey and Saudi Arabia'. *International Sociology*, 6 (3): 307–20.

Esposito, John (1980). *Islam and Development*. Syracuse, New York: Syracuse University Press.

—— (1982). *Women in Muslim Family Law*. Syracuse, New York: Syracuse University Press.

Hatem, Mervat (1993). 'Toward the development of post-Islamist and post-nationalist feminist discourses in the Middle East', in Judith E. Tucker (ed.), *Arab Women: Old Boundaries, New Frontiers*, pp. 29–48. Bloomington: Indiana University Press.

Helie-Lucas, Marie-Aimée (1990). 'Women, nationalism and religion in the Algerian struggle', in Margot Badran and Miriam Cooke (eds), *Opening the Gates: A Century of Arab Feminist Writing*, pp. 104–14. Bloomington: Indiana University Press.

Jaber, Nabila (1987). 'Modernization, legal reforms and the place of women in Muslim developing countries'. Ph.D. dissertation, Southern Illinois University: Carbondale, Illinois.

—— (1995). 'From unveiling to re-veiling: Islam and the Women's Movements'. *Journal of Arabic, Islamic and Middle Eastern Studies*, 2 (1): 15–27.

Jayawardena, Kumari (1986). *Feminism and Nationalism in the Third World*. London: Zed Books.

Kandiyoti, Deniz (1991). 'End of empire: Islam, nationalism and women in Turkey', in D. Kandiyoti (ed.), *Women, Islam and the State*, pp. 22–47. Philadelphia: Temple University Press.

Kristeva, Julie (1980). *Language and Desire*. Oxford: Oxford University Press.

Lewis, B (1981). 'The return of Islam', in M. Curtis (ed.), *Religion and Politics in the Middle East*, pp. 9–29. Boulder, Colorado: Westview Press.

Mernissi, Fatima (1975). *Beyond the Veil: Male–Female Dynamics in a Modern Muslim Society*. New York: Schenkman Publishing Company.

—— (1991). *Women and Islam: An Historical and Theological Enquiry*. Oxford: Basil Blackwell.

Minces, Juliette (1978). 'Women in Algeria'. In Lois Beck and Nikki Keddie (eds), *Women in the Muslim World*, pp. 159–71. Cambridge, Mass.: Harvard University Press.

Mosse, George L. (1985). *Nationalism and Sexuality: Middle-Class Morality and Sexual Norms in Modern Europe*. Madison: University of Wisconsin Press.

Parveen, Shaukat Ali (1975). *Status of Women in the Muslim World: A Study in the Feminist Movements in Turkey, Egypt, Iran and Pakistan*. Lahore: Aziz Publishing Company.

Pateman, Carole (1988). *The Sexual Contract*. Stanford, California: Stanford University Press.

Phillips, Anne (1991). *Engendering Democracy*. Cambridge, U.K.: Polity Press.

Radhakrishan, R. (1992). 'Nationalism, gender, and the narrative of identity', in A. Parker *et al.* (eds), *Nationalisms and Sexualities*. pp. 77–95. London: Routledge.

Rich, Adrienne (1980). 'Compulsory heterosexuality and lesbian existence'. *Signs*, 5 (4): 645.

Sabbah, Fatna A. (1984). *Women in the Muslim World*. New York: Pergamon Press.

Stowasser, Barbara (1993). 'Women's issues in modern Islamic thought', in J. Tucker (ed.), *Arab Women*, pp. 3–28. Bloomington: Indiana University Press.

Tessler, Mark A., with Rogers, Janet and Schnieder, Daniel (1978). 'Women's emancipation in Tunisia', in Lois Beck and Nikki Keddie (eds), *Women in the Muslim World*, pp. 141–58. Cambridge, Mass.: Harvard University Press.

Toubia, Nahid (1988). *Women of the Arab World*. London: Zed Books.

Tucker, Judith E. (ed.). *Arab Women: Old Boundaries, New Frontiers*. Bloomington: Indiana University Press.

Turner, Bryan (ed.) (1990). *Theories of Modernity and Postmodernity*. London: Sage Publications.

Unger, Roberto (1976). *Law in Modern Society: Toward a Criticism of Social Theory*. New York: The Free Press.

Vesey-Fitzgerald, Seymour (1955). 'Nature and source of the Sharia', in Majid Khadduri and H. Liebesny (eds), *Origin and Development of Islamic Law*, pp. 85–112. Washington, DC: Middle East Institute.

Youssef, Nadia (1976). 'Women in the Muslim world', in L. Iglitzin and R. Ross (eds), *Women in the World*, pp. 203–17. Santa Barbara, California: Clio Press.

Yuval-Davis, Nira and Anthias, Floya (eds) (1989). *Women–Nation–State*. New York: St Martin's Press.

Zuhur, Sherifa (1992). *Revealing Reveiling: Islamist Gender Ideology in Contemporary Egypt*. New York: State University of New York Press.

– 6 –

The Gender of Tradition: Syrian Women and the Feminist Agenda

Fiona Hill

The declaration of Marxist Syrian writer, George Tarabishi, that the female population of the Arab world is a 'paralysed' half,[1] reflects a belief held by radical socialists and feminists that the future integrity of the Arab world is dependent upon an overthrow of the patriarchal order. However, some find that the intersection of tradition and modernity in Arab society in the late twentieth century has created little more than a modernised form of Arab cultural tradition. Hisham Sharabi, who characterises this phenomenon as modernised patriarchy, or 'neopatriarchy', finds that the dominance of the father-figure is a central 'psychosocial feature' of a neo-patriarchal society (1988: 7). This has a particular relevance to Syria, where the cult of the President as champion of the nation has his image reproduced in all manner of media, and his sayings (aqwal al-ra'is) heavily quoted in speeches and reproduced in slogans and booklets, so that his socialist government might be said to resemble a modern version of the Sultanate.

As for women's status within this milieu, Abdel Kader (1987: 7) observes that Western feminists[2] have long realised that such issues cannot be divorced from broader political issues, and she insists that focusing particularly on women's position in Arab society 'is neither feminist chauvinism nor superfluous intellectualism', but rather an integral part of understanding the culture of the region, its forms of government, and its relationship with Europe. Syrian women, in common with other Arab women, are figured as the locus of trad-itional cultural values; but they are also the locus of specifically Ba'thist (socialist) objectives, and this fact may challenge their inclusion in a broader (Arab) feminism.

In this chapter I discuss the advance of Arab, and in particular Syrian, women in the light of nationalist and Islamist discourses, and with regard to Western and Arab formulations of feminism. While the chapter's focus is primarily on Sunni Muslim women, it is not intended to homogenise or delimit the experiences of those women, nor to exclude other Syrian women from feminist concerns. I argue that the cultural, political, and religious codes of the region create points of intersection, and of tension, for all women.[3]

Arab Feminism Divided

One might ask, as has Mai Ghoussoub (1988: 107), if a method of analysing and portraying women and their rights has a particular nationality. Yet it is clear from the nature of Arab feminist debate that aggressive nationalist agendas play a particularly pivotal role. These agendas can be abetted by the attitudes even of officially independent agencies. For example, although no other regional report did so, a United Nations Commission into social issues in West Asia[4] began with a cultural definition of the region, stating that it shared an Arab and Islamic heritage.[5] The espoused ideologies of religious conservatives and modernists, of nationalists and of socialists in the region are premised on the specificity of this Islamic/Arab heritage. Any commitment to issues of particular concern to women within this heritage must therefore remain secondary to other political and confessional concerns, to the extent that some critics within the Arab world insist that the subject of women's rights falls into the same artificial category as women's art, or women's literature (Hijab 1988: 167).

Fatima Mernissi (1993: 168) goes further than this to tie human, and women's, rights to notions of a Western, imperialist agenda. Suad Joseph (Stork, 1993: 26) critiques this Western construct of human rights by pointing out that it is premised on 'the autonomous, detached, contract-making, individualised person that emerged out of liberal bourgeois thought'. However, Reza Hammami and Martina Rieker (1988: 99) altogether reject the utility of such formulations, and argue that the dichotomy of the active/male/West against the passive/female/Third World is one that Marxist-feminist scholarship has been deconstructing for the last decade.

In its superficial manifestation of social change, many find that the Arab 'awakening' (*nahda*) of the late nineteenth century did no more than reorganise patriarchal structures and give them new and modern forms (cf. Sharabi, 1988: 4). Qasim Amin, an early champion of Arab women's 'liberation', whose radical writings created controversy in turn-of-the-century Egypt,[6] has been described by Marxist-feminists today as 'an ideologue of bourgeois domestic economy, rather than feminism' (Hammami and Rieker, 1988: 98). And Arab feminism remains a bourgeois phenomenon inasmuch as it involves women who have most often received both Arabic and European educations, and who have become 'visible' to men by being pro-active in public policy-making. Where Marxist feminists argue that only the struggle of Third World women is capable of a total sexual revolution, conservative Arab feminists argue that such a revolution forces a woman to extricate herself from her social milieu, occupied in part by men, and that this is unnatural and unrealistic.

Thus there resides a tension between formulations of Arab feminism in Western/imperialist and Third World/Marxist paradigms. Yet one might better argue that it is neither the advances of their Western sisters, nor the Arab man as a social partner, from whom Arab women must divorce themselves, but rather the paradigm of patriarchy in the Arab world, which displays so many points of convergence with orientalist/imperialist epistemology in its conscious and politically effective fixing of difference between the sexes.

The Arab Man and Feminism

The tension between capitalist (read Western) and socialist (read Eastern) formulae of feminism can neutralise, to some extent, the efforts of indigenous feminists, as much as does the overriding patriarchal order in the Arab world. Neopatriarchy in the Arab world is seen by indigenous feminists as a postcolonial phenomenon, and Joseph (Stork, 1993: 23) observes that 'contemporary patriarchy is a product of the intersection between the colonial and indigenous domains'. That this intersection should pass directly over the bodies, and persons, of women is perhaps of little surprise.

The potential for an analysis of the 'libidinal' motivation of certain facets of the colonial enterprise, which include notions of repressive Victorian sexuality and the promise of sexual liberation in the East, has been exploited by critical scholars of colonialism and the orientalist genre. Wayland Young's theory (1964) that repressed sexuality was one source of the imperialist drive in 'the East' has been balanced by Evelyne Accad's equally extraordinary thesis (1990) that Arab culture is the most sexually repressive of all societies, and that this fact is responsible for the violence, physical and psychological, of the Arab man.[7]

Since it is played out on the body of woman, the intersection between indigenous and colonial chauvinism has engendered competition and enmity. Attempts to elicit empathy of one with the other are often branded as neo-imperialism, even (or particularly?) now when they appear in *belles-lettres*. The Algerian writer Tahar Ben Jalloun, for example, writes in French, and is said (Abdel-Jaouad, 1990: 36) to bring the Western reader closer to understanding the Arab/Muslim as a subject, instead of as 'the other's' (in this case the French colonialist's) object of observation. His novels are said to be characterised by an 'oriental mood', which Abdel-Jaouad (1990: 36) considers to be a stylistic device to correct orientalist presumptions of the Arab/Muslim. However, (Algerian) critics find it a sacrilege that Ben Jalloun express what he does in 'the other's' language (that is, French), and the writer is criticised for being typical of Maghribi men who champion women's liberation but who, in fact, constitute a 'subtle but nonetheless pernicious neo-patriarchy' (Abdel-Jaouad, 1990: 35).

It is apparent that Arab men champion 'rights' in their society in terms of a shared responsibility, and that they do not conceive of women's needs as being separate from their own. In contemporary Syrian literature, Vial (1980: 418) has found that where women prefer to speak of themselves as a special category, men speak of the dispossessed in general, in order to show *'combien le monde est dur aux déshérités'*. Similarly, Mernissi (1993: 151) finds that, although initially 'petrified' by feminist concerns, Arab men are now comfortable with the 'apocalyptic renaissance' of which feminism is a part, and that promotes the future, rather than the past, as the locus of power. She quotes the Syrian poet Adonis[8] in his belief that the Arab man must now 'rethink himself in cosmic terms' (Mernissi 1993: 152), become unattached, and be comfortable with uncertainty.

Yet while Arab men are developing expressions of the new freedoms experienced in the wake of feminism, some feminists find that it is man who poses the greatest mystery. Helen Grace (1991: 118) remarks that women have worked hard to let themselves be known, whereas a man's world remains 'filled with the most bizarre rituals, posing as reality'.

Chodorow has proposed (1974: 44) that, in any given society, feminine personality defines itself through other people more than masculine personality does. That is to say that a woman's personal relationships with others define who she is. On the other hand, it has always been not only possible but largely the norm to speak of the world of men without speaking equally, and relatedly, of women. A man can, and does, identify himself independently of woman. Indeed, in some situations he must do so in order to be considered fully masculine.[9]

In his speech inaugurating the Year of the Woman in 1975 (which began the United Nations Decade of the Woman), the Syrian President, Hafez al-Assad, proposed that 'Woman is mother, wife, sister, daughter. How is it that the celebration of the Year of the Woman will not be our celebration for all?'[10] The Syrian President thus succinctly stated the familial definitions of woman, which demand that any celebration of woman is the celebration of her relationships with a man, so that any promotion of woman is also the promotion of man.

Western feminists regard the reflexive nature of female identity, which has femininity defined as the lack of masculinity, and which demands the repression of the feminine in order to augment the definition of the masculine, as a formulation against which to fight. For Arab feminism, Mernissi (1993: 126ff) takes up this fight, arguing that there has been a concerted effort to erase 'the feminine' from the political processes in the Arab world, in order that 'the feminine should never again be seen where power is exercised'.

Woman as Citizen

Egypt and Iraq had their first female government ministers in the 1950s. Syria has had hers since the 1970s. The Ministry for Culture has been under the direction of a woman, Najah Attar, since 1976, and there are at present thirteen women in Parliament. At the founding congress of the Syrian Ba'th Party in 1947 (at which there were no women present: Devlin, 1983: 32), it was declared that, 'The Arab woman enjoys all the rights of citizenship. The Party struggles to raise up woman's levels in order to make her fit to exercise these rights.'[11] Since the United Nations Decade of the Woman (1975–85), the Syrian Ba'thists have promoted literacy programmes, and allowed women greater access to education, industry and politics. Yet Shaaban (1991: 56) notes the irony that, while women's political and economic opportunities in Europe have seen slower progress than those of Syrian women, Syrian women's personal freedoms remain curtailed.

A publication of the achievements of the General Union of Syrian Women (Al-Itihad al-'Am al-Nisa'i, 1983b) points to the women's unions (*wahdat*) and associations (*rawabit*) that are found throughout Syria. In these, as well as in the cadre schools and training centres, the regional industrial centres and the women's clubs, lectures, seminars and classes are held on issues of employment, health, nutrition, household management, consumer information, literacy, and programmes for handicapped children, and these often result in Union publications of tables of statistics and small information booklets.

Statistics published by the Union of Syrian Women in 1987,[12] for example, indicated that in 1970 50.3 per cent of Syrian women aged between 10 and 14 years, and 91 per cent of women under 45 were illiterate, with a total of 42 per cent in the nation's capital of Damascus, and 90 per cent in the far north-eastern region of Hassake. Compulsory education in Syria helped decrease illiteracy in women from 64 per cent in 1975 to 49 per cent in 1983 (Altoma, 1991: 80), although these latter figures do not consider the ages of the women, nor the regions in which they live. In the late 1980s, the literacy rate was higher in Syria (25 per cent of all women) than in Jordan, Iraq and Egypt (Hopwood, 1988: 129). Mernissi (1993: 159) reports that, for the Arab world in general, education has offered women 'a legitimate way out of mediocrity'. In 1987 in Syria almost half of all medical students were women.

Yet, while the Ba'thist regime in Syria, as well as that in Iraq (cf. Ingrams 1983), is promoting women and advancing them into responsible positions in public institutions, the Union of Syrian Women as a government auxiliary has no political voice of its own. Shaaban (1991: 18) criticises the regional Unions for being more concerned with 'winning women recruits' and 'defending their own partisan positions' than they are with feminist issues, and she claims that most Syrian women do not see the Union of Syrian Women as radical or feminist (Shaaban, 1991: 79). Although as yet in its infancy, the Australian branch of the Union is already attracting the same criticisms.

Similarly in Australia, the Office for the Status of Women (OSW), based at the seat of government in Canberra, has been regarded by some as an organisation impervious to the needs of the 'average' woman.[13] In order to prepare the Australian Government for the United Nations Assembly of Women in Beijing in 1995, the Australian Women's Council (AWC) was formed, and its members travelled the country to make contact with independent women's groups and learn of their concerns, all of which were condensed into two or three main objectives. It is notable that the Secretary of the OSW spoke[14] of sifting through the 'vested interests' of the various women's groups with whom the AWC conferred, thereby implying that women could (or should?) experience their 'rights' in a context broader than their own lived experiences.

In Syria it would be reasonable to suggest that women experience their 'rights' in terms of their place in a family, and in a co-local, and often confessional, community rather than in terms of their position as citizens of the state. Since Syrian families and communities of all ethnic and confessional backgrounds are acutely patriarchal, the rights of women within these communities are, for the most part, defined accordingly. Despite the concerted efforts of the Ba'thists, it is questionable whether Syrian women can fully define their rights in their own communities, let alone feel the impact of state policy in their daily lives.

Woman as the Essence

Traditional and conservative notions of woman's secondary place and limited domestic power in relation to man are as entrenched in the urban centres of Syria as in the rural areas. Arranged marriages, dowry or bride price, polygamy, gender segregation, and submission and obedience of women to men, even to the extent of death for sexual transgressions, are documented, and feminists of all persuasions assume that such conditions perpetuate the subservience of many Syrian women to men, both domestically and in public life. In her collection of interviews with Arab women, Shaaban (1991: 27) finds that, although they may have become professionals and excel in many fields, at home Arab women are 'still considered the weaker sex' and are expected to behave as such – an attitude that Hijab (1988: 7) describes as being 'somewhat schizophrenic'.

A recent study on the work patterns of women in Jordan, Egypt and the Sudan finds that '"traditional" patterns and relationships are in fact reinforced by "modern" forces of labour migration and market-oriented production' (Shami *et al.*, 1990: xiv).[15] It also finds that women's entry into the labour market has not automatically led to empowerment and emancipation from patriarchal structures. Because feminist debate takes place within an Arab–Islamic framework, at the same time as women are encouraged to be part of national development and to participate 'in building socialist Arab society',[16] they are held back 'in their place as secondary actors within the family context' (Hijab, 1988: 7).

One way to overlook woman's social ambiguity in the Arab world, through official 'folk' culture, has been to reconcile the domestic sphere, as it is personified in woman, with the glories of antiquity. Such a reconciliation is made possible through woman's domestic stability and her perceived timelessness as a nurturer, enabling her to stand as an eternal figure and to transcend temporal boundaries. As the paragon of domesticity, this trope of Arab woman can pull the ancient and the future together into the present with considerable ease and profound effects. Such attempts at reconciling domesticity with 'glorious' antiquity are common in the Mediterranean basin. Egyptian nationalist stirrings early this century spawned (in the 1920s) a sculpture by the great Egyptian artist, Mukhtar, which is illustrative of woman's place in such reconciliations. Entitled *Nahdat Misr* ('Egypt's Awakening'), the commissioned sculpture depicts a disveiling peasant woman who, standing beside a Sphinx (also feminine), is viewing the distance. The sculpture juxtaposes the 'essence' of Egyptian indigenous culture, as embodied in the peasant woman, with notions of awakening and unveiling the glories of a Pharaonic past that belongs, somehow, to modern Egypt also.[17]

Similarly, an effective veiling of the sometimes appalling marginality of women in Syria has been achieved by eulogising their unique status as the locus of Arab traditions. Just as Ba'thist policy advocates the peasant (*fellah*) as forming the basis for rural social reform, the peasant woman (*fellaha*) has been glorified in Arab nationalist agendas for over a century.[18] Huda Sharawi, the mother of Arab feminism, together with Qasim Amin, contributed to this glorification of the *fellaha* by declaring that she ought be emulated by her urban sisters, whereas in reality, as was noted frankly by Abdel Kader (1987: 132–3), the peasant woman was/is the traditional beast of burden and, like all rural women, bears 'the brunt of conservatism and sexual subordination'.

It is a universal experience of feminism that hierarchy is genderised, and just as 'tradition' in the Arab world is located in woman, Joseph (Stork, 1993: 24) observes that the minority in a nation-state is also generally 'feminised'. In the West, casting women as the minority, or the disenfranchised, has the effect of allocating peculiarly 'feminine' characteristics to all minority groups, as well as to areas that traditionally have had a low political profile. The environment is a case in point. The image of a raped 'Mother Earth' has become a commonplace in Western societies, and for many is a received truism. Yet critics – including feminists – of eco-feminist movements in the late twentieth century object that these are built upon an essentialist falsification of woman, and that identification of women with nature 'speciously biologises the personality traits that patricentric society assigns to women' (Biehl, 1991: 3).[19]

Rural Women and Feminism[20]

Badran and Cooke (1990: xxxvi) note that feminist expression in the developing Arab countries is pioneered in an agrarian society involved in 'modern urbanisation', where religion remains a 'regulator of everyday life and a source of identity'. In Syria, while the government is suspicious of Sunni anti-government elements that linger, if they do not flourish, in the rural towns and villages, Islam is considered generally to be an urban-based religion. As for feminist expression, the relevance of rural women to Islamist agendas in the Arab world in general has been ignored by conservatives, while the modernists present rural women as the paradigms of strength and independence, using what Stowasser (1993: 24) terms an 'acculturationist and utopian language'. There is evidently a connection in Syria (and perhaps in the rest of the Arab world) between Islamist and feminist agendas, where both are urban-centred, both, in their radical forms, are suspected of destabilising the regime, and both ignore the needs and realities of rural women.

Some domestic traditions in the Arab world are reviled for constricting women's full realisation as social beings, and for retarding their contribution to economic development. In other quarters, technological and ideological developments are blamed for disempowering those same women, undermining their traditional domestic power-bases. Sharabi (1988: 31) promotes capitalism and the nuclear family as the source of women's emancipation from patriarchal hierarchies, whereas feminists Hammami and Rieker (1988: 97) find that it is Marxist ideology that conserves an already existing egalitarianism. But when Marxist feminist economists argue that the transition from subsistence to a market economy marks the loss of economic roles and independence for peasant women (cf. Abdel Kader, 1987: 33), they appear to advocate underdevelopment as a valid expression of resistance, and to promote traditional indigenous social custom over technological advances (cf. Ghoussoub, 1988: 108). One might legitimately question where the liberation is in this curious formulation of 'struggle'.

Hatem (1993: 44) argues that the 'complexity of patriarchal domination' in the Middle East is oversimplified by relating underdevelopment to gender inequality, and finds that concentration on women and development 'presents a dehumanised and degrading picture of Middle Eastern women'. Hatem (1993: 40) also argues that, although socio-economic conditions vary from one class to the next, the situation of all Arab women has been improved by the de-segregation of some. Hatem finds that those who 'try to trivialise' the effects of de-segregation by pointing to the fact that most rural women were never secluded, are ignoring the horrors of 'the old system' of sexual harassment and abuse. But despite Hatem's insistence, the way in which rural women are affected, let alone positively aided, by any improvements in the lives of urban women remains unclear.

For Syria, while the government seeks by way of health programmes, education, and agricultural policies to create new possibilities for rural women, there is as yet little exploration of what those possibilities may mean for those women.[21] The improvement of their conditions, particularly as regards their new economic opportunities, can directly challenge the traditional authority of men over women, and women's economic independence can be seen by men as breeding insubordination. Because female domestic production is socially defined, and therefore generally imbued with cultural values, for some communities a woman's production outside the domestic domain can be seen as asocial. A Syrian Bedouin man, for example, described women who labour outside their own homes, in pilot farms and cottage industries specifically established to benefit rural women, as 'prostitutes'.[22] Conversely, Hopkins (1991: 117) notes that the disinclination of women in one Egyptian village (Musha) to work in the fields, reportedly because it would be 'shameful', had more to do with the women's disinclination to work than with the men's concern for family honour. Hopkins proposes that the maintenance of this notion of 'shame', rather than being male-imposed, is in fact 'a form of female resistance'.

Overall, the move from subsistence to a cash economy is allowing rural Syrian women either more leisure or greater earning power. Ironically, in both cases, the women's dependence upon men is increased. A woman's ability to stay indoors has become a symbol of modernity, and, by association, femininity, in so-called traditional societies. This experience is witnessed in Syrian villages, where confinement to the house precincts also reduces threats to a woman's chastity and to the 'honour' of her menfolk.[23] While the less economically advantaged women in these villages remain almost fully responsible for agricultural production, the physical strictures that are imposed by the community remain equally relevant for women of all economic situations. Many rural Syrian women simply lack the ability, or indeed the will, to become fully independent social beings, or citizens, in a Ba'thist state.

Setenyi Shami (Shami *et al.* 1990: xiii) notes that generalisations about Arab women's 'position' are hampered by the variations in 'locality, group and class'. For rural Syria, the fact that a woman's ability to stay in the house becomes a symbol of modernity, femininity, and her heightened allure as a woman, suggests that, rather than devalued, she is re-valued, and her status is elevated by such a situation. The argument of Marxist feminists that subaltern women should be the focus of oppression, because they struggle against the 'process of hierarchisation' (Hammami and Rieker, 1988: 101; cf. Leacock, 1977: 9), is seriously flawed by overlooking aspects of relative security and relative power in the lives of those subaltern women.

The Veil as Feminist Indicator

Hammami and Rieker (1988: 96) argue that Middle Eastern Studies is the only field of scholarship that is restricted to an 'elaboration of a profoundly backward spectre of Islamic sentiment waiting to rear its head'. While their challenge is thrown to the Western academy, it might equally be posed to the indigenous populations of the Middle East, where such essentialisations can also hold sway. Religion, and religious custom, can be a locus of change. Yet, while religiously conservative women in Syria cannot be assumed to be passive or repressed, their place in a feminist agenda is uncertain.

Discussion of Arab/Muslim communities in terms of 'segregation', 'private sphere', 'modesty' and 'submission' is eternally controversial.[24] The term 'submission' is a loaded one, and its connotations are foreign to the non-Muslim ear.[25] For Muslims, submission is not conceived of as subordination, but rather as a resignation to the prescribed harmony. But, because it is prescribed from beyond them, specifically by the patriarchal order, it is this prescription of harmony that feminists see as problematic for women.

Hammami and Rieker (1988: 93 note 1) find that the most historically constant meaning of the veil is one of class, and that a failure to appreciate this fact confines Arab feminist debate to a focus on the domain of bourgeois women. While there are many reasons for wearing it, for many Arab working-class women de-segregation amounts to an adoption of *hijab* (which, among other things, translates as 'the veil'). Increased economic opportunities for peasant women in some rural areas imply strict use of the veil to affirm their chastity (Tillion 1983: 30), and urban Muslims who are experiencing an increase in population density, as well as greater opportunities for women to find work, share this same concern.[26] In Syria, the adoption of the veil runs against Ba'thist objectives, and as such may prove an effective mode of defying the regime (cf. Hatem 1993: 31).

It is notable in this regard that so-called Muslim 'fundamentalism' has been dubbed a patriarchal defence against feminism. While Mernissi (1993: 161) warns against dismissing feminism from the Islamic fundamentalist realm, pointing to the emergence of 'a virulent feminist leadership' within fundamentalist parties, assertions that the *hijab* gives a woman any heightened sense of self remain controversial in feminist circles (cf. Lazreg, 1988: 348 note 56), where it is doubted that the veil could be integral to a woman's persona. Yet it must be said that veiled Muslim women in Syria argue that this physical, and cultural, manifestation of *islam* (submission) constitutes a certainty of person and of community that is lost, or impoverished, without it.

Of course, an ignorance of the full significance of a veil is akin to the ignorance of many observers of the meaning of chastity, and assumptions about the sexuality of Arab/Muslim women that are based on the use of the *hijab* can alienate both Arab and Western feminists. I have often heard Western and Arab women and men alike scorning the 'hypocrisy' of veiled women seen purchasing lingerie in the Syrian market-place, or talking or behaving bawdily or flirtatiously in private, as if they had no right to do so. Misreading veiling as sexual repression, and regarding veiled women as somehow sexually neutered and voracious at once, is acutely reminiscent of the orientalist figuring of the Arab/Muslim woman, and says more about the observer than the observed.

Islam and Female Sexuality

Mernissi declares (1993: 127) that Muslim women have been veiled, not to create the fiction of an homogeneous and undifferentiated *'umma*, but because the Arabs of the *jahiliyya* knew that 'it is the body and its unconquerable sexuality that is the irreducible fortress of sovereign individuality'. Leila Ahmed (1984: 122) states that 'one's sexual identity alone . . . is more inextricably oneself than one's cultural identity', and that this forces Arab feminists into an opposition of loyalties, so that they are 'forced almost to choose between betrayal and betrayal'.

Women's sexual and emotional needs are not outside the realm of national political and economic development. While the Union of Syrian Women produces socio-legal studies in conjunction with such official bodies as the Syrian Ministry of Justice and UNICEF, specific consideration of the emotional and psychological needs of women is most evident in popular Syrian radio and television broadcasts. One recently produced television serial drama,[27] which revolves around an 'average', but long-standing, Damascene household in an old quarter of the Syrian capital, is extremely frank in its portrayal of women's emotional needs. The neighbourhood is besieged by honey-tongued property developers seeking to buy up all the old houses so as to raze them to the ground. At the same time, or perhaps as a consequence, these proud city families who cloister their women (one man even chains his simpleton daughter to keep her from 'harm') are confronted with their own suffocating conservatism, which is keenly defined in the emotional and physical lives of the women.

While this television serial highlighted women's perspectives, sentiments and voices, indeed poignantly so, feminists might argue that the happy resolution (which saw mother and daughter placed under the sensitive care of a man devoted to the conservation of traditional Arab artistic and, needless to say, cultural forms) still retained the prescribed connubial order. Overall, the men's protection and physical and moral guidance of the women, although queried as to modes of application, were not intrinsically challenged. For many feminists, this only confirms what Mai Ghoussoub describes (1987: 18) as 'the rule of official Arab machismo'. Since an (albeit fictional) woman's independence of mind and action would more likely be interpreted negatively as insubordination than as something to be applauded, while female leads in Syrian dramas do not lack strength of character, neither are they rebellious.

Yet one must remember that intellectual criticisms of State-imposed feminism can be countered by grass-roots praise for it. In Egypt, the perception among 'average' women was that, before Nasser, women had no rights, and that it was this popular President's policies that promoted women's status (cf. Hatem 1992). In Syria, *'arab* village girls in the eastern Jezira reported to me that, although the female characters on television were not insubordinate, they managed to express facets of their personalities that won them respect on more counts than were commonly allowed in Syrian villages. One girl confided that 'Television serials have done a lot for girls' (self-esteem).'[28]

Pernicious Customs

Nevertheless, certain Arab/Muslim customs that impact on women's sexuality are supported by those women, yet Western, and some Arab, feminists and intellectuals (Mernissi 1975, 1993; al-Saadawi 1980; al-Samman 1980; Shaaban 1991) agree that these customs must be subverted if women are to be liberated in any sense. Such customs are encapsulated in the visible, and dramatic, institutions of the veil (in its narrowest sense), the *harem* (in its broadest sense), clitoridectomy, and the killing of a woman to maintain 'honour'.

Clitoridectomy is neither an Arab nor an Islamic custom in essence, although it is in fact. Nawal al-Saadawi (1980: 40) dates female circumcision to the Pharaonic era, and notes that Herodotus mentioned it as a custom in the seventh century BC. Sherifa Zuhur (1992: 34) notes that there are no reliable sources for the custom in the Arabian Peninsula in pre-Islamic times, although she goes on to say that it was 'prevalent there, in Yemen, and further north in the Syrian desert later on'. Today some Islamists are reviving thirteenth- and fourteenth-century texts of Islamic scholars who found that circumcision was integral to Islam's stance on women.[29] While the World Health Organisation (WHO) finds that clitoridectomy is practised in Syria, for the past decade I have found rural and urban women of my acquaintance to be both ignorant of the practice, and horrified at the thought. In Australia, where the practice exists (although its incidence is not yet well documented), attitudes in public debates on the subject have been described as racist and bordering on hysteria.[30]

As for the *harem*, Lila Abu-Lughod (1989: 288) describes her use of the word as provocative because of its connotations of the orientalist 'imaginative world of Middle Eastern women'. I use the word in its original sense of *hurma* (from *haram*, sacred or forbidden), which denotes a wife, or wives, who are 'inviolable' under the protection of a male. It could be said that the inferiority that is implied by a multiplicity of wives augments the man's dominance, and reinforces the hierarchy, not only within his family, but within his entire community also.[31] Popularly thought to be dying a natural death in the Arab world in the face of economic exigencies and enlightened civil codes, polygamy is alive and thriving in Syria.[32]

Similarly, in some populations in Syria, both rural and urban, where woman represents the essence of the group's identity, the killing of an illicitly pregnant woman is the only recourse for the restoration of a family's 'honour'. Such homicide is not considered a crime by the community, and, while Ba'thist policy unambiguously declares this form of social and moral control as criminal, local civil administration is more lenient, and the extent of Ba'thist influence is questionable. However, Arab artists and intellectuals continue to be uncompromising in their damning of such social customs. In a short essay about a young woman who seeks to murder her sister to restore the family honour, Ghada al-Samman (1980) identifies a dramatic instance of what she calls 'masculinised behaviour', which she sees certain women displaying in pursuit of emancipation. In the vocal opposition to 'honour killing', recognition of the relationship between sexual abuse and male dominance is made explicit.[33]

In order to reverse such a relationship, al-Saadawi (1972: 168) declares that a change in the relations between male and female is necessary, and that this demands 'new modes of upbringing' at all stages of the life cycle. Syrian writers al-Samman (1961) and Shaaban (1991) agree that the truly liberated woman is one who believes that she is as human and as valuable in herself as is a man. But al-Samman (1980: 83) also sees men as victims who are equally as oppressed as women by the dictates of Arab/Muslim society.

Conclusion

In 1973 the Institute for Women's Studies in the Arab World (IWSAW) was established in the Beirut University College. Its researches and publications, in English and in Arabic, have been challenging and controversial, creating a healthy forum for debate and the illumination of all sorts of issues that concern the women of the area. Similarly in Jordan there is a plethora of social studies focusing on women.[34] Even allowing for the cultural overlap that one would expect to find between the countries of the region, the absence from such forums of Syrian women as a discrete group with locally specific concerns is remarkable.

While non-governmental, non-confessional women's organisations have emerged in some Arab countries, there are none as yet in Syria.[35] The Syrian Ba'thist Government emphasises certain ideals for women that are for the good of society as a whole, and these ideals could be challenged and jeopardised by independent feminist agendas. Therefore, any speculation about women's location in the dominant, socialist, patriarchal ideology must consider women as an integral part of that ideology (cf. Abu-Lughod, 1989: 291). Syrian Ba'thist philosophy stresses the importance of women's contribution to public life, yet the actual progress of Syrian women in education, matters of marriage, work and economic opportunities is retarded by traditional and conservative attitudes in the region. All manner of educational programmes, public forums, and constitutional articles enjoin women to contribute to the development of Syria, while at the same time they are restrained by the resilience of entrenched attitudes and normative modes that control their behaviour and ways of thinking of themselves.

In his preface to a Union of Syrian Women publication, George Tarabishi (1987: 10) urges men's emancipation along with women's, declaring that no real progress can be achieved in Syria until men consider their rights as men, and thus throw off the traditional Arab chauvinism. Similarly, until Syrian women see themselves as human beings first and foremost, they will remain the locus of traditional social values and, despite their place in modern public institutions, will only achieve what al-Samman (1980 [1961]: 142) calls 'the modern version of life in the harem'.

Notes

1. George Tarabishi (n.d.) *Women and Socialism* (Arabic), Beirut. Cited in Mernissi (1975: 103).
2. In this paper, 'Western' is used as a generic term for non-Arab, and indicates origins in, or associations with, Europe.
3. The concerns of Muslim women are not foreign to those of women in other confessional groups in Syria. However, outside the arena of the educated bourgeoisie, differences in cultural orientation, and the various communities' attitudes towards one another, defy the fixing of a common political premise to Syrian women's perceived needs and concerns.
4. The Economic and Social Commission for West Asia (ESCWA), 1985.
5. Report of the Secretary General: recommendations of regional inter-governmental preparatory meetings. A/CONF. 116/8, 21 February 1985 (cited in Hijab, 1988: 3).
6. *Tahrir al-Mar'a* (1899) and *Al-Mar'a Jadida* (1900), both of which are reprinted in Muhammad 'Imara (ed.) (1976). *Al-A'mal al-Kamila li-Qasim Amin*, in 2 vols. Beirut: al-Mu'assasa al-'Arabiya lil-Dirasat wal-Nashr.
7. Accad proposes that this is responsible for the violence in Lebanon, since such violence originates in the aggressive masculinity of the male, and in his lust to dominate and oppress women, and, presumably, other vulnerable entities. See Rana Kabbani (1986) and Malek Alloula (1987) for alternative discussions of the 'libidinal' nature of the colonial enterprise in the Middle East.
8. 'Ali Ahmed Sa'id.
9. The psychoanalyst Lacan proposed that the essential moment in the constitution of the self is when one distances oneself from the mother, in order to become oneself. Lacan discovered in women 'the danger of too much closeness', so that for self-development to take place, the 'correct distance is the opposite of the feminine' (Clement 1983: 78). However, a disciple of Lacan further proposes that if woman disappears then so too does the symptom of man, and when there is no longer a symptom, 'there is no longer a language, and therefore there is no longer a man either' (Lemoine-Luccioni 1987: 4).
10. My translation. From *al-Itihad al-Am al-Nisa'i* (1983a: no page numbers).
11. Article 12 of the Syrian Ba'thist Constitution, cited by President Assad in *République Arab Syrienne Union Générale des Femmes* (1989: 45).

12. *Al-Mar'a al-'Arabiyya al-Suriyya fi aqd al-Mar'a al-Dawli: 1975–1985* ('The Syrian Arab Woman in the International Decade of the Woman: 1975–1985'. 1987).

13. The OSW was called 'the Office for Women of Status' by Senator Amanda Vanstone when she criticised it for lacking relevance to the average Australian woman, and for doing 'nothing to raise the status of the great bulk of ordinary women performing ordinary jobs': *News Weekly*, 6 November 1993: 7.

14. Ann Sherry in an interview with Ranald MacDonald on Radio 3LO: Melbourne: 26 April 1994.

15. The research in this publication arose from recommendations of the UNESCO Regional Working Group on Women's Participation in Public Life in the Arab States Region, and was conducted by eminent women scholars of the Arab region.

16. Article 45 of the Syrian Constitution, cited by President Assad in a speech commemorating the 'liberation' of women through the 8 March Revolution (*République Arabe Syrienne . . .* 1989: 45).

17. For more on the context of this work by Mukhtar see Gershoni and Jankowski (1986).

18. In nationalist rhetoric, the *fellah* are seen as embodying the nobility and simple morality of the indigenous culture. For Egyptian nationalists, the very spirit of the nation was exemplified in rural life and characters (see Hanna, 1930; Hakim, 1933; Mahfouz, 1967). In Syrian school textbooks, there is a pronounced presence of the peasant as the only rural entity. A survey of these textbooks (36 primary and 32 secondary) between 1967 and 1976 (Sulayman 1978) offers a coincidental mosaic of Syrian women moving towards emancipation, equality with men, and participation in the national struggle (cf. Altoma, 1991: 80).

19. Jacobs (1994: 171) notes that environmentalism's dependence upon Western rational thought might be interpreted as dependence also upon 'masculinist knowledges' in the defence against exploitative, masculinist, colonialist approaches to the environment. The turning to 'women's knowledges' and 'indigenous knowledges' is a legacy of this interpretation.

20. Rural women in Syria cannot be spoken of homogeneously, for rural communities identify themselves variously as peasants, *'arab* (of tribal organisation and with a Bedouin legacy), and (rural) townspeople, or as Kurds, Turkmen, Circassians, and so on. The cultural legacies of each group pose varying challenges to Ba'thist programmes.

21. Citing FAO and UNESCO reports of 1979, Hinnebusch (1989: 282) notes that 'an exploited female proletariat' threatens

developing countries such as Syria with a 'feminisation of poverty'. There are few anthropological or sociological studies that specifically include women in Syria (see Sweet, 1960; Chatty, 1978; Rabo, 1986; Hill, 1994), but some excellent discussion papers written for the International Centre for Agricultural Research in Dry Areas (ICARDA) are concerned with gender-related aspects of farm labour in Syria and how new technologies may/do affect that labour (see Rassam, 1985; Rassam and Tully, 1986). A joint ICARDA and University of Hohenheim (Germany) study of land use management in dry marginal farming and pastoral areas of Syria (in press) includes a study of Bedouin women's role in domestic production.

22. Personal communication, 1990.
23. The present writer spent protracted periods between 1984 and 1990 living in villages on the banks of the northern Syrian Euphrates river, and has spent shorter sojourns in villages in the far north-eastern Jezira.
24. Marnia Lazreg (1988: 344 note 12) remarks the free use of the terms 'private sphere' and 'women's subordination' in what she describes as 'academic feminism's market for "Middle Eastern women"', whereby even writers who do not identify themselves as feminist use this (according to Lazreg) feminist language.
25. In anything but submission to Allah's will, it is also foreign to the Muslim, who is urged to assert his/her rights and to rise up against oppression by whatever means necessary. There are many verses in the Holy Book that indicate this. See for example *Qur'an* 22: 40ff; 4: 73, 91; and 3: 195.
26. Veiling as a socio-economic phenomenon has been discussed by many since the sixties. See for example J. Abu-Lughod (1961) and Williams (1980). As a religio-political offensive in the nineties, veiling is analysed by Zuhur (1992).
27. Haitham Haqqi's production of *Da'irat al-Nar* (Circle of Fire), Rahiba lil-Intaj al-Fanni, Damascus.
28. See Hill (1994: Appendix 10).
29. This is noted by Fatima Mernissi in *Le Harem Politique: Le Prophète et les femmes* (Paris: Albin Michel, 1987: 126), where she discusses al-Jawzi's *Kitab Ahkam al-Nisa'* (Beirut: 1980) and Ibn Taymiyya's *Fatawi'an al-Nisa'* (Cairo: 1983).
30. Such was the majority opinion after the National Conference on Female Genital Mutilation (4 July 1994, held at the Council of Adult Education Management Centre, Melbourne). The conference, attended by about 100 invited medical and legal professionals,

academics, Islamic and Christian scholars, immigration policy makers and others, found out that the issue engendered racial discrimination, and resolved that a five-year education programme should precede any legislation on the practice.

31. Olivier Richon (1985: 40) posits that with polygamy a man does not possess the other sex but rather its multiplicity, and this multiplicity may be said to characterise woman's inferiority to man.

32. Despite Shaaban's (1991: 60) assurance that, although it is still legally and religiously permissible, Syrian women 'have already succeeded in almost abolishing it', informal inquiry by the present writer in rural and urban Syria in 1996 revealed polygamy to be far from rare or outdated as an option.

33. This relationship is not unique to the Arab world. It has its reported correlations in Australia, among all communities, indigenous and immigrant. Burnam Burnam (1987: 92) states for the Australian Aboriginal woman that her 'spiritual strength, born out of tradition, is also acquired from male abuse, mainly sexual'. As with most of the debate on clitoridectomy and 'honour killing' in Australia, Jacobs (1994: 182) finds that sexual violence within Aboriginal society is taken up as 'a general political issue for the women's movement'.

34. A select bibliography of such studies can be found in Shami *et al.* (1990: 74ff).

35. Nor are there any in Qatar, the UAE, Saudi Arabia, Oman, Jordan, (former) North and South Yemen, Iraq and Libya (Hatem 1993: 37).

References

Abdel-Jaouad, Hedi (1990). 'Sacrilegious discourse'. *Middle East Report*, 163 (March–April): 34–6.

Abdel Kader, Soha (1987). *Egyptian Women in a Changing Society 1899–1987.* Boulder and London: Lynne Rienner Publishers.

Abu-Lughod, Janet (1961). 'Migrant adjustment to city life: the Egyptian case'. *American Journal of Sociology*, 67 (1): 22–32.

Abu-Lughod, Lila (1989). 'Zones of theory in the anthropology of the Arab world'. *Annual Review of Anthropology*, 18: 267–306.

Accad, Evelyne (1990). *Sexuality and War, Literary Masks.* Washington Square: New York University Press.

Ahmed, Leila (1984). 'Early feminist movements in the Middle East, Turkey and Egypt', in F. Hussain (ed.), *Muslim Women.* Beckenham: Croom Helm.

Al-Itihad al-'Am al-Nisa'i (General Union of [Syrian] Women), Maktab al-Thaqafa wal-'Ilam al-Markazi (1983a). *Aqwal al-Rafiq al-Munadil Hafez al-Assad (fi Qadaya al-Mara')*. Damascus: Majalla al-Mara' al-'Arabiyya.

Al-Itihad al-'Am al-Nisa'i, Maktab al-Thaqafa wal-'Ilam al-Markazi (1983b). *Munjazat al-Itihad al-'Am al-Nisa'i*. Damascus: Majalla al-Mara' al-'Arabiyya, 1980–3.

Alloula, Malek (1987). *The Colonial Harem*. Manchester: Manchester University Press.

al-Saadawi, Nawal (1972). *Al-Mar'a wal-Jins*, 2nd edn. Cairo: Maktab Madbuli.

—— (1980). *The Hidden Face of Eve*. London: Zed Press.

al-Samman, Ghada (1961). 'Our Constitution – We the Liberated Women'. In *Jaridat al-Nasr al-Suriyya* (November), trans. and reproduced in Ghada Al-Samman (1990), *Al-A'mal Ghayr al-Kamila, Saffrat Indhar Dakhli Ra'si*. Beirut: Manshurat Ghadah al-Samman.

—— (1980). *Al-A'mal Ghayr al-Kamila, Saffrat Indhar Dakhli Ra'si*. Beirut: Manshurat Ghadah al-Samman.

Altoma, Salih (1991). 'The emancipation of women in contemporary Syrian literature', in R. Antoun and D. Quataert (eds), *Syria, Society, Culture and Polity*, pp. 79–97. New York: State University of New York.

Badran, Margot and Cooke, Miriam (eds) (1990). *Opening the Gates, A Century of Arab Feminist Writing*. London: Virago.

Biehl, Janet (1991). *Finding Our Way, Rethinking Ecofeminist Politics*. Black Rose Books: Montreal.

Burnam, Burnam (1987). 'Aboriginal Australia and the Green movement', in D. Hutton (ed.), *Green Politics in Australia*, pp. 91–104. Melbourne: Angus and Robertson.

Chatty, Dawn (1978). 'Changing sex roles in Bedouin society in Syria and North Lebanon', in L. Beck and N. Keddie (eds), *Women in the Muslim World*, pp. 399–416. Cambridge, Mass: Harvard University Press.

Chodorow, Nancy (1974). 'Family structure and feminine personality', in Michelle Zimbalist Rosaldo and Louise Lamphere (eds), *Woman, Culture and Society*, pp. 43–66. Stanford, California: Stanford University Press.

Clement, Catherine (1983). *The Lives and Legends of Jacques Lacan*. New York: Columbia University Press.

Devlin, John F. (1983). *Syria, Modern State in an Ancient Land*. London: Croom Helm.

Gershoni, Israel and Jankowski, James P. (1986). *Egypt, Islam, and the Arabs, the Search for Egyptian Nationhood 1900–1930*. New York: Oxford University Press.

Ghoussoub, Mai (1987). 'Feminism – or the eternal masculine – in the Arab world'. *New Left Review*: 161: 3–18.

—— (1988). 'A reply to Hammami and Rieker'. *New Left Review*, 170: 107–9.

Grace, Helen (1991). 'Business, pleasure narrative, the folktale of our times', in R. Diprose and R. Ferrell (eds), *Cartographies, Poststructuralism and the Mapping of Bodies and Spaces*, pp. 113–25. Melbourne: Allen & Unwin.

Hakim, Tawfiq (1933). *'Awdat al-Ruh*, 2 vols. Cairo: Maktabat al-Adab, al-Matbaah al-Namudhajiyah.

Hammami, Reza and Rieker, Martina (1988). 'Feminist orientalism and orientalist Marxism'. *New Left Review*, 170: 93–106.

Hanna, Yusuf (1930). 'al-Da'wa ila al-Adb al-Qawm'. *al-Siyasa al-'Usbu'iyya* (Cairo), 10 (9 August).

Hatem, Mervat (1992). 'Economic and political liberalization in Egypt and the demise of state feminism'. *International Journal of Middle East Studies*, 24: 231–51.

—— (1993). 'Toward the development of post-Islamist and post-nationalist feminist discourses in the Middle East', in Judith E. Tucker (ed.), *Arab Women, Old Boundaries, New Frontiers*, pp. 29–48. Bloomington and Indianapolis: Indiana University Press.

Hijab, Nadia (1988). *Womenpower, the Arab Debate on Women at Work*. Cambridge and New York: Cambridge University Press.

Hill, Fiona (1994). Remaining Bedouin, ambivalent traditions in a Syrian Euphrates village. Unpublished Ph.D. thesis (anthropology), University of Melbourne, Parkville.

Hinnebusch, Raymond (1989). *Peasant and Bureaucracy in Ba'thist Syria*. Boulder, San Francisco and London: Westview Press.

Hopkins, Nicholas S. (1991). 'Women, work and wages in two Arab villages'. *The Eastern Anthropologist*, 44 (2): 103–23.

Hopwood, Derek (1988). *Syria 1945–1986, Politics and Society*. London: Unwin Hyman.

Ingrams, Doreen (1983). *The Awakened: Women in Iraq*. London: Third World Centre.

Jacobs, Jane M. (1994). 'Earth honouring: Western desires and indigenous knowledges', in Alison Blunt and Gillian Rose (eds), *Writing Women and Space: Colonial and Postcolonial Geographies*, pp. 169–97. New York: The Guilford Press.

Kabbani, Rana (1986). *Europe's Myths of the Orient*. Bloomington: Indiana University Press.

Lazreg, Marnia (1988). 'Feminism and difference, the perils of writing as a woman on women in Algeria'. *Feminist Studies*, 14 (1) (Spring): 81–107.

Leacock, Eleanor (1977). 'Women, development, and anthropological facts and fictions'. *Latin American Perspectives*, 4 (1 and 2).

Lemoine-Luccioni, Eugenie (1987) [1976]. *Partage des Femmes*, trans. by M.-L. Davenport and M.-C. Réguis as *The Dividing of Women, or Women's Lot*. London: Free Association Books.

Mahfouz, Naguib (1967). *Miramar*. Dar Misr lil-Taba'a: Maktaba Misr.

Mernissi, Fatima (1975). *Beyond the Veil, Male–Female Dynamics in Muslim Society*. Cambridge, Mass.: Schenkman Publishing.

—— (1993). *Islam and Democracy, Fear of the Modern World*. Cambridge, Mass.: Virago Press.

Rabo, Annika (1986). *Change on the Euphrates, Villagers, Townsmen and Employees in Northeast Syria*. Stockholm: Stockholm Studies in Anthropology: 15.

Rassam, Andre (1985). *Farm Labour by Age and Sex in North Western Syria, Implications for Two Proposed Technologies*. Aleppo: ICARDA Discussion Paper: 16.

Rassam, Andre and Tully, Dennis (1986). *Gender Related Aspects of Agricultural Labor in North Western Syria*. Aleppo: ICARDA Discussion Paper: 20.

République Arabe Syrienne Union Générale des Femmes (1989). *La Cause de la Femme vue par le Président Hafez El-Assad, Propos du Président Hafez Al-Assad à l'Occasion des Fêtes Nationales; Messages addressés par le Président El-Assad aux Conférences Mondiales de la Femme*, 2nd edn. Damascus: République Arabe Syrienne Union Générale des Femmes.

Richon, Olivier (1985). 'Representation, the harem, and the despot'. *Block* (Middlesex Polytechnic): 10: 34–44.

Shaaban, Bouthaina (1991). *Both Right and Left Handed, Arab Women Talk About Their Lives*. Indiana: Indiana University Press.

Shami, Setenyi *et al.* (1990). *Women in Arab Society, Work Patterns and Gender Relations in Egypt, Jordan and Sudan*. Paris: Berg Publishers and UNESCO.

Sharabi, Hisham (1988). *Neopatriarchy, A Theory of Distorted Change in Arab Society*. Oxford and New York: Oxford University Press.

Stork, Joe (1993). 'Gender and civil society, an interview with Suad Joseph'. *Middle East Report*, 183.

Stowasser, Barbara F. (1993). 'Women's issues in modern Islamic thought', in Judith E. Tucker (ed.), *Arab Women, Old Boundaries, New Frontiers*. pp. 3–28. Bloomington and Indianapolis: Indiana University Press.

Sulayman, Nabil (1978). *Al-Niswiyya fi al-Kitab al-Súri al-Madrasi 1967–1976*. Damascus: Ministry of Culture.

Sweet, Louise (1960). *Tell Toqa'an, A Syrian Village*. Ann Arbor: Michigan University Press.

Tarabishi, George (n.d.). *Women and Socialism* (in Arabic). Beirut: no publisher cited.

Tarabishi, George (1987). 'Introduction', in Union of Syrian Women. *Al-Mar'a al-'Arabiyya al-Suriyya fi 'aqd al-Mar'a al-Dawli, 1975–1985*. Damascus: Regional Command Press.

Tillion, Gertrude (1983 [1966]). *The Republic of Cousins*, trans. Q. Hoare. London: Al Saqi Books.

Vial, Charles (1980). 'La Littérature Contemporaine en Syrie'. In André Raymond (ed.), *La Syrie d'Aujourd'hui*, pp. 407–29. Paris: Centre National de la Recherche Scientifique.

Williams, John Alden (1980). 'Veiling in Egypt as a political and social phenomenon', in J. L. Esposito (ed.), *Islam and Development, Religion and Sociopolitical Change*, pp. 71–85. Syracuse, New York: Syracuse University Press.

Young, Wayland (1964). *Eros Denied*. London: Weidenfeld and Nicolson.

Zuhur, Sherifa (1992). *Revealing Reveiling, Islamist Gender Ideology in Contemporary Egypt*. New York: State University of New York Press.

– 7 –

Islam, Culture and Nationalism: The Post-Soviet Experience of Turkmenistan, Uzbekistan and Tajikistan[1]

Shahram Akbarzadeh

In the last years of the Soviet Union and following its collapse, we have witnessed a rising tide of interest in traditional religion in Central Asia as well as elsewhere. Open expressions of faith have become a daily occurrence in Central Asia. Ashgabat, the capital city of Turkmenistan, is covered with posters of President Niyazov in *al-Ihram* (the white robe worn by pilgrims in Mecca). President Karimov of Uzbekistan swore allegiance on the *Qur'an* at his inauguration ceremony (Brown, 1992). But only a short time ago, these people were leading Communist Party members.

The leadership in Central Asia has remained virtually unchanged. It has shown a clear determination to stay in power. Evoking the native traditions of these Muslim societies is quite important for the attainment of this goal. But the same leadership was earlier involved in the suppression of Islam. This was the official line. The rise of the Bolsheviks to power was followed by the closure of mosques, *madrassahs*, and *Shari'ah* courts and the confiscation of *awqaf* (religious lands and endowments), and evoked an armed resistance known as *Basmachi*. Leaders of the *Basmachi* resistance movement were often *mullahs* and Sufi *pirs* or *ishans*. The bulk of the movement was made up of peasants who regarded the new rulers as anti-Muslim, that is, enemies of their and their fathers' traditional way of life. Their struggle with the Soviet regime was not about Islam *per se*; it was about preserving their identity, which was manifested in their Islamic traditions and institutions.

The failure of anti-Islamic campaigns stands witness to the misguided Bolshevik approach, which attacked Islam as a faith. This could not undermine Islam's social role. Islam retained its prominence in cementing the community of believers. It was Islam's cultural significance that helped unite Central Asian Muslims and prepare them for the challenge posed by Soviet cultural imperialism. It is in reference to this feature that an explanation for the return of Islamic traditions may be sought.

It seems that the Bolshevik leadership failed to grasp the importance of Islam in Central Asia's identity. Official measures to eradicate the faith overlooked Islam's cultural attributes. Nonetheless, by the 1970s and early 1980s Soviet scholars were grappling with the phenomenon of Islam/culture unity on an academic level (see Ashirov, 1975; Saidbaev, 1984). Islamic precepts, it was argued, had become customary and fixed in people's consciousness over the years, to such an extent that Islamic and non-Islamic traditions were inextricable (Bazarov, 1982: 172–3; Ro'i, 1984: 31). Vagabov, a Soviet sociologist, observed this unity in every aspect of Central Asian life. Taking marriage as an example of important socio-cultural events, he observed that: 'marriage ceremonies of the people of the Soviet East consist of secular culture, national traditions, religious [Islamic] rituals and even pre-Islamic pagan activities. Here differentiating between religious and national is exceptionally difficult' (1988: 194).

This feature, in particular, helps to illuminate the underlying reasons for the strong hold of Islamic traditions on Central Asian societies. Gapurov, the First Secretary of the Central Committee of the Communist Party of Turkmenistan, in April 1973 gave a detailed, albeit hostile, account of the magnitude of Islamic tradition in Turkmenistan. At a Central Committee plenum Gapurov seriously criticised the failure of the party *apparat* to carry out effective campaigns against this 'reactionary' threat to the unity of the Motherland (*Rodina*, used interchangeably for the USSR and one's constituent republic) (1973).

The state of affairs was, really, more serious than Gapurov was willing to admit. The local party *apparat* not only neglected their anti-Islamic responsibilities, but at times were involved in traditional Islamic activities. In 1975 a Turkmen party secretary (*charshanga raion*) registered the local communists' complicity in unlawful performances of Islamic/traditional marriage, and the use of official vehicles to transport pilgrims to a local *mazar*, or Saint's tomb (Murtazakulov, 1975: 2).

In spite of overconfident promises about the eradication of religion, Islam remained intrinsic to Central Asian cultures. Islam was a point of reference, a source of self-identity to bond and differentiate Central Asians from the infidel Russians. In this sense even Communist Party membership could not impair the self-perception of Central Asians as Muslims (Ro'i, 1987: 172–3). That, in effect, meant admitting to being Muslims and participating in Islamic/traditional acts of male circumcision, *nikah* (Islamic marriage), celebration of *Kurban Bairam* and *Uruza Bairam* (*'Id al-Adha* and *'Id al-Fitr*), and visiting *mazars*. Reaffirming the compatibility between self-identification with a Muslim community and party membership Khaidar Sharifzode, Imam of Kulob region, stated: 'a Communist can be an orthodox Muslim' (Rotar, 1992b: 3).

A recent recognition of this feature was expressed by the Russian academician Malashenko, who rejected as groundless Russian hopes for the dissipation of Islam. To paraphrase, his proposition is to argue that Islam will only die away with the people of Central Asia (1993a: 3).

This is indeed a recognition of the strength of the native culture in the minds and hearts of the people. Islam's contribution to cultural cohesiveness could be invoked to explain the process in which Soviet attempts at social engineering were so fundamentally undermined. The Central Asian Soviet Man was a thin layer of conformity that concealed a deeper source of identity, that of traditional culture. Preserving a distinct culture, often containing a blend of Islamic and pre-Islamic traditions, throughout the Soviet period allowed the native élite to identify itself with its own community while performing the standard Soviet rites of attending May Day and International Women's Day celebrations. The post-Soviet experience of the independent states in Central Asia stands witness to the durability of culture, not in spite of, but especially because of, external pressure.

It is this deeper sense of attachment to a Muslim community, now organised in completely separate political entities, that allows former party members simply to cast aside the superficial Soviet traditions and adapt to new conditions. The void following the break-up of the Soviet Union was filled by native cultures. And Presidents Karimov and Niyazov are two good illustrations of a native élite in search of indigenous traditions. (Though the historical past is not fixed; it is, in fact, often presented in particular ways to suit their authoritarian rule.) The fact of relying on (their Islamic) history, whether factual or fictitious, spiced with modern ideas of parliamentarianism and secularism, consolidates the sense of a national community ready to take off for a glorious future.

Here, the native élite can also rely on a Soviet legacy. Present national groups in Central Asia are a direct consequence of the Soviet nationalities policy. The 1924 division of the region into separate so-called national republics was the first step to put in place social infrastructures for the formation of national identities. Separate languages were developed and distinct histories were written, to establish the separateness of Uzbeks, Turkmens and Tajiks. Soviet schooling, conducted in the language of the titular nationality of each republic, was instrumental in inculcating the novel language-based national identity. Central Asian élite groups, in the course of Soviet rule, emerged to closely identify with their national territories. They were trained in their republican political structures and, as a rule, functioned in their titular territories (Miller, 1977). 'National' borders determined the limits of authority for the élite groups. Though subordinate to Moscow in vital matters of economic planning, security and foreign relations, native élites operated within their titular republics in the wake of the Soviet collapse.

Since the emergence of the independent states in Central Asia and the freeing of Central Asian politics from the restraining Soviet models and terminology, native leadership has returned to supposedly traditional modes of government. In particular, it has exhibited a clear propensity to employ traditional/Islamic terminology. Linking the present (often authoritarian) politics with traditions that are presented as indigenous has been largely successful in circumventing sociopolitical instability.

The fate of Tajikistan is an exception. Although similar nation-building policies were pursued in that republic in the Soviet period, once the Soviet regime was gone the 'national' élite failed to grasp the significance of national community and Islam's importance in that community. Linguistic and religious diversities in Tajikistan also appear to have been at fault in undermining the dynamic of Tajik nationalism and fuelling regional rivalry (Akbarzadeh, 1996).

This chapter is a study of the three states of Tajikistan, Turkmenistan and Uzbekistan.[2] It is an attempt to explore the post-Soviet efforts of élite groups to consolidate their national communities and the role of Islam in this process. The chapter examines the ways in which Islamic and quasi-Islamic traditions have been invoked to justify and benefit the hitherto 'atheist' élite in its nationalist drive.

Soviet Legacy of Successor States

Even before the collapse of the Soviet system, Central Asian Muslims found ways to compensate for the restrictions imposed on performing traditional and Islamic rites. Friday congregations in public gathering places such as *chaikhane* (or teahouses) were not unusual in the countryside. There were also non-'working' mosques (that is, mosques converted into secular places such as museums or clubs) that still served Muslims as assembly halls. 'Little *haj*', a phrase coined by Igor Belyaev

(1987) to describe visits to local *mazars*, was widely practised by Central Asians, since performing *haj* (pilgrimage to Mecca) was next to impossible in the Soviet era.

Central Asians and their élites for the most part found Soviet attempts at separating Islamic traditions from their national identities, created since the 1920s and now accepted, to be impossible. The tension was further exacerbated by Moscow's tenaciously anti-Islamic line. Soviet authorities condemned *sheikhs* (usually unregistered custodians of *mazars*) for presenting Islam as a national heritage (Murtazakulov 1975:2). This remained so even during Gorbachev's reign. In his speech at the Twenty-Seventh Congress of the Communist Party of the Soviet Union (CPSU), Gorbachev attacked Islam as a 'feudal vestige of the past', and as incompatible with socialist goals and 'the scientific world outlook' (Ro'i, 1987). Islam was assessed as an undesirable feature that had to be eradicated.

Retaining Islamic traditions, therefore, was a form of implicit resistance to assimilation into the Soviet mould; it was a common effort by party and non-party Tajiks, Turkmens and Uzbeks to develop and retain an identity distinct from the Russian/Soviet dictated one, though bearing the national imprints of the Soviet period.

Here a complication arises from the fact that all Central Asian republics, to a greater or lesser extent, have embraced their cultural traditions and are engaged in a determined process of reviving and renewing their pre-revolutionary cultures. This is a quest for identity. Examples of this process are abundant, particularly in Turkmenistan and Uzbekistan, where the rediscovery of the past, critical to the revival and cohesion of their culture, is advancing under direct state auspices. This process cannot ignore Islam. Central Asian cultures are unimaginable without Islamic traditions. And the nationalist governments of Central Asia are fully aware of this characteristic. In fostering cultural traditions, therefore, ruling parties also nurture Islam. A salient manifestation of this process is the rising number of officially sanctioned mosques, and the establishment of academic agreements with Turkey and Arab states for training future Central Asian *mullahs*, as Allamyrat Miradov, Chairman of the Council for Religious Affairs attached to the Turkmen Cabinet of Ministers, has indicated (Allamyrat Miradov, pers., comm., Ashgabat, 2 November 1992).

The current Islamic revival in the republics of Turkmenistan, Uzbekistan and Tajikistan is a double-faceted phenomenon. Firstly, it draws strength principally from the fusion of Islam and pagan cultural traditions, with few political repercussions. Secondly, it attains ideological importance in the absence of alternative universalist world outlooks. After the failure of Marxism, which has proved the most attractive twentieth-century political ideology and programme for development with its promise of equality and justice, Islam finds welcoming signs in the political scene. It has the potential to develop into a popular and militant political ideology. In such circumstances its rival, liberal (or authoritarian) secularism, cannot offer a viable challenge to the universal appeal of Islam.

However, for at least two reasons, Islam as a political ideology has remained underdeveloped. Firstly, the Muslim clergy in Central Asia belong to the Sunni sect, which has traditionally submitted to the supremacy of lay rulers and accepted the separation of Church and State. Secondly, over seventy years of Soviet rule have placed limitations on the knowledge of Islam and its precepts. This experience has undermined the self-confidence of the *ulema* to challenge political authorities. Islam in Central Asia has not posed any significant challenge to the predominant order. Instances of Islamic assertiveness with clear political overtones are too few and far between to justify a fear of 'political Islam'. Instead, the native élites in Central Asia have seized upon the cultural weight of Islam to secure social cohesion and political stability.

Turkmenistan

The year 1992 was a busy one for the Turkmen state. After recovering from the initial shock of Soviet disintegration the Turkmen leadership realised that its future hinged on aligning its efforts with the cultural revival process. This process had been initiated independent of the state, mainly by the Turkmen literary intelligentsia and the Muslim clergy. State auspices for cultural revival invariably took a classic form of post-Soviet bureaucratic nation-building. A clear example of this deliberate campaign was the signing of the presidential decree on the restoration of Turkmen history and culture in February 1992 (*Turkmenskaya Iskra* (henceforth *TI*), 1992c: 1–2). Earlier that year President Niyazov had visited Geok-Tepe (*TI*, 1992a: 1), the site of the 1879 defeat of Russian troops at the hands of the Teke Turkmens, and announced the official intention to build a museum in Geok-Tepe on the theme of Turkmen resistance to Tsarist Russia. The Turkmen ministries of culture, finance, Gosplan (State Planning Committee) and the Academy of Sciences were named as the participants in this project (*TI*, 1992b: 1).

With the fading of all hopes for the restoration of the Union, the Turkmen state embarked on a comprehensive campaign to eliminate Soviet titles. So the parliament of Turkmenistan was changed from the Supreme Soviet to the *Mejlis* (Zhukov, 1992: 3), and oblasts (or

Soviet administrative divisions) came to be known as *velayatlar* (RFE/
RL 1992). The ruling party also created a completely new assembly
based on cultural traditions, which were presented as specifically Turkmen. The advisory assembly of *Khalq Maslehati* consists of 60 elected
deputies, called *Khalq Vekillar* (Musaev, 1992: 1). *Khalq Vekillar*, the
government stresses, are elected on a strictly traditional basis. That,
according to the party First Secretary, Ondzhuk Musaev, means the
election of the *Yagsholi* (or *Aqsaqali*, literally the 'white-bearded') elder
men of different communities to the assembly (Ondzhuk Musaev, pers.,
comm., Ashgabat, 26 October 1992). This is a clear attempt to draw
on clan/family affiliations and utilise them for the legitimisation, and
hence the preservation, of the ruling élite.

Khalq Maslehati is, in practice, made up of some parliamentarian
deputies, members of the cabinet of ministers and *hakims* (*velayat*
leaders, appointed by the President). The assembly is chaired by
President Niyazov (*TI*, 1992f: 1). The Turkmen political system is
claimed to be unique in the world (Podalinsko, 1992: 2).

A further feature of the Turkmen post-Soviet politics is the personality cult that President Niyazov has built around himself. After their
unsolicited independence, the Turkmen leadership began an extensive
campaign to present Saparmurat Niyazov as a national hero. The main
boulevard in the capital Ashgabat is decorated with Saparmurad
Niyazov's name. Life-size pictures of the President are present in most
public places. And the state-owned daily paper (*Turkmenskaya Iskra*)
scrupulously carried pictures of Niyazov on its first page throughout
1992 and 1993. Since 1 January 1994, however, Niyazov's picture has
been included in the permanent masthead of the first page, along with
the official Turkmen flag and emblem. Ondzhuk Musaev, the First
Secretary of the ruling Democratic Party of Turkmenistan, compares
Niyazov with the sixteenth century poet Makhtumquli (Ondzhuk
Musaev, pers. comm., Ashgabat, 26 October 1992), who is treated like
a god in the proposed pantheon of Turkmen nationalism. Niyazov's
cult of personality has a Soviet precedent, but it is also rooted in
traditional Turkmen society. The favoured title of *Turkmenbashi* (Chief
of Turkmens) for Niyazov (Zhukov, 1993: 4) is a clear reference to
the patriarchal legacies of Turkmens. Indeed, Niyazov sees his role as
the chief and arbitrator of all Turkmen clans (Ondzhuk Musaev, pers.
comm., Ashgabat, 26 October 1992). There is no historically recorded
evidence, however, for a native Turkmen chief arbitrator for
the Turkmen clans. This task was, however, often performed by the
Khan of Khiva, who ruled over Turkmen land prior to the Bolshevik
takeover.

Invoking, and in this case shaping, Turkmens' historical memory in respect of the indigenousness of their political organisation, allows the Turkmen propaganda machinery to dismiss criticism of Niyazov's personality cult as misguided and based on a lack of understanding for the 'profound *aqsaqal* traditions' that are the basis of the modern Turkmen polity (Dovgoryat, 1992: 1).

The earlier-mentioned presidential tour of Geok-Tepe was completed after a visit to the newly built Chary-Akhun mosque (*TI,* 1992a: 1). President Niyazov pursues amicable relations with Islamic authorities and has presented himself as the champion of the faith. He even performed a highly publicised pilgrimage (*haj*) to Mecca while on an official visit to Saudi Arabia in April 1992. For the first time in the history of Central Asia the Islamic feast of *'Id al-Adha* (known as *Kurban Bairam* in Central Asia) was celebrated as a national holiday and widely publicised (*TI,* 1992e: 1). The grand *Qazi* of Turkmenistan explained this celebration in the following manner: 'This public holiday helps us to restore the representation of our *culture and customs* that have been accumulated over many centuries of history' (Kurbanova, 1992: 2; my emphasis). It is noteworthy that here the *Qazi* is making no distinction between Islam and culture.

Niyazov's approach has proved fruitful, for it has ensured general loyalty among *mullahs*. The registration of the office of *Qaziat* (ecclesiastical leadership) for the Muslims of Turkmenistan in June 1992 provided the best occasion for the clergy to reaffirm their loyalty to President Niyazov. Qazi Nasrulla ibn Ibadulla's endorsement of Niyazov's candidacy in the first state-wide presidential election in Turkmenistan was brandished in bold on the front page of the Turkmen daily (*TI,* 1992d). Here the Turkmen state is conscious of the risks involved in fostering Islam, and is at pains to point out the secular basis of its polity (Niyazov, 1992: 1).

An additional factor that could have contributed to the absence of anti-establishment militancy in the ranks of Turkmen *mullahs* is the benign character of the Islamic revival in Turkmenistan. This is perhaps explained by reference to the loose nomadic structure that was predominant in pre-1920s Turkmen society. Their nomadic lifestyle, governed by unwritten customary laws, often escaped the more rigid/orthodox aspects of the Islamic establishment. In comparison with sedentary Uzbeks and Tajiks in the Bukharan khanate, nomadic Turkmens were far less Islamicised. This seems to confirm Niyazov's assertion that 'Turkmenistan was never a fanatical Islamic society' (Niyazov, 1992: 1).

Uzbekistan

A similar process of nation-building is under way in Uzbekistan. The official daily paper (*Pravda Vostoka*) often carries stories on the *Aqsaqali* and their traditions, although no Turkmen-like assembly has been formed for the 'white-beards'. In a transparent bid to revive an image of traditional authority for the state, local leaders have been renamed *hakims* (*Pravda Vostoka*, 1991). In 1992, the Uzbek parliament made *Kurban Bairam* and *Uruza Bairam* national holidays (*Pravda Vostoka* (hereafter *PV*), 1992a); the Uzbek President issued a decree which, in effect, strengthened traditional community cohesiveness. *Mahalla*, an urban evolution of rural clan communities (Poliakov, 1992: 76–80), has been assigned the task of establishing some kind of a social security fund in each locality (*PV*, 1992c).

In reviving and championing pre-revolutionary traditions, the native élite is making a calculated effort to find a substitute power-base and a corresponding legitimation for its rule. Despite the fact that Uzbek nationhood is a recent creation of Moscow,[3] the notion provides comfort for people of diverse political trends. Nationalism is professed by all parties in the political spectrum; it is not confined to the leadership. The only quasi-popular movement in Central Asia, Birlik (Unity), with its strong links with Uzbek literary circles, also emphasises Uzbekness and everything pertaining to Uzbeks. In this respect, Birlik pays particular attention to Islamic traditions, as was best shown in one of its gatherings (1990) to discuss the promotion of the Uzbek language, where the assembly hall was decorated with green banners and the meeting opened with the reading of a verse from the *Qur'an* (Ro'i, 1990: 59; RFE/RL, 1994b).

Muhammad Salih, the leader of the Erk opposition party who contested the December 1991 presidential election, is a staunch secularist and Uzbek nationalist. However, he expresses a compelling need to respect Islamic tradition, and teaches the *Qur'an* to his son (Muhammad Salih, pers. comm., Tashkent, 5 October 1992). Here Muhammad Salih shares an understanding with his political rival, President Karimov; and that is the undeniable significance of Islam for the Uzbek identity. The appreciation of this feature, therefore, prompts Karimov, who is himself a product of Soviet secularism, to swear allegiance on the *Qur'an* and conclude a political speech by wishing Allah's blessing for his audience (Karimov, 1992b: 1).

Even more noteworthy is the tacit utilisation of Islam in foreign relations. When the Tajik Government looked set to be run by Uzbek-hostile politicians, the Uzbek president sent a message to that republic and reminded them of their common history and traditions and also the common philosophy of Islam that bound Tajiks and Uzbeks (*PV*, 1992b: 1). In another instance, the Uzbek Government invited the Mufti of Tashkent to play host to the Iranian delegation at the belated opening ceremony of the Iranian embassy in Tashkent (*PV*, 1992d: 1). Examples like these point to the familiar use of Islam and Islamic institutions as public relations tools. The days of labelling the growing interest in Islamic expressions 'cancerous' and associating Islam with feudal customs are long gone.[4]

Official sanctions are welcomed by Islamic leaders. In return for state auspices and the return of their authority most *mullahs* are prepared to offer the government the blessing sought after, and advise Uzbeks against drawing Islam into politics, as Imam Sheikh Abdulghani Abdullo of Tashkent did in his interview (1991). But the threat of an Islamic political movement appears to have pushed the Uzbek state to review its policy toward Islam. After the mayhem of independence, the state is trying to re-establish its complete control over Islamic institutions. The recently adopted law 'On Freedom of Conscience and Religious Organisations' granted extensive powers to *hakims*, local government and state agencies at the local level to control the activities of Islamic institutions. Even the content of sermons at mosques is claimed to fall under the control of local administrators (Usmanov, 1994: 3).

This latest shift in policy could prove unsettling, disenchanting the otherwise politically apathetic *mullahs*. The Uzbek authoritarian mode of government has already paralysed opposition movements, placing severe restrictions on the freedom of assembly. Erk and Birlik can no longer publish their papers legally (RFE/RL, 1994b). In this milieu, a *rapprochement* between the restricted but functioning mosques and the practically illegal secular opposition movement is not unlikely. As the still-expanding number of mosques serve as venues for public gatherings, secular opposition activists may find no other alternative but to rely on the Islamic network (Olcott, 1993: 93).

Tajikistan

Two seemingly unrelated phenomena appear to be at the root of the Tajik crisis in the aftermath of the Soviet implosion: regionalism and Islam. Evidence pointing to these as contributory factors to the continuing political instability is not hard to come by.

Firstly, regional affiliations that were the hallmark of pre-1917 Central Asia appear to have retained their hold on the popular psychology of the inhabitants of this republic. Soviet policy-makers may have expected their rule to have overcome local and regional loyalties, but if so they were mistaken; whether a survival from pre-revolutionary days, or because something in the Soviet experience strengthened them, such loyalties were clearly vigorous in the 1990s. Local affiliations correspond roughly with the four regions of Leninobod, Kulob, Kurgan Teppe and Pamir. The concentration of political power in the hands of Leninobodi leaders, who often co-opted complacent Kulobis but excluded public figures from Kurgan Teppe and more effectively from Pamir from governmental posts, was often a source of tension. The more economically prosperous Leninobod (producing 65 per cent of Tajikistan's GNP in the post-Second World War period) dominated the Tajik state (Martin, 1993: 19). This was a well-established feature in Tajik politics, reflected even in a Tajik folk saying: 'Pamir dances, Kulob guards, Kurgan-Teppe ploughs, Dushanbe produces, and Leninobod trades and governs.'

The main opposition parties include: Rastakhiz (Renaissance) Popular Movement, Democratic Party of Tajikistan, Islamic Renaissance Party (IRP) and La'li Badakhshon (Ruby of Badakhshon). The last is clearly a Badakhshoni regionalist party. The others also generally enjoy popularity in Kurgan Teppe and the mountainous region of Badakhshon (Pamir), with the Kulob and Dushanbe regions torn between loyalty to the northern region of Leninobod and solidarity with their neighbours. Signs of a mounting regional/clan conflict were transparent in the first displays of public discontent with the government in 1992, so much so that the union of public servants was moved to issue a public warning (not against Islamic fundamentalism, but) against the dangers of *klanovoi nenavisti*, clan hatred (*Narodnaya Gazeta*, 1992c). The publication of this warning in the Tajikistan Communist Party's daily paper was an unprecedented admission of the failure of the Soviet project to eradicate this pre-revolutionary feature in Tajikistan. The ensuing civil war that erupted after the overthrow of the coalition government in November 1992 served to entrench the significance of clan politics in the psychology of Tajiks. Emomali Rahmonov, head of the present government, admitted that in his speech delivered to the eighteenth session of the Tajik parliament in December 1993 (*Sadoi Mardum*, 1994a).

Secondly, the governments of Russia, Uzbekistan and Tajikistan have also accused Tajik opposition parties of favouring an Islamic model of government, hence destabilising Tajikistan and the region. Calls for the establishment of an Islamic republic in Tajikistan were certainly heard. In 1986 Mullah Abdullo was imprisoned after agitating for the creation of a *Musulmanabad* (Muslim-land) in Tajikistan (Hetmanek, 1990: 37). In a later case, Mirbobo Mirrahimov, a member of the Tajik Academy of Sciences, was widely quoted as advocating an Islamic regime for Tajikistan (Hetmanek, 1990: 37).

Accusing opponent dissidents of Islamic fundamentalism was a favoured tactic of the KGB. At times these fabrications aroused the indignation of even high-ranking party members (Brown, 1990b: 26). Highlighting the Islamic manifestations of opposition, then by the KGB and now by the Tajik, Uzbek and Russian states, tends to overlook the ill-defined but emotionally appealing nature of Islamic traditions. In Eden Naby's words 'centuries of old customs and habits . . . [have been] imbued with an Islamic cast' (1986: 289). This renders Islamic terminology a more popular medium than the remote and irrelevant Soviet/European vocabulary. It is plausible that profound feelings are likely to be articulated in traditional (that is, Islamic) phraseology. Moreover, after *perestroika* relaxed the rigid guidelines for accepted forms of political discourse, the native intelligentsia no longer feared to utilise a more diversified language. Mirrakhimov's case (1989) is then a good illustration, for he began his controversial speech by reference to chronic housing shortages in Tajikistan. Only then did he move to advise his audience not to elect Russians to the post of people's deputy and to predict the consequent out-migration of Russians, leading to the establishment of an 'Islamic republic' (Ro'i, 1990: 61). There was little in Mirrahimov's speech to suggest that his reference to an 'Islamic republic' meant anything more than a Russia-free Tajikistan.

Indeed, there have been no visible provisions for the establishment of an Iranian-style polity by the Islamic opposition in Tajikistan. In May 1992 the coalition of Islamic/democratic forces attained power in Dushanbe (capital of Tajikistan). This was a dramatic event, for the feared Islamic state appeared to be on the threshold of power. Neither before attaining power nor after, however, did the opposition advocate Islam as a ruling ideology. At a press conference, two weeks before becoming part of the government, the opposition's list of demands contained no reference to Islam. Present at the conference were the highest Islamic authority in Tajikistan, Qazikalon (Grand *Qazi*) Akbar Turajonzoda, and leaders of the IRP (*Narodnaya Gazeta*, 1992b). This was a reaffirmation of Turajonzoda's earlier position on the separation of religion and the state, expressed in an interview the previous year (Vyzhutovich, 1991: 2). The May–November 1992 coalition government made no attempt at establishing *Shari'ah* courts, let alone a fully-fledged Islamic regime.

Consequently, calls for an Islamic republic should be interpreted as a mere negation of the status quo. Just as the discourse of democracy was/is often used by the European population of the former USSR to negate the abhorred Soviet system, Islam was/is utilised in Taji-kistan to express mass enmity to an unpopular political establishment. This is made possible because Islam best represents the most indigenous and uncontaminated set of values. Islam is undisputedly theirs. This is not, in the least, a pointer to the nature of the proposed 'Islamic' state.

This should explain the position of Shodmon Yusupov, Chairman of the Democratic Party of Tajikistan. Writing from exile, Yusupov rejected the accusation of Islamic fundamentalism as 'simply absurd' (1993). According to Shodmon Yusupov none of the parties in the coalition of opposition forces called for the establishment of an Islamic regime.

The failure of the Tajik state to champion Islam in the crumbling phase of the Soviet model had a detrimental effect on the politics of continuity. In 1992 motions to adopt Islamic holy days as official holidays, to slaughter livestock according to Islamic law and to exempt mosques and other religious institutions from land tax were rejected by the Tajik parliament, leading to the disillusionment of the Tajik Qazikalon Akbar Turajonzoda (Martin, 1993: 21). The government of President Nabiev was then forced by mass demonstrators to declare *Idi Kurban* and *Idi Fitr* national holidays (*Narodnaya Gazeta*, 1992a). This was in stark contrast to the alert leadership of Uzbekistan and Turkmenistan. Indeed, President Karimov held the 'feeble leadership' of the late President Nabiev of Tajikistan responsible for the escalation of the Tajik conflict (Karimov, 1992a: 3). The leadership in both Uzbekistan and Turkmenistan adopted similar measures in regards to Islamic holy days without causing undue concern. Indeed, the celebration of *Idi Kurban* in Tajikistan, like its Muslim neighbours, should be viewed as nothing more than an open acknowledgment of Islam's significance to the native culture. It is important to note also that the same decree acknowledged the two pre-Islamic celebrations of *Mehregan* and *Sada* as important dates in the Tajik calendar.

But the official line remained hostile toward Islamic conventions. This could not be more damaging to a state dependent so heavily on Islamic authorities for legitimacy. As late as 1991, it is noted, there existed an implicit coalition between rural party bosses and the *mullahs* that ensured the latter's endorsement of party candidates for the Supreme Soviet. Considering the fact that almost 70 per cent of the population in Tajikistan live in rural areas, the political implications of this coalition were far-reaching. Perhaps it was in appreciation of this precarious balance of interests that Kahar Mahkamov, the First Secretary of the Communist Party of Tajikistan, in 1986 proposed the legalisation of unofficial *mullahs* (Brown, 1990b: 26). This was not achieved.

In the short period that Mirbobo Mirrahimov headed the Tajik State Radio and Television under the coalition government he cancelled Russian and Uzbek programmes, in a gesture of triumph. The promotion of the Tajik language at the expense of Russian and Uzbek was indicative of an underlying characteristic. The opposition appears committed to Tajik nationalism. The Tajik 'nation' appears to have become the third source of identity and a relatively novel object of loyalty. As early as 1990, Rastakhiz was active in hoisting the banner of 'Tajikistan for the Tajiks' (Brown, 1990a: 30). National consciousness seems to have been the cement that united the opposition parties. The regionally inspired groups sought cohesion through national unity and equality. An indigenous (that is, Tajik/Islamic) state was expected to address the misdeeds of the Soviet era. It was not to be an Islamic state, for Uzbeks were also Muslims who had lived in the region long before its Stalinist demarcation. The goal appears to have been a Muslim Tajik state. Here, the stress was evidently on the second adjective, while the first remained a statement of the obvious; there simply could not exist a non-Muslim Tajik state. Hence, the importance of Islam was not rooted in its divinity, but in its indivisibility from the incipient Tajik identity.

What further complicates the quest for nationalism in Tajikistan is the republic's ethnic make-up. The overwhelming concentration of Tajikistan's Uzbek-descended population in Leninobod[5] could not but contribute to the fusion of national and regional crises. Concurrent regional hostility to the ruling Leninobod on the one hand and Tajik national rivalry with Uzbeks (living predominantly in Leninobod) on the other seem to have been mutually reinforcing. For reasons stemming either from regional hostility or national inspirations, the two have coincided in their opposition to Leninobod's rule. This is an intricate case of mutual dependence, with the balance tipped slightly in favour of nationalism, making it an evolution of regional aspirations.

To add another dimension to the Tajik riddle, the post-coalition government of Emomali Rahmonov seems involved in advancing a fourth object of loyalty. *Vatan* (motherland) is a favourite point of reference for the present government. In an open invitation to all refugees and expatriates, Rahmonov reminded them of the plight of the motherland to encourage their return. This emotionally charged appeal was addressed to Tajikistan's *hamvatanon*: fellow countrymen and women (*Sadoi Mardum* (hereafter *SM*), 1994b). Rahmonov appears determined to deal with the ethnically fragmented Soviet legacy through a supra-ethnic civil accord. Consequently, political stability is sought through the promotion of a supreme identity, not regional or national (though his rhetoric is not completely free of nationalist references), but supra-national. This is a republican identity to incorporate the full spectrum of Tajikistan's colourful ethnic make-up. The role of the Tajik language daily paper, *Sadoi Mardum* (People's Voice), is noteworthy in this project, for it often publishes (Soviet-type) material on the friendship of the people. In a series of interviews, on the theme of Rahmonov's parliamentary speech, entitled 'Taji-kistan is the *Vatan* of us all', Uzbeks and Russians are presented as equal citizens of the republic. Predictably, the interviewees proclaim their allegiance to Tajikistan as their motherland (*SM*, 1994c).

In a later issue *Sadoi Mardum* published an appeal by labour collectives in which all citizens (*shahrvandon*) were invited to work collectively for the future of the motherland regardless of their regional, clan, national and religious differences (*SM*, 1994d). It continued: 'We should be faithful children of our history. This is a matter of honour (*nomus*)' (*SM*, 1994d). *Nomus* is the most profound form of honour in Tajik society. It refers to the traditional protectiveness of men for female members of their immediate family. Invoking *nomus* (used twice in the text), instead of *sharaf*, which also indicates honour, but in more general terms, is perhaps a pointer to the significance that the authorities attach to the success of their supra-national project.

Islam is present in the very fabric of the proposed supra-national identity. In February 1994 Rahmonov's government banned TV programmes that upset 'traditional values' (for example, erotic movies and programmes containing scenes of alcohol and tobacco consumption) (RFE/RL, 1994a), exhibiting his awareness of the weight of Islam in the popular culture. Early in the year Rahmonov, in his parliamentary speech, had identified Tajikistan as a member of the Muslim world, evidently seeing the future of the republic in close contact with other Central Asian republics, Iran, Afghanistan and Arabic states (*SM*, 1994a). In a symbolic gesture, the Tajik Government condemned the Hebron massacre of Palestinians (*SM*, 1994e).

The persistence of overt regional loyalties in Tajikistan has made the task of nation-building more difficult in comparison with Uzbekistan and Turkmenistan. In the last two cases clan-based communities appear to have been undermined, with relative success, throughout the Soviet period. Peculiar characteristics, founded on linguistic, religious and geographical diversities, however, seem to have impaired this process in Tajikistan. The consolidation of a Tajik national community, attempted by the Islamic–democratic forces, and the supra-national project advanced by the present government depend on an essential prerequisite: an efficient centrally administered state bureaucracy is critical to both these processes. And the present government seems committed to just that. President Rahmonov, in his parliamentary address, stressed the need to cleanse the corrupt and malfunctioning state administration, to hold a state-wide referendum for the adoption of the first post-Soviet constitution and to organise parliamentary elections in 1994 (*SM*, 1994a).

In the mayhem of rivalry between competing identities in Tajikistan, Islam is an invariable constant. Regional, national and supra-national identities have a common denominator. Islam is a component of all: hence, it is not a defining parameter. In this sense, then, Islam is a subsidiary (secondary) point of reference, a flexible component that can be moulded in various shapes, though it may lend itself more readily to supra-national and national frameworks than regional.

Indeed, the Islamic ideology, except for a limited number of devout activists, is a loose term with no definite meaning. Hence its general appeal. It is also a prime source of confusion when examining Tajik politics. Although one can assume that an equivocal understanding of an Islamic state exists (one that is guided by the *Qur'anic* Laws), and the example of the Islamic Republic of Iran has perhaps contributed to the solidification of this perception, Islam in Tajikistan is a negating phenomenon. It is far from becoming a formative ideology standing on its own merits.

Conclusion

With the exception of the Tajik leadership, the native élite in Central Asia managed to pass unscathed through the uncertain period immediately after the Soviet collapse. The Central Asian leadership (Uzbek and Turkmen in particular) seems to have managed this by reverting to (and to a certain extent fabricating) indigenous modes of government. The official advancement of traditions and cultures, now presented as national, is pivotal to legitimation and social harmony.

In contrast to their Tajik counterpart, the Uzbek and Turkmen élites have relied heavily on their Soviet legacies to retain the status quo. State-orchestrated efforts at fostering the Soviet-initiated national identities in these two republics stand in stark contrast to the absence of any state programme to encourage national sovereignty in Tajikistan. Both Uzbek and Turkmen élites appear to have made considerable progress in instilling the idea of a homogeneous national community among their titular groups. Uzbeks and Turkmens, or at least those in urban centres and closer to state propaganda machinery, seem to have adopted the official version of their histories. It appears that the Uzbeks believe in the commonality of their fate, as do the Turkmens.

Republican leaderships in Central Asia are keen to present themselves as champions of national culture. This invariably relates to Islam. Presidents Karimov and Niyazov of Uzbekistan and Turkmenistan openly proclaim, as President Rahmonov of Tajikistan may grudgingly admit, that Islam is a national heritage. Accordingly, their governments need to accommodate Islam and its symbols, for they cannot have any claim on legitimacy based on championing national interests while suppressing a key feature of their cultural identity. This realisation complicates the picture, for no section of the élite groups is ready to compromise the tradition of state control over the Islamic hierarchy. Relations with Islam in these states, therefore, are becoming characterised by the dual policy of reverence and watchful supervision. Islam is being celebrated as a national asset; but states reserve for themselves exclusive rights to draw on it.

Notes

1. Tremendous difficulties still confront the researcher in rendering correctly the languages of the Central Asian states into English. No standard method of transliteration has been achieved in English-speaking countries. In this chapter the author has attempted to render the words phonetically.
2. The author wishes to thank Mr John H. Miller for his thoughtful and thought-provoking commentary and guidance, and Ms Sheila Davies for her editorial suggestions. Any shortcomings of this paper are, however, entirely the responsibility of the author.
3. It must be noted that the name 'Uzbek' was used in the fourteenth-century as a pejorative term by Tajik/Turkic inhabitants of Transoxiana. Mir Alishir Navoi, Zahiriddin Muhammad Babur and Muhammad Salih Mirza, all of whom are revered as fathers of Uzbek literary and historical heritage, were contemptuous of (*Özbek*) nomads to the north of the Aral Sea and the Syr Dar'ya. In the 1930s and 1940s Alishir Navoi, in particular, became the focus of Soviet writers; he was often referred to as the father of the Uzbek language, distorting the fact that he considered himself a Turk and wrote in a Turkic language distinct from modern Uzbek, known as *Chaghatay* (see Allworth, 1990: 36–43, 228–31). New rulers of Uzbekistan have pedantically followed this Soviet tradition.

4. The Uzbek state has also used references to Islamic fanaticism to discredit forces it deems destabilising for its authority. As Vali Akhmed Sidur, a leading member of the Islamic Renaissance Party, argues, Karimov's cries of Islamic fundamentalism have found 'a strong echo in the Western press' (Rotar, 1992a: 3). President Karimov implicated the Islamic republics of Iran and Afghanistan in his speech delivered to the UN General Assembly on the continuing instability in Tajikistan and the region (*Aziya*, 1993: 2). The Russian Government has shown particular attention to the potential threat of Islamic fundamentalism. According to academician Malashenko the scarecrow of fundamentalism is used to keep the weak Central Asian states close to Russia (1993b: 3). A similar view was expressed on the eve of an official visit to Tajikistan by the American Secretary of State, James Baker, to explain the United States' interest in Central Asia (Karpov, 1992: 4). Related to the question of the Islamic spectre hanging over the Muslim states of Central Asia is also the threat of a tightening 'Turkic belt' on the southern tier of the Russian Federation.

5. At the time of the last Soviet census in 1989, Uzbeks constituted 23.5 per cent of the total population of the republic; and 40.5 per cent of all Uzbeks in Tajikistan live in the Leninobod oblast.

References

Abdullo, Sheikh Abdulghani (1991). *Vera uchit dobrote* ['Faith teaches kindness']. *Pravda Vostoka*, 11 December: 1.

Akbarzadeh, S. (1996). 'Why did nationalism fail in Tajikistan?'. *Europe–Asia Studies*, 48 (7).

Allworth, Edward A. (1990). *The Modern Uzbeks*. Stanford: Hoover Institute Press.

Ashirov, N. (1975). *Islam i natsii* ['Islam and nations']. Moscow: Politizdat.

Aziya (1993). *Vystuplenie prezidenta respubliki Uzbekistan I. Karimova na 48-i sessii general'noi assamblei OON* ['Address of the president of the republic of Uzbekistan I. Karimov to the 48th session of the general assembly of the UN']. 39 (77): October.

Bazarov, A. (1982). *Osobennosti musul'manskikh religioznykh perezhitkov* ['Characteristics of Islamic religious vestiges']. *Sotsiologichestkie issledovaniya*, 2: 172–3.

Belyaev, Igor (1987). *Islam i politika* ['Islam and politics']. *Literaturnaya Gazeta*, 20 May: 12.

Brown, Bess (1990a). 'Unrest in Tajikistan'. *Report on the USSR*, 23 February: 28–31.

—— (1990b). 'Religion and nationalism in Soviet Central Asia'. *Report on the USSR*, 20 July: 25–7.

—— (1992). 'The presidential election in Uzbekistan'. *RFE/RL Research Report*, 24 January: 23–5.

Dovgoryat, N. (1992). *Glavnoe – stabil'nost' i mir* ['The main thing is stability and peace']. *Turkmenskaya Iskra*, 7 July: 1.

Gapurov, M. (1973). *Ideologicheskuyu rabotu – na uroven' sovremennykh trebovanii partii* ['Ideological work: to the level of the current party requirements']. *Turkmenskaya Iskra*, 3 April: 1–2.

Hetmanek, Allen (1990). 'The reawakening of Soviet Islam'. *Middle East Insight*, 7(2/3): 34–40.

Karimov, Islam (1992a). *Suverennost', kotoraya ob'edinyaet* ['The sovereignty which unites']. *Vek*, 11, 22 October: 3.

—— (1992b). *Plechom k plechy – po puti progressa* ['Shoulder to shoulder on the path to progress']. *Pravda Vostoka*, 2 December: 1.

Karpov, A. (1992). *Dushanbe khochet sotrudnichat' s Amerikoi* ['Dushanbe wants co-operation with America']. *Izvestiya*, 12 February: 4.

Kurbanova, A. (1992). *Ot vorot mira – k domu soglasiya* ['From the gates of peace to the house of consensus']. *Turkmenskaya Iskra*, 22 June: 2.

Malashenko, Aleksei (1993a). *Islam nepobezhdennyi* ['Islam unvanquished'] *Nezavisimaya Gazeta*, 21 July: 1, 3.

—— (1993b) *Islam kak faktor vosstanovleniya SSSR* ['Islam as a factor in the restoration of the USSR']. *Nezavisimaya Gazeta*, 18 August: 3.

Martin, Keith (1993). 'Tajikistan: Civil war without end?'. *RFE/RL Research Report*, 2 (33): 18–29.

Miller, John (1977). 'Cadres policy in nationality areas, Recruitment of CPSU first and second secretaries in non-Russian republics of the USSR'. *Soviet Studies*, 29 (1).

Murtazakulov, I. (1975). *Ateisticheskoi rabote – vysokuyo boevitost* ['Atheistic work: high militancy']. *Turkmenskaya Iskra*, 16 April: 2.

Musaev, Ondzhuk (1992). *Dempartiya Turkmenistana – Partiya reform* ['Democratic party of Turkmenistan is the party of reform']. *Turkmenskaya Iskra*, 16 December: 1.

Naby, Eden (1986). 'The concept of jihad in opposition to communist rule: Turkestan and Afghanistan'. *Studies in Comparative Communism*, 19 (3/4): 287–300.

Narodnaya Gazeta (1992a). 9 April: 1.

—— (1992b). *Press-konferentsiya oppozitsii* ['Opposition's press conference']. 28 April: 1.

—— (1992c). *Obrashchenie* ['Appeal']. 1 July: 1.

Niyazov, Saparmurat (1992). *Turkmenistan ne budet ni kommunisticheskim, ni islamskim* ['Turkmenistan will neither be Communist, nor Islamic']. *Turkmenskaya Iskra*, 24 February: 1.

Olcott, Martha Brill (1993). 'Central Asia on its own'. *Journal of Democracy*, 4 (1): 92–103.

Podalinsko (1992). *Kakaya u nas vlast?* ['What kind of power do we have?'].
Turkmenskaya Iskra, 9 July: 2.

Poliakov, Sergei P. (1992). *Everyday Islam*. New York: M. E. Sharpe.

Pravda Vostoka (1991). 6 December: 1.

Pravda Vostoka (1992a). *Zakon respubliki Uzbekistan o prazdnichnykh dnyakh v respublike Uzbekistan* ['Law of the republic of Uzbekistan on holidays in the republic of Uzbekistan']. 16 July: 1.

—— (1992b). *Uchastnikam Vsemirnogo foruma predstavitelei Tadzhikov* ['To the participants of the world-wide forum of Tajik representatives']. 10 September: 1.

—— (1992c). *Zakon prezidenta respubliki Uzbekistan* ['Law of the president of the republic of Uzbekistan']. 15 September: 1.

—— (1992d). *Otkrytie posol'stva* ['The opening of the embassy']. 7 November: 1.

RFE/RL (Radio Free Europe/Radio Liberty) (1992). *Daily Report*. 21 May (97).

—— (1994a). *Daily Report*. 28 February.

—— (1994b). *Daily Report*. 7 March.

Ro'i, Yaacov (1984). 'The task of creating the new Soviet man: "Atheistic propaganda" in the Soviet Muslim areas'. *Soviet Studies*, 36 (1): January: 26–44.

—— (1987). 'Religion as an obstacle to *sblizhenie*: the official perception'. *Soviet Union/Union Sovietique*, 14 (2): 163–79.

—— (1990). 'The Islamic influence on Nationalism in Soviet Central Asia'. *Problems of Communism*, 39 (4): 49–64.

Rotar, Igor (1992a). *Zapad i vostok na oblomkakh imperii* ['West and East on the debris of the empire']. *Nezavisimaya Gazeta*, 21 May.

—— (1992b). *Kommunist mozhet byt' pravovernym musul'maninam* ['A Communist can be an orthodox Muslim']. *Nezavisimaya Gazeta*, 5 June: 3.

Sadoi Mardum (1994a). *Bunyadkori murodu maqsadi most* ['Construction is our aim and objective']. 1 January: 2.

—— (1994b). *Murojiatnomai sardori davlat, Raisi Shurai Olii Jumhurii Tojikistan Rahmonov E. Sh. ba hamvatanoni khoriji Tojikiston* ['Appeal of the head of state, Chairman of the Supreme Soviet of the republic of Tajikistan Rahmonov E. Sh., to expatriates of Tajikistan']. 16 January: 1.

—— (1994c). *Tojikiston vatani hamai most* ['Tajikistan is the motherland of all of us']. 26 February: 1.

—— (1994d). *Murojiatnomai ishtirokchieni mashvarati jumhuriyavii namoyandagani kollektivhoi mehnati va ahli jomeai jumhuri ba hamai shahrvandoni tojikiston* ['Appeal of the participant deputies of labour collectives and members of the republican society to all citizens of Tajikistan']. 2 March: 1, 3.

—— (1994e). *Izhori hamdardi* ['Expression of sympathy']. 4 March: 1.

Saidbaev, T. S. (1984). *Islam i obshchestvo* ['Islam and society']. Moscow, Nauka.

Turkmenskaya Iskra (1992a). 14 January: 1.

—— (1992b). 15 January: 1.

—— (1992c). *Zakon ob okhrane pamyatnikov istorii i kul'tury Turkmenistana* ['Law on the protection of the historical and cultural monuments of Turkmenistan']. 6 March: 1–2.

—— (1992d). *Zaregistrirovan Kaziat* ['*Qaziat* is registered']. 3 June: 1.

—— (1992e). *Kurban bairam – prazdnik narodnyi* ['*Kurban bairam* is a people's holiday']. 14 June: 1.

—— (1992f). *Ukaz Prezidenta Turkmenistana o sozyve khalk maslakhaty* ['The decree of the President of Turkmenistan on the convocation of *Khalk Maslakhaty*']. 23 June: 1.

Usmanov, Lerman (1994). *Opredelit li 'Islamskii faktor' budushchee strany?* ['Will the "Islamic factor" determine the future of the country?']. *Nezavisimaya Gazeta*, 6 January: 3.

Vagabov, M. V. (1988). *Islam i voprosy ateisticheskogo vospitaniya* ['Islam and the question of atheistic education']. Moscow: Vysshaya shkola.

Vyzhutovich, V. (1991). *Krasnoe znamya kommunizma ili zelenoe znamya islama?* ['Red flag of communism or the green banner of Islam?']. *Izvestia*, 5 October: 2.

Yusupov, Shodmon (1993). *Chego zhe khochet rossiiskoe pravitel'stvo v Tadzhikistane?* ['What does the Russian government want in Tajikistan?']. *Nezavisimaya Gazeta*, 25 August: 1, 3.

Zhukov, Igor (1992). *Sozdanie narodnogo soveta-put' k prezidentskoi respublike* ['Formation of the people's soviet is the path to a presidential republic']. *Nezavisimaya Gazeta*, 17 December: 3.

—— (1993). *Turkmeniya ne narushit printsip 'pozitivnogo neitraliteta'* ['Turkmenistan will not violate the principle of "positive neutrality"']. *Segodnya*, 6 August: 4.

Economic Development and the Search for National Identity in Central Asia[1]

Derek Verrall

The former Soviet Union was a multinational state made up of some 126 nationalities and over 200 languages. The claim of the revised party programme in 1986 that 'The national question, a legacy of the past, has been successfully solved' was soon to be called into question. National sensitivities were exposed in Kazakhstan in December 1986 when the long-time head of the party organisation, Kunaev, was replaced by a younger, energetic reformer in the Gorbachev mould, G. Kolbin, an ethnic Russian. Widespread rioting, resulting in the loss of life, ensued. This and other outbreaks of nationalism, particularly in the Baltic States and Georgia, suggested that long-suppressed grievances were coming to light in the more open atmosphere that prevailed during the Gorbachev era.

It is useful to indicate briefly the treatment of nationalities within the former Soviet Union as a backdrop to current problems. In principle, loyalty to a smaller nationality, based on ties of language, culture and tradition, was encompassed within a broader political loyalty to citizenship of the USSR. The attempt to create a collective identity in the USSR based on international working-class solidarity, rather than national identities, led to the mobilisation of socialisation agents and mass literacy campaigns. The attempt simultaneously to grant the symbols of nationhood to the republics, while insisting on the supremacy of the central state and proclaiming the aim of transcending national separateness and ethnic identity, resulted in an inherently unstable dualism, which eventually collapsed following the weakening of the Soviet centre. It also resulted in the drawing of the maps of the various republics without much heed to consolidating natural regions or national units for the ethnic communities, which did not yet think of themselves as distinct nationalities. The boundaries set in Soviet Central Asia resulted in the presence of large irredentist populations in each republic. While the present borders have been accepted by current Central Asian leaders, the potential for territorial disputes is apparent. Thus Central Asia's two main Persian-speaking cities, Samarkand and Bukhara, were included in Uzbekistan, leaving the republic of Tajikistan to establish its capital in Dushanbe. Moreover, Uzbeks have periodically staked a claim to all of the Ferghana Valley, which includes Kirghizstan's Osh oblast and part of the Khojent oblast in Tajikistan (Olcott, 1992: 256).

Republican élites, drawn from the titular nationality, who had risen through the system by balancing the demands of Moscow against the needs of their republic while maintaining a regime of strict control, sought to defend and advance the interests of their locality and clan. This they did primarily through the defence of regional economic interests, by asserting a degree of local autonomy in the control of the republic's economy, by seeking a greater share of investment from the centre, and by gaining greater access to consumer goods and in general seeking to modify national economic policy to the advantage of the locality. The degree of their success varied depending on the programmes being pursued by the centre. Thus Khrushchev's policy of economic decentralisation, through the establishment of regional economic councils in the period 1957–65, concentrated resources in the hands of the leaders and managers at the level of the republics. Brezhnev abolished the regional economic councils, but allowed the republics' political élites greater political control to an extent that permitted widespread corruption. In Central Asia the best-known of the corruption scandals involved the leadership of the Uzbek Communist Party, which stood accused of falsifying production figures and fabricating the existence of millions of tons of cotton that were never produced or distributed to state purchasing agents. Billions of roubles were reportedly funnelled into the shadow economy of the republic (Cavanaugh, 1992a).

While the former Soviet Union was able to deliver the benefits of economic growth the nationality question was to some extent blunted, as the government tried to equalise levels of economic development throughout the single economic space by centralised resource allocation. However, during the Brezhnev era the Central Asian republics declined in their relative capacity to attract new investment. Since the mid-1960s Central Asia, home to more than 11 per cent of the Soviet population, received only about 6.5 per cent of the total USSR investment. Much of the investment that has flowed in has been directed to the development of export resources in specific republics. Thus in former Soviet Turkmenia oil and gas investments kept per capita investment near the Soviet average (Monyak, 1993a), while Kazakhstan, a beneficiary of Stalin's heavy industrialisation and Khrushchev's agricultural policies, appeared less attractive to central planners looking for new projects in an exhausted economy. The exception to this was the Gur'ev oblast in Kazakhstan, where central-ised investment was allocated for oil production. Such investment did little to stimulate development of the local economy, and its benefits eluded local residents. Those, mainly ethnic Russians, brought into the region to establish the industry in the 1970s left in the 1980s (Monyak, 1993b). Gorbachev's plans for economic revitalisation were based on investment flows to the European portion of the USSR, where the return to capital and labour could be maximised. The sub-sequent collapse of the Soviet economic system and the disruption of the transportation and distribution system only heightened anxiety. The traditional system of assisting the poorer republics by resource transfers appeared to be directly under threat in the context of Gor-bachev's rhetorical denunciations of 'parasites' and 'profiteering' in the context of corruption scandals.

The earlier drive to economic development had resulted in rapid upward social mobility for those who left agriculture for factory work in the cities or preferably for service and administrative jobs. Children gained a degree of education and training in modern skills. In Central Asia expenditure on education was higher than the national average, as attempts were made to iron out historic inequalities (Sakwa, 1989: 312). Despite these attempts, Russian and other immigrant nationals continued to be disproportionately employed in industry because of patterns of ethnic occupational preference and the quality of their higher education. These differing occupational patterns have given rise to ethnic tensions. Modern industrial cities have attracted immigrant workers with the requisite skills through high wages, forming ghettos of apparent privilege, while natives living on the fringes continue to exist in rural squalor. In the military a high proportion of conscripts from Central Asia were assigned to construction units because of their poor language and other skills (RFE/RL *Daily Report*, 29 May 1990). Moreover, as indicated in the National Profile appendices to the pre-sent article, the Central Asian republics maintained a high proportion of their population and economic activity in agriculture. This reflects the fact that there was no technological revolution in Central Asian agriculture.

More manual workers – largely women and children – were picking cotton by hand in the early 1980s than twenty years before. In the USSR in 1981, about 35 per cent of the overall harvest, that is about 2,150 thousand tons of cotton, was hand-picked. In 1962, about 70 per cent of the harvest, that is about 2,100 thousand tons, was hand-picked (Gleason, 1991: 348).

The modernisation experience in Central Asia was brutal. The civil war, all but concluded by the early 1920s, continued as the *Basmachi* revolt, one of the consequences of which was the flight of Tajiks over the border into Afghanistan. Today they continue to involve themselves in the smuggling of arms and cross-border raids into Tajikistan, continuing to fuel that republic's civil war. The anti-religious campaigns and forced collectivisation, with its attendant starvation, not only generated additional refugees but left a legacy of bitterness expressed in the upsurge of popular nationalism of the late 1980s and in the rejection of the ethnic groups forcibly relocated in Central Asia by Stalin in the 1940s.

Recent figures on health, poverty and unemployment reported by Diuk and Karatnycky (1993: 47–50) indicate the appalling conditions in Central Asia, which affect overwhelmingly the peoples of the titular nationality. Thus in 1986 infant mortality in the Russian republic was 19.3 deaths per 1,000 births, while comparable figures for Uzbekistan were 46.2; Tajikistan, 46.7; Turkmenistan, 58.2; Kirghizstan, 38.2; and Kazakhstan, 29.0. In large part these figures are the product of inadequate health care and the shocking environmental devastation of much of Central Asia. Deputies at the 1989 Congress of People's Deputies pointed to the effects on the Kazakh population of nuclear testing at Semipalatinsk and the consequences of the devastating misuse of toxins and irrigation in the cotton industry (Glebov and Crowfoot, 1989: 147–52). In 1988, using a poverty level of 78 roubles per month per capita, some 6.3 per cent of the population of the RSFSR lived below the poverty line. Comparable figures for the Central Asian republics were Tajikistan, 36.6 per cent; Turkmenistan, 58.6 per cent; and Uzbekistan, 44.7 per cent. Unemployment rates in Central Asia in 1986, at a time of official full employment in Russia, were 26 per cent in Tajikistan; 23 per cent in Uzbekistan; 19 per cent in Turkmenistan; and 16 per cent in Kirghizstan. Such discrepancies, falling as they did most heavily on the titular nationalities, created a volatile social basis for ethnic violence. While education provided a source of social mobility for some of the children of the Central Asian republics, advancement was most rapid for those who adopted Soviet ideology and the Russian language – a distinct minority.

Although there was no consistent policy that might be termed 'Russification', in the sense of a strident promotion of one ethnic group at the expense of the others, the advantages to be had by learning the language of the bureaucracy led to fears of a 'creeping Russification' and language becoming a politically salient issue within the newly independent states. The fact that membership of the titular nationality usually conferred an advantage in terms of obtaining official positions and access to higher education points up the disadvantage of non-Russian national minorities within the republics, and constitutes an additional source of ethnic division within the newly independent republics.

The former Soviet Union appeared able to maintain a reasonable degree of integration while the economy grew and the party maintained its unity and cohesion. In retrospect this appears to have been the result of adopting an attitude of 'bow to the master and go your own way'. The anti-corruption campaign caused a backlash in the republics because of the widespread belief that, whatever their crimes, local leaders were first and foremost members of their republics, and an attack on the leaders was but a thinly veiled attempt to reimpose central Russian control. Indeed, in Uzbekistan a major rehabilitation programme was undertaken in the case of Rashidov and his disgraced followers (Cavanaugh, 1992).

While the Central Asian republics were under-represented in the Communist Party itself, making up only 5.7 per cent of the Communist Party of the Soviet Union (CPSU) in 1986 as compared with their 9.9 per cent of the total population in 1979, in the 1970s and 1980s the rate of increase in membership was higher than average (Sakwa 1989: 130–1). Moreover, it appears as though titular ethnic groups within the Union republics consolidated their position within each republic at the expense of other ethnic groups excepting the Russians. This has resulted in major ethnic tensions within republics, not only in respect of immigrant minorities, but also with respect to minorities from neighbouring republics. When reinforced by economic changes, such as land reform in rural areas or the allocation of apartments in the cities, that favour one group at the expense of others, these tensions can have disastrous consequences. Following the June 1990 decision of the Kirghiz-dominated soviet in the city of Osh, located in the then Kirghiz SSR near the Uzbek border, to reassign land of a collective farm that local Uzbeks had been farming for years, a riot ensued. At least 300 people died in this incident and over 1,000 were injured. The intervention of troops was necessary to regain order (RFE/RL *Daily Reports* Nos. 107–10, 6–11 June 1990; Gleason, 1993).

Derek Verrall

The Economic Legacy of Dependence

Economic integration is measured in terms of the flow of goods, services, labour and capital between nations or regions. In a market setting this involves the reduction of barriers to the movement of the above factors and theoretically leads to production's becoming regionally specialised in line with cost differences. However, 'once the market is replaced by central planning, all movement of goods and factors within the region requires an explicit action by the governments involved' (Marer and Montias, 1980). In the Soviet Union integration was a component of national economic development. Not only did planners succeed in creating highly interdependent economies with high trade flows between the various republics, but enormous sums of investment were centralised and redistributed within the Union. Transfers from the central budget as a percentage of republican spending in 1991 were 44 per cent for Tajikistan, 42 per cent for Uzbekistan, 34 per cent for Kirghizstan, 23 per cent for Kazakhstan and 22 per cent for Turkmenistan (Marnie and Whitlock, 1993).

This was officially regarded as economic specialisation of the regions, taking advantage of unique local factor endowments in a way that integrated the specialised economies of the republics into the all-Union economy so as to maximise both local and central interests. However, a convincing case has been made by Gleason (1991) that the experience of the Central Asian republics represents an almost textbook case of neo-Marxist internal dependency theory, the central features of which are:

1. A relatively powerful core establishes exchange relationships with a weaker periphery to the initial benefit of both.
2. Commerce comes under the control of the centre and the peripheral economy is forced into complementary development with the core – a development that is reinforced through legal, political and repressive measures.
3. A division of labour develops in which the dependent area concentrates its efforts on supplying raw materials to the centre, and in the case of agriculture the concentration on one major export crop, while the centre concentrates on processing, manufacturing, service, and finance.
4. This leads to a concentration of trade for the periphery and a reliance on the centre for the supply of technology. The dependent area serves as a captive market, buying back goods processed from the primary commodities which it supplied.

5. As the exchange relationships become less favourable to the periphery, and more beneficial to the centre, incentives are distributed in such a way that periphery managers and political élites acquire an interest in sustaining what has become an inequitable relationship.

6. As the economic power of the centre grows, the cultural values of the centre threaten to supplant local cultural values and, where salient ethnic cleavages exist between the centre and the periphery, differential educational and employment opportunities produce ethnic stratification.

Thus the high degree of integration of the Soviet economy came at the cost of structural flaws that have exacerbated the problems the states of Central Asia have to contend with as they move to more market-based systems and to new patterns of trade. Moreover, the general organisation of economic activity under the Soviet system provided for large-scale enterprises, presumably to achieve economies of scale, a system of incentives that led to the ossification of production techniques once the initial investment had been made, and the vertical structuring of the economy such that horizontal links between enterprises were either stifled or irregular and based on personal contacts. When the top layers of the administrative hierarchy were eliminated or otherwise divested of their former power, there were few alternative mechanisms for the distribution of goods and services between enterprises and across the borders of what are now independent sovereign states. Falls in inter-republican trade as a result have been substantial, as have falls in GDP for each republic (see Appendix: National Profiles). The high export to GDP ratios suggested by the figures in the National Profiles for the late Soviet period are not a measure of the international competitiveness of these export-oriented enterprises, and completely ignore the artificially low price of transportation.

The major distortion of the Soviet development policy was its impact on the sectoral structure of the region's economies, which transformed Central Asia into a specialist supplier of raw materials, especially cotton. This continued a trend established in the late 1880s under the Tsarist regime, which produced the region's first grain deficits (Rywkin, 1982: 14–15) and currently makes much of the region dependent on food imports (Glebov and Crowfoot, 1989: 150–2). One of the most noticeable changes in the region has been the reduction of sowing areas in cotton-producing regions and the consequent reduction in cotton production. In 1992 6.5 million tonnes of raw cotton was harvested, 17 per cent less than in 1991. Uzbekistan produced 518,000 tonnes, 11 per cent less than in 1991, Turkmenistan 132,000 tonnes, 9 per cent less, and Tajikistan 409,000 tonnes, 50 per cent less. (Azerbaijan produced 210,000 tonnes, 39 per cent less: *Delovoi Mir*, 2 March 1993: 10–11.) Gradual increases in the production of foodstuffs are occurring in areas not so polluted as to be non-viable for agriculture, although, given the capacity to utilise the cotton crop for export and foreign currency earnings, there may be an economically imposed limit as to how far this trend is allowed to proceed.

As can be seen from the National Profile appendices, the Central Asian republics maintain very high rural populations, high degrees of non-industrial employment and a high level of agricultural output. The Central Asian trade pattern of raw material and agricultural goods being exchanged for industrial goods is obvious in the case of Uzbekistan and Kazakhstan, both of which depend on other Commonwealth of Independent States (CIS) countries for machine tools. Tajikistan imports all its tractors, cars and trucks; Kirghizstan all its fertiliser and gasoline; while Turkmenistan, where agriculture accounts for 46 per cent of net material product (NMP) and 42 per cent of total employment, imports 65 per cent of the grain it consumes, 45 per cent of the milk and dairy products, and 70 per cent of the potatoes. Cotton accounts for 50 per cent of the nation's arable land and 60 per cent of its agricultural production (Marnie and Whitlock, 1993).

In a region dominated by agricultural production and seeking to move toward economic reform, the absence of private property conventions presents a major constraint on land reform. In the absence of individual rights the importance of group rights, especially clan and family rights, dominates the issue of land reform. In the Soviet era agricultural production was based on local clan structures, and within the communal farm work brigades were organised on the basis of extended families, with smaller work units of about ten people based on immediate family units (Dimitry Mickulsky, pers. comm., Moscow, 10 October 1993). Whatever reservations might be held by free marketeers, political leaders are probably correct in their assessment that this represents the limits of what is possible and what will work. In essence, the state appropriates the property of state and collective farms and reassigns these to particular groups. Shares are distributed to those who had worked on the farm in question, which may be inherited but not freely bought or sold. Shareholders may withdraw farm assets for individual use, redistribute assets among smaller co-operative enterprises, or continue to farm within the large enterprise (Gleason, 1993). While it is true that governments that have the power to create and enforce property rights also have the power to abrogate them, Central Asian officials and leaders are probably genuinely convinced that increased incentives designed to improve farmers' output are necessary and that such a system, sensitively handled, may make agricultural reform possible without major ethnic disturbances.

This legacy constitutes a major problem for all CIS states, which they seek to overcome through new trade and financial relationships and external assistance. These include the re-establishment of ties within the CIS, but on a different economic and institutional basis, the formation of linkages with neighbouring countries in an expanded Economic Co-operation Organisation (ECO), leading to regional economic integration, and the active encouragement of economic relations on a global basis, primarily through seeking investment and joint development ventures with firms from both the West and the developing nations of East and South-East Asia.

CIS Integration

The short-term benefit of maintaining integration in the CIS is to minimise disruption to trade-dependent economies, while rebuilding on a more market-oriented basis. In the longer term, open borders between the Central Asian republics and the remainder of the CIS can be expected to result in increased economic activity, lower costs and prices and more diversified production. This has led to efforts, varying in intensity from country to country among the Central Asian republics, to maintain trade relations with the CIS. Since June 1990 there have been a series of meetings of Central Asian republican leaders designed to set up a degree of regional co-ordination of economic policy, to urge such co-ordination within the wider CIS, and to gain whatever advantage might be had from adopting a common stance at CIS forums.

Despite statements of intent, few specific steps have been taken to implement the declarations. Following the collapse of President Gorbachev's attempts to salvage the Union in December 1991 and the proposal to establish a Slavic economic union of Russia, Ukraine and Byelorussia, the Central Asian presidents met in Ashkhabad on 12 December to discuss relations with the proposed new entity. The resulting declaration signed by all five presidents stated their willingness to join the CIS, but insisted that the Central Asian republics should have equal rights to the three founding states, that the CIS should not be based on ethnic or confessional criteria, and that existing borders should be regarded as inviolable, and called for the unified command and control of the strategic forces. At a press conference following the meeting, Uzbek President Karimov declared that the most urgent task ahead was economic development (RFE/RL *Daily Reports*, Nos 231–7, 6–16 December 1991). It has been suggested that subsequent meetings of the Central Asian leaders have been designed to put pressure on other CIS members to adopt co-ordinated policies on range of issues, not the least of which is economic policy, or risk the disintegration of the CIS (Brown, 1993a).

To secure continuity of delivery in the most important commodities, a series of bilateral trade agreements have been signed by individual states with Russia. While many are barter deals, and hence prone to inefficiencies, they are the foundation of energy and agricultural product delivery. There has also been some progress in establishing a more liberal customs regime with other CIS members and among the Central Asian republics themselves, from which Turkmenistan has held aloof. In March 1992 CIS members agreed to the principles of free movement of goods across each others' boundaries, and a common customs policy with third countries was agreed. However, while import and export tariffs have been kept low, formal and informal quantitative restrictions on trade continue to inhibit the free flow of goods. Inter-governmental trade agreements represent a form of state control on trade, while payments restrictions to balance trade have reduced trade volume. While state orders are still used extensively for the distribution of important commodities in Central Asia, solemn treaties on customs policy will remain statements of intent.

Russia's decision on 1 January 1993 to charge world prices for oil and gas represented the withdrawal of the implicit subsidy provided to other CIS nations through underpriced energy products. To date this has not affected sales under pre-existing inter-state trade agreements, which exempt most energy consumption in the Central Asian republics, but it would seem to be a matter of time before world prices prevail in the region, thus rectifying a major price distortion in regional trade.

A Central Asian Commonwealth?

It is possible to point to geography, a common Turkic background, a historic 'Turkestan' that predated the Tsarist conquests, and the brief existence, until 1925, of a Turkestan Autonomous Soviet Socialist Republic. Nevertheless, there is little to suggest the basis of an economic union, despite the series of Central Asian conferences that have been held. While the region certainly has the resources for energy self-sufficiency, abundant raw materials and agricultural capacity to suggest the feasibility of processing industries, the prospect of economic independence from Russia seems remote and at best a long-term prospect. The present infrastructure radiates from Russia, and there are few cross-linkages within the region, which limits the capacity to find outlets to markets other than the former Soviet one. Indeed Uzbekistan's decision to leave the Central Asian power grid, because of 'the diminishing exchange of electricity between the region's republics and the introduction of transaction practices between them' (Brown, 1993a, citing *Izvestia*, 13 January 1993), suggests an unravelling of some forms of interconnection. The legacy of Soviet-inspired regional specialisation means that much of the raw material processing capacity is located outside Central Asia. Again, considerable initial investment would be required to establish regional storage, processing and transportation facilities – which appears to be beyond the capacity of the region. The intra-regional agreements on trade and economic co-operation entered into are limited in scale, and this suggests that they are of less significance than the more extensive interactions with Russia or the attempts to forge new linkages with the outside world, which it is hoped will supply the necessary investment, technology and equipment to build the processing and manufacturing plants.

In addition to these economic obstacles to regionalism, reluctance to move beyond rhetorical declarations stems from fears that any such association would be dominated by Uzbekistan. While meetings of the Central Asian leaders continue and declarations on regional economic and financial co-ordination are issued, little in the way of practical steps toward implementation has been achieved. After the Tashkent summit of 3 and 4 January 1993, agreement was reached on refining some of Kazakhstan's oil in Uzbekistan and Turkmenistan; committees of experts were established on energy, oil, cotton and grains, each to be headquartered in a different regional capital; and an Aral Sea fund was created (RLA-*Novosti*, 4 January 1993). In addition, moral support was offered to the constitutional authorities in Tajikistan and humanitarian aid was promised. While a common information region for the five republics has been established, agreement has apparently been reached on using the Tashkent Television and Radio Centre as a base for transmissions to all of Central Asia, and a regional newspaper is to be published in Alma-Ata, there is no indication of the language or languages to be used or how the great variation in information policies in Central Asia is to be handled (see Brown, 1992a and 1993a, for details).

What seems clear is that the potentially divisive issues, radically different interpretations of democracy, and different concepts of economic reform, are not addressed. Such issues are likely to prevent the emergence of a Central Asian common market. It seems likely that the statements suggesting the formation of a Central Asian common market were primarily designed to issue a warning as to the future potential for disintegration of the CIS if more resolute steps were not taken to co-ordinate policy. However, such warnings contained a great deal of bluff, given the obstacles to closer integration, and states in the region are seeking individual economic linkages outside the region in an uncoordinated manner.

Central Asia and the Organisation of Economic Co-operation

The Organisation of Economic Co-operation (ECO) was originally founded by Iran, Pakistan and Turkey. In November 1992 it was joined by the Central Asian states together with Azerbaijan and Afghanistan. It has the potential to strengthen multilateral links between a bloc of countries sharing the Islamic faith and culture, and has as its objective the elimination of trade barriers between member states. In addition, it is proposed to establish an investment bank and a common airline (*Izvestia*, 27 November 1992). While a degree of integration is likely over time, given that in the immediate past it was artificially suppressed, this appears most likely in the development of transport and communication links and the creation of a network of power grids and pipelines. The landlocked nature of the Central Asian republics suggests that access to ports of neighbouring regional countries and the creation of alternative transportation routes to those already established through Russia is to be expected. However, these infrastructural projects are long-term, and none of the Central Asian republics' ECO partners are in a position to offer the scale of credits necessary to give a shorter-term boost to their economies. What can be expected is that the organisation will provide a forum for bilateral negotiations, an area in which Turkey has been particularly active.

Turkey's attempts to create economic and cultural links with the Central Asian states has been encouraged by the West in order to steer them toward a secular model of an Islamic state rather than the Iranian alternative. Despite Turkey's apparent willingness to play a role in Central Asia and the tendency for the Turkic republics to look to Turkey for assistance, there are obvious economic limits to Turkey's capacity to assist (RFE/ RL *Daily Report*, No. 229: 4 December 1991).

Besides offering loans and credit guarantees, Turkey has granted $1 billion in aid and trade credits for projects, including a linked telephone network with the Central Asian republics (Turkey's state-owned telecommunications manufacturer will supply small-capacity exchanges to each country) and a gas deal under which Turkey receives gas from the former Soviet republics in exchange for goods and services. Perhaps of greater long-term significance are the thousands of scholarships established at Turkish universities and high schools (Waltzman, 1993: A29), the training of bankers and diplomats and the beaming of television programmes to the area in Turkish (Marnie and Whitlock, 1993). These programmes appear to have the enthusiastic support of the republics' leaders (RFE/ RL *Daily Report*, No. 154: 14 August 1991).

Links with the West

The Central Asian republics seeking immediate economic results are increasingly looking to the market economies as a source of foreign investment to develop, process or refine their raw materials for export. They have also successfully sought acceptance by international financial organisations such as the International Monetary Fund, the World Bank and the European and Asian development banks. Together with this export orientation has come a recognition of the need to diversify, so that the reliance on cotton can be reduced. The major vehicle for achieving these goals appears to be through the development of joint ventures with external partners, typical of which has been Uzbekistan's barter deal with a Danish company, which involved the exchange of 16,000 tons of cotton for the establishment of a jeans factory (AFP, 23 February 1993, cited in Marnie and Whitlock, 1993).

On a larger scale are attempts to establish joint venture arrangements in raw materials development. Nowhere is this more the case than in attempts to exploit the region's growing reserves of oil, which were neglected during the Soviet era. In August 1991 Kazakh President Nazarbaev had refused to sign a contract with the US Chevron Corporation giving it development rights at the Tengiz oil fields, arguing that the USSR Government had not been sufficiently conscientious in negotiating the transaction (RFE/RL *Daily Report*, No. 155: 16 August 1992). By late 1992 Chevron, British Petroleum, Mobil and others were all involved in the development, with Chevron reported to be investing over $1.5 billion in the next three years. British Gas and the Italian Agip company have signed an agreement to explore and exploit the Karachaganak oil and gas fields in western Kazakhstan. Current reports suggest that Soviet estimates of reserves of three billion tonnes in the Caspian region need to be trebled (see Appendix).

What remains in doubt is the timescale and costs required to bring this oil onto the world market. Specifically, problems of extraction and the remoteness of the potential fields from ports and markets make for high costs. Suggested pipeline routes have aroused objections from varying quarters. Thus a route across Iran is opposed by the United States, which has pressured international financial institutions effectively to boycott this scheme (Hyman, 1994: 32). Russia is opposed to a route via the Caucasus to the Mediterranean coast of Turkey. Russian commentators have speculated that one of the factors motivating Russia's military intervention in Chechnya is to strengthen its claim to have the pipeline cross Russian territory to the Black Sea (*Moscow News*, 23–29 December 1994: 2). Moreover, Russia has vigorously reasserted its claims in what Moscow sees as its rightful sphere of influence. Specifically, Russia has claimed joint ownership and a full share in all gas and oil operations in the Caspian Sea, arguing that its role in oil development during the Soviet era entitles it to participate in future developments. Such intervention has slowed the finalisation of agreements between Western oil and gas companies and the Central Asian republics with oil reserves. Recent reports suggest that British Gas is reconsidering its $6 billion investment in Kazakhstan's Karachaganak natural gas field because of uncertainties occasioned by Russian intervention (Hyman, 1994: 32).

Another major project has involved the European Bank for Reconstruction and Development in a joint venture arrangement with a US company to develop Uzbekistan's largest gold-mining enterprise, Muruntau. Independence has also allowed the national authorities to introduce legislation providing guarantees against nationalisation of foreign investments and granting tax exemptions for the import and export of industrial equipment.

Notions of Identity and Ethnic Conflict

While the political élites and their economic advisers have embraced this new orientation, in which they have been supported by Western perceptions of a competition between Iran and Turkey for dominance in the region, it is less certain where the mass of the population find their identity. Despite over a hundred years of Russian domination, the last seventy under the Soviets, the dominant cultural influences are Turkic (in all except Tajikistan, whose ethnic origins can be traced to Iranian roots) and from the Islamic faith, which remains the strongest cultural link among the people of the region as a whole. Prior to the Soviet era there was no widespread national consciousness of being Uzbek, Turkmen, Tajik, Kirghiz or Kazakh.[2] However, seventy years of census-taking, registration of ethnic identification and the Soviet policy of promoting national cultures, through developing the languages, cultures and histories of the various nationalities in the republics, while simultaneously centralising political and economic power in all-Union structures, resulted in the flowering of national cultures, undermining the project of creating a Soviet identity. The titular republican nations had two identities, two languages, two cultures, two histories and two sets of institutions. In particular the existence of republican Academies of Science, television and radio networks and communist parties provided important channels for élite and mass communication and reinforced a collective identity (Shearman, 1993: 31). The people who constituted these nationalities and ethnic groupings failed to identify psychologically with the Soviet nation, and regarded the Soviet state as an extension of Russia. The repressive conditions that permitted the assumption that republican nationalism could be contained in the cultural sphere broke down under the Gorbachev reform agenda. Nationality-based feelings of resentment and victimisation arose out of the anti-corruption campaigns conducted from Moscow under Andropov and Gorbachev. This was particularly strong in Uzbekistan, where the campaign resulted in the overturn of the whole hierarchy in the republic, involving hundreds of officials and thousands of employees, and led to a tarnished representation of the Uzbek people and their politico-social traditions in the Russian and centrally-controlled media (Carrère d'Encausse, 1993: 16–21).

The first serious manifestation of national sentiment occurred in Kazakhstan following the appointment of the Russian, Kolbin, to replace the corrupt Kazakh, Kunaev, upsetting the long-standing practice of appointing nationals to the position of party first secretary. This move was interpreted as indicating Moscow's distrust of the Kazakh leadership cadres, a preparedness to ride roughshod over local sensitivities, and an attempt to assert greater central control over the periphery. On 17 December 1986 mass demonstrations broke out in Alma-Ata, the capital, demanding 'Kazakhstan for the Kazakhs'. While dismissed in initial press reports as the acts of drunken hooligans urged on by the Kanaev clan, the resurgence of nationalist demands appears to have been a genuine response. It also reflected the shifting demographic balance in the republic, which had resulted in the re-emergence of the Kazakhs as the largest ethnic group after decades of minority status *vis-à-vis* ethnic Russians and other immigrants. (This followed the loss of one-quarter of the Kazakh population, a million people, following the nomad resettlement drives of the late 1920s, the colonisation of the most fertile lands by Russians, Ukrainians, and Byelorussians, and the resettlement of ethnic groups considered unreliable during the Second World War.) In addition, the desperate material conditions of the Kazakhs became more obvious as the Soviet economy collapsed.

Current developments in Central Asia are occurring against a backdrop of shifting demographic factors, which has seen the population of Central Asia triple to thirty-three million in the forty years since 1951, and, since the late 1980s, by large-scale population shifts. The demographic explosion has produced a distorted age distribution, with over 50 per cent of the population below the age of nineteen and only 42 per cent in the 20 to 59 years age bracket. In the 1990s this will lead to an exacerbation of housing and employment opportunity shortfalls. Moreover, the impact of increased population is leading to an expansion of the rural relative to the urban population (Monyak, 1993a). There has been an outpouring of ethnic Russians, occasioned by fears that the republics would pass legislation mandating the use of the indigenous languages as the official state languages, and in response to the inter-ethnic violence that rose throughout the region in the late 1980s.

While the initial ethnic disturbances consisted of demonstrations against the centre and the dominance of Russian immigrants, Central Asia has been rocked by a series of increasingly violent incidents, which in 1989 and 1990 escalated to the wholesale slaughter of minority immigrant groups. In June 1989 Meskhes in the Ferghana Valley were massacred by Uzbek youths in the course of a full-scale riot in which the participants defied government, police and militia units, seized weapons and trains and immobilised public transport. The resulting casualties consisted of over 100 dead, 1,000 wounded and hundreds of houses and public buildings burnt. Over 34,000 Meskhe refugees were generated, and they continued to be subject to attack in the refugee camps created by the authorities. The clear objective of the Uzbeks was to drive all Meskhes out of the republic.

Similar disturbances have occurred in all other republics. In Kazakhstan Daghestani immigrants at the oil drilling centre of Novy Uzen were the primary targets, although rioting spread to other sections of the republic. In Kirghizstan and Tajikistan recent Armenian refugees have been targeted. These attacks were initially attributed in the Russian and centrally-based press to hooliganism and extremist nationalists. However it is likely that the real causes were to be found in the marked socio-economic differences between migrants and natives, their differential access to resources such as housing, employment and education, and the lack of assimilation among the immigrant groups, based on feelings of cultural superiority. Thus the 60,000 Meskhes in Uzbekistan were widely perceived as holding jobs at the expense of Uzbeks and, through their ownership of co-operatives and shops, exploiting the indigenous population by charging high prices for foodstuffs in increasingly short supply. In other cases the immigrant groups have held the best jobs in technologically sophisticated industries such as the Kazakh oil industry. As economic conditions deteriorated in the Soviet Union the indigenous peoples of Central Asia faced a desperate future, in contrast to the comparative prosperity of the displaced immigrants.

Not all violence has been directed at regional outsiders, and not all immigrants have suffered to the same extent. Thus Russians may be leaving the area in ever-increasing numbers, fearing among other things the introduction of new language requirements and the rejection and harassment to which they are increasingly subject; but there are no reports of massacres against them. Moreover, relocated persons of German ethnicity have not suffered. This suggests that the most vulnerable are those immigrant groups who have no powerful republican base. Again, this suggests a degree of selectivity in the targeting of minority groups and implies a degree of manipulation, at least during 1989 and 1990. The incident at Osh, continuing hostility between Tajiks and Uzbeks, and the continual involvement of the formerly displaced Tajiks who fled to Afghanistan during the war in Tajikistan, suggest that there is considerable scope for intra-regional ethnic conflicts within Central Asia, despite a common adherence to the Islamic faith.

Besides the broad economic challenges facing the political leadership of the Central Asian republics, the creation of a series of nation states – each with a unique collective national identity – appears to be a major concern for the region's leaders. If a nation is a portion of the human population that shares a historic territory and common myths and memories giving it a shared cultural identity, and a state is a political unit comprising public institutions in some sense representing and ruling over the population of a bounded territory, then the nation-state legitimises the political institutionalisation of the state on the basis of its claim to embody the nation. It is not surprising that leaders of the new republics, former communist party officials, have sought the mantle of nationalism in the attempt to capture the popular imagination and create their own bases of political legitimacy under increasingly adverse economic circumstances. The Soviet legacy established a national culture that, even if distorted, provided the basis for the creation of a collective community based on a psychological perception of belonging, a sense of shared identity that may transcend other divisions and cross-cut other identities such as religion.

National identity is an emergent phenomenon. Its formation is an ongoing process rather than a resultant fixed set of attributes. As such it is a combination of conceptions and stories of the past shaped by current economic, geopolitical, political, cultural and contemporary factors. It is therefore able to be shaped to some extent by domestic political groupings within a state, and can be mobilised and drawn on by political élites for their own purposes. Those leaders who symbolically associate with the national identity and mobilise it possess a monopoly of popular support. Yet the construction of a national identity risks alienating the large ethnic minorities in the republics. In the case of the approximately 10 million Russians living in the region in 1990, over 50 per cent of them second generation, yet with only 1 per cent able to speak one of the titular languages, this minority comprises the educated technical élite. Faced with the need to re-evaluate their status, given that they now find themselves Russian nationals residing in and subject to the laws of a foreign state, many have sought to return to Russia. Accounts in popular magazines, based on interviews, suggest that those who remain do so because of prevailing economic conditions and shortages in Russia. Individuals are liable to leave given the personal opportunity. Signs of an outbreak of ethnic hostility directed against Russians could lead to further large-scale out-migration.

While it is possible that the Central Asian republics might themselves fragment or be wrecked by inter-republican conflict, the example of Tajikistan and the attempt to create a political environment conducive to large-scale long-term infrastructural investment suggests that republican political élites have an interest in maintaining existing borders. This has led to the imposition of authoritarian measures designed to quell ethnic tensions and to curb Islamic fundamentalists. In Kirghizstan, recognised as the most democratic of the Central Asian republics, this involves imposing limitations on the media and banning organisations on the basis of their tendency to sow ethnic discord. In Uzbekistan and Turkmenistan all political opposition has been repressed by governments in which the former power structure remains largely intact, albeit under a different name (for details see Brown (1992b) and the RFE/ RL *Research Reports* by Bess Brown (1992c, 1993b, c), Cassandra Cavanaugh (1992b) and Christopher Panico (1992)).

There is no denying the impact of Islam on the identity, behaviour, attitudes and way of life of the peoples of Central Asia and its influence on the demographic explosion. However, this is not to subscribe to exaggerated fears of an upsurge of Islamic fanaticism or the creation of a united Islamic bloc. Rather than a force for regional integration, Islam is being used by political, intellectual and religious leaders of each republic to provide a religious value system on which to base each nation's moral recovery and solidarity. As such, it provides a means of legitimising the nation-state, but unites only members of the same national community. Islam serves to bind the members of a given community against all outsiders, including Muslims from different communities (Rwykin, 1982: 89; Carrère d'Encausse, 1993: Chapter 6 ff). It seems certain that current national élites, having gained independence, are anxious to strengthen allegiance to the nation and utilise all sources of allegiance, including religion, to further that objective. Rather than regarding Central Asian Muslims as a unified *Homo Islamicus* (a category suggested by Hélène Carrère d'Encausse in 1979 in the context of explaining the almost total lack of assimilation of Central Asians into Soviet society), it is more useful in present circumstances to attend to the multiple identities available to Central Asians, which include clan and tribal loyalties, national identity and religious faith (Bennigsen, 1979). Such a perspective suggests that the peoples of the former Soviet Central Asian republics are continuing to construct their distinct national identifications.

Notes

1. I should like to thank Linda Creek and Jan McCosh in Warrnambool, who prepared the tables, Ted Smith III of the School of Mass Communications at Virginia Commonwealth University, who allowed me to use his study to prepare the first draft of the paper while I was on sabbatical from Deakin University, and Vladimir Rusavayev at the Centre for Europe in Moscow for his friendship and unfailing patience as we argued about the nature of the Soviet regime and its relations with the former constituent republics. I am sure he still thinks I have got it wrong.
2. The notion of belonging to a political entity called 'Uzbekistan', 'Turkmenistan', 'Tajikistan', 'Kirghizstan' or 'Kazakhstan' was foreign to the overwhelming majority of people living in what

were to become the Central Asian Republics. Loyalties were to the clan, tribe or extended family. The five autonomous republics were Soviet constructions, the number and boundaries of which fluctuated from the period of the Civil War until the mid-1930s.

References

Bennigsen, Alexandre (1979). 'Several nations or one people'. *Survey*, 108.

Brown, Bess (1992a). 'State of the Media: Central Asia'. Radio Free Europe/ Radio Liberty (RFE/RL) *RFE/RL Research Report*, 16 September.

—— (1992b). 'Kazakhstan and Kirgizia on the Road to Democracy'. *RFE/ RL Research Report*, 13 November.

—— (1992c). 'Turkmenistan asserts itself'. *RFE/RL Research Report*, 1 October.

—— (1993a). 'Regional co-operation in Central Asia'. *RFE/RL Research Report*, 29 January.

—— (1993b). 'Tadjik opposition to be banned'. *RFE/RL Research Report*, no date, but late March.

—— (1993c). 'Tadjikistan; the conservatives triumph'. *RFE/RL Research Report*, 12 February.

Carrère d'Encausse, Hélène (1979). *Decline of an Empire: The Soviet Republics in Revolt*, trans. Martin Sokolinsky and Henry á la Farge. New York: Newsweek Books.

—— (1993). *The End of the Soviet Empire*, trans. Franklin Philip. New York: Basic Books.

Cavanaugh, Cassandra (1992a). 'Uzbekistan reexamines the cotton affair'. 4 August.

—— (1992b). 'Uzbekistan looks South and East'. *RFE/RL Research Report*, 21 August.

Delovoi Mir (2 March 1993). 'The economy of the CIS in 1992'. Translated in *Soviet Economics Bulletin*, University of Melbourne, May 1993: 2–4.

Duik, Nadia and Karatnycky, Adrian (1993). *New Nations Rising: The Fall of the Soviets and the Challenge of Independence*. New York: Wiley.

Gleason, Gregory (1991). 'The political economy of dependency under social-ism: the Asian Republics in the USSR'. *Studies in Comparative Communism*, 24 (4): 335–53.

—— (1993). 'Central Asia: land reform and the ethnic factor': *RFE/RL Research Report*, 30 November.

Glebov, Oleg and Crowfoot, John (eds and trans.) (1989). *The Soviet Empire: Its Nations Speak Out*: London: Harwood Academic.

Hyman, Anthony (1994). 'Kuwait by the Caspian?'. *Middle East*, 238.

Izvestia (27 November 1992). 'Central Asian Republics join the Islamic Trad-ing Bloc'. Translated in *Soviet Economics Bulletin*, University of Melbourne, January 1993: 25.

Marer, Paul and Montias, J. M. (1980). 'The theory of East European integration'. In *East European Integration and East–West Trade*. Bloomington: Indiana University Press.

Marnie, Sheila and Whitlock, E. (1993). 'Central Asia and economic integration'. *RFE/RL Research Report*, 26 February.

Monyak, Robert (1993a). 'Geographic Perspectives on Soviet Central Asia: report of a lecture by Robert Lewis, Columbia University, 7/12/90'. *Nationality Papers*, 21(2): 151–4.

—— (1993b). 'Post-1985 internal migration: spatial patterns and issues. Report of a lecture by Beth Mitchnek, Columbia University, 25/1/91'. *Nationality Papers*, 21 (1): 154–6.

Moscow News, 23–29 December 1994.

Olcott, Martha (1992). 'Central Asia's post-empire politics'. *Orbis*, 36 (2): 253–68.

Panico, Christopher (1992). 'Turkmenistan unaffected by winds of democratic change'. *RFE/RL Research Report*, 3 November.

Radio Free Europe/ Radio Liberty. *Daily reports*. 29 May 1990; 6–11 June 1990; 14 August 1991; 4 December 1991; 6–16 December 1991; 16 August 1992.

RLA - *Novosti*, 4 January 1993.

Rywkin, Michael (1982). *Moscow's Muslim Challenge: Soviet Central Asia*. Armonk NY: M. E. Sharpe.

Sakwa, R. (1989). *Soviet Politics: An Introduction*. London and New York: Routledge.

Shearman, Peter (1993). 'Reimagining Russian national identity': Paper to 'State in Transition' conference. LaTrobe University. Melbourne. 6–8 August.

Waltzman, H. (1993). '7,000 Central Asian students enrol at Turkish institutions'. *Chronicle of Higher Education*, 39 (42): A29.

Appendix: National Profile

Kazakhstan

Declared sovereignty: 25 October 1990; Independence: 16 December 1991

Population:	16,793,000
Area in sq. km.:	2,717,300
Urban population (%):	57
Rural population (%):	43
Industrial production as % of Net Material Product (NMP):	28

**Agricultural production as %
of Net Material Product (NMP)**: 40
Capital, with population: Alma-Ata: 1,161,000

Ethnic Groups: Kazakhs 40%, Russians 38%, Germans 6%,
Ukrainians 5%

Major Religions: Sunni Islam, Russian Orthodox, Roman
Catholicism, Baptist

Main Agricultural Products: grain, wool, meat

Main Industries: metallurgy, heavy machinery, machine tools,
petrochemicals, agro-processing, textiles

Natural Resources: coal, iron ore, oil, chrome, lead, wolfram,
copper, zinc

Kirghizstan

Declared sovereignty: 15 December 1990; Independence: 31 August
1991

Population: 4,422,000
Area in sq. km.: 198,500
Urban population (%): 38
Rural population (%): 62
**Industrial production as % of Net
Material Product (NMP)**: 30
**Agricultural production as % of Net
Material Product (NMP)**: 40
Capital, with population: Bishkek
(formerly Frunze): 642,000

Ethnic Groups: Kirghiz 52%, Russians 22%, Uzbeks 13%,
Ukrainians 3%, Germans 2%, Tartars 2%

Major Religions: Sunni Islam, Russian Orthodox

Main Agricultural Products: livestock, cotton, wool, leather,
hemp, vegetables, fruit, grain

Main Industries: metallurgy, agricultural and other machinery,
food processing, electronics.

Natural Resources: coal, gold, mercury, uranium.

Tajikistan

Declared sovereignty: 24 August 1990; Independence: 9 September 1991

Population:	5,358,000
Area in sq. km.:	143,100
Urban population (%):	33
Rural population (%):	67
Industrial production as % of Net Material Product (NMP):	29
Agricultural production as % of Net Material Product:	38
Capital, with population: Dunshanbe:	592,000

Ethnic Groups: Tajiks 62.3%, Uzbeks 23.5%, Russians 7.6%

Major Religions: Sunni Islam: many Pamiris are Ismaeli Muslims

Main Agricultural Products: cotton, wheat, dairy products

Main Industries: hydro-electricity, food processing

Natural Resources: aluminium

Turkmenistan

Declared sovereignty: 22 August 1990; Independence: 27 October 1991

Population:	3,714,000
Area in sq. km.:	488,100
Urban population (%):	45
Rural population (%):	55
Industrial production as % of Net Material Product (NMP):	16
Agricultural production as % of Net Material Product (NMP):	46
Capital, with population: Ashgabat:	416,000

Ethnic Groups: Turkmans 72%, Russians 9.5%, Uzbeks 9%, Kazakhs 2.5%

Major Religion: Sunni Islam

Main Agricultural Products: livestock, cotton

Main Industries: textiles, petro-chemical and chemical, gas and oil processing, electricity

Natural Resources: gas, oil, iodine, sodium sulphate, mineral salts

Uzbekistan

Declared sovereignty: 20 June 1990; Independence: 31 August 1991

Population:	20,708,000
Area in sq. km.:	447,400
Urban population (%):	49
Rural population (%):	51
Industrial production as % of Net Material Product (NMP):	33
Agricultural production as % of Net Material Product (NMP):	43
Capital, with population: Tashkent:	2,120,000

Ethnic Groups: Uzbeks 71%, Russians 8%, Tajiks 5%, Kazakhs 4%, Tartars 2%, Karakalpaks 2%

Major Religion: Sunni Islam

Main Agricultural Products: cotton, grain, vegetables, fruit, silk cocoons

Main Industries: agricultural and textile machinery, chemical products, metallurgy, aircraft

Natural Resources: petroleum, gas, gold, silver, copper, lead, zinc, uranium

Source: *IMF Economic Review*, Washington 1992

– 9 –

Iran's Foreign Policy Since the Gulf War[1]

Adam Tarock

The importance of Iran to the Middle East, because of its size, population, and political and cultural influence, is often compared with China's importance to South-East Asia or with that of Germany to Europe. What this comparison implies is that Iran, as a major regional power, cannot be ignored or kept out of the political game, for what happens in Iran makes a significant impact not only on the Persian Gulf but also on the Middle East as a whole. This was so under the shahs, and it is more so under the ayatollahs. For the past eighteen years, however, except for a brief period during and after the Gulf War, Iran has been the favourite villain of the conservative Arab states and of the West. In the literature it is often described, ominously, as a 'regional superpower'. According to Martin Indyk, the special assistant to President Clinton for Near East and South Asian Affairs and now United States Ambassador to Israel, Iran is 'a real threat to Israel, to the Arab world, and to Western interests in the Middle East' (Law, 1993: 4). Yet despite the rather flattering 'regional superpower' status bestowed on it by some Middle Eastern experts, Iranians genuinely feel apprehensive about the intentions of the outside powers towards them. In other words, the would be 'mother of all threats' feels herself threatened.

Since the end of the Persian Gulf War of 1991, Iran's relations with the outside world have, on balance, improved. This point will be made clearer as this chapter progresses. Briefly, however, Iran now has good working relations with most Western countries (Britain and the United States being exceptions), with its new neighbours to the north, the independent Muslim Central Asian republics, with Turkey, Pakistan, and the Persian Gulf States. But good relations with the Gulf States can hardly be taken for granted. Nor is the unstable situation in the Muslim republics reassuring to the Iranians. The six republics

(Kazakhstan, Uzbekistan, Azerbaijan, Turkmenistan, Tajikistan, and Kirghizstan) are the object of intense competition for influence by regional powers such as Turkey, Pakistan, Saudi Arabia and Iran, as well as by the United States and even China. Should Iran be marginalised as a result of the competition, its northern border could become much less secure. Iran has 1,750 kilometres of common border with the Central Asian republics, about 2,500 kilometres of sea lanes in the Persian Gulf, and 1,500 kilometres with Iraq. It is important to note here that, six years after the end of the war with Iraq in August 1988, Baghdad continues to be of particular security concern to the Iranians, for there is still no peace treaty signed between them. This concern was expressed by President Rafsanjani in his Friday prayer sermon on 6 August 1994 (*Kayhan Havai*, 10 August 1994: 29).

Furthermore, Iran's relations with Turkey, an ally of the West and a member of NATO, can hardly be described as 'truly' friendly, despite the fact that both countries, along with Pakistan, are members of the Economic Co-operation Organisation (ECO), formed in 1985. The Turks have accused Iran of fomenting Islamic fundamentalism in Turkey, and the Iranians have blamed the Turks for harbouring and aiding Iranian monarchists and other opposition groups in attacking Iranian border towns from bases in Turkey, and of following America's anti-Iranian policy in the Middle East. Thus, since the Persian Gulf War, relations between the two countries had until August 1994 remained tense, if not hostile. As will be discussed later, the Iranians generally speaking believe the Turks are acting as a stalking-horse for the United States in the Middle East and in particular in the Transcaucasian and Central Asian regions. However, in early August 1994, President Süleyman Demirel visited Tehran and, after talks with President Rafsanjani, said that his visit 'opened a new chapter' between Tehran and Ankara and that the two countries were 'determined to boost co-operation in all aspects' (*Kayhan Havai*, 3 August 1994: 32).

But relations between them soured again in February 1996 when Turkey signed a military agreement with Israel allowing Israeli planes to use Turkey's airspace. The security implication of the agreement for Iran is that for the first time it brings Israel right next to the Iranian border. The agreement alarmed the Iranians so much that soon after it became known, the Iranian Foreign Minister, Ali Akbar Velayati, visited Ankara, bearing a message from President Hashemi Rafsanjani to his Turkish counterpart Süleyman Demirel. Although Ankara has assured Tehran that it would not allow its airspace to be used by Israel against Iran, the Iranians remain suspicious, and are unhappy with the turn of events in their relations with Turkey. Finally, neighbouring

Afghanistan continues living through a period of intense uncertainty caused by a brutal civil war. But perhaps more worrying for Iran is the strong US military presence in the Persian Gulf and the Clinton administration policy of 'containment of Iran'.

This chapter will primarily concern itself with Iran's foreign policy since the Gulf War, except when, for the purpose of the present discussion, it is deemed necessary to refer to events that took place prior to that war. The chapter is divided into three sections: Iran's foreign policy in the Persian Gulf; Iran's foreign policy towards the Central Asian republics; and Iran's relations with the West, particularly with the United States.

Iran and the Persian Gulf States

In general, Iran's present relations with the Persian Gulf States should be looked at in the context of the latter's relations with Baghdad during the eight-year war between Iran and Iraq and the developments in the region since the Gulf War. Students of Middle East politics are well aware of the very generous financial and political assistance that the Arab Gulf States, Saudi Arabia and Kuwait in particular, gave to Saddam Hussein during that war. Details of that assistance need not be elaborated here. Suffice it to say that there is now irrefutable evidence to support the assertion that had it not been for the Saudis' and the Kuwaitis' financial backing of Saddam Hussein, Iraq would have been unable to pay for the mass-destruction weapons used against Iran. So, an examination of Iran's foreign policy *vis-à-vis* the Gulf States cannot be divorced from the latters' support of Iraq prior to the Gulf War. That support is bound to have left a deep scar on the national psyche of the Iranians.

Iran's reaction to Iraq's attack on its southern neighbour was quick and unequivocal support for Kuwait, as is reflected in a statement by the Iranian Foreign Minister, Ali Akbar Velayati: 'We detest Iraq's occupation of Kuwait' (*The Iranian Journal of International Affairs*, 1991: 2). At the same time, Iran condemned the deployment of American troops in the region. However, the strong condemnation of Iraq and the subsequent endorsement of the United Nations resolutions concerning the Kuwait crisis were noted with satisfaction and gratitude by the Gulf States and their Western allies. Iran's support came despite the fact that some radical groups in Iran opposed this policy on the grounds that, notwithstanding Saddam Hussein's hostility towards Iran, the Iraqi people now faced aggression from America, considered Iran's number one enemy. The support came also despite Saddam's cynical 'conversion' to Islam and the sudden discovery by Iraqi 'Islamic' scholars of a family tree that linked him with the house of the Prophet Muhammad. Nor did the Iranians take seriously Saddam's conversion when he placed on the Iraqi flag the Islamic credo, 'God is most great.'

Iran's stance during the Gulf crisis was not, of course, so much inspired by purely altruistic motives or heart-felt affection for the Kuwaitis and the US-led coalition forces as by its desire to see Saddam Hussein removed from power. Iran could not acquiesce in Iraq's acquisition of Kuwait and the ensuing improvement in its wealth and geostrategic position without deep anxiety. In fact, with Saddam Hussein's history of aggression, Iran could not be sure that after consolidating his position in Kuwait, he would not again turn his attention to the Iranian province of Khuzistan. Shireen Hunter argues that a major worry for Iranian foreign policy-makers was that the United States and its allies could not or would not eliminate Saddam Hussein and would settle for a compromise, thus leaving Iran to face an even more vengeful Iraq (Hunter, 1992a: 129). Whatever its rationale and motives for endorsing the United Nations resolutions, Iran's condemnation of the Iraqi invasion of Kuwait, as has already been pointed out, was appreciated universally.

Dividends for Iran

The Iraqi loss in the Gulf War, however, brought certain dividends for Iran. The most important was that the Iraqi Government finally accepted the peace terms that Iran had sought to impose at the end of the Iran–Iraq War in 1988. This included the recognition of joint sovereignty over the Shatt al-'Arab waterway as embodied in the Algiers agreement of 1975, and the withdrawal of Iraqi troops from Iranian territory. Using Islamic symbols and anti-Zionist rhetoric in his letters of 19 May 1990 and 30 July 1990[2] to President Rafsanjani, Saddam Hussein solicited the support of Iran for his occupation of Kuwait, implying that after the Gulf crisis was over the two countries could co-operate in the security of the Persian Gulf. Iran, however, would not take the bait.

Another important dividend was, and has been since, that it enabled Iran to increase oil production so dramatically that for a while it became the world's second-largest exporter, after Saudi Arabia. Also, not long after the Gulf War, the European Community lifted its economic sanctions against Iran, Britain and Canada restored diplomatic relations with Iran, and the French announced that they would rebuild the Kharg Island terminal, badly damaged during the Iran–Iraq War.

Perhaps more important than material gain was the moral victory over the Gulf States, who had applauded Saddam Hussein for his attempts at halting 'Persian expansionist hordes'. Iran now claimed that it too had been a victim of Iraqi aggression and that the Arabs' support of him was morally wrong. In fact, after the invasion, Kuwait's foreign minister, who was visiting Tehran, expressed regret at his country's past support of Iraq (FBIS/NES, 1990: 59; Hunter, 1992a: 129). Iran's regional diplomacy scored a success when the Gulf Co-operation Council (GCC) members (Qatar, Bahrain, Kuwait, Saudi Arabia, Oman, and the United Arab Emirates) declared, following their summit meeting held in Qatar in December 1990, that the GCC would welcome better ties with Iran and that Iran should be included in any future regional security system. The Iranians' response was: 'This [communiqué] could be regarded as a welcome beginning for some fundamental collaborations between the countries of the region to end the need for the presence of foreign troops in the region. Iran would be ready to collaborate *in all aspects of the Gulf security plan*' (emphasis in the original) (Malek, 1991: 17).

In addition, Dr Velayati told the Third Conference on the Persian Gulf, held in Tehran in January 1991: 'We hope the Persian Gulf countries maintain [Gulf] security without foreign intervention. . . . Let us manage our own affairs' (*The Iranian Journal*, 1991: 5).

To allay fears among the Gulf Arab States that Iran did not intend to play the 'big brother' role in the region, the Iranians apparently even suggested the possibility of Turkey and Pakistan joining a Gulf security arrangement. Nothing much came of this suggestion, but it was a clever diplomatic move for, on the one hand, Turkey and Pakistan are traditional allies of the United States and therefore, theoretically, acceptable to the Arabs and, on the other, they are Iran's partners in the ECO. Soon after these diplomatic initiatives, relations between Kuwait and Iran and Iran and Saudi Arabia, which had reached a high level of hostility during the 1980s, improved considerably. For example, in April 1991, President Rafsanjani made a rare visit to Riyadh and met with King Fahd. This resulted in the resumption of diplomatic ties between Iran and Saudi Arabia on 19 March 1991.

The trend towards improving Iran's relations with the Gulf States continued for most of 1991. For example, in September, Iran's foreign minister met the Emir of Kuwait, who was attending the UN General Assembly meeting in New York City. In the same month, the foreign ministers of the Gulf Co-operation Council and Dr Velayati met to discuss issues related to Gulf security and Iran's role therein, as well as co-operation between Iran and the GCC. According to Hunter (1992a: 133), following these contacts the Foreign Minister of Saudi

Arabia, Prince Bin Faisal, told reporters that if current positive trends in Iran's diplomacy continued, Iran and the GCC could develop mutually beneficial relations during the 1990s. Furthermore, so as to avoid creating new apprehension about Iran's intentions in the Gulf, Iran did not intervene militarily or add fuel to the fire when its co-religionists, the Shi'ites in southern Iraq, were being brutally repressed by Saddam Hussein after the war.

Hopes Dissipated

So there is enough evidence to suggest that during and for a short while after the Gulf crisis, Iran and the Gulf States were heading towards some kind of regional co-operation, if not by way of a *de jure* agreement then at least by way of a *de facto* one. But Iran's attempts at reaching a new security arrangement with the Gulf States failed, as the atmosphere of co-operation that had emerged following the Gulf War was dissipated by the end of 1991. The residue of old distrust and suspicions about Iran's designs for 'expansionism' had won the day. The suspicion was further reinforced by the West's view that the Iranian system of government was (is) inherently a threat to Western interests in the region and by extension to its allies in the Gulf. It became clear to the Iranians that the Western powers, in particular the United States, preferred to keep Iran out of future security arrangements. For example, a press report quoted British Foreign Secretary Douglas Hurd as saying that post-war Gulf security should be 'mainly Arab-led' (*Financial Times*, 1991: 2), the implication being that non-Arab Iran should not be allowed to be a party in such arrangements.

The Iranians were further disappointed when a 10-year security pact was signed between Kuwait and the United States on 10 September 1991, and also a separate security pact between Bahrain and the United States, allowing the latter's forces access to bases there. According to Amin Saikal, under the pact 'the Kuwaiti leadership has sought to guarantee the country's long term security by agreeing to full co-operation on defence matters. This includes allowing the United States to stockpile and pre-position military hardware in Kuwait and to have full access to the country's infrastructural facilities for military operations' (Saikal, 1992: 117). Saikal further argues that by forming the security pact with the Persian Gulf States, the United States wants (a) to keep Iran weak, and (b) to isolate Iran from the international community. The United States hopes that the isolation or containment of Iran would force Tehran to adopt a more accommodating foreign policy *vis-à-vis* the West and its allies in the Persian Gulf. In signing separate security treaties with these states, the United States, it appears, has this time decided to take direct responsibility for the security of its allies in the region.

The GCC Divided on Iran

However, not all the GCC members want to keep Iran at arm's length. For example, the group's more southern members (Oman, the UAE, and Qatar) are geographically closer to Iran. They have a tradition of trying to work with the larger country to the east, not against it. During the Iran–Iraq War these sheikhdoms, unlike Kuwait and Saudi Arabia, maintained a relatively good working relationship with Iran. In fact, after the Iran–Iraq War Oman and the United Arab Emirates sought to act as mediators between Iran and Iraq. But the invasion of Kuwait rendered the mediation irrelevant. In general, in the post-Khomeini era, and especially since 1991, the GCC member states have viewed Iran as less of a threat to their security. Considering the fact that Iran spends only about $2 billion a year on rebuilding its armed forces, as compared with their own spending of several times that amount on purchasing the most sophisticated weapons, the GCC have reasons to believe that Iran has no intention of embarking on an expansionist policy in the region. They have also noted that Iran, along with Turkey and Syria, has not attempted to divide Iraq by supporting the Kurdish and Shi'ite separatists. Furthermore, they have noted Iran's increasing emphasis on trade and economic development with them. But they have been unwilling to assist Iran in its post-Iran–Iraq War reconstruction programmes. As John Anthony says, the GCC countries, with their vast financial resources and influence in several national and international developmental agencies (that is, the World Bank, the IMF, the Arab Monetary Fund, the Arab Fund for Social and Economic Development) have assisted a great many countries, but not Iran (Anthony, 1993: 115–16).

A particular issue that divides the Persian Gulf States and Iran is the peace accord between the Palestine Liberation Organisation (PLO) and the state of Israel. While the Gulf States have virtually accepted the peace agreement, Iran continues to reject it on the grounds that it does not meet the aspirations of the Palestinians for a genuine independent state. However, neither Iran nor the Gulf States have made this issue a public bone of contention between them.

As we have already noted, Iran is in principle opposed to the presence of foreign forces in the region. For the present, however, Iran appears to have adopted a two-edged policy on this issue. The first is that it has recognised, though not accepted, the fact that the United States is going to maintain a strong presence in the Persian Gulf for the foreseeable future, and that there is little that it can do about it. Secondly, Iran seems to have grudgingly recognised that the sheikhs and the emirs, with their small territories and populations, may have logic on their side in wishing to secure themselves against stronger neighbours (that is, Iran and Iraq) and therefore seeking security protection from great powers. Constructing its foreign policy within the framework of these two realities – a permanent US presence in the Gulf and the rulers' vulnerability to regional forces – Iran has since the Gulf War been engaged in confidence-building exercises with the Gulf rulers and has to a good degree succeeded in its efforts. For example, when the Saudi Minister of Defence and Civil Aviation, Prince Sultan ibn Abdal 'Aziz, told the Iranian ambassador in Riyadh that the Saudis did not believe that 'Iran poses any threat to either the region or to Saudi Arabia' (*Kayhan Havai*, 12 May 1993: 31), it was widely reported in the Iranian press. The intention was to show not only to the Gulf States but also to other states interested in the security of the region (that is, the United States) that Iran is far from a threat to their interests in the region. Also, in May 1993 Dr Velayati made a 'good will' visit to the Gulf States and met with King Fahd, who accepted President Rafsanjani's invitation to visit Iran. No definite date has been set for the visit, but Rafsanjani is on record as saying that his 'government is determined to improve relations with Riyadh' (*Kayhan Havai*, 2 June 1993: 4). But we should not be over-optimistic about the outcome of the new opening, for similar *rapprochements* even during the Shah's regime and since have ended in failure.

However, to say that Iran has been successful in securing the trust of the Gulf States is not to say that its success has been unqualified. For example, since 1992 relations between Tehran and some members of the GCC have continued to be troubled over three small islands – Abu Musa, the Greater Tunb and the Lesser Tunb – near the Strait of Hormuz.[3] Abu Musa Island (with 600 inhabitants), which was under British control, was 'returned' to Iran in 1971 under an agreement signed between Iran and Sharjah. Reportedly, these islands were returned to Iran after it had withdrawn its historic claim to Bahrain, principally because it believed, at the time, that its greater interests centred in the strategic Strait of Hormuz (Mojtahed-Zadeh, 1992: 485–500).

In April 1992, Iranian authorities prevented entry into Abu Musa Island[4] by a group of Indian, Pakistani and Arab workers employed by Sharjah. Not long after that some 100 teachers and their families from Sharjah tried to enter the island, but were again denied entry by the Iranians. The United Arab Emirates sent a representative to Tehran to discuss the issue, but Iran refused to talk with him, arguing that as far as Iran was concerned there was no issue to be discussed and that the 1971 agreement on Abu Musa was between Iran and Sharjah only. In the same month, April, the Iranian parliament, the Majlis, passed a bill extending Iranian territorial waters to 12 miles, thus placing the disputed islands well inside them. Technically, any claim by the UAE now could be viewed as an act of aggression against Iranian territory. This was not acceptable to the Arabs. So, the High Council of the UAE, meeting on 12 May to debate Iran's response to the issue, concluded that the commitments of each member of the UAE were to be treated as commitments of the UAE as a whole. The issue of the islands demonstrates the delicate nature of the relations between Iran and its Arab Gulf neighbours, and how problems that could be resolved through negotiations could quickly raise the political temperature in the Persian Gulf.

As is clear from the statement of a leading Iranian parliamentarian, Ata-ollah Mohajerani, Iran feels there is an urgency in settling its disputes over the islands with the Gulf States. Iran, he argues, is aware that it has 'to rush to settle its problems with its [Gulf] neighbours, otherwise the Americans will quickly intervene in the hope of aggravating the situation' (*Kayhan Havai*, 7 July 1993: 32). In general, the success or failure of Iran's policy towards the Persian Gulf Arab States hinges greatly on its relations with Saudi Arabia. These relations have not been very good since 1993, as was indicated by President Rafsanjani in a press interview he gave in the latter part of 1995. Referring to the two countries' ties, he said: 'It is not very good. An average relationship – even less than average – but we would like to see an improvement' (*Middle East Insight*, 11 (5): 14).

US Pressed for Action

Since the end of the Persian Gulf War, Egypt and Israel have adapted a far less compromising approach towards Iran than have the Persian Gulf States. Cairo and Tel Aviv have been arguing that with Iraq weakened and under international sanctions, the principal threat to US interests in the Middle East and to the Persian Gulf in the post-Gulf War era comes from Iran. They have been pressing Washington hard for a confrontation, military if necessary, to bring to a halt the perceived Iranian support for terrorism and Islamic fundamentalism in the Arab world. 'Israel is pressing very hard for such a confrontation, recognising Iran to be the most serious military threat it faces', according to Chomsky (1993: 1). In Israeli strategic thinking, Iran may be attacked so that the Muslim fundamentalist influence in the Arab world may diminish (Shahak, 1993: 19). In mid-April 1993, the then director of the CIA, James Woolsey, made a not-so-secret visit (it was widely reported in the media) to Egypt, during which President Mubarak warned him about Iranian-backed Islamic groups which – according to him – undermined stability in the Middle East, especially in Egypt and the Persian Gulf (*The Age*, 19 April 1993). He argued along the same lines when he visited the Gulf leaders in May to shore up support for his drive against the danger of Islamic fundamentalism. But a more serious and ominous warning was given to Iran by Shimon Peres in April 1996, through the good offices of France, that Israel will hold Iran responsible for any attack on Jewish or Israeli targets abroad (*Foreign Report*, 1996: 1). In theory, if not in practice, this warning means that a version of 'Operation Wrath' will visit Iran if it fails to control not only its own agents but also all the other individuals or groups throughout the world who for reasons of their own may attack, say a synagogue or a shop owned by a Jew.

This sort of alarm raised by conservative Arab leaders is not unlike the one they once raised about the threat of communism to the Arab world. Then, as now, the idea was to enlist the support of the West. This time, however, conservative Arab leaders have an easier job in convincing the West of the 'threat' of Islamic 'fundamentalism' not only to Middle East stability but also to Western security and commercial interests. The job of convincing the West is now easier because since the end of the Cold War Western Europe and the United States themselves feel threatened by Islamic revivalism and the political and economic impact that it is having on their Muslim immigrants. As Roberson (1994: 302) argues, 'Islam [and by extension Iran] is seen by many in the West as virulently anti-Western and a threat to governments and societal stability in the Middle East, with a potential carry over into international commerce'.

To sum up, it is accurate enough to say that Iran's relations with its Gulf neighbours have considerably improved since the Gulf War. But in spite of the occasional friendly remark or sentiment expressed by the Gulf rulers about Iran, the Iranians have as yet to persuade them to form a security alliance with Iran. Iran blames non-regional powers for continually nourishing the fears of the Gulf States and for portraying Iran as the source of subversion and terror and as a potential threat to their security. While there is a good degree of truth in the Iranians' argument, the fact remains that the smaller Gulf States have a lesser military capability than Iran, even though 60 per cent of the latter's military capability was destroyed during the war with Iraq, according to a report by the Congress (*Kayhan Havai*, 16 June 1993: 30).[5] Considering Iran's present economic and military weaknesses, it is hard to imagine that it would in the next 10 to 15 years be in any position to threaten, militarily, its Arab neighbours. In fact, rather than being a threat to its neighbours, Iran at present faces two worrying prospects. If, on the one hand, Saddam Hussein were to rearm himself, he might again invade Iran without the fear of the punishment he received from the West when he invaded Kuwait. If, on the other hand, he were replaced in a US-backed military coup, then there is a likelihood that Washington would dominate a future Iraqi regime. Perhaps a hated, internationally isolated Saddam would be Iran's best bet.

Iran and the Muslim Republics of Central Asia

The collapse of the Soviet Union was a great relief to the Iranians, because it brought to an end the century-old deadly rivalry, first between Great Britain and Russia and then between the United States and the Soviet Union, for the domination of Iran. In other words, for the first time in more than a century the Iranians now feel no apparent threat to their national sovereignty and security coming from their former superpower neighbour. But the break-up of the Soviet empire and the end of the Cold War has at the same time deprived them of the East versus West card that they had successfully used for maintaining Iran's independence. With the disintegration of the Soviet Union, the United States can now act more boldly towards Iran. For instance, the United States naval confrontation with Iran in the Persian Gulf during the last stages of the Iran–Iraq War would probably not have happened but for Gorbachev's foreign policy in the late 1980s in accommodating rather than challenging Washington's assertive policies in the Third World. Also, the 'containment' policy directed against Iran by the Clinton administration may have a greater chance of success than it would have had during the Cold War. It is worth noting that at present (June 1996), relations between Iran and Russia are very good; indeed they 'have never been so good in the past 500 years', according to Dr Velyati, who met President Yeltsin in Moscow in March 1996 (*Iran News*, 9 March 1996). It should be remembered that Russia has persistently resisted strong pressure from the United States to cancel a one billion dollar contract to build a nuclear power station in Bushir, Iran.

At present, however, the Iranians are concerned about the six newly independent but politically unstable Muslim republics in Central Asia. The emergence of these republics, which historically have been within the sphere of Iran's and Turkey's cultural and political influence, has rekindled the old Ottoman–Persian competition. Moreover, the disappearance of the common fear of the Soviet Union, which had united Turkey and Iran (under both the Shah and the Islamic Republic) has given new saliency to these divergences. Also, Iran's Islamic activism versus Turkey's secularism have further oiled the wheels of competition for influence in the republics. A third Muslim country vying for influence there is Saudi Arabia. It has been active in spreading funds for the distribution of about a million copies of the *Qur'an*. The Saudis see themselves in a leadership position in the Islamic world and seek to propagate their version of Islam (which the Ayatollah Khomeini called 'American Islam') in competition to that of Iran, which they see as subversive and ultimately a threat to their standing and security. And, of course, Saudi Arabia has the financial resources to use as an inducement to the republics.

It is too early to declare the winner in the competition for 'influence', but in this race Turkey has a number of advantages over Iran. For example, in its attempts to win the hearts and minds of the republics, Turkey, as a member of NATO, can draw, and indeed has drawn, on the political and propaganda support of the West, that is the depicting in the Western media of Turkey as a 'moderate', 'democratic' state and of Iran as a 'terrorist', 'anti-democratic', and 'anti-Western' state. Furthermore, in assisting the republics, Turkey could theoretically draw on Saudi Arabia's financial resources. In contrast, Iran, presently engaged in a massive (estimated at between $600 and $700 billion) reconstruction programme, can offer them little economic assistance in the way of loans, investments or grants. Moreover, as Hunter has argued, most political élites in these republics are likely to side with the West, not only because of their acute financial problems but also because of their technological needs. So, when dealing with Third World countries, they are likely to favour those that adhere to a Western-style democracy (that is, Turkey), even if only in words (Hunter, 1992a: 329). In its competition with Iran, Turkey has two other important advantages. One stems from the fact that in international relations countries feel less secure with powerful neighbours, so that they try to keep them at arm's length. Turkey, though politically more influential and militarily stronger (by virtue of its alliance with the West) than Iran, has no common border with the republics. The second is that decades of religious suppression by the communists have inevitably turned the masses in these states more towards secularism than to religious activism. What this means is that Islamic ideology on the Iranian model has little attraction for the people of Central Asia. This is particularly so when secular Turkey and its Western supporters are trying to portray Islamism not as a liberating socio-political force but as an oppressive doctrine similar to that of communism – plus 'terrorism'.

More Cultural than Religious

But Iran's limitations in influencing the republics do not lie only in the latters' interest in aligning themselves with the West. Iran's limitations lie also in the fact that the republics have a different perception of Islam from that which is prevalent in the Muslim world. Seyyed Rifaat Hussein, a Pakistani academic, argues that Islam in the Central Asian context is more cultural than ideological. Its ethos is neither medieval nor feudal. Quintessentially it is secular, egalitarian and rational. He quotes Nursultan Nazarbayev as saying: 'I do not think fundamentalist Islam has much chance . . . It is not possible to build a civilised relationship between sovereign states which see themselves as democratic on religious grounds' (Hussein, 1992: 629). It was perhaps because of the republics' interest in engaging in economic co-operation rather than in religio-political matters that Turkey and Iran, as well as Pakistan, have succeeded in incorporating these countries into the Economic Co-operation Organisation (ECO), an economic and trade alliance between Turkey, Iran and Pakistan. Their incorporation into the ECO should be regarded as one of Iran's successes in its foreign policy in the post-Gulf War period.

Iran played a crucial role in bringing the Central Asian republics into the ECO. At a summit meeting held in Tehran in February 1992, the meeting granted membership to the five republics, and gave observer status to Kazakhstan and Turkish Cyprus. With the induction of these republics into the ECO, the organisation has certainly acquired a new momentum. These developments have opened up immense vistas of regional co-operation and development, which, if grasped properly, could radically transform the entire spectrum of life in the region in a very short span of time. After the European Union, it is now the largest economic alliance in the world – comprising eight countries with a total population of over 250 million. Despite low levels of technological and industrial development, it is a resource-rich area with a strategic location, being at the crossroads that link Europe with the Asia–Pacific region. The members of the enlarged ECO have much in common: besides being geographically close and economically well-resourced, they partake of a rich cultural heritage and a general Islamic orientation. The link with the ECO has provided the republics with an important transit route to the outside world through the Persian Gulf; it also has given Iran new routes to Europe.

Adam Tarock

Iran's Edge over Turkey in Central Asia

But as a transit route to the world market, Iran is more valuable to the republics than the other way round. Most Central Asian republics have signed bilateral economic and transport agreements with Iran, as, in the words of Uzbek Foreign Minister, Sadyk Safaev, 'Iran is the only route to the Persian Gulf and the Mediterranean' (Dorsey, 1993a: 15). Similarly, Turkmenistan sees Iran as its most important gateway for the export of natural gas to Europe. With the help of the World Bank and the European Bank of Reconstruction and Development, as well as financial assistance from Iran, Turkmenistan is planning to build a 5,000-kilometre gas pipeline across Iran that would link it with Western Europe. So as to link Iran with the republics, Iran in May 1996 completed a 165-kilometre railway connecting the Iranian railway network to of Turkmenistan. For their part, Western transport companies see Iran as a cheaper and safer route to Central Asia than Russia and the Ukraine, from where travel is only possible in protected convoy. Thus, Central Asian dependency on Iranian ports for much of their imports and exports would give Iran a great edge over Turkey in regional influence.

Politically, too, by presenting itself as 'neutral', Iran scored a qualified point over Turkey for its mediation between Azerbaijanis and Armenians. However, in August 1993 Iran appeared to have ended its neutrality over Nagorno-Karabakh and sided with Azerbaijan, amid mounting concern over the human and political cost of the Armenian offensive near its border. Velayati, on a visit to Baku in August, said Iran was 'committed to the territorial integrity' of Azerbaijan and called on the Armenians to withdraw from Azerbaijani lands. In September 1993 the situation in Azerbaijan became worse when in a new offensive the Armenians occupied 20 per cent of Azerbaijan and made at least 100,000 people homeless in the southwest of the country, between Karabagh and the Iranian border. Iran then set up a 20-kilometre security zone inside the country for the Azeri refugees. Turkey has made no objection and has talked of 'co-ordination' in the region with its rival for regional influence, Iran. Turkey has no common border with Azerbaijan proper, but only with the small Azerbaijani enclave of Nakhichevan. There are good economic relations between Iran and Armenia. They have signed an agreement for the supply of Iranian oil and gas to Armenia through the construction of a pipeline, and Armenian scientific personnel, including 1,000 health workers, have found employment in Iran (Dorsey, 1993b: 17–18).

In short, Iran's visible diplomacy has been cautious. It has established trade offices and opened embassies with a view to building a broad relationship. The emphasis has been on cultural and economic relations within the framework of the ECO as well as on a bilateral basis. Also, as has already been mentioned, the visit of Turkish President Demirel to Tehran in August 1994 to improve security and economic co-operation between the two countries and President Rafsanjani's remark that Iran has 'confidence' in the Turkish government (*Kayhan Havai*, 3 August 1994: 32) are likely to lessen the intensity of their competition in the Central Asian Republics. However, Iran's bigger challengers for political and economic influence in the region are Moscow and Washington; but that is another story.

Perhaps the most difficult issue confronting Iran and some of the republics is over the use of the natural resources of the Caspian Sea. Prior to the disintegration of the Soviet Union, the sea was jointly managed by Iran and the Soviet Union. Now three other states – Turkmenistan, Kazakhstan and Azerbaijan – border the sea. Iran and Russia argue that the Caspian is a 'lake' and not a sea – and is therefore not subject to standard international practice and law with regard to delimitation of offshore areas. As a 'lake', so goes the legal argument, the Caspian is the property of all the states bordering it, and so agreements on oil or gas production have been agreed to by all the littoral states. This legal argument was raised by Iran when in 1995 Azerbaijan signed a $7.4 billion dollar agreement with Western and non-Western oil companies for the exploration for oil in the Caspian Sea. Under pressure from the United States, Iran was excluded from being a partner in that agreement.

Iran, Western Europe, and the United States

When we talk about Iran's relations with the West, we are basically referring to the turbulent US–Iran relations over the past sixteen years. The acrimonious relationship, or perhaps a more accurate description would be 'mutual demonisation', between the two countries continues to affect political developments in the Middle East on the one hand and the relationship between the Middle East and the West on the other. To begin with, Iran at present has normal diplomatic and trade relations with almost all the European nations. A major bone of political contention between the Iranians and the Europeans, more specifically between Tehran and London, is the Salman Rushdie affair. Relations between the two capitals have remained below ambassadorial level primarily, but not exclusively, because of the Rushdie affair. In July 1992, Britain expelled three Iranians on the suspicion that they were involved in an attempt to kill Rushdie, though no hard evidence was produced. Relations took a turn for the worse when Prime Minister John Major met Rushdie in May 1993, perhaps to indicate clearly to the Iranians that as long as the Rushdie affair remained unresolved, normalisation of relations between the two countries was not possible. On the other hand, the Iranians view this affair as a political whip used by the West to lash out at Iran whenever its suits them. To the argument by Britain that relations between the two countries cannot be fully normalised until Iran rescinds Ayatollah Khomeini's *fatwa*, the Iranians say that 'theologically' this cannot be done, since the author of the *fatwa* who had the authority to do so is no longer alive. The Iranian authorities have repeatedly assured the West that they are not going to do anything to implement the *fatwa*.

Trade and diplomatic relations with other major European states, namely France, Italy and Germany, are good on the whole, despite their many difficulties. One such difficulty was the assassination of the former Iranian Prime Minister, Shapour Bakhtiar, in Paris in July 1991. Paris implicated Iran in the murder, but Tehran denied any involvement in it. A French court investigating the case in December 1994 acquitted the only one among the accused who was an administrative secretary at the Iranian embassy in Switzerland at the time of Bakhtiar's assassination.

Also, cultural relations between Iran and Germany suffered a setback in 1993 when Germany banned Iranian publishers from the Frankfurt Book Fair, the world's largest, after German writers protested about Iran's policy with regard to Rushdie. On balance, however, Iran is pleased with its relations with France, Italy and Germany, and particularly that these states have resisted the US pressure to cut or at least downgrade their trade and economic ties with Iran. Unlike the US, Europe believes that dialogue with and not containment of Iran will eventually moderate Iran's policy towards the West. In short, Iran's relations with Europe have improved since the Gulf War. We now turn to Iran–US relations – or rather the lack of such relations.

A decade of hostility between the two appeared to be abating shortly before and for a while after the Gulf crisis. In Washington's view, Iran had by then become less of the 'big bad wolf' of the region. Iran had, for example, pressed its Lebanese supporters to free the Western hostages held in Beirut, and had thus helped to end the hostage crisis that had so much damaged Iran's image in the West. Furthermore, Iran had opened to the West by seeking loans from the World Bank as well as by inviting foreign investors to participate in the country's reconstruction programme, involving billions of dollars. Moreover, because of the collapse of the Soviet Union, there was no longer the potential (if there ever was) of Iran's conniving with Moscow and thus facilitating the Soviets' entry into the 'warm waters' of the Persian Gulf. Equally importantly, by the time of the Gulf crisis Iran had launched its reconstruction programme and needed to focus its attention more on domestic than on external issues. In other words, by the end of the 1980s, the Iranian leaders were 'doing a Gorbachev': concentrating more on economic and social reforms at home and less on 'exporting' Islamic ideology. So in the early part of 1991 there was, for a short while, a ray of hope that Iran–US relations might gradually improve. That opportunity was missed (as will be discussed later), as was the one that had presented itself two years before.

At the end of the Iran–Iraq War in 1988, the United States had had the chance to influence Iran's internal policies and thus its foreign policy. Had the United States taken this chance and sent the right signals to regional states that it fully supported the implementation of the UN resolutions on the Iran–Iraq conflict, the tragic miscalculations of the following years, such as the invasion of Kuwait, would have been prevented. The most important signal would have been an unequivocal insistence that Security Council Resolution 598 be applied in its entirety. An important aspect of the Resolution related to the withdrawal of Iraqi troops from Iranian territory. The United States not only did not insist on the implementation of Resolution 598, but remained silent, thus giving tacit support to the Iraqis' continued claim that they must have full sovereignty over all of the Shatt al-'Arab waterway. The United States' insistence on the withdrawal of Iraqi troops from Iranian territory would have had a very positive impact on Iran. However, by and large, the Bush administration followed the past policy and refused to take any positive step towards Iran (Hunter, 1992b: 16).

Hostility Given New Licence

It appears that the old hostility is now given a new licence under the Clinton administration. So, we are now left with the questions: What is the US policy towards Iran? Putting it differently, how does it view Iran in relation to Persian Gulf security and to Western interests in the region as a whole? Equally, what is Iran's present policy towards the US and what are its conditions for the normalisation of relations with Washington?

As a general guideline it should be pointed out that, like its three predecessors, the Clinton administration continues to regard the

Islamic Republic of Iran as inherently irrational, diabolical, and inimical to United States interests in the Middle East. As to Iran's view of the US in the post-Khomeini era, America is still regarded as the 'Great Satan'; but in the political rhetoric of pragmatic Iranian leaders, America is now less frequently referred to by that name. Given that the two countries have that kind of perception of each other, we now can proceed to the specific political issues that divide them.

'Containing' Iran

The United States takes issue with Iran on the following: alleged Iranian support of international terrorism; its attempt to export revolutionary ideology to other Muslim countries; its opposition to the Arab–Israel peace process; and its determination to rearm and, worse, to achieve nuclear capability – in short, to pose a threat to Western interests in the Middle East. Clinton's policy towards countries like Iran – 'backlash states', as they are called by Anthony Lake, Assistant to the President for National Security Affairs – is to confront them head-on: 'As the sole superpower the United States has a special responsibility for developing a strategy to neutralise, contain and, through selective pressure, perhaps eventually transform these backlash states into constructive members of the international community' (Lake, 1994: 46).

In confronting and containing Iran, the administration has adopted a two-edged – internal and external – policy towards Iran. The internal one is to give political and moral support to Iranian opposition groups residing overseas. For example, in December 1992, President Clinton wrote a letter to Mass'ud Rajavi, leader of the Iranian Mujahedin-e Khalq, in which he set out his commitment to furthering the cause of democracy in Iran, as a cornerstone for his foreign policy (Walker, 1993: 8). The letter followed an earlier meeting between Mujahedin officials and Al Gore. Moreover, in 1995 the CIA asked for, and Congress approved, 20 million dollars for 1996, to continue covert operations aimed at destabilising Iran, while in July 1996 United States legislators passed a secondary boycott law, prohibiting foreign-owned companies from investing more than 40 million dollars in Iran's oil and gas industries.

It is ironic that the Mujahedin – with their Marxist leanings and history of anti-American terrorist activities – have been able to enlist the tacit support of the administration. However, while the Mujahedin can certainly cause discomfort to the Iranian government at home or politically embarrass it abroad (as in the case of attacks in 1992 on Iranian embassy buildings in Europe and Australia), they neither have the military capability nor sufficient support inside the country to be able either to topple the government or to affect its political behaviour. In other words, if by supporting Iranian dissident groups the intention is to make Iran modify its foreign policy, then that is unlikely to succeed. However, containing Iran 'externally' could be much more effective.

The Clinton administration appears to believe that containing Iraq is much easier than containing Iran. This is reflected in a 10 November 1992 telephone conversation between King Fahd and Clinton, in which both agreed that 'emergent powers in the Gulf needed containing' (Jaber, 1992: 8–9) – neither side left any doubt in anyone's mind that they were talking about Iran. This mode of thinking about Iran is also reflected in much of the writings of Middle East experts. For example, in comparing Iran's threat to the US interests in the Persian Gulf with the Soviet threat to the US interests worldwide, Daniel Pipes and Patrick Glawson argue that Washington has two basic policy options with regard to Iran's threat: *détente* or containment. Their advice is to opt for 'containment hoping that the internal problems will eventually cause the regime to implode' (Pipes and Glawson, 1993: 128). In fact, in May 1993, Martin Indyk said the United States was changing its historic policy in the region. According to Indyk, in the past the Americans had tried to use the power of Iraq to counter Iran, and vice versa. From now on, America would accept that both regimes are fundamentally hostile to its interests. 'Both would in the future be opposed, as part of a "dual containment" policy. . . . America hopes that the loyalty of American friends – Egypt, Israel, Saudi Arabia, the Gulf emirates and Turkey – can maintain a balance of power in our favour' (*The Economist*, 29 May 1993: 40). He reiterated that policy at a symposium on US policy towards Iran and Iraq a year later (Pipes, 1994: 1–26).

A drawing of President Rafsanjani in *The Washington Post* (reproduced in *The Guardian Weekly* of 9 May 1993: 18) very much reflects Washington's perception of the post-Gulf-War Iran. It shows Rafsanjani's face partly black and partly white, but with the black part overshadowing the white part, suggesting that since the Gulf War Iran has been pursuing a two-edged policy: a little moderation but more terror. This view of Iran is reflected not only in statements by US officials but also in commentaries by most American academics specialising in the Middle East (Green, 1993: 12–16). As Gary Sick has argued, the dark side or the ugly side is painted by Egypt, Israel and the CIA who 'all have concluded that their interests are served by the propagation of a new enemy – Islamic fundamentalism in general and Iran in particular' (Sick, 1993: 18). In the United States' view,

Iran's dark side comprises its support of terrorism in the Middle East, in Europe and even in the United States. This view of Iran as a 'terrorist' state has become so much part of American (and of Israeli) political rhetoric that any act of terrorism anywhere in the world is automatically blamed on Iran even before the local police have had a chance to investigate the case. For example, the bombings of some Jewish buildings in Argentina and England in July 1994 were blamed on Iran only hours after the incidents. Then a couple of weeks later the local police said that in their investigations they found no evidence of Iran's involvement in the bombings.

Washington also takes issue with Iran for trying to undermine the Middle East peace process. Two things can be said about this. First, though Iran has certainly a degree of moral and ideological influence among the Islamic movements in the Arab world, its capacity to affect the peace process is highly exaggerated, one would suspect for political reasons, by the United States. Second, if the continuing clashes, since the Israel–PLO peace accord, between the Israeli security forces and the Palestinians and the general discontent of the Palestinians are anything to go by, then Iran has little need to urge the Arabs to reject the peace accord.

Finally, the United States alleges that Iran is trying to acquire long-range missiles and nuclear capability. The Iranians have denied it, and if they are cheating on nuclear weapons, the International Atomic Energy has yet to catch them out. However, it should be noted that Iran is trying to rebuild its military strength at least to the level that it was at before the start of the Iran–Iraq War. As Kamal Kharazi, the Iranian ambassador to the United Nations, has pointed out, much of the present arms build-up may be justified as a prudent measure against a re-occurrence of the beating that the country took at the hands of Saddam Hussein in the 1980s. As Sir Anthony Parsons, a former British ambassador to Iran and the UN, has argued, the rearmament programme is, to an objective observer, understandable given the nature of Iran's neighbours – Saddam Hussein, unstable post-Soviet Central Asia and chaotic Afghanistan. 'If there were a different regime in Tehran, Western governments would be invoking precisely these reasons for justifying a massive arms sales drive to Iran – legitimate self-defence needs' (Parsons, 1993: 17).[6]

Sir Anthony Parsons argues that there is a school of thought dev–eloped in Washington, where paranoia about Iran has reigned for 14 years. According to this school of thought, a renascent Iran presents as big a threat to Western interests as did the pre-Gulf-War Saddam Hussein, and therefore he should remain in power so that some kind of power balance can be reconstructed. Parsons maintains that Arab states and the West should not overestimate the Iranian danger, and should resist any temptation to compare it with the Iraqi regime. 'Unlike Iraq, Iran has no territorial ambitions on the Arab shore . . . It is important to get things in proportion and to differentiate between the demon in Baghdad and the demons in Tehran' (Parsons, 1993: 16).

Still, compared with other Middle East countries, Iran's expenditures on its armed forces are indeed small. According to the International Institute for Strategic Studies, Iran, with a population of 60 million and armed forces of 528,000 had a defence budget of $4.6 billion for the years 1991 and 1992. The comparable statistics for Israel are 5.1 million, 175,000, $5.8 billion; for Saudi Arabia 7.6 million, 157,000, $13.9 billion; and for Jordan 4.4 million, 99,000, $0.6 billion, respectively (Atkeson, 1993: 115). As these figures show, Iran's military expenditure is much below that of other Middle East states. While it cannot be said that Iran has an 'aversion' to allocating a much larger budget for its defence forces, the fact is that Iran simply cannot afford to compete in the 'arms bazaar' with the other Persian Gulf States. Its military and economic situation is neatly and accurately described by Gary Sick thus:

> The reality is that Iran is in no position to mount a sustained foreign policy challenge outside its borders and will not be able to do so for years to come. Its domestic economy was thrown into chaos first by the revolution and then by the double whammy of its long war with Iraq, and international sanctions. Its military forces were decimated, and much of its economic infrastructure was devastated. Its oil fields experienced extensive damage . . . Refugees [about four million] from Afghanistan and Iraq have added to the burdens of dealing with large numbers of Iran's own population displaced by war. In addition, Iran has been plagued by earthquakes and floods of biblical proportions over the past few years. As a result, its military budget has declined steadily to the point where it is one of the least militarised countries in the region by almost any measure (Sick, 1993: 18–19).

In short, unless Iran puts its own house in order and improves markedly its economic situation by the end of this decade, the very survival of the regime would be at risk (*Kayhan Havai*, 23 June 1993: 9).[7]

It is perhaps because of this dire situation that the Iranians have on several occasions sent out some strong signals indicating their interest in improving relations with the United States. For example, Iran's ambassador to the United Nations is on the record as saying: 'We can see no problem with establishing relations [with America], if such relations were based on reciprocal respect . . . I believe the United

States continues to see Iran from the perspectives of pre-revolutionary conditions, but that era is gone' (*Kayhan Havai*, 19 May 1993: 7). And no less a person than President Rafsanjani has on two occasions since 1993 said he saw no difficulty in restoring relations with the United States 'if our assets [frozen by President Carter] are released, then we can begin thinking about future relations' (*Kayhan Havai*, 2 June 1993: 31).

As a further step towards improving relations with America, the Iranians invited a group of leading American journalists and editors to visit Iran in July 1994 to counter, in the words of Rafsanjani, 'the many lies said about Iran in the United States' (*Kayhan Havai*, 15 June 1994: 25). It is interesting to note that in 1994 the United States became Iran's third trade partner, surpassing Italy and France (*Kayhan Havai*, 3 August 1994: 32). Clearly, Iran is interested in normalising its relations with America, as it seems concerned about Clinton's 'dual containment' policy, with Israel adding its influential voice to argue that Islamic fundamentalism is now a world threat, so as to justify its claim to be protecting the Middle East against it.

Conclusion

Iran's foreign policy since the Gulf War has been a mixture of setbacks and relative successes. The Iraqi invasion of Kuwait was a blessing in disguise for Iran, as it forced Saddam Hussein to accept Tehran's terms for a peace treaty. It also improved Iran's image abroad and especially among its Gulf Arab neighbours. However, Iran failed to persuade the Gulf States to form some kind of regional security arrangements comprising regional states only, without the participation of foreign powers, that is, the United States. Following the security arrangements signed between Kuwait and the United States and Bahrain and the United States, it became obvious to the Iranian government that the Arabs would prefer to keep Iran at arm's length.

Similarly, Iran's foreign policy towards the Central Asian republics has been a mixture of disappointments and successes. In its effort to influence the politics of these republics, it has run into stiff competition from Saudi Arabia, Pakistan, and especially Turkey. It has become evident to, and accepted by, the Iranian leadership that the republics place much greater importance on economic co-operation with Iran than on ideological (Islamic) ties. Hence the many economic agreements signed between Tehran and the republics.

Perhaps a great concern to the Iranian foreign policy-makers is that the 'good will' (George Bush's words) that was generated between

Tehran and Washington at the very beginning of this decade enjoyed only a short life. The old hostility now seems to have been rekindled under the Clinton administration, which hopes that, by 'containing' Iran, the Islamic regime will implode. However, should that policy fail, it is not altogether unreasonable to think that the US might take military action against Iran by 'finding' (or, as critics of the US would say, 'manufacturing') some kind of 'compelling evidence' of Iran's involvement in international terrorism or of its developing a nuclear capability. Although US military action against Iran is unlikely at the present time, nonetheless Iran feels apprehensive about the US policy towards it.

Notes

1. This is an updated version of an article by the same name published in the *Australian Journal of International Affairs* (*AJIA*), (48 (2): 267–80). The present version is published with the permission of the *AJIA*.
2. This author has photocopies of the letters referred to here.
3. 'MOU [Memorandum of Understanding] on Musa'. It is worth noting here how some Middle East experts like Daniel Pipes and Patrick Glawson distort the facts. In 'Ambitious Iran, Troubled Neighbours', they say that in April 1992 Tehran 'expelled several hundred residents' from Abu Musa, whereas in fact Iran 'prevented' the entry of non-residents of Abu Musa. The authors also say that in September 1991 Iran 'declared sovereignty' over three islands; in fact Iran's sovereignty over these islands was established in 1971.
4. Abu Musa Island is jointly ruled by Iran and Sharjah under the 1971 agreement. See the excerpts from the agreement in *Kayhan Havai*, 1 June 1994: 30.
5. The figure of 60 per cent for Iran's military losses during the Iran–Iraq War cited in the text is attributed to Barry Rosen, of Brooklyn College, in an interview with the Voice of America.
6. See also by the same author (1993), 'Iraq, Iran and the West's Policy of Demonisation', *Middle East International* 452: 16–17.
7. For an analysis of Iran's social, economic and military situation after the end of the Iran–Iraq War, see in the said newspaper

Rafsanjani's Friday's sermon. According to him, when the guns of war were silenced, more than half the country's production capacity – that is factories, power stations and power lines, ports, airports, oil installations, and so forth – was destroyed. As were ten cities and 20,000 villages. The cost of reconstruction is estimated at $1,000 billion.

References

Anthony, John Duke (1993). 'Iran in GCC dynamics'. *Middle East Policy*, 11 (3): 107–20.

Atkeson, Edward B. (1993). 'The Middle East. A dynamic military net assessment for the 1990s'. *The Washington Quarterly*, 16 (2): 115–33.

Chomsky, Noam (1993). 'The Mideast, fundamentalism, terrorism, and US foreign policy'. *Z Magazine*, 6 (5): 1–16.

Dorsey, James (1993a). 'Iran and Uzbekistan'. *Middle East International*, 449: 15.

—— (1993b). 'The growing entente between Armenia and Iran'. *Middle East International*, 439: 17–18.

Economist (29 May 1993): 40.

FBIS/NES (21 November 1990). 'Kuwait Foreign Minister meets Hashemi Rafsanjani': 59.

Financial Times (7 February 1991): 2.

Foreign Report (1996). 2396: 1.

Green, Jerrold D. (1993). 'Iran's foreign policy. Between enmity and conciliation'. *Current History*, 92 (570): 12–16.

Hunter, Shireen (1992a). *Iran After Khomeini*. New York: Praeger.

—— (1992b). 'The Bush–Baker legacy: Iraq, Iran and the Gulf'. *Middle East International*, 439: 16–17.

Hussein, Seyyed Rifaat (1992). 'The political economy of Pakistan's relations with Central Asia with special reference to the ECO'. *The Iranian Journal of International Affairs*, 4 (3–4): 628–42.

Iranian Journal of International Affairs (1991). 3 (1) (Spring): 2–5.

Iran News (1996). 9 March: 3.

Jaber, Nadim (1992). 'All eyes on Clinton'. *Middle East International*, 438: 8–9.

Kayhan Havai: 12 May 1993; 19 May 1993; 2 June 1993; 2 June 1993; 16 June 1993; 23 June 1993; 7 July 1993; 1 June 1994; 15 June 1994; 3 August 1994; 3 August 1994 and 10 August 1994, President Rafsanjani's Friday prayer sermon: 'Reconstruction of war devastated areas without foreign assistance shows Iran's [technical] power'.

Lake, Anthony (1994). 'Confronting backlash states'. *Foreign Affairs*, 73 (2): 45–66.

Law, John (1993). 'Martin Indyk lays out the Clinton approach'. *Middle East International*, 452 (11 June): 4.

Malek, Mohammad H. (1991). 'Iran after Khomeni: perpetual crisis or opportunity'. *Conflict Studies*, 237: 17.

Middle East Insight (1995). 11 (5): 14.

Mojtahed-Zadeh, Pirouz (1992). 'Political geography and history of island of Abu Musa'. *The Iranian Journal of International Affairs*, 4 (3–4): 485–500.

Parsons, Anthony (1993). 'Iraq, the US and the UN, the unanswered questions'. *Middle East International*, 443: 16.

Pipes, Daniel (1994). 'Symposium of dual containment. US policy toward Iran and Iraq'. *Middle East Policy*, 3 (1): 1–26.

Pipes, Daniel and Glawson, Patrick (1993). 'Ambitious Iran, troubled neighbours'. *Foreign Affairs*, 72 (1): 124–41.

Roberson, B. A. (1994). 'Islam and Europe, an enigma or a myth?'. *Middle East Journal*, 48 (2): 288–308.

Saikal, Amin (1992). 'The United States and Persian Gulf security'. *World Policy Journal*, 11: 117.

Shahak, Israel (1993). 'How Israel's strategy favours Iraq over Iran'. *Middle East International*, 446 (19 March): 19–20.

Sick, Gary (1993). 'The two faces of Iran, Rafsanjani's moderation and Mullah's holy terror'. *The Guardian Weekly*, 9 May 1993: 18–19.

The Age (19 April 1993).

Walker, Martin (1993). 'Clinton refines policy on Iran and Islam'. *The Age* (20 January).

– 10 –

Turkey: From Total War to Civil War?

Paul J. White

Ever since its foundation in 1923, the modern Turkish state has always been hostile to any notion of Kurdish ethnic or national particularism. The infant Turkish Republic declared unequivocally: 'There are no Kurds in Turkey, but mountain Turks, and each person who lives within the borders of Turkey is considered a Turk' (Özoğlu, 1993: 115).[1] (Today Kurds make up roughly 12 million of Turkey's overall population of around 60 million.)

Previously, under the Ottoman Empire, the situation had been different. Both the Turks and the Kurds took their identity, overwhelmingly, from their religion – orthodox Sunni Islam. Each group showed allegiance to the Ottoman Sultan, who was, conveniently, also the Caliph, or leader of all the Sunni Muslims. The word 'Türk' was considered an insult in Ottoman times – denoting a half-wild, thoroughly rural person. The Kurds had no distinct national identity then either, although works such as Ahmet Xani's seventeenth-century epic poem *Mem-u Zîn* are evidence of awareness of ethnic difference from at least this time – at least among élite layers of Kurds.

Turkey today presents a starkly different picture. While armed nationalist conflicts in other parts of the world (Ireland, Israel/Palestine) are supposedly giving way, at least temporarily, to political solutions, the Kurdish problem in Turkey is going from bad to extremely worse. A sharp polarisation between Turks and Kurds is under way throughout Turkey, as Kurdish nationalist guerillas fight to carve an independent Kurdistan out of eastern and south-eastern Anatolia. The guerilla war alone has taken thousands of lives. This conflict is now supplemented by anti-Kurdish urban death squads and openly anti-Kurdish demonstrations by Turkey's armed forces. Turks and Kurds are far from any political solution.

This chapter begins by examining the origins, founding strategy and aims of the principal Kurdish nationalist organisation in Turkey today, the Partiya Karkerên Kurdistan (PKK – Kurdistan Workers' Party), and recent Turkish state attitudes towards Kurds and the PKK. The different avenues presented by circumstances for 'resolving' the PKK insurgency are investigated, against the background of events over the past four years: popular Kurdish uprisings, proposed ceasefires and the more recent drift towards total war on both sides. Nevertheless, it is argued that a 'political settlement' of the type currently being attempted between the PLO and Israel and the IRA and Britain plus the Irish Republic is highly unlikely in the short term. The more likely outcome is a descent into a full-blooded ethnic civil war between Turks and Kurds.

The chapter demonstrates how the inability of the nationalist Turkish polity to accommodate Kurdish nationalism led to a wide-scale, spontaneous upsurge of militant Kurdish nationalism, which connected with the emerging PKK insurgency. Nationalism, it is further argued, has not served the Kurds well, however. As both the guerilla and civilian 'mass action' wings of Kurdish nationalism in Turkey have blossomed, timid cultural and political reforms have been withdrawn by the Turkish state and military pressures on guerillas and civilian nationalists alike have intensified. This increasingly strident state repression pushed the Kurdish population even closer to the militant Kurdish nationalist camp, and produced a deepening spiral of violence and devastation. Most worrying of all, a dangerous polarisation of Turks and Kurds has emerged throughout Turkey. The result of this extreme ethnic polarisation may well be a full-blooded civil war between the two communities. This, if it occurs, will surely be the final grim proof of the common failure of nationalism on both sides.

Emergence of the Partiya Karkerên Kurdistan

Kurdish nationalist organisation in Turkey is a very straightforward matter today. If a Kurdish nationalist group is not connected with the PKK, it is of no consequence. The PKK's major (and only serious) political rival in Turkish Kurdistan has been the Partiya Sosyalist a Kurdistan (PSK). Originally known as the Socialist Party of Kurdistan of Turkey (Partiya Sosyalist a Kurdistana Tirkiyê – PSKT – in Kurdish), this organisation was formed in complete secrecy in 1974. The party is led from exile in Sweden by Kemal Burkay (More, 1984: 70; Gunter, 1988: 394; Heinrich, 1989: 33). Armed clashes occurred between Burkay's organisation and the PKK in 1975 and 1980. Naturally, the PSK blames the PKK entirely for these, and the death of a PSKT militant, Mustafa Camlibel, in one of the clashes. The PSKT/PSK has even gone as far as accusing the PKK of being infiltrated (and, by implication, directed) by Turkish secret police (More, 1984: 185).

At its Third Congress in October 1992, the PSKT reorganised itself under a new name – the Partiya Sosyalist a Kurdistan. In recent years, however, the organisation has been completely marginalised by the increasingly successful PKK, to the point where there must be serious doubt that the PSK continues to function inside Turkey. An examination of the present-day Kurdish nationalist movement in Turkey must therefore concentrate upon the PKK and its fronts and satellites.

The initial nucleus of what eventually became the PKK grew out of a 'political–ideological current' whose members included Kemal Pir (More, 1984: 185; Heinrich, 1989: 42–3). By about 1974, this current was distributing leaflets. Over the next four years it evolved into a political party – the PKK was formed in November 1978. The PKK claims to be Marxist and Leninist, but its ideology, strategy and tactics are a mixture of Stalinism and nationalism. The organisation consciously fosters a Stalin-like personality cult around its leader, Abdullah Öcalan.

The main difference in practice between the PKK and other Kurdish nationalists in Turkey has been its attitude to the use of political violence. In a 1977 document written in preparation for the PKK's founding, it calls for the 'persistent mobilising of a broad force', to force revolutionary change, since the 'indispensable method of struggle is based on extensive violence' (More, 1984: 188).[2] In the party's founding manifesto the following year, it envisaged a very Guevarist or even Maoist-sounding strategy of long-term 'people's struggle'. The first task of this clandestine guerilla network is to smash 'the network of agents and secret service organisations by a pitiless struggle' (Heinrich, 1989: 44).

The party has its own army, the ARGK (People's Liberation Army of Kurdistan), as well as being the leading element in a broader political front, the ERNK (National Liberation Front of Kurdistan) (Heinrich, 1989: 43–4). The PKK has used violence against the Turkish right wing and the state apparatus, but also against 'feudal' Kurds (More, 1984: 188; Van Bruinessen, 1988: 40ff). The PKK's guerilla war against the Turkish state began on 15 August 1984, and has continued up to the present. Then, as now, actions have been mostly classical guerilla hit-and-run actions. The guerilla war has brought the PKK considerable support from Turkish Kurds – including Turkish Kurds exiled in Europe (Van Bruinessen, 1988: 41).[3] The PKK has also gained considerable notoriety for its armed clashes with other Kurdish nationalist organisations and Turkish leftist groups, and even its alleged assassinations of PKK dissidents and ex-members,[4] not to mention its killing of many civilians.[5]

The PKK was hit particularly hard by the military repression following the September 1980 military coup in Turkey. For some time the activities of the PKK were severely curtailed (More, 1984: 188). By the late 1980s, however, a PKK resurgence occurred. PKK military successes enhanced its reputation, as did its ability to support militarily the string of spontaneous uprisings that swept Turkish Kurdistan in March/April 1990.

The party has declared its opposition to all the mainstream Turkish parties of the Right and of the Left (such as the Communist Party), which refuse to support Kurdish independence. It has also denounced Kurdish 'reformist nationalist' organisations, which it accuses of being based on feudal and bourgeois pro-imperialist elements (More, 1984: 190–1). The PKK says that it can only work with 'genuine Marxist-Leninists'. To this end, it has concluded working relationships with at least some Turkish far-left organisations such as the small Devrimci Birlik group (More, 1984: 189–92).[6]

The PKK has always been motivated by extreme Kurdish nationalism. Thus, while claiming that the PKK enjoyed 'good relations' with almost all the parties of the Turkish Left, Abdullah Öcalan also accuses the latter of 'social chauvinism' towards Kurds, adding, in an interview with the author:

> AÖ: We have developed not with the support of the Turkish Left, but by struggling against it. If we had waited for the Turkish Left, the Kurdish movement wouldn't have developed. The Turkish Left has the function of stopping the Kurdish movement, of being an obstacle to it.
>
> PW: What sort of relations do you have with the Turkish Left?
>
> AÖ: If there were no PKK, then there is no Turkish Left. But they have a lot of shortcomings. They haven't made a turn [that is, they have not changed]; that's why they are staying very small (Abdullah Öcalan, pers. comm., Lebanon, 2 July 1992).[7]

A leading cadre at what was formerly the PKK's main guerilla training school, the Mahsum Korkmaz Akademisi (Academy) in Lebanon, stated in a lecture to young trainee guerillas on 29 June 1992[8] that the Turkish Left had never wanted to change the whole system. It had always told Kurds to fix up Turkish problems first, 'then we'll give you some rights'. Unlike the Turkish Left, he claimed, the PKK was not chauvinist. It has tried several times – unsuccessfully – to work with the Turkish Left, he asserted.

The PKK has also been marked by a pragmatic, populist streak. There must therefore be considerable doubt about the PKK's ability – or desire – to follow a Marxist strategy. Öcalan is himself quite explicit that his is not a movement basing itself on any particular social class – despite the reference to workers in the PKK's name – stating to the author: 'We have got [workers'] strikes [in PKK strategy], but they are not the main action.' A few moments later, he was even more explicit:

PW: What place does specifically *class* politics play in your strategy, at this stage?

AÖ: The role of the poor peasants, the workers, the intellectuals, everybody who has got the will to develop, could shape our policy. We are not only a class movement. You should call our movement a humanitarian movement – not a class movement, but a movement for the freedom of the human being. So, you can't understand the movement, by looking at the PKK only through the spectacles of class struggle (Abdullah Öcalan, pers. comm., Lebanon, 2 July 1992).

Özal Appeals to the Kurds

Like all other Turkish Kurdish nationalists, the PKK periodically accuses the Turkish state of human rights violations. Whatever the precise facts are about these allegations, it is clear that Ankara has not been solely pursuing a policy of naked aggression against Kurdish nationalists in Turkey. During 1991, Turkey's president at the time, Turgut Özal, began to make (admittedly clumsy) overtures to the Kurdish minority. The President announced that laws outlawing the use of the spoken Kurdish language would be repealed, and he offered an amnesty to all Turkish Kurdish guerillas – including Abdullah Öcalan.

In early 1991, the then President Özal openly discussed (*Yüzyil*, 24 February 1991: 8–13)[9] transforming the Turkish Republic into a series of confederated states, on the United States model, with each state having a certain degree of latitude in local affairs. The new confederation might even have a new name (*Yüzyil*, 31 March 1991: 8–16).[10] Özal had four stages in his scheme for gradual confederation, according to *Yüzyil*: '1) Freedom for the Kurdish language, 2) Cultural rights, 3) Presidency system, 4) Federation' (Gresh, 1991; *Middle East Times*, 5–11 November 1991; *Yüzyil*, 24 February 1991: 8).

Özal confronted some considerable difficulty within his own National Motherland Party (ANAP) for these proposals (*Middle East International*, 22 March 1991: 8). Many conservative parliamentarians regarded the president's scheme as representing at least a partial unravelling of the monocultural identity first set in place as the basis of the Turkish Republic by Atatürk himself. These MPs were probably correct, although it is hard to see what else the president could have done, given the growth in Kurdish support for the PKK's guerilla war.

Kurdish nationalists generally reacted to President Özal's proposals with scepticism, pointing out, for instance, that the cultural laws passed (with considerable difficulty) by the legislature still did not permit the printing or circulation of Kurdish printed materials. A common response from Kurdish nationalists was to demand that Ankara show its sincerity by declaring a general amnesty towards all Turkey's estimated 3,000 political prisoners. The president did release many political prisoners, following the passing of limited amnesty legislation early in 1991. Most of those released, however, were politically identified with the far right; only a handful of leftists were able to take advantage of the new law, leaving very many leftists and over 1,000 Kurds imprisoned (Gresh, 1991; *Yüzyil*, 24 February 1991). As the ANAP Mayor of Hakkari, Naim Geylani, commented: 'When the PKK gets weak, we'll have an amnesty. If we have an amnesty now, they'll say we're frightened of the PKK' (*Yüzyil*, 24 February 1991).

Legislation outlawing the advocacy of Kurdish nationalism, communism or Islamic 'fundamentalism' was lifted during April 1991 – only to be immediately replaced by a new 'anti-terror' law that one specialist of the region has accused of being open to a multitude of interpretations (Gresh, 1991). Meanwhile, Ankara had made it quite clear that it still had no intention of tolerating Kurdish political opposition; armed clashes continued in the wake of these reforms (*Middle East International*, 3 May 1991: 5).[11]

This would seem to relegate talk of an imminent peaceful accord between the PKK and Ankara to the shadows for the foreseeable future, even though PKK leader Abdullah Öcalan had already shown that his party is capable of working for its goals by means other than pure and simple physical force. He revealed a 'soft' side of the PKK in interviews given during 1990. Öcalan raised the distinct possibility of his party working 'by legal means'. He claimed that – right from the beginning of the conflict – 'armed struggle has not been the only option' for the PKK. If the Turkish state 'had accorded us our freedom of organisation and our political rights, if it had renounced violence, the armed struggle would never have started', he added (*Dossier du Kurdistan*, November 1990: 9). Öcalan also called for the formation of a new, legal mass democratic party, which pushes Turkey towards democracy' (*Dossier du Kurdistan*, November 1990: 9–10).

He added that the group of ex-Sosyaldemokrat Halkçı Parti (SHP – Social Democrat People's Party) MPs behave amicably towards the PKK and say they are interested in the formation of such a broad legal party (*Dossier du Kurdistan*, November 1990: 9–10). These MPs were expelled or otherwise forced out of their party for their moderate championing of the Kurds' democratic rights. They went on to form a new party, the Halkın Emek Partisi (HEP – People's Labour Party). HEP was active in large Turkish urban centres (including Istanbul), but it was basically a Kurdish social democratic party, based in Diyarbakır. Most of HEP's rank-and-file campaigners were reportedly[12] PKK supporters – perhaps even secret PKK members. If this is true, and Öcalan's interview hints that it might be, it would show that the PKK is not an irrevocably militarist party, committed only to victory through force of arms. Further evidence of a strong connection between the PKK and HEP's successor organisation, the DEP (Democratic Party), was provided in late September 1994, when three ex-DEP deputies and the DEP vice-chairman, Remzi Kartal, attended a PKK/ERNK festival in the Netherlands (*Milliyet*, 27 September 1994).

A balanced view of the HEP and its successor organisations seems to be that it is a party increasingly dominated by PKK supporters and members, but with important sections of it quite distinct from – if not hostile to – pro-PKK politics. This was somewhat dramatically shown by a spate of resignations from the party in the wake of a pro-PKK speech by one of its MPs, Hatip Dicle, on 12 December 1993 (*Turkish Daily News*, 14 December 1993, 16 December 1993; *Le Monde*, 16 December 1993).

In the 1990 interview cited above, Öcalan seemed to be determined to convey a quite pacific view of his party, which has been accused not only of violence against the Turkish government and its supporters, but also against the Turkish Left and rival Kurdish nationalists. He stressed:

> We would like to have done with the artificial division and the confrontations between left groups. We want them to unify. Our popular movement has as its objective to bring the Turks, the Kurds and the minorities in Turkey to unify, to elaborate a common platform for all.
>
> Our movement will be a peaceful movement. It will work with peaceful methods. It will be built from the base and organised from it, contrary to all the other forces, which have always been organised from the top down to the base (*Dossier du Kurdistan*, November 1990: 9).

He stressed that this broad movement should not be 'an ideological party', but a broad movement which must take root throughout Turkey. 'The other parties, the parties of the state, cannot do this. They have capitulated before the generals' (*Dossier du Kurdistan*, November 1990: 10).

In another, earlier, interview with *Hürriyet* newspaper (*Hürriyet*, 1 April 1990) Öcalan offered on behalf of his party to lay down arms, provided the government would allow the PKK to operate legally, and declared an amnesty of political prisoners, as a sign of good faith. The PKK leader also renewed calls for ceasefire negotiations with the Turkish government. Öcalan also explained: 'There's no question of separating from Turkey. My people need Turkey: we can't split for at least 40 years . . . unity will bring strength' (*Hürriyet*, 1 April 1990).

With such a patient, hopeful perspective of co-operation with the Turkish state, it should not be surprising that the PKK would make serious attempts to achieve its strategy through offering to abandon its armed activities.

From Uprising to Ceasefire

The test of real events has demonstrated that – whatever one thinks about it – the PKK now commands real support among Turkish Kurds. An uprising (*serîhildan*) in the Turkish section of Kurdistan that began in mid-March 1990 had serious effects on many aspects of politics in Turkey as a whole, which require examination at this point, as these events illustrate the degree to which the Kurdish national movement has developed spontaneous militant forms 'from below' (*Middle East International*, 13 April 1990: 13–14; *Human Rights in Turkey*, April 1990; *Kurdistan Liberation*, April 1990: 5–6; *The Independent*, 7 April 1990; *Middle East Times*, 3–9 April 1990, 27 March 1990).

The uprising began on 12 March 1990, following a battle between PKK guerillas and Turkish troops in the district of Savur in Mardin province. Some 40 troops and 13 guerillas were killed in the clash. During the battle, helicopters bombed fields adjacent to the village (*Voice of Kurdistan*, May 1990: 19).[13]

The battle occurred at the start of Newroz, the Kurdish New Year. For Kurdish nationalists, Newroz has long been the most important annual national celebration. The coincidence of the particularly savage battle in Mardin province with Newroz sparked a regional uprising.

On 14 March 5,000 people participated in the funeral demonstration at the city of Nusaybin of Kamuran Dundar, a guerilla killed at the earlier battle of Savur. Turkish special units attacked the funeral, killing a 22-year-old man, Semsettin Cifti, and causing a stampede in which a child was trampled to death. More than seven hundred people were arrested and tens of demonstrators were wounded by troops (*Kurdistan Liberation*, April 1990: 5; *Voice of Kurdistan*, May 1990: 19–20; *Middle East Times*, 27 March 1990).

Protests were organised the following day in Nusaybin. Workers struck, shops remained shut, and students boycotted schools and colleges. Demonstrators fought security forces on the streets of Nusaybin. Mass solidarity demonstrations were quickly organised across Turkish Kurdistan and even in Turkey itself. Almost 1,000 demonstrators were arrested, including some in Ankara and Istanbul. General strike action spread throughout Mardin province (*The Independent*, 7 April 1990; *Human Rights in Turkey*, April 1990: 1–2; *Kurdistan Liberation*, April 1990: 5).

A 15,000-strong demonstration of residents in Cizre in Mardin province (a town with only 30,000 people) was attacked by army and police special units during March. Many people were wounded in apparently indiscriminate shooting by the state's forces and one demonstrator was crushed to death beneath a tank. Over eighty people were injured and hundreds arrested. State hospitals reportedly refused to treat the wounded (*Kurdistan Liberation*, April 1990: 5).

Nevertheless, the rebellion continued in Cizre and throughout the province. Other solidarity action during March 1990 included hunger strikes by 500 political prisoners in Diyarbakır (who were later joined in their strike by their relatives) and by one hundred political prisoners in Van and in Antep. University students in Dicle, Istanbul, Ankara, Eskişehir and in Erzurum also staged demonstrations (*Middle East International*, 13 April 1990; *Voice of Kurdistan*, May 1990: 20–1; *Kurdistan Liberation*, April 1990: 5).[14]

On 23 March 1990, literally thousands of people are reported to have marched in Cizre's streets chanting slogans like 'Down with Turkey!' and 'Long live free Kurdistan!' (Gunter, 1990: 90).

The mayor of Nusaybin, who had described conditions in his town and admitted that people willingly participated in protest demonstrations, was suspended from his post by President Özal. 'There didn't even have to be a leader of the protests. Everything has come to the point of explosion from the inside, because of bad policies, state terrorism, and torture', Mayor Yildirim told reporters (*Middle East International*, 13 April 1990: 13, 27 April 1990: 14; *The Independent*, 7 April 1990). One seasoned observer of the region commented: 'The escalation of demonstrations in south-east Turkey, with thousands of ordinary people taking part, suggests that the local population is gradually becoming sympathetic to Kurdish nationalist aspirations' (*Middle East Times*, 27 March 1990).

Michael Gunter cites the assessment of a Turkish intelligence report of this period: 'that the PKK was now operating in major cities, encouraging popular opposition to the state, and urging organised demonstrations, strikes, boycotts, and seizures of public buildings. A senior government official declared: "This is beginning to turn into a new and different situation"' (Gunter, 1990: 90).

Reflecting on this turn of events, a press statement issued by the Central Headquarters of the ARGK, the PKK's guerilla force, on 15 August 1991 claimed that the PKK's forces were now 'at a stage of preparing to proclaim a revolutionary government in those parts of Kurdistan, where the political and military authority of the enemy has already been broken' (*Kurdistan Report*, October 1991: 1, February 1992: 10–12).

The PKK was certainly aided by the turn of events at this point. The spontaneous nationalist uprising had provided fertile terrain for the PKK to organise in – and it was the only Kurdish nationalist organisation really in a position to do so. The mass exodus of Iraqi Kurds at the end of the 1990–91 Gulf War generated chaos along the Turkey–Iraq border, enabling the PKK to establish bases deeper inside Iraqi Kurdistan than ever before, as well as benefiting from a fortuitous enhancement of its weaponry (*Middle East International*, 26 July 1991: 24). This enabled it greatly to enhance its military operations inside Turkish Kurdistan, and made it appear as the only Kurdish nationalist organisation in Turkey with a real chance of success. This, in turn, attracted more support to the PKK than ever before (*Middle East International*, 26 July 1991: 24).[15]

By August 1991 the Turkish military had begun armed cross-border raids, to hit alleged PKK bases in Iraqi Kurdistan. The first operation, on 5–19 August 1991, ventured only a reported ten kilometres into Iraqi territory, according to one source (*Middle East International*, 30 August 1991: 12); but later operations were soon going as much as 30 kilometres inside, according to another (*Keyhan International*, 10 October 1991). The *New York Times* reported that Turkish warplanes dropped napalm on targets, 'apparently wounding several civilians' (*New York Times*, 20 October 1991). These raids continued into 1994, when they again intensified in frequency, with tens of thousands of Turkish infantrymen and F16 warplanes venturing much further than earlier.

Meanwhile, events behind the scenes militated to cut off the PKK's Iraqi bases. Independent Kurdologist Vera Beaudin Saeedpour claims: 'Months before the Persian Gulf War, Jalal Talabani and Masoud Barzani, leaders of the Iraqi Kurdistan Front, were invited to Turkey and given to understand that Ankara might not look unfavourably on a political entity for Iraqi Kurds' (Saeedpour, 13 November 1991). As part of this deal, she added: 'Iraqi Kurds would have to secure their borders against incursions of their brethren across the border'. The way was now clear for Turkish forces to raid Turkish Kurdish guerilla bases inside Iraq (Saeedpour, 13 November 1991).

President Özal visited Hakkari on 13 October 1991, conceding that there are Kurds in Turkey, and they must be respected – although stressing that there was no need to separate (BBC World Service, 13 October 1991). Irrespective of whatever the president said, however, even cultural manifestations of Kurdishness were now being clamped down on. Kurdish musical cassettes were by this point again being seized by police (*The Militant*, 6 September 1991). Even more ominously, an HEP MP, Vedat Aydın, was kidnapped by a '*kontrgerilla*' (counter-guerilla) death squad and murdered. Police opened fire at Aydın's funeral procession, killing and wounding several people. Many people were also abducted at the funeral (*The Militant*, 6 September 1991; *Kurdistan Report*, February/March 1994: 28–30).[16]

In the face of these reversals in the Kurdish national movement's fortunes, the PKK's activities intensified in severity and scope. Since August 1991, claimed the *New York Times*: 'Rebel bands now stop buses on the roads, pulling off suspected collaborators, civil servants and soldiers, usually for swift execution' (*New York Times*, 20 October 1991). The PKK's stepped-up activity began to paralyse the south-east (*New York Times*, 20 October 1991).

A December 1991 PKK firebomb attack on a Turkish department store in Istanbul was widely reported internationally. Notes found at the store identified the attackers as PKK members (*New York Times*, 26 December 1991). This incident apparently happened the day after security forces in Turkish Kurdistan machine-gunned eight Kurds to death (*New York Times*, 26 December 1991; *Herald-Sun*, 27 December 1991).

The election of a new government headed by Süleyman Demirel as Prime Minister in October 1991 raised many hopes. After all, Demirel was himself a victim of the military. (Demirel was overthrown as Prime Minister in both the 1971 and the 1980 military coups.) Şırnak residents had welcomed the new PM with shouts in Kurdish of 'Long live Demirel' (*'Bijî Demirel!'*), when he visited there in 1991 (*Turkish Probe*, 27 March 1992; *In These Times*, 5–11 February 1992). Hope was further encouraged by one of Demirel's first statements as Prime Minister. Speaking in Diyarbakır in January 1992, he told reporters: 'Turkey has recognised the reality of the Kurds' (*New York Times*, 26 December 1991). Demirel's Justice Minister, Suat Bilge, went even further, promising that 'Turkey will be number one among the countries that have no human rights problems . . . we are about to become a totally clean human rights champion and others will be lagging behind' (*Candle*, December 1992: 1).

Demirel promised to repeal repressive laws, to improve the human rights situation for Kurds. These hopes were soon dashed, however, as security forces continued killing Kurds in Turkish Kurdistan, the PKK retaliated, and Turkish death squads began operating systematically. Demirel was simply not willing (or not able) to attempt to pull the military into line (*In These Times*, 5–11 February 1992).

As the Kurdish death toll mounted, at least one Kurd a day was killed by police or death squads in Turkey, according to Kurdish scholar Cemsid Bender. In the first four months of 1992 alone, he claimed, there were 225 assassinations of Kurds (*Crescent International*, 1–15 February 1992).[17] Yet, even now, mass Kurdish unrest still failed to reach the proportions of the new, sustained popular uprising for which Abdullah Öcalan called, to be launched at Newroz 1992 (21 March). In comparative terms, the nationalist movement was at a lower level than it had been 12 months earlier.

In spite of this, the PKK was still able to wreak much damage on the Turkish state and economy in south-east Anatolia. Turkey does not have very many high-grade petroleum deposits – but what it does have are important to its under-developed economy. In 1992 the PKK was able to damage this. Several PKK attacks on oil installations and vehicles during 1992 were successful enough to threaten a complete halt to the operations of the oil industry in Turkey's Kurdish region (*Middle East Times*, 14–20 April 1992).

Such PKK military successes were not without their cost, however, as the state's measures against its Kurdish citizens multiplied. A statement on 3 March by the HEP Chairperson for the main Kurdish city of Diyarbakır, Hüseyin Turhallı, claimed that the Turkish state was escalating its war against Kurdish civilians, on the pretext of combating the PKK's guerillas. As the government 'declared war' on the PKK, he asserted, it also: 'bombed all the mountainsides of Tunceli, Kulp, Muş, Bingöl, Gabar, Cudi, Herekol and Namaz [Kurdish population centres] using military aircraft and helicopters. According to official announcements between 500 and 700 people were killed as a result of these bombardments' (Turhallı, 1992).

In the week preceding Newroz 1992, Prime Minister Demirel promised in media broadcasts: 'The Kurdish community would celebrate this year's festival in freedom' (Helsinki Watch, July 1992). But, even as the broadcasts were occurring, his government was ordering increased troop concentrations in Kurdistan, for a 'Spring Operation' against Kurdish nationalists. President Turgut Özal declared in late January that the 'armed forces with super power will go to the [southeast] region next term. This will be an extraordinary power. These forces will not let the bandits live there . . . We have to remove the roots of all these events. This is the solution' (Helsinki Watch, July 1992).[18]

Clearly, the state did not wish to see a recurrence of the 1991 Newroz – especially since PKK leader Abdullah Öcalan had called for Newroz celebrants 'to join in mass uprisings throughout the country as of March 21' (*The Militant*, 1 May 1992).[19] The PKK's popular political front, the ERNK, later denied that this was a call to a military offensive, but, by implication, merely a political assault through mass demonstrations and the like. As proof, the ERNK statement asserted that there had, in fact, been no military attack on the Turkish state by the PKK's forces (ERNK European Spokesperson, *Press Statement*, 23 March 1992).

In the early hours of 21 March, Newroz celebrations began throughout Kurdistan. Diyarbakır, Cizre and Siirt in particular were centres for large celebrations. Kurds in Istanbul, Ankara, Izmir and Adana celebrated as well. In both Turkish Kurdistan and in western Turkey very many Kurds were killed or injured by police and security forces. Many more were summarily arrested – including those in western Turkey (Helsinki Watch, July 1992, *passim*). Many houses and shops were set on fire in several towns in Kurdistan, and much of Cizre was ablaze for several days.

Turkish authorities claimed that troops were forced to shoot when attacked by armed demonstrators. However, only three fatalities were reported by the government among their own forces. The report of an investigative team despatched to Turkey by the United States-based human rights monitors, Helsinki Watch, could find no evidence of provocative or illegal acts, not even firing on Turkish security forces, by demonstrators (Helsinki Watch, July 1992: 11).[20]

Citing the events of Newroz 1992 as proof that the 'Demirel-Inönü government' was simply a civilised front for 'the special military chamber and the army', which was really in charge of Kurdish policy, the PKK's European popular political front's spokesperson announced on 23 March 1992 that, as a result, there was 'absolutely no other alternative but to fight'. He also outlined the PKK's ambitious strategy and goals at the time. Under the PKK's leadership, he promised, 'the dimensions of mass popular uprising will expand to the utmost degree' (ERNK European Spokesperson, *Press Statement*, 23 March 1992).

The state's offensive that began on Newroz continued over the following months, however (Helsinki Watch, July 1992: 11). Most notable was a Turkish military assault on the Kurdish city of Şırnak, beginning on 18 August 1992. The authorities claimed that the PKK had occupied the city. While this appears far-fetched – it was simply not within the PKK's capacity to do this – it does seem that the PKK did attack buildings in the city from outside the city itself. There is general agreement among Western observers, however, that the Turkish army, not the PKK, was responsible for the virtual destruction of the city (*Middle East International*, 11 September 1992: 14–15; *Middle East Times*, 8–14 September 1992).[21]

Şırnak was reduced to little more than rubble. A twenty-two-hour artillery barrage, followed by soldiers setting alight whatever was left, forced its population of 25,000 to evacuate the town (*Middle East Times*, 8–14 September 1992; *Middle East International*, 11 September 1992; *New York Times*, 30 March 1992; ERNK Statement, n.d).

PKK attacks also continued throughout the south-east, as well as in western Turkey's large cities. A Western reporter who visited the PKK's main bases in north-eastern Iraq near the Iranian border reported them planning further battles, and said 'they appeared well-fed, well-armed and ready to fight' (*Middle East International*, 17 April 1992).[22] However, perhaps hundreds of PKK guerillas and Iraqi Kurdish civilians were killed when the next Turkish incursion into Iraqi Kurdistan began on 4 October. The Turkish military's anti-PKK assault in Iraqi Kurdistan was joined by *peshmerga* guerillas of the Kurdish Democratic Party of Iraq and the Patriotic Union of Kurdistan (PUK), who accused the PKK of helping Saddam Hussein's Government to enforce an economic blockade of Iraqi Kurdistan (*Middle East International*, 7 August 1992: 11, 19).[23]

Bombing raids into Iraqi Kurdistan by Turkish warplanes also began again immediately after Newroz 1992 (*New York Times*, 30 March 1992; *Middle East International*, 17 April 1992: 8).[24] The Turkish government sent at least 20,000 troops, backed by tanks and armoured personnel carriers, into northern Iraq (*Financial Times*, 29 October 1992). By the end of November, Iraqi Kurds and Turkish military detachments had reportedly succeeded in crushing PKK forces in Iraq. Both the Iranian and Syrian governments allegedly mobilised troops to close their borders, in the hope of preventing PKK guerillas from fleeing into their territory (*New York Times*, 24 November 1992).

Back in Turkey, the slaughter continued on both sides. By the start of October 1992 the death toll in the Kurdish war had reached an estimated 5,000 civilians, guerillas and Turkish military personnel (*Middle East Times*, 10–16 November 1992), As the casualties stacked up, Turkey noticeably polarised. The editor of *Milliyet* noted: 'Funeral ceremonies of servicemen killed by the guerillas are turning into manifestations [demonstrations] against the PKK and Kurdish militants. In some provinces the backlash is, for the time being, limited to Turks refusing to serve or to talk to ethnic Kurds' (*Middle East Times*, 8–14 September 1992).

In Turkish Kurdistan, however, the mood only hardened:

> But much has changed among the Kurds in recent years. There is a strong sense of national identity that supports demands for greater autonomy and cultural rights. Their determination may cost them dear, but with the economy of the south-east in tatters and the youth thoroughly alienated, some feel they have little to lose (*Middle East International*, 9 October 1992).

Nevertheless, there are signs that something that should have always been apparent to the PKK – that it could not hope to win a guerilla war against the vastly larger and more sophisticated Turkish military – began to dawn on it at about this time.

Ceasefire

It was noted above that Öcalan went on record at least as early as 1990, as being possibly supportive of a legal Kurdish political party (*Dossier du Kurdistan*, November 1990: 9). And, during the previous Newroz bloodlettings, of course, Abdullah Öcalan had declared that the PKK did not want war, but that it was forced on to this course by its enemy. In a war, such remarks are too easily disregarded as political man-oeuvring, designed only to apportion blame for casualties to one's opponent. The first serious indication of a more pacific alternative in the mind of the PKK was a statement issued by the latter's popular political wing on 4 March 1993. The 4 March 1993 ERNK statement was notable for its direction to PKK supporters 'To take steps to secure a ceasefire between the parties with a view to holding a referendum so that the Kurdish people can freely express their wishes' (Kurdistan Information Centre, 4 March 1993).

The immediate political background for this declaration was a meeting between Öcalan and the Iraqi PUK leader Jalal Talabani in late February 1993. This produced a proposal from Öcalan for a peace deal between the PKK and Turkish authorities, which Talabani was asked to convey to the latter. Several factors probably contributed to this momentous step, but a key one must have been the growing *rapprochement* between Syria (the PKK's best protector in the past) and Turkey. The PKK was finally forced out of its training camp in the Bekaa Valley in September 1992, for instance. Most significant, however, was the deadly toll of the guerilla war on the PKK itself: 'Above all, it has not been a good year for the PKK inside Turkey or contiguous areas inside northern Iraq, where it once had major training camps for an army variously estimated at between 5,000 and

15,000 guerillas' (*Middle East International*, 19 March 1993: 10–11).

Despite almost 100 deaths in Newroz 1992, the much-vaunted Botan–Behdinan liberated area in Turkish Kurdistan failed to take shape. When interviewed by this author at the PKK's training camp in Lebanon's Bekaa Valley on 2 July 1992, it is instructive that Öcalan was noticeably vague on this question. The following exchange took place:

> PW: Does your organisation have any liberated zones in Turkey-Kurdistan? What's life like in them? What social relations predominate?
>
> AÖ: There are areas where our control has been developed, and the people there have respect for our decisions. We could say that people take our word into account, more than they take the word of the Turkish government. The people see our authority and they have respect for the decisions we take. We could say that in Kurdistan the control is fifty-fifty. In some areas we have finished the political, military and social control of the enemy, or minimised it.

Unfortunately for the PKK, however, the Turkish authorities were still not interested in a political solution to the Kurdish war while the PKK still retained significant striking power. Instead, the government intensified its military attacks, by land and air, including deep, renewed pushes against alleged PKK bases in Iraqi Kurdistan. By October 1993 the PKK was clearly on the defensive (*Middle East International*, 19 March 1993: 10–11).

The PKK unilaterally declared a ceasefire on 17 March 1993, on the eve of the annual Newroz bloodshed. This probably accounts for the fact that Newroz passed with only 'one boy killed, a handful of people wounded and some scores of arrests', compared to the ninety-four deaths in 1992. This seems to indicate both that the PKK's militant political intervention into the previous year's Newroz was a factor in the 1992 casualties, and that its political authority was such in Turkish Kurdistan that it could create the opposite result if it wished, by ordering its supporters to exercise political self-restraint. As well, there was also 'an element of repression fatigue among the Kurdish populace that could have been a factor influencing Öcalan's decision' (*Middle East International*, 2 April 1993: 10).

Whatever its immediate cause, however, Öcalan's proposal contained a radical political departure for the PKK:

> Öcalan strongly implied that if his ceasefire initiative drew signals that Ankara was ready to talk about a political settlement of the Kurdish

problem, the truce could be quietly extended indefinitely. Most importantly of all, he signalled clearly that the PKK was now willing to envisage the future of the Kurds of Turkey being settled within the framework and borders of a unified, democratic Turkish republic, effectively laying aside (though not formally renouncing) a key element of the PKK's ideology – the demand for an independent state embracing the whole of Kurdistan (*Middle East International*, 2 April 1993: 10).

The ceasefire announcement, as one observer put it, 'was unilateral and unhedged by conditions, save that the PKK would defend itself if it came under attack' (*Middle East International*, 2 April 1993: 10).[25] 'Öcalan called on the Kurds of Turkey to celebrate Newroz peacefully and to avoid provocations which the security forces might seize upon. And that, by and large, was the way it turned out' (*Middle East International*, 2 April 1993: 10).

On 20 March 1993 Abdullah Öcalan met with Kemal Burkay of the PSK in Damascus. They issued a statement calling for all 'Kurdish patriots' to improve their relationship and to work together for the sake of Kurdistan. Öcalan and Burkay agreed to fight together for a 'democratic federation' in Turkey, as the only solution to the Kurdish problem. They also called for a further meeting in mid-April of several diverse Kurdish nationalist groups, around these same aims (*Nokta*, 3–9 July 1994). Such a 'broad-minded' attitude was a new departure, especially for the PKK, since both parties had a previous history of sectarian hostility towards each other. It was especially noteworthy with relation to the PKK, given the latter's record of violence towards political rivals.[26]

Originally intended to run from 20 March 1993 to 15 April 1983, the ceasefire was extended 'indefinitely' on 16 April, after it failed to elicit a positive response from Turkish authorities (*Kurdistan Report*, April/May 1993, back cover).

In an unusual display of Kurdish nationalist unity that must have been quite difficult to cobble together – and is indicative, it might be argued, of the pressures the PKK was suffering – the press conference called to announce the indefinite ceasefire brought together on the same platform: PKK General Secretary Abdullah Öcalan; PUK leader Jalal Talabani; PSK General Secretary Kemal Burkay; the leader of the small Kurdistan Democratic Party – Hevgirtin – and the HEP leader Ahmet Türk (*Kurdistan Report*, April/May 1993, back cover).[27]

Total War

The Turkish government ignored the PKK's ceasefire, despite the ceasefire being extended by the PKK, in the hope of eliciting a favourable response.[28]

The statement by the PKK and allied groups formally announcing the end of the ceasefire on 8 June 1993 demanded that the authorities abolish the state of emergency in Turkish Kurdistan, stop torture and military attacks on Kurds, release detainees and recognise the Kurdish identity. 'Then alone can we talk about the ceasefire continuing', the statement said (Kurdistan Information Centre, n.d. [1993]). This declaration added: 'War is the only means by which we can liberate ourselves from this bloody dictatorship which intends our total destruction. . . . In 1993 the war will intensify to an unimaginable extent. . . . The PKK has decided that this year all means will be used to hit those economic targets that enrich the Turkish state.' Turkey's tourist industry would be especially targeted for violent attacks, the statement concluded (Kurdistan Information Centre, n.d. [1993]).[29] Öcalan commented a few days later that thousands of people ('maybe 15,000 to 20,000') could die in the renewed conflict (Öcalan, 12 June 1993). The PKK's most senior military commander, Cemil Bayık, explained the following day that the PKK's martial escalation was designed to force Ankara to the conference table (*Turkish Daily News*, 10 June 1993).

Declaring on 24 June 1993 that the government 'will not take the terrorists and blackmailers as interlocutors', however, Turkey's then Foreign Minister, Hikmet Çetin, expressed the Turkish state's continued refusal to deal with the PKK nationalists politically. Instead, the authorities' offensive against the Kurds of Turkey became more intense than ever before in history. A policy of 'total war' was declared against the PKK. This consisted of far more than purely 'military' measures. Thus, the government and the military conferred with the mainstream media, to secure their co-operation in what was termed a 'psychological war' against the Kurdish nationalists (*Turkish Daily News*, 12 July 1993; *Turkish Probe*, 24 August 1993). Leftist and pro-Kurdish publications that worked against the grain of this campaign were once again crushed; their editors were jailed and the publications banned (US State Department, 1994). All expressions of Kurdishness – even singing Kurdish songs at weddings – were again physically punished by the authorities (*Turkish Probe*, 27 July 1993).

For a growing section of the powerful Turkish military hierarchy, however, even these extraordinary measures were inadequate. By mid-1993, a clear trend surfaced within the military establishment that demanded total control of the Kurdish war.[30] In early July 1993, General Doğan Güreş, then the supreme military figure in Turkey, warned openly of martial law throughout Turkey by the end of the 1994 Turkish winter, if the PKK insurgency were not crushed by then (*Turkish Probe*, 13 July 1993). This and other statements by leading military figures – plus the sheer intractability of the situation for Ankara – seemed to do the trick. By the end of July 1993 Prime Minister Çiller was reported to have 'cleared the way fully for military-backed policies to "solve" the regional issue which the government insists on not calling "the Kurdish problem"' (*Turkish Probe*, 27 July 1993).[31]

The fortunes of the parliamentary voice of Kurdish nationalism in Turkey are indicative of the rapidly decaying political situation. The HEP was outlawed by Turkey's Constitutional Court in August 1993. The court alleged that the HEP advocated separatism. The ex-HEP MPs quickly formed an interim replacement organisation, the Özgür Demokrasi Partisi (Free Democracy Party – ÖZDEP), which was very soon renamed simply the Demokrasi Partisi (DP). By the end of 1993, however, the DP also found itself under investigation by the Constitutional Court. The DP was outlawed on early 16 June 1994, and a total of eight DP MPs jailed for treason – a crime carrying the death penalty in Turkey (US State Department, 1994).[32]

The HEP and its successor parties also had to contend with violent extra-legal opposition to themselves. A United States State Department document, *Country Report on Human Rights Practices, for 1993 [for Turkey]*, appears to lend some credibility to the claim of the Turkish Human Rights Association:

> that five hundred and twenty-four people were killed in 1993 by unidentified attackers mostly in the east and south-east of the country. The majority were leaders or prominent members of the Kurdish community . . . Human rights groups reported the widespread belief that at least some 'mystery killings' are carried out by a counter-guerrilla group associated with the security forces . . .
>
> In the past two years, at least fifty-four members of the DEP and its predecessor, the HEP, have been assassinated. Amnesty International (AI) states that it has received persistent and credible reports of members of security forces threatening to kill Kurdish activists.

Turkey's İnsan Hakları Derneği (Human Rights Association) asserts that unsolved political 'murders at the hands of Turkish death-squads claimed nine hundred and sixty-seven victims among the Kurdish population since the beginning of 1990 until October 1993' (İnsan

Hakları Derneği, 1993a, b).[33] In addition, the ethnic polarisation between Kurds and Turks increased, as funerals for Turkish military personnel killed in clashes with the PKK turned into anti-PKK rallies throughout the south-east, and other anti-Kurdish manifestations multiplied in central and western Turkey during 1993 (*Turkish Daily News*, 30 June 1993, 14 July 1993; US State Department, 1994).[34]

Militarily, however, the PKK/ARGK was clearly under intense attack by mid-1993, as 'additional troop, tank and armoured vehicle[s]' were deployed 'to support the existing 140,000 security forces' in Turkish Kurdistan. Turkish military forces concentrated in the three main ARGK catchment areas: 'Mt. Cudi, Gabar and Tanin Tanin where the PKK has most of its manpower . . . The second front is identified as the provinces of Bingöl, Muş and Diyarbakır. The third is the provinces of Van, Erzurum and Ağri' (*Turkish Daily News*, 19 July 1993).

As the authorities' relentless campaign continued throughout 1993 and did not stop in 1994, a new exodus began from Kurdish areas. This was of two kinds. In some cases, Kurds simply streamed out of their towns or villages owing to the heavy fighting and devastation (*Turkish Daily News*, 19 July 1993). But, increasingly, they flooded out as a result of being directly ordered out by the military. By September 1994 the Turkish military was placing these new Kurdish refugees in massive encampments – similar to what were called during the Vietnam war 'strategic hamlets'. These are conglomerations of the populations of several villages, who are relocated in an area which military authorities consider more secure. At least four mass military detention camps were established in Turkish Kurdistan for Kurds forced out of their villages by the military offensive. Camps were set up at Topçular, Damlatepe Mezra and Şırnak Darê (Akçay).[35]

Kurdish nationalist sources close to the PKK were claiming by 20 August 1993 that 25,000 Kurds had already become refugees as a result of the new military offensive in the provinces of Yuksekova and Çukurca alone. These refugees took refuge in the mountains from tank bombardments and attacks by Turkish special forces, according to the report (Agence France Presse, 20 August 1993).[36]

A great number of Kurdish refugees also took shelter in major Turkish conurbations like Diyarbakır, whose size shot up 300 per cent, reaching 900,000 by August 1993 (*Turkish Probe*, 3 August 1993).

Turkish military commanders reportedly stated in August 1993 that they would 'finish off the PKK in a year' (*Turkish Daily News*, 10 August 1993). While this has clearly not been achieved, the statement nevertheless underlines the severity and determination of the authorities' campaign.

A joint statement by Öcalan and Burkay on 30 August 1993 again called for a ceasefire and 'a political dialogue process' to commence, which could result in a political solution, through the recognition of the 'Kurdish national reality' (*Turkish Daily News*, 2 September 1993).[37] This was not to be, however. Instead, the PKK paid heavily in terms of lives lost for the unprecedented Turkish offensive. By the end of August 1993, the military was claiming 1,000 PKK fighters had been killed (*Turkish Daily News*, 27 August 1993, 2 September 1993). However the pro-nationalist Kurdish population of the Kurdish part of Turkey appears to have only been driven further into the PKK's arms as a result. As one commentator explained in August 1993: 'Even the hardline commander of Şırnak, Gen. Mete Sayar, agrees that the PKK has grown at least twofold over the past two to three years' (*Turkish Probe*, 3 August 1993).

Abdullah Öcalan's brother, Osman, himself a senior PKK/ARGK leader, commenting on the support received by the organisation in the PKK stronghold of Cizre, claimed: 'we have to thank Turkey. We won half of the town. The other half has been delivered to us on a silver platter' (*Turkish Probe*, 13 July 1993). It seems that: 'People are joining its ranks, mostly from among the unemployed, either in reaction to the absence of state services and opportunities in the region or in revenge for human rights violations' (*Turkish Probe*, 13 July 1993).[38]

According to sources like independent journalists – for example, the moderate Ismet G. Imset of the daily *Turkish Daily News* and the review *Turkish Probe* – not to mention both Turkish and international human rights bodies, the violations consist of 'raiding villages, evacuating the population and burning down their houses' (*Turkish Probe*, 3 August 1993). Şırnak, as mentioned earlier, was almost completely destroyed by bombardment in August 1992. The Institut Kurde de Paris reports that next 'Varto and Kulp were subject to a similar fate, while Lice and Silvan, victims of permanent terror, were emptied of their inhabitants'. In addition, the Institut continues, the inhabitants of the towns Yuksekova and Çukurova 'were obliged to seek refuge in the mountains to escape . . . blind bombardments' (Institut Kurde de Paris, August–September 1993: 3).[39]

The thinking behind this is obvious – to deny the guerillas any possibility of access to their local material supporters. The PKK has acknowledged the effect of this tactic, to a certain extent:

ARGK Military Council Chairman and PKK Central Committee member Cemil Bayık agrees that this will – to an extent – make life difficult for his mountain units, referred to normally as *'Savasçı'*, or fighters.

'But', he adds, 'they are so tough that they can live even without supplies, eating what the mountains have to offer and drinking melted snow in place of water' (*Turkish Probe*, 3 August 1993).

It is only natural, of course, to expect that a person in Bayık's position would try to play down the effects of his enemy's offensive. But, by any reckoning, the future is potentially ominous for Turkey's Kurds overall. In a macabre latter day replay of the Vietnam war (now complete with strategic hamlets and, some claim, even napalm), the government forces are pursuing an elusive guerilla foe. The casualties of the first ten years of an ascending spiral of violence are quite shocking; according to Agence France Presse and the *Middle East Times*, the death toll calculated by them 'from official statistics' for the period 15 August 1984 to 15 August 1994 comes to '15,000, including 3,500 civilians, and 2,500 security troops' (*Middle East Times*, 22–28 August 1993).

Neither side can win,[40] but they both are contributing to the realisation of a chilling future situation, which might well eventuate. This turn of events reaps the bitter fruits of over ten years of increasingly bloody confrontation, leading to total war on both sides, the forcible evacuation and relocation of whole communities, the sinister executions of the death squads and the consequent development of poisonous racist moods on both sides.

Such a situation is ripe for an even bloodier conclusion. The vast numbers of Kurds in the strategic hamlets and the newly swollen cities like Diyarbakır could find themselves confronted with a full-scale civil war. The PKK envisages an ever grimmer eventuality. ARGK Military Council Chairman Bayık claims that the military is consciously forcing the Kurds into large concentrations – even though it knows that the younger Kurds always escape to join the guerillas. Bayık claims the military has 'a master plan': 'To force as many as possible into enemy lines and deal with them en masse' (*Turkish Probe*, 3 August 1993).

Conclusions

In the normal course of events, the main players in a country's business sector succeed in determining the general course of its state apparatus. Turkey, however, is not a normal Western-style democratic state. Turkey is what scholars have dubbed a 'praetorian state' – that is, one in which military, para-military or semi-military forces operate independently of the civilian political apparatus. Such forces exercise their independent political power by virtue of the use of force or, sometimes, merely by the threat to use force. Typically, praetorian military classes arise when civilian political institutions are not strong enough to contain sectional interests. When competing sectional interests threaten to explode, a praetorian military intervenes violently, on behalf of the irresolute civilian political apparatus (Landau, 1974; Karakartal, 1985).

Modern Turkey has already seen no less than three clear examples of extreme 'praetorian' action – the military coups in 1960, 1971 and 1980, respectively. In the case of the 1971 coup, the military simply needed to threaten military force, in order to obtain its wishes. (The 1971 coup is known in Turkey as the 'coup by memorandum'.)

In Turkey, the armed wing of the state apparatus is regarded as the supreme guardian of society. Under the dominant Kemalist ideology (named after Kemal Atatürk), the armed wing of the state is even obligated to step in, if one section of society threatens to upset the status quo set in place in 1923 with the establishment of the Turkish Republic.

Despite the fact that Turkey has gone through a period of considerable stabilisation since the last military coup in 1980, there are familiar danger signals again reappearing. In addition to the rise of Kurdish insurgency in the countryside since 1984, Left/Right political violence has begun again. Ultra-rightist death squads are killing leftist intellectuals and journalists, leftist urban guerillas are bombing and strafing their opponents, and Kurdish guerillas are operating now in both urban and rural areas. As inflation and unemployment rise, the level of political violence increases.

Increasingly, there is discussion among students of Turkish affairs about whether there will be another coup. This misses the point – which is that the higher echelons of the military, who now own a considerable slice of Turkish industry and business, have themselves become a very central part of the political apparatus of the state, as well as remaining its physical guardians. This situation allows the military to act with considerable autonomy from the rest of the ruling political apparatus for the present. The generals are even able to resist the demands of the otherwise powerful industrialists' association TUSAID, which is agitating for political democratisation at present (as the foundation for a strong economy), instead of descending into a costly civil war (*Le Monde Diplomatique*, June 1994).

Eventually, of course, even the most praetorian state must heed the imperious exigencies of the market-place, and thus Turkey must seek to come to terms with the PKK, by seeking a political settlement. One suspects that the generals are quite aware that their war with the PKK can never be completely won, for a number of reasons – principally 'geographic' (the mountainous terrain of Turkish Kurdistan) and political–cultural (the ethnic polarisation pushes Kurds to support the PKK). The generals must know that it is impossible to continue their Kurdish war, which has cost Turkey US$25 billion since 1984 – US$6 billion of which was spent in the first five months of 1994 alone (*Le Monde Diplomatique*, June 1994).

So, in the end, Turkey's generals will have to negotiate with Kurdish nationalists. But, in a desperate attempt to prevent this, the military is determined to destroy the PKK physically. One surmises that they must reckon that they can only win from this approach, since they will at least succeed in further weakening the PKK. To the military mind, the time for 'peace' talks is when your enemy is down for the count.

The great danger for Turkey's Kurds is that the impossibility of completely eliminating the PKK by military means – and the equal impossibility of the PKK's militarily defeating the Turkish state – will convince the security forces and the PKK alike to resort to increasingly desperate measures. As outrage follows outrage, the result might well be the horror of a full-blown civil war.

Acute ethnic polarisation has already been the fruit of ten years of steadily bloodier war between the PKK and the Turkish state. The upshot may well be a full-blooded civil war between the two communities (as in ex-Yugoslavia), given that the ingredients for this are fast maturing: a rising death-toll on both sides; political intransigence on at least one side and a chaotic economic situation throughout the state, especially in the insurgent sector. As usual, civilian Kurds and Turks will be the losers.

Notes

1. For a scholarly attempt to give some support to this view, see Fahrettin (1963: 6).
2. According to More (1984: 189), the PKK's founding document states: 'Against reactionary violence we propose revolutionary violence, to protect and defend the national dignity of the Kurdish people.'

3. This is also confirmed by my own interviews with Kurdish nationalists in the Middle East, Europe, Britain and Australia. The opinion that the PKK is the 'only' Kurdish group opposing the Turkish state is repeatedly heard.

4. Naturally, the PKK denies specific allegations, although in recent years it has admitted in a somewhat vague manner that it made some 'mistakes' earlier on in its relations with other political tendencies. Hugh Pope claims that 'more than a quarter' of the PKK's cadres were 'eliminated' during the 1991 Gulf War, after challenging Öcalan's refusal to consider dropping the organisation's steadfast opposition to any sort of Kurdish autonomy scheme. See *Middle East International* (5 April 1991: 6). For a critical view by rival leftists, see *International Viewpoint* (7 May 1990: 180).

5. PKK guerillas admitted this to me, when I visited their training camp in the Bekaa Valley in Lebanon, in June–July 1992. However, they also claimed: (1) that many of the alleged killings of civilians are actually carried out by Turkish army 'dirty tricks' squads, dressed like PKK guerillas; (2) that they only killed Turkish schoolteachers in Turkish Kurdistan after the latter ignored their warnings to leave; (3) that some killings of innocent civilians (for example, the entire families of a Village Guard, not just the Guard) had taken place in the past, but that these were mistakes; (4) that any PKK guerilla caught carrying out such actions would be severely punished; (5) that all PKK guerillas have the responsibility to arrest their commanders for such actions – or to shoot them, if this is not possible; and that (6) the PKK's Fourth Congress adopted the death penalty for such practices. Some ARGK commanders charged with this offence have been executed by the ARGK. The full facts in this matter are difficult to obtain, although it is clear that the PKK has killed innocent civilians.

6. For more information on the PKK's programme and its relations with other Kurdish and Turkish organisations, consult: *Partiya Karkerên Kurdistan. PKK Kürdistan Devriminin Yolu (Manifesto); Berxwedan* (Resistance) – fortnightly popular PKK newspaper; and *Serxwebûn* (Independence) – monthly PKK ideological paper. Both newspapers are written in Turkish and Kurdish and published in Germany.

7. Interview with Öcalan by the author, at the Mahsum Korkmaz Akademisi, 2 July 1992.

8. The lecturer was a member of the Camp Management Committee. The account of his remarks given here is a summary of his speech to trainee guerillas, as noted down by the present author, at the M. K. Akademisi on 29 June 1992.

9. Faced with a hostile response from sections of the Turkish power structure, Özal later denied his proposal.
10. This has been proposed by a retired Army commander. See 'Türkiye'ye yeni isim' (*Yüzyil*, 31 March 1991: 8–16).
11. The *Middle East Times* article adds that Turkish Kurdish guerillas acquired a great deal of extra weaponry from Iraqi Kurds fleeing into Turkish Kurdistan. It also reports that the PKK staged a series of attacks, following the Turkish raids, that included the execution of three ranking provincial officials in Sohal, on 28 April 1991.
12. Information given to the author in a discussion with a BBC journalist just returned from Turkish Kurdistan, 31 May 1991. The fortunes of the HEP will be covered further below.
13. The *Middle East Times* article cited here gives 13 March as the date of the uprising's beginning; I am using the date stated by PKK supporters, in the *Voice of Kurdistan* journal.
14. See also the 'Regional Review' (*Middle East Times*, 5–11 June 1990: 11), which reports on repression of a hunger strike by Kurds in Diyarbakır.
15. Levitt notes: 'A qualitative change has taken place; the PKK has now succeeded in winning itself popular support inside the towns of the south-east, like Mardin.' The *Sydney Morning Herald* (21 October 1991) concurs with this: '"A year ago they were little more than a rag-tag terrorist band", a Western diplomat said of the [Turkish] Kurds. "Now they have become a viable guerilla army."' The *New York Times* (20 October 1991) said of the PKK: 'Before the Gulf War, it was more of a nuisance than a security threat.'
16. The *Kurdistan Report* article cited here is clearly a pro-PKK commentary on these *kontrgerilla* murders. According to the US State Department, *Country Report on Human Rights Practices for 1993 [for Turkey]*:

The Human Rights Foundation of Turkey (HRF) claimed that government security forces were responsible for 91 extrajudicial killings in the first 9 months of 1993. A substantial number of 'mystery killings', in which the assailant's identity was unknown, occurred as well. Human rights groups, journalists, and other independent observers continued to allege the complicity of security forces in a number of these killings.

17. Perhaps significantly, the Kurdish journalist M. Altun was killed on 24 February 1992, after linking the supposedly Islamic

'*Hizbullah*' or '*Hizb-i-kontra*' counter-guerilla death squads with the Turkish state, as was a journalist from the weekly magazine *İkibin'e Doğru,* on 18 February 1992.

18. Doğu Perinçek (1992), at the time the president of the Socialist Party (Turkey), adds: 'On Feb. 22nd, the General Commander of military forces Mr Güreß, has given the date of the operation to the newspapers and said all the preparations will be ready by March 15th.'

19. Letter by Abdullah Öcalan to the *Turkish Daily News,* cited in *The Militant* (1 May 1992). See also: Helsinki Watch (June 1992: 2); *Kurdistan Report* (April 1992: 2).

20. Helsinki Watch added (footnote number 8: 11) that 'Helsinki Watch receives almost daily reports of violence and bloodshed in towns throughout the Turkish south-east, and on occasion the fatalities in these incidents may actually exceed the highest reported death count from any one municipality during Newroz (25 in Şırnak)'.

21. According to a press release at the time issued by British supporters of the PKK (Kurdistan Information Centre, London (1992)), *Massacre by Turkish State in City of Sirnak Continues,* 21 August 1992:

> There is not one guerilla in the city of Şırnak. This is merely an excuse to kill Kurdish civilians. An inhabitant of Şırnak managed to make a telephone call to the Human Rights Association in Diyarbakır saying that the Turkish government was using helicopters and German-made Panzers to bombard the city and destroy it. He also said[:] 'In the attack, which has now lasted more than 48 hours, more than half of the city has been destroyed. The house of the mayor, and the shop underneath are burning. There are large numbers of dead. The massacre is continuing'.

According to Amnesty International, Şırnak police had marched through the town shouting 'Blood for blood!', 'Şırnak will be the grave of the Kurds!', and 'Human rights are the enemy of the people' (*Candle,* 5 March 1992).

22. Abdullah Öcalan boasted to a reporter from a Turkish daily newspaper (*Milliyet,* 22 March 1992): 'Even if 100,000 people die this year, our movement cannot be disrupted.'

23. The KDP and the PUK are the main parties in the Iraqi Kurdistan Front mentioned earlier. The KDP and the PUK were at the time on good terms with both the Ankara and Washington govern-

ments. For accounts of the clashes in northern Iraq, see: *Middle East Times* (13–19 October 1992); *Middle East International* (23 October 1992); *Middle East Times* (10–16 November 1992). For Abdullah Öcalan's view on relations between Iraqi Kurdish nationalists and Ankara, see the extracts from a speech by him in *Kurdistan Report* (July 1992).

24. Agence France Presse stated in a dispatch from Ankara on 18 March 1992 that 'the Turkish government has reportedly carried out more than 30 air raids against PKK positions in Iraq since September 1991'.

25. In contrast, a speech by Öcalan on 16 April 1992 very clearly stated that the guerilla war would continue even if negotiations began with Turkish authorities (*Kurdistan Report*, July 1992):

> If anyone calls a halt in the name of the PKK, then he is a liar and does not belong to us. Even while political negotiations proceed the freedom march will go on. Our goal is complete independence and freedom. We will do everything to attain this goal; war is a part of this, just as truce or political negotiations. No other policy can be made in the name of the PKK.

26. When interviewed by this author on 3 June 1992, Kemal Burkay acidly denounced the PKK in very unflattering terms, using 'Marxist' language: 'The PKK is not a proletarian movement. Maybe the PKK is a movement of poor peasants, also of the lumpen proletariat in [its] majority – a kind of lumpen proletarian movement' (Burkay, pers. comm., Stockholm, 3 June 1992).

27. See *Kurdistan Report* (April/May 1993). As recently as late 1992 Talabani was being described by PKK mouthpieces as someone who had sold his country to colonialism and imperialism. See, for instance, 'Barzani and Talabani Conspiracy Unmasked', in *Kurdistan Report* (November/December 1992). These allegations are not without foundation; there is evidence of direct contact between Ankara and Iraqi Kurdish leaders going back as far as September 1988 (see the report by Y. Doğan, in *Cumhuriyet*, 16 September 1988).

28. See US State Department, *Country Report on Human Rights Practices for 1993 [for Turkey]*, which states: 'Renewed PKK violence in May ended a 2-month ceasefire declared by the PKK but never acknowledged by the Government. Violence in south-east Turkey has since reached unprecedented levels.'

29. See also: *Kurdistan Report* (October–November 1993); *Middle East Times* (6–12 July 1993); *Turkish Daily News* (10 June 1993).

30. According to one source (*Turkish Daily News*, 12 July 1993): 'Although Çiller has recently declared that she will give every kind of political support to the army's campaign, officers argue that this does not have the same meaning as "a free hand to deal with terrorism in their own way".'

31. This did not stop the proliferation of groups in or close to the military advocating extreme solutions, however. See *Turkish Daily News on Sunday* (15 August 1993) and Ismet G. Imset in *Turkish Probe* (3 August 1993), which cite an officer promoting 'using napalm on the Ararat, Tendürek, Cudi and Herekol mountains'.

32. See also: İnsan Hakları Derneği (1993a, b); Amnesty International (1994a, b); *Middle East International* (9 July 1994: 14).

33. See also: Amnesty International (1994a, b); *Middle East International* (9 July 1994: 14).

34. According to an Agence France Press report (24 July 1993), soldiers at funerals not only shouted slogans such as 'Death to the PKK!', but also 'Death to the Kurds!' and 'Down with the Kurds!'

35. *Özgür Ülke* (19 September 1994) states:

> A *vali* [provincial governor], Ünal Erkan, who visited the 2,000 villagers in the Şırnak Darê (Akçay) camp, reportedly warned them to tell any human rights investigators visiting the camp that the PKK – not the Turkish army – had burned down their villages. When some Europeans did visit the camp and one inmate stated that the army burned down his village, he was later tortured for a week, according to *Özgür Ülke*. Camp inmates were reported to be grossly underfed. Youth were reportedly forced to don military dress and go on military operations with the army, against the PKK.

36. See *Milliyet* (19 October 1994) and Reuters (7 November 1994) for more recent reports.

37. Similar sentiments were reiterated by Öcalan some eight months later, when he called for problems to be settled peacefully, in the context of a Turkish–Kurdish federation (*Middle East Times*, 25 April–1 May 1994).

38. The same article also claims that the PKK has not attracted Turkish Kurdish support 'in recent years', either owing to 'its Marxist-Leninist ideology' or because of 'its promises for an independent land'. The first of these assertions is undoubtedly true (the PKK's Stalinism has always been particularly shallow), but the second claim runs completely contrary to the reasons given to this author for joining the PKK by Kurdish youth at the Mahsum Korkmaz Academy in Lebanon in June–July 1993.

39. The Diyarbakır branch of the İnsan Hakları Derneği compiled an eight-page 'List, by Name, of Kurdish Villages Evacuated by Force and Destroyed by the Turkish Army', up until August 1993. This list is reproduced in Institut Kurde de Paris, *Information and Liaison Bulletin* (August–September 1993: 20–7).

40. General Doğan Güreş boasted that the PKK would be 'finished' by September. A journalist in the right-of-centre *L'Express International*, commenting on this boast, asked ironically 'In September, very well, but of which year?' (*L'Express International*, 23 June 1994: 10).

References

Agence France Presse (18 March 1992). Ankara.

—— (24 July 1993).

—— (20 August 1993). '*Offensive Turque: 25,000 personnes dans les montagnes, selon le Comité de Kurdistan*'.

Amnesty International (1994a). *Amnesty International Report 1994*. London.

—— (1994b). *Turkey: Security Offensive Cloaked by Information Blackout – Torture: 'Disappearance' and Extrajudicial Execution in the Southeast Province* (Special Statement, 14 January).

BBC World Service. News broadcast (13 October 1991).

Candle [Amnesty International Australia Bi-annual Supporters' Bulletin] (5 March 1992).

—— (December 1992). 'This Charade is no Game'.

Crescent International (1–15 February 1992). 'News in Brief'.

Cumhuriyet (16 September 1988).

Dossier du Kurdistan (November 1990). Interview with PKK General Secretary Abdullah Öcalan: '*Notre mouvement doit être un mouvement pacifique*'.

ERNK European Spokesperson (23 March 1992). *Press Statement*.

ERNK statement. (Undated – probably March 1992). 'They are freedom fighters, not terrorists.'

Fahrettin, Kırızoğlu M. (1963). *Kürtlerin Kökü*. Vol. I. Ankara: Ayyıldız Matbaası.

Financial Times (29 October 1992).

Gresh, Alain (1991). 'Nouvelle Donne au Proche-Orient et en Union Soviétique: La Turquie ébranlée par les mutations régionales'. *Le Monde Diplomatique*, July.

Gunter, Michael M. (1988). 'The Kurdish problem in Turkey'. In *The Middle East Journal* (Summer).

—— (1990). *The Kurds in Turkey: A Political Dilemma*. Boulder: Westview.

Heinrich, Lothar A. (1989). *Die Kurdische Nationalbewegung in der Türkei*. Hamburg: Deutsches-Orient Institut.

Helsinki Watch (1992). *Kurds Massacred: Turkish Forces Kill Scores of Peaceful Demonstrators* (June).

Herald-Sun (27 December 1991).

Human Rights in Turkey (1990). 'An 'Intifada' in Turkey?' (April).

Hürriyet (1 April 1990).

İnsan Hakları Derneği (1992). Diyarbakır branch. 'List, by name, of Kurdish villages evacuated by force and destroyed by the Turkish army'. (Up until August 1993.) Reproduced in Institut Kurde de Paris (1992). *Information and Liaison Bulletin* (August–September).

—— (no date, c. 1993a). *Balance of Turkish State Repression in Kurdistan*. Distributed by the human rights group Autonome Forum, Toronto, Canada.

—— (no date, c. 1993b). *The Attacks and Repression Against the Kurdish People Continue*. Distributed by the human rights group Autonome Forum, Toronto, Canada.

Institut Kurde de Paris (1993). *Information and Liaison Bulletin* (August–September): 'After mountain villages, the Turkish army bombards and destroys Kurdish cities'.

International Viewpoint (1990). 'Two, three, many intifadas' (7 May).

In These Times (1992). 'The "Kurdish Question" is being reformed in Turkey' (5–11 February).

Karakartal, B. (1985). 'Turkey: The Army as Guardian of the Political Order'. In C. Clapham and G. Philip (eds), *The Political Dilemmas of Military Regimes*. London and Sydney: Croom Helm.

Keyhan International (1991). 'Turkey rejects Iraqi protest over territorial infiltration' (10 October).

Kurdistan Information Centre, London (1992). *Massacre by Turkish State in City of Sirnak Continues* (21 August).

—— Leaflet (4 March 1993).

—— (No date [1993]). *Press Statement to World Public Opinion*.

Kurdistan Liberation (1990). 'Popular uprising in Kurdistan' (April).

Kurdistan Report October 1991; February 1992; April 1992; November/December 1992; April/May 1993; October/November 1993; February/March 1994.

Landau, Jacob M. (1974). *Radical Politics in Modern Turkey*. Leiden: E. J. Brill.

L'Express International (1994). 'Guerre aux Kurdes' (23 June).

Le Monde (1993). 'Le principal parti pro-Kurde radicalise sa position' (16 December).

Le Monde Diplomatique (1994). 'Guerre au Kurdistan, pousée Islamiste et crise économique. Dangereuses dérives en Turquie' (June).

Middle East International 13 April 1990; 27 April 1990; 'Furore over Ozal's decree'; 22 March 1991; 5 April 1991; 3 May 1991; 26 July 1991; 30 August 1991; 17 April 1992; 7 August 1992; 11 September 1992; 9 October 1992; 23 October 1992; 19 March 1993; 2 April 1993; 9 July 1994.

Middle East Times 27 March 1990; 3–9 April 1990; 5–11 June 1990; 5–11 November 1991; 14–20 April 1992; 8–14 September 1992; 13–19 October 1992; 10–16 November 1992; 6–12 July 1993; 25 April–1 May 1994; 22–28 August 1994.

Milliyet 22 March 1992; 27 September 1994; 19 October 1994.

More, Christiane (1984). *Les Kurdes aujourd'hui: mouvement national et partis politiques*. Paris: Éditions L'Harmattan.

New York Times 20 October 1991; 26 December 1991; 30 March 1992; 24 November 1992.

Nokta 3–9 July 1994.

Öcalan, Abdullah (1992). 'Kurdistan and the Kurdish people are not for sale! The march for freedom goes on!' *Kurdistan Report* (July).

Özgür Ülke (1994). 'Bir toplama kampı daha' ('One More Concentration Camp') (19 September).

Özoπlu, Hakan (1993). 'Winds of change: the Kurdish Workers' Party and Turkish nationhood'. *The Turkish Studies Association Bulletin* (Fall).

Partiya Karkerên Kurdistan. *Berxwedan* (Resistance) – fortnightly popular PKK paper.

—— (n.d.). *PKK Kürdistan Devriminin Yolu* (*Manifesto*).

—— *Serxwebûn* (Independence) – monthly PKK ideological paper.

Perinçek, Doπu (1992). Press release, 22 March.

Reuters. (7 November 1994 [Atrush, Iraq]).

Saeedpour, Vera Beaudin (1991). Letter to the *New York Times* (13 November).

The Independent (1990). 'Kurds "on the Point of Explosion"' (7 April).

The Militant (6 September 1991). '40,000 Kurds protest killings by Turkish police'; (1 May 1992). 'Turkish Government transforms Kurdish areas into war zones'.

Turhallı, Hüsseyin (1992). Press statement. *Appeal* (3 March).

Turkish Daily News 10 June 1993; 30 June 1993; 12 July 1993; 14 July 1993; 19 July 1993; 10 August 1993; 27 August 1993; 2 September 1993; 14 December 1993; 16 December 1993.

Turkish Daily News on Sunday (1993). PKK is finished if contained in Botan' (15 August).

Turkish Probe (27 March 1992); (13 July 1993). 'Differentiating between PKK and Kurdish issues'; (27 July 1993). 'Is the southeast lost?'; (3 August 1993). 'As the PKK grows . . . and grows'; (24 August 1993). 'Realizing the "Kurdish problem"'.

US State Department (1993). *Country Report on Human Rights Practices for 1992 [for Turkey]* (January). Washington.

—— (1994). *Country Report on Human Rights Practices for 1993 [for Turkey]* (January). Washington.

Van Bruinessen, Martin (1988). 'Between Guerilla War and Political Murder: the Workers' Party of Kurdistan'. *Middle East Report* (July–August).

Voice of Kurdistan (May 1990). 'Uprising and Newroz: the chronology of actions'.
Yüzyil (24 February 1991). 'Özal federasyon dusünüyor'.
Yüzyil (31 March 1991). 'Türkiye'ye yeni isim'.

– 11 –

The Role of the United States as an Initiator and Intermediary in the Arab–Israeli–Palestinian Peace Process: Comparing the Approaches of the Bush and Clinton Administrations

David Beirman

The September 1993 handshake on the White House lawn in Washington between Israeli Prime Minister Yitzhak Rabin and Palestine Liberation Organisation (PLO) Chairman Yasser Arafat represented a triumph of pragmatism over ideology. If we examine the major political events of the 1990s – the collapse of the Berlin Wall, the fragmentation of the Soviet empire, the denouement of apartheid and the first tentative steps towards a comprehensive reconciliation of the Arab–Israeli conflict – there is a common thread. Advocates of maximalist solutions to international conflict have failed.

Although the Clinton Administration could not claim credit for originating the Israeli–PLO agreement, there is no doubt that the Clinton administration's role will be as crucial to its ultimate implementation as was Jimmy Carter's in guaranteeing the Camp David Accords between Israel and Egypt in 1979. Attempts to resolve the Arab–Israeli–Palestinian conflict have involved many players, but the United States has been the binding element essential to all successful peace initiatives in this conflict since 1973. Both the Bush and Clinton administrations have played and are currently playing a major role in being both initiators and intermediaries in resolving the Arab–Israeli–Palestinian conflict. In the case of both administrations there have been cyclical fluctuations between the predominance of an active initiating role and a passive intermediary role.

The Palestinian Arab demand, voiced since 1932, for all Palestine, which was enshrined in the Palestine National Charter of 1964, has been eroded by the fact that the State of Israel has become an irrevocable and viable element within the Middle East. Egypt formally recognised this fact in 1979. Jordan has unofficially recognised it since 1949, and the Syrians have tacitly done so since the 1973 Yom Kippur War. The PLO leadership's *formal* advocacy of a two-state solution to the Palestinian–Israeli conflict was ratified by the Palestine National Council in Algiers in November 1988. That meeting endorsed United Nations Resolution 181 of November 1947, which called for the partition of Palestine into a Jewish and an Arab state.

It was a sobering reminder to Palestinians that their official accept-ance of this resolution was forty-one years too late, and had amounted to one of many lost opportunities to achieve Palestinian Arab sover-eignty during the twentieth century.

In December 1988, PLO Chairman Yasser Arafat responded to pressure from United States Secretary of State George Shultz and declared his acceptance of Israel's right to exist and the PLO's accept-ance of UN Resolutions 242 and 338 as the appropriate framework for peace. Additionally, Arafat stated his preparedness to renounce terrorism. Arafat's statement was made at a UN meeting in Geneva. A rider to the latter renunciation was that it would not apply to acts within Israel and Israeli–occupied territory. The significance of Arafat's statement was that it facilitated the opening of an *official* dialogue between the United States and the PLO. The final days of the Reagan administration signalled the beginning of a United States dialogue with *all parties* to the Arab-Israeli conflict.

The United States has been an active element in Middle East politics since the First World War. Woodrow Wilson's advocacy of self-determination in the 1919 Versailles Conference applied to the Middle East as much as to anywhere else. However, American advo-cacy of self-determination for Arab nationalism in the Middle East was overridden by the British and French grabs for domination over the region.

It was not until the post-Second World War era that the United States exercised a truly significant influence in shaping Middle East politics. The Truman administration favoured the immediate admis-sion of 100,000 Jewish immigrants to Palestine in the wake of the Holocaust, in defiance of the provisions of the 1939 *White Paper*. Chaim Weizmann's personal intervention with President Truman overcame the United States State Department's reluctance to back Zionist demands for a Jewish state in Palestine. The State Depart-ment's opposition to Zionism was founded on its view that United States economic interests were better served by maintaining close relations with the Arab oil-producing states with which the United

States had substantial oil interests. Truman's decision to support the 1947 partition resolution resulted from a combination of local Jewish lobbying, his personal regard for Zionist leader Chaim Weizmann and the more potent need to counter Soviet support for partition. In fact, United States and Soviet recognition of Israel in 1948 was almost simultaneous.

The Cold War was to be the most significant element guiding United States Middle East policy from 1945 to 1990. The shared Soviet and United States opposition to the Israeli, French and British actions in Sinai and Suez in 1956 resulted in the withdrawal of the British and French from the Suez Canal Zone and the Israeli forces from Sinai in 1956 and 1957. The Eisenhower administration intervened in Lebanon in 1958. The United States and the Soviets actively competed for influence in the Middle East and North Africa during the 1950s and 1960s.

Until 1967 there was relatively little direct involvement of the United States in the Arab–Israeli conflict. President John F. Kennedy was the first United States President to approve the sale of advanced weaponry to Israel. The sale of HAWK anti-aircraft missiles was approved because they were primarily a defensive weapon. Germany supplied Israel with American tanks from its own stocks. Until 1967 the Soviets were the main supplier of weaponry to the Arab states confronting Israel. Egypt and Syria were largely equipped with Soviet arms. Jordan and Lebanon were equipped with British, American and French weapons. Israel's military forces were mainly equipped with French-produced weapons and a collection of British, French and American armour.

The 1967 Six Day War heightened the Cold War element in United States policy towards the Arab–Israeli conflict. The severance of diplomatic relations with Israel by the Soviet Union and its satellites resulted in the Soviets' playing a pro-active role in support of Egypt, Syria, Iraq and the PLO. The United States under the Johnson and Nixon administrations was an active and overt supporter of Israel. The French boycott of arms sales to Israel in the wake of the Six Day War resulted in the United States' becoming the primary financial supporter and arms supplier to Israel. The United States maintained strong relations with Jordan, Iran and the Gulf States throughout the 1970s. The United States support for UN Resolution 242 enabled it to maintain relations with much of the Arab world. United States support for Jordan in its 1970 civil war against the PLO engendered hostility between the United States and the PLO.

During the 1973 Yom Kippur War, the United States was the only state to support Israel's war effort. The Soviets actively supported both

Egypt and Syria. As Israel gained the military initiative against Egypt towards the end of October 1973, Soviet threats to intervene were countered by the United States raising its state of nuclear alert. The Yom Kippur War bought the world closer to a Soviet–American nuclear confrontation than at any time since the 1962 Cuban Missile crisis.

In the wake of the 1973 Arab–Israeli War, the United States assumed the diplomatic initiative by negotiating disengagement agreements between Israel and Egypt in Sinai and Israel and Syria on the Golan Heights. Henry Kissinger's shuttle diplomacy during 1974 and 1975 under Presidents Nixon and Ford was the progenitor of larger-scale conflict-resolution methods utilised in resolving the Arab–Israeli conflict. Although Israel's territorial concessions under the disengagement agreements were relatively minor, their political import was substantial. They enhanced the influence of the United States in the region as an essential element in any peace process.

From a Cold War perspective, the Soviet Union's severance of diplomatic relations with Israel in 1967 proved to be a major miscalculation. It effectively removed the Soviets from any role in brokering an Arab–Israeli peace. The Soviets were increasingly identified with the rejectionist elements within the Arab world.

Given this position it was hardly surprising that they joined the Arab world's condemnation of Egyptian President Anwar Sadat's visit to Israel and the subsequent Camp David Accord, which involved thirteen days of Jimmy Carter's presidency. Carter was the first United States President since 1948 to advocate a solution to the Arab–Israeli conflict in which Palestinian Arab interests would play a significant part. In one of history's ironies, the Camp David Accord, so bitterly condemned by most of the Arab world and the PLO in 1979, is the model on which the peace process to which the PLO agreed in September 1993 is based.

There is another parallel between the origins of the Camp David Accord and the September 1993 autonomy process. In both cases the United States acted as an arbiter and a guarantor, but in both instances the lead-up to the agreement was achieved through backchannel diplomacy that involved some unlikely initiators. Romania's late and unlamented ex-president, Nicolai Ceausescu, played an important role in supporting the Sadat initiative. The backchannel diplomacy that led to the Israeli–PLO agreement was largely brokered by a Norwegian academic and the Norwegian Foreign Minister.

George Bush's initiation into the complexities of the Arab–Israeli conflict came during his term as United States Ambassador to the UN between March 1971 and January 1973. Bush recalled his initiation in the UN when Soviet Ambassador Yakov Malik accused the United States of taking orders from Israel in refusing to push for an immediate Israeli withdrawal from the territories Israel gained in the 1967 War. Bush further recalled what he described as 'a one-sided irresponsible UN resolution condemning Israel's attacks on Palestinian bases in Syria and Lebanon'. Bush's objection to the resolution was that it ignored the cause of those attacks, 'the murder of Israeli athletes at the Munich Olympics'. Bush vetoed the resolution on behalf of the United States in 1972.

When George Bush was appointed as Ronald Reagan's Vice-President in 1980, he once again came to face to face with the Arab–Israeli conflict in one of its more complex stages. The bilateral elements of the Camp David Accords between Israel and Egypt were implemented and Israel withdrew from the Sinai according to schedule. This proceeded despite the assassination of Anwar Sadat in October 1981 and the fact that the rejection of the accords by the PLO and most of the Arab world prevented implementation of the Palestinian autonomy elements of the accord.

Bush was involved in promoting a continuation of United States peacekeeping involvement in Lebanon following Israel's 1982 invasion of Lebanon. Bush's support for maintaining the United States presence was rejected by Reagan after 240 marines were killed in late 1983 by Shi'ite fundamentalists in a suicide raid in Beirut.

The Reagan administration's approach to resolving the Arab–Israeli conflict was to subsume Palestinian claims within a Jordanian-dominated framework. In 1988, King Hussein's renunciation of Jordan's claim to the West Bank and East Jerusalem in favour of the Palestinians and his acceptance of the PLO as the legitimate representative of the Palestinians made the United States approach a politically unsustainable foreign policy.

Israel's invasion of Lebanon in 1982 and its handling of the *intifada*, which broke out in December 1987, were subjected to intense criticism by the United States' media and public opinion – including significant elements of the American Jewish community. Relations between Israel and the Reagan administration had undergone significant strains during Reagan's second term. While Reagan and his Secretary of State George Shultz were pro-Israel, they were frustrated with Israeli Prime Minister Yitzhak Shamir's insistence on expanding West Bank settlements. The Jonathan Pollard spy scandal, in which an American Jewish naval officer was convicted of spying for Israel, concerned the United States Administration. What concerned them more than Pollard's actions was the fact that Pollard's Israeli minders were promoted. The PLO leadership and Yasser Arafat in particular were quick to act on this shift in mood, and the late-1988 PLO 'peace offensive' received a cautiously positive reception from the incoming Bush Administration when it assumed office in January 1989.

The PLO's desire to improve relations with the United States was, in part, a response to events in Eastern Europe. After Mikhail Gorbachev assumed the Soviet leadership in 1985, Soviet support for rejectionist Arab regimes and the PLO waned.

Gorbachev liberalised emigration procedures for Soviet Jews and tolerated Poland, Hungary and other Eastern European countries resuming diplomatic relations with Israel by the end of the 1980s. The Soviets themselves were on the verge of resuming relations with Israel. The Soviet Union's relaxation of restrictions against the Soviet Jewish population resulted in a massive influx of Soviet Jews to Israel. While this created problems for the Israeli economy in the short term, it greatly restored Israel's demographic balance in favour of the Jews. Gorbachev was anxious to disengage from many of the Soviet Union's foreign involvements such as Afghanistan, defuse the Cold War, and concentrate on internal reform.

The changes in Soviet policy undermined an important foundation of Arab rejectionism. The PLO leadership and the governments of countries such as Syria could no longer rely on unqualified Soviet moral, political or military support for a belligerent policy against Israel.

The first year of the Bush presidency was accompanied by an accelerating collapse of the Soviet Empire. Poland, Hungary, Romania and East Germany abandoned communism. Within the Soviet Union itself the Baltic States of Lithuania, Latvia and Estonia were the first of the Soviet republics to declare independence.

The Bush administration's response to the altered situation in the Middle East was to maintain and encourage the dialogue with the PLO during the first half of 1989. The administration also began to demand a more flexible approach to Palestinian nationalism from the Israelis. In April 1989 Israeli Prime Minister Yitzhak Shamir released Israel's peace plan. It called for elections in the West Bank and Gaza, and an implementation of autonomy for the Palestinians in the West Bank and Gaza. It excluded Palestinians from East Jerusalem from the process. Additionally, it rejected any suggestion of sovereignty for the Palestinians and advocated a continuation and expansion of Jewish settlement on the West Bank and in Gaza. The Shamir plan rejected any negotiations with the PLO, but expressed a preparedness to talk with elected Palestinian officials in the territories. The Shamir plan was rejected by the PLO and the Arab states, and was received without enthusiasm by the Bush administration.

The main decision-makers in United States Middle East policy during the Bush Administration were the President, the Secretary of State James Baker, the Deputy Secretary of State Lawrence Eagleberger, the Director of Near East, African and South-East Asian Affairs Richard Haass, and Dennis Ross of the Department of Policy Planning. The Bush administration owed little to Jewish communal support and, while sympathetic to Israel, it viewed Israel within the broader perspective of United States regional interests in the Middle East.

All these key officials supported an incremental approach to resolving the Arab–Israeli conflict. James Baker broke the mould of the Reagan administration's Israel-centric approach to the conflict when he suggested in May 1989 that the United States should learn to look at the Middle East from a Palestinian perspective. The rapid collapse of the Soviet Union altered the United States view of Israel as a Cold War strategic asset. James Baker expressed his frustration with Israel's refusal to either deal with the PLO or countenance territorial compromise on the West Bank and Gaza. In 1990 he was quoted as telling the Israelis that 'if they are serious about discussing peace, the White House number is . . .'.

By May 1989 the PLO was making a strong impression on the Bush administration. In Paris, Arafat declared that the articles in the Palestine National Covenant rejecting Israel's right to exist were void. Arafat's statement was welcomed in the West but carried little weight. The Covenant could only be amended by a two-thirds majority vote of the Palestine National Council. In fact, despite Arafat's stated commitment to alter the covenant by September 1994, this has not been done. The dialogue between the PLO and the United States Government was abruptly suspended in May 1989 following an abortive seaborne raid on Tel Aviv by the Abu Abbas faction of the PLO. Although Arafat distanced his Fatah faction from the raid, the Bush administration viewed the attempted raid as a renunciation of the PLO's stated intention to renounce terrorism.

Between May 1989 and August 1990 the Arab–Israeli conflict became a secondary concern of the United States Administration's foreign policy. The reunification of Germany and the seminal changes occurring within Eastern Europe were of greater concern to the United States than resolving an Arab–Israeli conflict that was politically at a stalemate. In 1989, Syria completed its dominance of Lebanon with the signing of the T'aif Agreement, which resulted in the disarming of all the militias except for Hezballah. The death of the Iranian leader Ayatollah Khomeini in 1989 was perceived by the Bush administration as an opportunity to restore relations with the more pragmatic Rafsanjani regime.

Iraq's invasion of Kuwait in August 1990 restored the Middle East to the centre stage of United States foreign policy concerns. The ensuing Gulf War was the first opportunity for the United States to deal with an international crisis in the post-Cold-War era. The Gulf War was to have a major impact on the direction of the Arab–Israeli conflict resolution process.

Bush and Baker totally rejected Iraq's call for linkage between an Iraqi withdrawal from Kuwait and Israeli withdrawal from the West Bank, Gaza and the Golan Heights. As the Bush administration viewed it, Iraq's aggression against Kuwait was completely wanton and unprovoked, whereas Israel's conquest of the territories captured in the 1967 war was a response to a series of belligerent acts on the part of Israel's Arab neighbours. The terms of Resolution 242 obliged Israel to withdraw from *territories* captured in the 1967 war, but also obliged Israel's neighbours to end the state of belligerency and to recognise the sovereignty and integrity of all states in the region. Israel's return of Sinai to Egypt was clearly in the spirit of Resolution 242, but Israel's return of territory required simultaneous reciprocal guarantees of peace and normalisation of relations. The Bush administration's opposition to linkage was accompanied by an equally strong condemnation of the expansion of Israeli settlements in the West Bank and Gaza. This stance was important in demonstrating a sensitivity to Arab interests.

The Bush Administration successfully recruited many Arab nations to lend their moral and military support to the coalition of nations arrayed against Iraq. From the perspective of the Arab–Israeli peace process that followed the Gulf War the most important of these nations was Syria. The Syrian regime harboured a long-time antagonism towards Saddam Hussein's regime in Iraq, despite the many ideological similarities between the two Ba'thist regimes. The collapse of the Soviet Union, which hitherto had been Syria's main source of political and military support, obliged Syria to improve its relations with the United States, so as to obtain political support for its claim to the Golan Heights. Syria's support for the coalition was clearly in its interest. Syrian involvement in the coalition silenced United States criticism of Syrian hegemony in Lebanon and Syrian sponsorship of terrorism.

The PLO's position in the post-Gulf-War peace process was weakened by its alignment with Iraq. Although the PLO denied supporting Iraq's invasion of Kuwait, the PLO was widely perceived as Saddam's most enthusiastic supporter outside Iraq.

The Palestinians actively supported Saddam Hussein's call for linkage. Saddam's rhetoric, in calling for the liquidation of Israel and the liberation of Palestine, appealed to Palestinian Arabs in Jordan and the Israeli-controlled territories.

Jordan's uncomfortable neutrality stemmed from its fears of openly opposing Iraq, of alienating its Palestinian majority, and of being totally excluded from Western aid. Jordan's position was publicly condemned, but privately accepted, by the Bush administration. Jordan proved to be a convenient conduit for freed hostages, refugees, negotiators and the media prior to the outbreak of hostilities in January 1991.

The Bush Administration was careful to maximise the level of international legitimisation for its prosecution of the Gulf War in 1991. It was to follow this trend in its handling of the Arab–Israeli peace process after the Gulf War. It sought support from Arab states, Iran, the Soviet Union, the European Union nations and, most significantly, the UN. Bush, the former United States Ambassador to the UN, who during his term had had a jaundiced view of the world body, had no hesitation in using it to legitimise his pursuit of the Gulf War and Arab–Israeli peace.

The Gulf War resulted in a significant upturn in relations between the United States and Israel. Israel's exercise of military restraint in the face of Iraqi Scud attacks was largely a political decision by Israeli Prime Minister Shamir. From an Israeli perspective it was a very sage investment. Israel's 'restraint' earned it significant financial and diplomatic dividends. One of the most important of these was that Israel exercised a powerful influence in determining both the form and substance of the Peace Conference agenda and the Palestinian representation, at least in the early stages.

The Bush administration gained considerable political power in the Middle East from its victory in the Gulf War. By March 1991 the discord within the Soviet Union had reduced the former superpower to an impotent bystander. The Bush administration actively interceded with all the parties to the Middle East conflict in gathering them to the Madrid Conference. Bush and Baker were accommodating to the Israelis in the organisation of the conference. There was no official PLO presence. The Palestinian delegates were part of a joint Jordanian–Palestinian delegation. The administration also acceded to Israeli requests for no preconditions to the discussions. This accommodated Shamir's rejection of a 'Land for Peace' basis for negotiations.

However, the Bush administration was prepared openly to oppose Israel on certain key policies. In September 1991 the United States rejected an Israeli request for loan guarantees worth over US$10 billion. The guarantees were rejected in opposition to the Shamir Government's continued expansion of Jewish settlements in the West Bank and Gaza. The Bush administration linked any loan guarantees to a settlement freeze. The Bush administration's actions angered the Israelis, but convinced Arab delegations that the United States was prepared to impose and capable of imposing financial pressure on Israel and resisting the 'power' of the Israel lobby. The Bush administration's approach to the Middle East peace process was a reflection of its globalist outlook. Bush was an internationalist. His vision of the American Presidency was to help shape a world order. Flushed with hubris in the wake of the military victory over Iraq, Bush harboured visions of a 'new world order'. These would quickly fade. It was his globalism that would result in his ultimate election defeat by a candidate who would emphasise domestic issues.

Baker had intimated to the Syrians that he would seek a more conciliatory approach by Israel on the Golan Heights. The participation of the Gulf States was ensured through the United States' action of 'protecting' Saudi Arabia and the Gulf States from Iraq. The Egyptian Government was a strong supporter of the conference as a vindication of its own accord with Israel. Jordan felt obliged to attend as a means to ensure future Western financial support. The fact that the Syrians had agreed to attend eased Jordan's path.

The PLO was left without any effective bargaining chips in the wake of its support for Iraq during the Gulf War. Immediately prior to the Madrid Conference, the PLO blundered again when it expressed its support for the abortive coup that attempted to overthrow Mikhail Gorbachev in Russia. The PLO reluctantly agreed to the Palestinian negotiating group. Although no members of the Palestinian delegation were formally members of the PLO, virtually all were sympathetic to it. There was regular communication between the delegation and Tunis. Although formally a part of the Jordanian delegation, it was clear that, in practice, they were a separate entity. The participation of a Palestinian delegation in any form effectively, if unofficially, resumed a PLO dialogue with the United States. It also meant that the issue of Palestinian autonomy and sovereignty would be a central part of the agenda.

In the early stages of the peace conferences the United States Administration, and James Baker in particular, adopted an assertive approach in seeking to find common ground between the delegations. It was clear that the early sessions of the peace conferences involved more posturing than substance.

Israel's Likud Party's stance of peace without any land concessions and the Syrian and Palestinian demands for Israeli territorial concessions as a precondition for peace left little room for common ground.

During the first half of 1992 the stalemate in the peace process continued. James Baker was appointed as Bush's presidential campaign manager. Lawrence Eagleberger, who succeeded James Baker as United States Secretary of State, lacked Baker's assertiveness to advance a Middle East settlement. He was also pre-occupied with the Russian crisis of late 1992. Irrespective of his skills, Eagleberger was a stop-gap Secretary of State in a lame-duck administration. The peace process stalled while the participants awaited the outcome of the Israeli elections of June 1992.

In June 1992, the atmospherics of the peace process changed. The Israeli Labor Party-led coalition's narrow victory in the Israeli elections fundamentally altered the prospects for a breakthrough. Yitzhak Rabin had been elected on a mandate to advance a 'land for peace' formula. Rabin and his new negotiating team were quick to offer a range of concessions, which were rejected by the PLO and the Syrians. Rabin promised a partial freeze on Jewish settlements, which prompted the Bush administration to approve loan guarantees for Israel. However, between the Israeli and the United States elections the Bush administration failed to play an assertive role in brokering an agreement. In truth the positions of the Israelis and the Palestinians were now bridgeable.

There were differences in specifics, such as the size of the projected Palestinian police force and of the governing organisation. These would have been resolved with active intervention by the United States, but were complicated by a lack of will to involve the PLO through a backchannel.

The lack of progress in the pivotal issue of an Israeli–Palestinian accord in the framework of the Washington peace process led to exploration of a resolution through what became known as the Oslo backchannel. The Oslo backchannel began in mid-1992 with the involvement of Terje Toed Larsen, Director of the Norwegian Institute for Applied Social Science, his wife Mona Juul, Marianne Heilberg, a respected scholar on Palestinian society, and her husband Johan Jorgen Holst (then Norway's Defence Minister and later Foreign Minister). The four Norwegians were exceptionally well briefed on the Israeli–Palestinian conflict and had access to a wide range of Israeli and Palestinian contacts. The Oslo talks began as a secretive academic exchange between left wing Haifa University Political Science Professor Yair Hirschfeld and PLO economic spokesman Ahmed Suleiman Krai (better known as Abu Alaa). The meetings between Hirschfeld and Abu Alaa were held with the full support of

both the Israeli Cabinet and the PLO leadership in Tunis. The two
sought to thrash out a political and economic framework that could
lead to a formal accord.

The Oslo backchannel negotiations were conducted in secrecy.
Apart from a limited circle of senior Israeli and PLO officials only the
Norwegians, United States President Bill Clinton and Egyptian President Hosni Mubarak were informed of the talks. The initial stages of
the talks between Abu Alaa and Hirschfeld covered economic issues
and a framework of political principles. It was quickly established
that the first area of broad agreement was on the level of economic
infrastructure co-operation. In this context, tourism infrastructure and
co-operation in the field of tourism presented many opportunities for
economic development, rapid job creation and cash flow for both
Israel and the fledgling Palestinian economy (Perry, 1992).

The peace process experienced yet another hiatus during the final
months of the United States presidential election process and during
the early weeks of the incoming Clinton administration. The election
of Bill Clinton to the Presidency introduced a significant change of
emphasis in the United States Administration's approach to the Middle
East peace process. Clinton offered himself as a mediator and as an
approachable President. In reality he had made it clear that his election
mandate was an 'America-first' approach. Whereas the Bush administration had a globalist outlook, the Clinton administration's prime
concern in its foreign policy was to subordinate United States foreign
involvements to American interests.

Clinton was far more sensitive to the American Jewish vote than
Bush. As a Democratic candidate, Clinton was obliged to consider the
Jewish vote. During the campaign Clinton attacked Bush for 'using
pressure tactics against Israel. In the process, he [Bush] has raised Arab
expectations that he'll deliver Israeli concessions and fed Israel's fears
that its interests will be sacrificed to an American-imposed solution.'

Clinton's choice of Chief Middle East adviser, Dr Martin Indyk,
aroused controversy in some quarters. Indyk, an Australian-raised
Jewish academic, possesses outstanding academic credentials. Indyk's
critics claimed that, because of the few months he spent working as
a researcher for the America–Israel Public Affairs Committee, his sole
concern would be for Israel. His ten years as head of the Washington
Institute for Near East Studies, a high-powered conservative think
tank, demonstrated his broader interest in American Middle East
policy.

Clinton's Secretary of State, Warren Christopher, was one of a small
number of senior officials who had been part of the Carter Administration. Christopher was Baker's opposite. His preferred role was that

of a mediator rather than an initiator. In his dealings with the Arab–Israeli peace process, he would adopt a quiet approach until July 1993, when he engaged in an active round of shuttle diplomacy to end the Israeli bombardment of southern Lebanon and obtain Syria's co-operation in restraining Hezballah in southern Lebanon.

One of the greatest concerns of the Clinton administration has been the growing support for Islamic fundamentalist groups in undermining the peace process. The growth of Hamas among the Palestinians, Hezballah among the Lebanese and the Muslim Brotherhood in Egypt were all factors that were resulting in a growing caution among the Arab states and preventing the Palestinian delegation from openly moderating their stance at the formal peace talks. Indyk expressed strong concern about the Iranian influence in undermining the peace process through its sponsorship of Hamas, the Muslim Brotherhood and Lebanese Hezballah. The Clinton Administration would retain the Bush Administration's uncompromising attitude to Iraq.

In 1993 the first Washington session of the peace talks did not take place until May. The Clinton administration had an inauspicious beginning with problems surrounding early appointments. Israel's expulsion of 415 Hamas leaders aroused voluble protests from all the Arab delegations. Although the PLO had little sympathy with the fundamentalist Hamas movement, it could not publicly endorse an Israeli action against Palestinians, even Palestinians who rejected the PLO. Consequently, formal sessions of the peace talks were subjected to an extended delay as the Arab states and the Palestinians maintained their protest.

It was clear that the formal sessions of the peace talks were achieving little in the way of concrete results. Akiva Eldar,[1] an Israeli journalist who had attended all the sessions of the peace talks, pointed out, however, that personal relations between the negotiators had improved. It was also clear that the Israeli Government's official sanction of contacts between Israelis and the PLO had legitimised the wide-ranging contacts that had been established between Israel and the PLO.

Israel's approval of Feisal Husseini as a part of the Palestinian delegation made the veil concealing Israeli–PLO contacts all but transparent. These moves were all supported by the United States. Until Operation Accountability,[2] the Clinton Administration adopted a hard-line approach to Iran, Muslim fundamentalists and Iraq. This policy identified what the United States perceived as the major barriers to a successful peace process.

In the wake of Operation Accountability, the United States placed increasing emphasis on attempting to draw Syria into the peace process. In a revealing paper, Barry Rubin, a fellow of the John Hopkins Institute, claimed that Syria's preferred policy was to participate in the peace talks on the one hand and avoid reaching an agreement with Israel on the other.

Rubin claimed that Syria's support for Hezballah and the anti-Arafat elements of the PLO aimed to prevent any agreement that would necessitate any Syrian agreement with Israel. Rubin recommended in his June 1993 paper that the United States should take a more interventionist role towards Syria, on the basis that the United States had the upper hand in the Syrian–United States relationship. One month later Warren Christopher followed this suggestion to the letter in his actions to resolve the conflict between Israel and Hezballah.

In the wake of the agreements signed between Israel and the PLO and Israel and Jordan, the Clinton administration is now engaged in drawing Syria into the web of a comprehensive agreement. The activism so strongly promoted by James Baker in 1991 to advance an Arab–Israeli peace was renewed at the end of 1993. The United States played an active role in resolving the differences between Israel and the PLO to advance to the beginning of the autonomy process in May 1994. The implementation of the Gaza–Jericho phase of autonomy was achieved with considerable implementation problems, but is making considerable progress. The PLO announced an election for Palestinians in Gaza and the West Bank for November 1994. This eventually took place in January 1996.

The signing of a non-belligerency agreement between Israel and Jordan as an initial stage towards normalisation between the two countries and the establishment of diplomatic relations between Israel and Morocco in September 1994 and between Israel and Tunisia in October 1994 were achieved with the active support of the United States. In September 1994 United States Secretary of State Warren Christopher conducted a series of talks with Syrian President Hafez al-Assad to bring Syria into the peace fold. Israel was involved in the Casablanca meeting of North African and Gulf Arab states in October 1994, which resulted in formal ties being established between Israel and Jordan, Tunisia and Morocco. The Arab economic boycott of Israel was also relaxed.

As progress has been made with the peace process, the rejectionist forces have resorted to international terrorism to vent their opposition. Iran's sponsorship of such groups as Islamic Jihad, Hezballah and Hamas has been a means to use these groups to fan the flames of anti-Israel and anti-Western sentiment among many disaffected Palestinian and Lebanese Muslims. It also gives justification to rejectionist elements within Israel who oppose the peace process on the grounds of its threat to Israel's future security and viability as a Jewish state. As the most deadly acts of fundamentalist terrorism, such as the August 1994 bombing of the Jewish Community Centre in Buenos Aires, have been targeted at Israelis, diaspora Jews and Jewish organisations, they are designed to provoke an Israeli military response. To date they have in fact not produced this result, and the Israeli Government under Rabin with an uncertain 1996 election in mind was determined to make the peace process an irreversible *fait accompli* by then.

It took a Gulf War to make the Bush administration adopt an interventionist role in advancing a peace process between Israel, the Arab states and the Palestinians. Formal ties between Israel and Jordan rapidly ensued from the Casablanca conference. Israel also commenced the process of diplomatic relations with Oman. In formalising ties between Israel and Jordan, President Clinton played a key role as the guarantor and sponsor.

By early 1995, the peace process stood at a critical hiatus. Yitzhak Rabin was fully committed to implementing the peace process with the neighbouring Arab states and the Palestinians (with obvious differences in relation to Jerusalem). The PLO leadership was similarly committed. The time-frame in which this could be actualised was restricted by growing opposition within the Israeli and Palestinian communities. In Israel's case, this was certainly limited by the prospect in mid-1996 of a general election. Within the Palestinian community, Hamas was increasing in power every day the peace process fell behind schedule. Consequently the Clinton Administration needed to take a more pro-active role within a very limited time-frame. The global role of the United States in many crises was a limitation on its ability to focus its attention on the Middle East.

The United States has the power and the resources to broker a peace accord between Israel, the Arab States and the Palestinians. The principal qualities it needs to maintain the process are stamina and will. In the final years of the twentieth century the Middle East region is slowly resolving its most irreconcilable conflict. The initiative behind that conflict resolution will ultimately stem from the region itself; but the United States is the only nation on earth that has the power and the regional contacts to be a reliable guarantor of the peace process.

Notes

1. Akiva Eldar is the Foreign editor of the Israeli newspaper, *Ha'aretz*, interviewed by the author in April 1993.
2. Operation Accountability was an attack on Hezballah and Islamic Jihad bases in south Lebanon launched by the Rabin government in July 1993, in response to rocket attacks on northern Israel. It was largely viewed as an Israeli over-reaction in the international media, but had the effect of the United States placing pressure on Syria to restrain fundamentalist forces in southern Lebanon.

References

Allen, Charles and Portis, Jonathan (1992). *Bill Clinton, The Comeback Kid*. New York: Birch Lane Book Press.

Atherton, Alfred Leroy (1992). 'Shifting sands of Middle East peace'. *Foreign Policy*, 86 (Spring): 242–69.

Bell, Coral (1989). *The Reagan Paradox. American Foreign Policy in the 1980s*. New Jersey: Rutgers University Press.

Bush, George (1987). *Looking Forward. An Autobiography*. New York: Doubleday.

Findlay, Paul (1989). *They Dare to Speak Out*. Natal: Islamic Propagation Centre.

Friedman, Robert (1992). *Zealots for Zion*. New York: Random House.

Green, Stephen (1988). *Living by the Sword*. Brattleboro, Vermont: Amanda Books.

Mandell, Brian (1990). 'Rethinking the mediators calculus. Challenges for American peacemaking in the Arab–Israeli conflict'. *International Journal*, Canadian Institute of International Affairs, Summer: 568–602.

Matter, Phillip (1989). 'The Arab world East and West'. *Foreign Policy*, Fall: 141–68.

Peck, Julianna (1984). *The Reagan Administration and the Palestinian Question. The First 1,000 Days*. Washington: Institute for Palestine Studies.

Perry, Mark (1992). *Fire in Zion. The Israeli–Palestinian Search for Peace*. New York: William Morrow.

Pipes, Daniel (1989). *The Long Shadow*. New Brunswick: Transaction Publishers.

Rubin, Barry (1993). *Radical Middle East States and US Policy*. Washington Institute for Near East Studies, Publication number 35 (June).

Shamir, Yitzhak (1994). *Summing Up*. London: Weidenfeld & Nicolson.

History and the Meaning of the Disaster: Arab and Palestinian Politics from 1948–1993

Jeremy Salt

Was Arab independence a dream, or for a brief moment did it really happen? If one were to apply a sporting metaphor to the Arab situation, the Arabs are not the runners in a relay race but the baton. For a brief period in the 1950s they appeared to be running on their own; but the changeover was merely fumbled by the British and French, and now the baton has been passed on to American hands. Almost at the end of the twentieth century the Arab people appear to have no more real freedom than they did at its beginning. They are being claimed by a form of imperialism little different in essence from the old, by a 'new world order' resting on the military and economic domination that has ensured the success of American policies for the past two decades, just as it ensured the ascendancy of Britain and France a century ago. American interests are now served by a range of client governments extending from the Gulf to North Africa, and including Saudi Arabia, Egypt, Jordan and Morocco. The United States and Israel are now able to refashion the Middle East according to their own interests.

The capitulation of Egypt through the Camp David agreement (1979) and the equally significant collapse of the Palestinian position in the 'interim agreement' reached between the Government of Israel and the Palestine Liberation Organisation (PLO) leadership (1993) are striking achievements on the road to a 'reconstructed' Middle Eastern order. In the absence of any countervailing force following the collapse of the USSR, the United States and Israel are now free to do what they want in and with the Middle East, from attacking Iraq again if the need arises to punishing Syria should it fail to join the 'peace process'. The 'interim agreement' reached between Israel and the PLO leadership is the golden key that will simultaneously enable Arab governments to unburden themselves of the vexatious 'Palestinian problem' and Israel to enter lucrative Middle Eastern markets. Based on the ability to impose solutions, the 'interim agreement' deliberately circumvents Palestinian rights as they are described in international law: every critical issue is excluded and every landmark United Nations resolution dealing with the rights of the Palestinians ignored. And even so far as it goes, the facts Israel is busy creating on the ground indicate that it has no intention of vacating even the last remnant of Palestine. Since the signing of the agreement the number of settlers in the West Bank has increased from 120,000 to 140,000 and, as of May 1996, a further 60,000 acres of land has been expropriated for such purposes as 'quarries' and 'nature reserves'. West Bank Palestinians estimate that 73 per cent of their land has now been seized. More roads and housing units are being built and 'Greater Jerusalem' is being extended even deeper into West Bank territory (Salt, 1994–5: 27). Not for the first time in the twentieth century a treaty is being imposed on the people of the Middle East: a treaty that they seem to have no choice but to accept.

The Arab State System

The Palestinian problem cannot be separated from the weakness of the Arab state system any more than the weaknesses of the latter can be understood apart from the deliberate dislocation of Muslim societies (Arab, Persian, Ottoman, Central Asian, African) by European governments in the nineteenth century. Superior firepower made the outcome inevitable wherever Muslims and Europeans came into open conflict; but to occupy as well as invade, the assault on the integrity of Muslim societies had to be comprehensive. Cultural engineering went hand in hand with the overthrow of governments, the penetration of economies and the adaptation of agricultural systems to meet European needs. The means differed but not the end: although Britain did not seek to emulate France's *mission civilisatrice* in Algeria, its educational policies in Egypt after the occupation in 1882 actually had the objective of restricting education and preventing the emergence of a rebellious native class. 'I want all the next generation of Egyptians to be able to read and write', wrote Lord Cromer. 'Also I want to create as many carpenters, bricklayers, plasterers etc. as I possibly can. More than this I cannot do' (Mansfield, 1971: 140). Egyptians were to be given enough education (primary and secondary) for them to be taken into the administration as clerks; but higher learning was regarded with the greatest suspicion. 'With few exceptions the British were unsympathetic to proposals for establishing an Egyptian university. They feared it would do even more to foster nationalism than the law school', which was regarded as a 'breeding ground' for nationalism and French-inspired subversion (Mansfield, 1971: 144–6).

The peoples of the Middle East resisted as well as they could; but the unity that Jamal al-Din al-Afghani saw in the nineteenth century as the stone that would shatter the 'glass house' of European power was never realised, despite continual uprisings against the French and the British in the Middle East and Africa and against the Russians in the Caucasus and Central Asia. The attempts of reformers to meet the West on its own terms (by importing European systems of government, law and education) disrupted traditions, to the dismay of many Muslims: if Islam did not describe their societies above all else, what did?

For many, the answer was secularised nationalism. What form it should take was far from certain, even in the twentieth century. There were specific loyalties to specific territories, sharpened by foreign occupation, but at the same time there was the desire to liberate the 'Arab nation'. The impossibility of separating Islam from the historical concept of the Arabs as a 'nation' (an interpretation even secular nationalists shared) immediately raised problems for Christians and other religious groups. And even apart from religion, just how were the Arabs to be defined? There were many who did not regard themselves as Arabs at all (the Maronites of Lebanon and, in the twentieth century, the followers of the Syrian Social Nationalist Party); indeed, all the Arab territories had a specific past that predated Islam and Arabism and provided an alternative pole of identity.

This search for identity was made immeasurably more difficult by continuing foreign occupation and domination in all its forms. The links between political domination, economic exploitation and cultural subversion over almost 200 years are clear: through the Treaty of Balta Limani (1838), the British finally managed to break down the tariff barriers Muhammad Ali had erected around cotton, sugar and tobacco and undermine the attempts of the Egyptian ruler to achieve the economic and industrial self-sufficiency he realised must be the cornerstone of political independence. Increasingly beholden to the British for financial advice, by 1876 his successors (especially the Khedive Ismail) had plunged Egypt so deeply into debt that Britain and France intervened to protect the interests of their bondholders. The country's finances were reorganised under a system of dual control, which redeemed the situation largely at the expense of the already impoverished *fellahin*: 'the main burden fell on the long-suffering *fellahin* and it soon became apparent that Egypt was being squeezed dry' (Mansfield, 1971: 10). Indebtedness – and Egypt was not the only country unable to meet its obligations to external financial interests even in the nineteenth century – increased the country's vulnerability (as the construction of the Suez Canal and the sale of Egypt's shares in the canal company to Britain had already done) and paved the way for invasion and occupation in 1882.

A similar situation of indebtedness in Istanbul forced the sultan to issue the Decree of Muharram (1881) allowing the European powers to control whole sections of the Ottoman revenue through the Public Debt Administration. Throughout the region foreign financial control and penetration of Middle Eastern economies undermined local industries and, given the organic connections between different sectors of society in their craft and religious organisations, subverted society at its very foundations.

For those Arab lands that had not yet known European occupation the collapse of the Ottoman Empire in 1918 meant merely a change of masters. Everything the Western powers did was calculated to advance their own interests at the expense of those they were supposed to be governing as a 'sacred trust of civilisation'. This is how the League of Nations described the obligations of the 'advanced nations' to 'those colonies and territories . . . not yet able to stand by themselves under the strenuous conditions of the modern world' in the Middle East, Central and South-West Africa and even 'certain of the South Pacific Islands'. Humbly accepting the territories they themselves had just parcelled out (for, even more than the United Nations in its early days, the League of Nations was a European club), the new masters of the Middle East then began creating the institutions that in their own interests they would eventually have to destroy. The history of the constitutional monarchy in Egypt from 1922 is punctuated by the repeated intervention of the British in the workings of government. The credibility of parliament and the political parties and the authority of the king were all mortally weakened: so much for the sacred trust.

In Iraq the British created a monarchy and a political system that they manipulated in the same fashion. Oil, imperial communications and Iraq's position at the head of the Persian Gulf shaped British policy in the same way that geographical position and the canal did in Egypt. The monarchy was created by Britain, the king was imported from outside, and Iraq was turned into a source of cheap oil for the home country and a bastion of regional influence. Here, as in Egypt, there could be no trust in a system manipulated by a foreign power in its own interests, any more than there could be in pliant politicians aligning themselves with 'the West' against communists and 'radical' nationalists across the region.

With the French the picture was much the same. The French began by dividing Syria (from which Palestine had already been separated) and establishing in Lebanon a territory and a regime that politically and demographically made confrontation and the civil wars of 1958 and 1975 inevitable. In the Syrian hinterland, with the aim of disrupting the Arab nationalism that they associated with Sunni Islam, the French created separate administrative enclaves that conformed to ethnic and regional divisions. They also brought minorities into the administration and the Troupes Spéciales du Levant in disproportionate numbers (van Dam, 1981: 18); and finally, they gave away the province of Alexandretta to Turkey: again, nothing further from the 'sacred trust' undertaken by France on behalf of the Syrians could be imagined.

The mandated territory of Palestine constituted a special case, with independence to be delayed until such time as the 'Jewish homeland' had been built up and the overwhelming Muslim and Christian majority overcome. But by supporting the Zionist programme against the wishes of the Palestinian population – 'Zionism, be it right or wrong, good or bad, is rooted in age-long traditions, in present needs, in future hopes, of far profounder import than the desires and prejudices of the 700,000 Arabs who now inhabit that ancient land', wrote Balfour (Ingrams, 1972: 73) – Britain further poisoned its own wells throughout the Middle East.

Thus did the modern Arab state system emerge. Here were societies whose older identities had been cast aside in favour of a secularised, unfamiliar and somewhat ambiguous nationalism. Here were states, political parties and individual leaders struggling to establish their legitimacy against the mutually irreconcilable aspirations of powerful European states. The outcome was the undermining of the hopes of the liberal nationalists that a balanced Middle Eastern order could emerge from the colonial period. Their humiliation at the hands of their colonial masters, their inability even to begin to deal with the massive social and economic problems that faced them, encouraged the rise of new ideological formations (Muslim, Arab nationalist and communist) and military cliques that saw no future in a dubious parliamentary process. The result was the 'radicalisation' of Middle Eastern politics after 1945 and the rise of regimes dispensing with open parliaments and imposing development from the top down.

The exhaustion of the European powers in a second war finally gave the Arabs their chance to make a run for real independence.

Unfortunately, the same developing power vacuum invited someone else to fill it. Unable to prevent the victorious European powers from soaking up the region's territory and resources in 1918, the United States had subsequently won the richest prize of all – Saudi Arabia. Soviet power (was it ever as great as the Western media led their readers to believe?) brought the United States into the Middle East in increasing strength after 1945. Determined to protect the region from 'communist subversion', the United States ended up carrying out numerous subversive programmes of its own in the years ahead – Operation Ajax, the successful overthrow of the Mossadeq Government in Iran in 1953, and Operation Straggle, the failed conspiracy against the Syrian Government in 1956, are two of them – as well as providing military and economic aid to favoured governments. Of a less official nature, the CIA had so many Arab politicians on the payroll at one stage, including the President, Prime Minister and Foreign Minister of Lebanon and the Prime Minister of Jordan – that 'if the CIA blanketed the rest of the Middle East the same way we'd soon be out of key politicians for CIA personnel to recruit' (Eveland, 1980: 250). Money for the Lebanese President was delivered directly to the presidential palace in a suitcase: 'soon my gold De Soto with its stark white top was a common sight' (Eveland, 1980: 252, also 217–23).

In the last two decades, playing on the cupidity and weakness of Arab rulers as successfully as the British and French did for more than a century, the United States has succeeded in creating a dependent state system in the Middle East. But this has been at the cost of an increasingly aggravated social environment arising from economic inequities, the unrepresentative nature of Arab governments and the knowledge that the United States ultimately calls all the shots in the Arab world. Even where there is an ostensibly open electoral system Arab governments are largely regarded by their own electors as being manipulative and corrupt. Their inability to take collective action in the name of an identifiable Arab interest, despite the obligations imposed upon them by membership of the Arab League, was demonstrated most painfully after Israel invaded Lebanon in 1982, when they could not even agree to meet, let alone agree on a course of action. They are frequently guided more by tribal, dynastic, sectarian and even family considerations than the interests of their people or 'the Arab world' – but the alarms are already sounding, and nowhere more loudly than in those countries bound most closely to the interests of 'the West'.

The Islamists have made immense gains in Egypt in the past decade, and only by debarring both the Muslim Brotherhood and Nasserist groups from direct participation in the political process can the National Democratic Party Government of Husni Mubarak be assured of retaining its grip on power. Chronic economic problems continue to have a corrosive effect on the political structure: while the economy 'seldom seems destined for sustained growth or complete collapse' (Roy, 1990: 161), indebtedness has returned Egypt to the days of the khedives:

> Foreign indebtedness now heads the long list of issues that have traditionally plagued Egypt. It looms as possibly *the* problem of the 1990s, raising serious questions about the country's future financial integrity. In the past twelve years Egyptian debt has increased tenfold to its present level of approximately $53 billion – about $42 billion in public and private sector debt and $11.4 billion in military debt. In total debtedness Egypt now ranks seventh in the developing world. In terms of government-to-government debt it ranks number one (Eveland, 1980: 250).

The United States is now Egypt's major trading partner, but while Egypt has 'benefited' from 'an uninterrupted and substantial flow of aid on highly concessionary terms' (Handoussa, 1990: 122), the cost has been high. The reduction of subsidies and the IMF's ideological attack on the public sector through 'reforms' – what Handoussa calls 'the indiscriminate condemnation of public enterprise' – has brought about a sharp increase in unemployment, a decrease in real income and a sense of 'unprecedented crisis, not only in the management of its [Egypt's] massive foreign debt but also in the finance of basic goods and services for over one third of the population who remain below the poverty line' (Handoussa, 1990: 122–3). And while 'free trade' dictates that the Egyptian market remain wide open to imports, strict quotas imposed on Egyptian manufactured goods (mostly cotton and textiles) have proved to be 'a major impediment to the growth of these exports to the United States and EEC markets' (Handoussa, 1990 : 119). Transformed through its dependence into an American client state, does Egypt have much if any more freedom of action than it did under the Khedive Ismail 120 years ago?

In Saudi Arabia, another supposed pillar of Western interests and Gulf security, fiscal mismanagement, corruption and the willingness of dissident *'ulama* to challenge an autocratic system are bringing the system to the point of crisis. The Gulf conflicts (an officially admitted $25 billion funnelled to Iraq during the Iran–Iraq War and $40 billion to get Saddam Hussein out of Kuwait) and profligate spending on arms that Saudi Arabia does not have the capacity to use (arms buying falls somewhere between $12 billion and $18 billion annually) have plunged the country into foreign debt of $60 billion. In 1980 Saudi Arabia was earning $100 billion a year ($300 million a day); by 1994 its annual income had fallen to $40 billion, much of it draining away into the arms industries of Britain, France and the United States: the Yamama 2 deal with Britain alone is estimated to involve between $60 and $150 billion (Aburish, 1994: 201), of which hundreds of millions of dollars have already been paid out in 'commissions'. To a small but increasing number of Saudi dissidents their government is no longer tolerable.

> Like a rotting carcass the House of Sa'ud is beginning to decompose. The reality is ignored by its members and their friends and as usual the people who are the source of decay are the last to admit their inability to halt it. For the first time ever the failures of the House of Sa'ud's internal, regional and international policies have converged to undermine it. Most significantly and dangerously it is the irreversible internal pressures – the willingness of the Saudi people to gather under an Islamic banner and their demands for a substantial change in the way they are governed – which are almost out of control (Aburish, 1994: 303).

Saudi Arabia has another government which will not – indeed *cannot* – defend Arab interests where they come into conflict with the ambitions of the United States and 'Western interests' generally.

These developments – in Egypt, Saudi Arabia, Algeria and indeed across the Middle East – should be taken as portents of the changes that are likely to come. Edward Said has referred to the 'mass uprisings' of the 1980s (in Iran, the Philippines, Argentina, Korea, Pakistan, South Africa, eastern Europe, China, the West Bank and Gaza) and the way they 'all challenged something very basic to every art and theory of government, the principle of confinement'. Against the power of governments 'the unresolved plight of the Palestinians speaks directly of an undomesticated cause and a rebellious people paying a very high price for their resistance' (Said, 1993: 396). It is not simply the state of the economy in a particular country, or corruption, or the unrepresentative nature of governments, or a specific historical question such as the fate of the Palestinians or the globalisation of Arab economies, but all of these issues combined that are taking away from the Arabs as people the right to define themselves, control their own territory and resources and determine their future. Applying this dilemma to any other people in history, can it be imagined that it would continue indefinitely?

The Palestinians

When Israel was created in 1948 the historian Constantine Zurayk applied the expression *'al-Nakba'* – the disaster – to the dispossession of the Palestinians from their homeland and the creation of a Jewish state in their place. No one then could have predicted how much worse the situation would become. Arab and Palestinian resistance to the imposition of Israel on the Middle East led to the wars, which the Arabs were destined to lose because of the complete asymmetry in the power balance between themselves and Israel and its Western backers. Not only the rest of Palestine but the territory of surrounding states was occupied, with the civil war in Jordan (1970) and Israel's onslaught on Lebanon (1982) adding to Palestinian and Arab difficulties. With the signing of the 'interim agreement' between the PLO and Israel in 1993 the region has been brought to another watershed in its modern history. By an increasing number of Palestinians – possibly the majority now – the agreement is regarded as one of the most serious blows they have experienced since 1948.

Upon its formation in 1964 the PLO based its strategies on armed struggle and the establishment of a secular democratic state for Muslims, Christians and Jews to replace the exclusivist 'Zionist entity' in Palestine. By 1974 – in the face of vehement opposition and considerable personal danger – the Palestinian mainstream had begun moving reluctantly towards accepting Israel as a *fait accompli*. This change of direction was opposed by virtually all groups on the left: two of its earliest public proponents (Said Hammami and Issam Sartawi) were assassinated for expressing their views.

The 'two-state' solution was developed stage by stage from 1974 to 1988 without any reciprocal gesture being made by either Israel or the United States. Not once in this period did the United States use its immense leverage to restrain or punish Israel for its continual breaches of the very international conventions and laws that the United States was sworn to uphold. The United States Government regarded the territories seized in 1967 as occupied, yet did nothing (as it could have done by scaling down arms and economic aid) to stop Israel from settling them. Israel's invasion of Lebanon and the use of proscribed weapons (cluster bombs) was met not with sanctions, but with even higher levels of military aid. Furthermore, American policies on the Middle East were indistinguishable from those of Israel itself: surely never before in history had such a small tail wagged such a large dog. American involvement in Middle East 'peace' efforts after 1967 was based on state-to-state relations and what Israel wanted rather than the core Palestinian issue: UN Security Council

Resolutions 242 and 338 were singled out for their importance, although neither refers to the Palestinians except indirectly as 'refugees'. Those UN resolutions that actually set out the rights of the Palestinians were studiously ignored, the object being to arrive at a settlement without the participation of the Palestinians rather than with them. The celebrated remark by President Carter's National Security Adviser, Zbgniew Brzezinski, 'bye-bye PLO', accurately summed up the dismissive American reaction to the risks being taken by Palestinian 'moderates'.

The refusal of Israel and the United States to deal with the PLO completely undermined the organisation's gradualist approach as well as the personal standing of its executive chairman; but not even capitulation by an Arab leader seems to be enough for Tel Aviv and Washington. When Anwar al-Sadat went to Jerusalem in 1977 he claimed to have the objective of a 'comprehensive settlement' in mind: had Israel responded in kind his extraordinary gesture could have led to one. At Camp David, Sadat: 'offered Israel peace, security, normal relations with its neighbours and whatever international guarantees it chose provided it withdrew from the territories occupied in 1967 and allowed the Palestinians to establish their own state. None of these preconditions survived the grinding months of negotiation' (Seale, 1988: 307).

Instead, Israel manipulated both Sadat and President Carter, taking advantage of Sadat's isolation and playing on Carter's rapidly diminishing domestic support. Where the negotiations touched on the West Bank and the Gaza Strip at Camp David, Menachem Begin agreed to grant autonomy to the people but not the land. This insistence that the land must remain under Israeli control and open to Jewish settlement foreshadowed the agreement imposed on Yasser Arafat in 1993. For agreeing to surrender the territory it had occupied in Sinai Israel was handsomely rewarded with more weaponry and a 'memorandum of understanding' that bound the United States even more tightly to its support. By removing Egypt from the 'confrontation states' Israel's hands were freed for action elsewhere: in Lebanon, which it invaded in 1982; and in the occupied territories, where Begin accelerated settlement programmes; the two were indeed tied together, the invasion and crushing of the PLO designed as a salutary lesson to the Palestinians of the West Bank.

The diplomatic path followed by Arafat from 1974 led to accolades in the international arena (the appearance by the PLO Chairman before the UN General Assembly and the diplomatic recognition of the PLO as the legitimate representative of the Palestinian people by an increasing number of governments), but nothing from Israel, until the PLO leader effectively surrendered nearly twenty years later by recognising Israel's 'right' to exist without extracting from Israel acknowledgment of the Palestinians' claim to have a state of their own. As others are doing, Yasser Arafat – stateless in Gaza – is no doubt reflecting now on the fate of those who take 'risks for peace' in the Middle East.

Israel is now using this agreement to consolidate its position in Jerusalem and the rest of the occupied territories at the small cost of giving the Palestinians 'autonomy' in carefully selected areas. There is nothing in the text of the 13 September 1993 agreement to justify the numerous declarations by Arafat that the Palestinians are finally on the way to a state of their own. The position of both the Israeli Government and opposition is that there will never be a Palestinian state between the Mediterranean and the Jordan river; that settlements will not be dismantled; and that Jerusalem will never be shared. These assertions are supported by what is happening on the ground: the expropriation of land and construction of houses on the West Bank continue unabated, and plans are under way 'to extend greater Jerusalem virtually to Jericho with vast construction projects, plans for tourist sites along the northern shore of the Dead Sea, some $700 million of investment in new roads to connect settlements with Israel and each other, bypassing Palestinian villages and towns' (Chomsky, 1994: 264). Steps are also being taken to 'obliterate the official border (the Green line) by settlement and road building' (Chomsky, 1994: 264). While the Palestinians are granted minimal autonomy, the object is clearly a form of territorial fragmentation that would eliminate the possibility of their ever having sufficient territory to create a viable state. Ultimate control of the territory, its foreign relations, its economy and its natural resources (most critically water) would remain in the hands of the Government of Israel.

Needless to say, the rights of the Palestinians ejected from their homeland during the formative stage of Israel's history are not to be taken into account at all in this 'peace' process: indeed, according to reports from the United Nations, a bloc of countries including Egypt are planning the rescission of all General Assembly resolutions 'critical' of Israel; this action would 'eliminate resolutions on Palestinian national rights, human rights violations under the military occupation, Israeli settlements, Israel's refusal to renounce nuclear weapons, Israel's (virtual) annexation of the Golan Heights etc.' (Chomsky, 1994: 265). For the first time – as well as now referring to the West Bank and Gaza as 'disputed' rather than occupied territories – the United States has voted against Resolution 194 of 11 December 1948, affirming the right of expelled Palestinians to return or otherwise to be repatriated

(Chomsky, 1994: 219). And according to Mark A. Bruzonsky (1994: 8), former Washington representative of the World Jewish Congress, Israel is now working towards the ultimate diplomatic prize of United States recognition of Jerusalem as its capital.

While their fate is being decided for them, West Bank and Gaza Palestinians continue to suffer at the hands of settlers and the military. In the first eight days after the massacre of thirty Muslim worshippers at the Ibrahimi mosque in Hebron in February 1994, thirty-three more Palestinians were killed by the Israeli military and, while the town was put under curfew, armed settlers continued to swagger around the streets as before. Their bullying and intimidation is designed to let 'the Arabs' know 'who the true rulers in Hebron are' (Chomsky, 1994: 258). The attempt by the late Prime Minister Yitzhak Rabin to distance his government from the embarrassment of the Hebron massacre and the actions of 'extremist' settlers ('sensible Judaism spits you out') does not change the fact that the Labor Government remains committed to the West Bank settlements, which the Labor Party and *not* Likud sanctioned in the first place: former Foreign Minister and now Prime Minister Shimon Peres has given repeated assurances that Israel has 'no intention of destroying existing Jewish settlements in the territories' (Peres and Arye, 1993: 27). Naturally the people stay, too. 'It would be unthinkable to force them to leave, unless we wanted to risk a civil war', writes Peres (Peres and Arye 1993: 20).

Within a year of the 'Declaration of Principles' being signed its fragility was even more evident than at the start. The continuing Palestinian reaction indicates that Arafat has accepted conditions that not only the 'extremists', who are the staple diet of the Western media, but also the Palestinian mainstream find unacceptable. 'In Gaza and increasingly in the West Bank Palestinians who once regarded Israel as the sole enemy have come to see the Palestine Liberation Organisation and its chairman, Arafat, as another enemy', Youssef M. Ibrahim wrote recently in the *New York Times*. He added:

Arafat, 65, his 10,000 PLO policemen and the few hundred PLO bureau-crats and supporters he brought with him from exile in Tunis are sinking into deeper isolation, becoming the object of derision and distrust. In the short space of time since he arrived here in July after three decades of struggling from Jordan, Lebanon and Tunisia, Arafat is finding little warmth among Gazans and evaporating support among Palestinians on the West Bank. It amounts to a state of open rebellion to which he has responded with repression and helplessness.

The Fatah militia and the PLO policemen, in the graffiti scrawled on Gaza walls, are now denounced as 'Israel's loyal servants' and Arafat's 'dogs'. The killing of fourteen demonstrators by Palestinian police in Gaza, and the armed attack by Arafat loyalists at the Ain al-Hilweh refugee camp in Lebanon, which took ten more Palestinian lives, caused anger across the Middle East. At Ain al-Hilweh, as elsewhere among Palestinians, Arafat's opponents were not just the Islamic activists, but older-style nationalists who were the backbone of the Palestine movement in the 1960s and 1970s. Even the Fatah Central Committee, in a statement whose signatories included the Palestine National Authority's Economic Minister Ahmad Quray (Abu Ala) and Foreign Minister Faruq Qaddumi, described the killings in Gaza as a 'massacre'.

The inability of the Palestine National Authority to attract more than a fraction of the promised international aid has compounded Arafat's problems in the occupied territories. He is criticised from within for his authoritarian methods and compromised from without by the humiliating way he is treated – not as the leader of a prospective Palestinian state, but as Israel's regent in territories it remains determined to control in all important aspects. As the limited scope of the autonomy Israel is prepared to grant the Palestinians becomes even clearer a resurgence of resistance to both Arafat and Israel seems inevitable.

The Fate of Israel

It is with feelings of the profoundest gratification that I learn of the intention of His Majesty's Government to lend its powerful support to the re-establishment in Palestine of a national home for the Jewish people. . . . I welcome the reference to the civil and religious rights of the existing non-Jewish communities in Palestine. It is but a translation of the basic principle of the Mosaic legislation: 'And if a stranger sojourn with thee in your land, ye shall not vex [oppress] him. But the stranger that dwelleth with you shall be unto you as one born among you, and thou shalt love him as thyself' (Lev. xix 33, 34) (Ingrams, 1972: 13).

Several years ago the American Jewish writer Roberta Strauss Feuerlicht wrote a book called *The Fate of the Jews*, in which she draws attention to the contradiction between the ethics of the early Jewish prophets and Zionism. 'Ethics, not monotheism or chosenness, was the Jews' great contribution to religion', she writes. Beginning with the Decalogue, and reasserted by Amos, Hosea, Micah, Isaiah and

Jeremiah: 'the transcendent concern of the prophets was social justice' – plus, inevitably, a revulsion at power and its trappings. The triumph of power at the cost of ethics led to disaster in Jewish history, with Judaism surviving 'not because of its kingdoms but because of its teachings'. Tracing the history of the modern political Zionist movement, and moving through the breaches of international law and ethics that have characterised the rise of Israel, the author writes that 'Zionists executed the psychological coup of the century by taking Palestine from the Arabs and then pretending Jews were Arab victims'. Dispersion and exile have so scattered the Jews that the ethical imperative is the 'single link' that binds them; but now 'that single link is in danger of being smashed by Israel'. Israel

> is not the Messiah but the Golem. Created to save the Jews it has turned on its creators, corrupting and destroying them by its very success at making them a nation like all others. Judaism as an ideal is infinite; Israel as a state is finite. Judaism survived centuries of persecution without a state; it must now learn how to survive despite being a state. . . . American Jews who care about Israel are concerned that it has made a covenant of death with its Masada mentality and reliance on direct action . . . not since the fall of the Second Temple have Jews been such an engine of death and destruction (Feuerlicht, 1984: 249–50).

What Feuerlicht's book succeeds in drawing out is the inconsistency between 'Jewish ethics' and the gradual fulfilment of the Zionist programme in Palestine from the late nineteenth century onwards. In a book first published in 1987, *The Birth of the Palestinian Refugee Problem 1947–1949*, Benny Morris, drawing on Israeli state archives, chronicled the deliberate expulsion of Palestinians from their homeland and the seizure of their land or – in the euphemistic language of the settlers – its 'liberation from the hands of tenant farmers' (Morris, 1989: 55). As valuable as the book was in confirming what the Palestinians already knew, Morris avoided the important question of prior intent going back as far as Theodor Herzl. The notion of transfer was propounded by both Herzl and Weizmann as well as the lesser figures who surrounded and followed them; indeed, the objective of removing land from Muslim and Christian ownership and labour was already being realised by the Jewish National Fund. There were many who had misgivings on moral grounds: the early Zionist colonial administrator Arthur Ruppin admitted that it was difficult 'to realise Zionism and still bring it constantly into line with general ethics' (Elmessiri, 1977: 132), but he eventually came to the conclusion that there was 'no alternative' to confrontation with the local people if the

Zionist programme was to be carried forward. The inability to buy more than a fraction of the land created a series of contradictions. It was soon obvious that a 'Jewish state' could not be established in Palestine except through force, and even the presence of the people and their ownership of the land would have to be overcome – as it eventually was when Palestinians were herded out of their homeland in 1948.

Against the ideological background and the strenuous efforts to clear the land of its people in 1948, the dispossession of the Palestinians can hardly be regarded as an accident or as a 'miraculous simplification of our task', as Weizmann would claim. To describe an armed uprising by a settler minority against the indigenous majority as a 'war of independence' subverts the meaning of language. Certainly it is a queer notion of democracy that rests on the prior expulsion of the indigenous majority; and indeed, only by being specifically anti-democratic did the Zionist programme in Palestine have any hope of being realised – a fact that Israel's imperialist backers acknowledged at the very beginning: 'The weak point of our position is that in the case of Palestine we deliberately and rightly decline to accept the principle of self-determination' wrote Balfour. '[I]n Palestine we do not even propose to go through the form of consulting the wishes of the present inhabitants of the country . . .' (Ingrams, 1972: 61/73).

To the initial costs of establishing Israel – the expulsion of 750,000 Palestinians, the expropriation of their land and property and its parcelling out for 'socialist' *kibbutzim* and *moshavim*, the destruction of 350 of Palestine's 450 villages, and the seizure of land even from those Palestinians who remained in Israel, theoretically under the protection of the law – must be added the attacks on the population of surrounding countries that followed. The loss of civilian life in southern Lebanon (occupied for seventeen years) continues until the present day. In the Palestinian territories seized during the 1967 war the humiliation of the people by religious fanatics protected by the military and encouraged to 'redeem' the land forms an additional láyer of their torment.

The Israeli annexation of Jerusalem following the seizure of the eastern half of the city in 1967 has been stamped with the same disregard for ethics and human rights. Homes and even villages on the outskirts of the city have been bulldozed, and land has been taken from Muslim and Christian Palestinians to make way for Jewish settlements. In 1977 a delegation from the National Lawyers Guild of the United States visited the Jewish Quarter of East Jerusalem:

where a ten year Israeli Government plan calls for reconstruction and substitution of Jewish families for Palestinians. By 1975 more than 6,000 Palestinians had been evicted after being offered some compensation and their homes were destroyed; 200 Jewish families had already moved in while only 20 Palestinian families remained. Delegation members also visited the Wailing Wall in the Old City. A large, paved open space adjacent to it required the destruction of hundreds of Palestinian homes and removal of more than 4,000 Palestinian residents (National Lawyers Guild, 1978: 14–15).

The 'Judaisation' of Jerusalem, the attempt to obliterate its Palestinian identity, and the 'thickening' of the 'Greater Jerusalem' area to include much of the West Bank has continued relentlessly. Slowly the boast made by Menachem Begin in 1983 is being realised: 'Gradually we have been managing to erase the physical distinction between the coastal area and Judea and Samaria . . . We haven't completely succeeded yet. But give us three or four or five years and you'll drive out there and you wouldn't be able to *find* the West Bank' (Aruri, 1984: 23, emphasis in original). Not since France invaded Algeria in 1830 has a Middle Eastern territory been so comprehensively colonised, its land parcelled out among the *colons* and its people reduced to such utter helplessness.

The final thread in this strand is the unequal status of the Palestinians who are now citizens of the state of Israel. They have equal rights neither in theory nor practice. They have the freedom to vote as they choose, but they can never have full equality in what the preamble to Israel's Declaration of Independence describes as the 'state of the Jewish people', simply because they are not Jewish. The 'Law of Return' granting citizenship rights to Jews who have no physical connection with the land while denying the right of return to Palestinians who actually lived there until 1948 further delineates the essentially second-class status of Israel's 'Arab minority'. Behind the democratic façade they do not enjoy the same rights and access to services: Ian Lustick's *Arabs in the Jewish State* is only one of many books that draw attention to the institutionalised discrimination in Israel and the legal means by which it is upheld. Discriminatory indices emerge at every level. In the economy, 'to the structural and institutional factors involved in the continued backwardness of the Arab sector must be added the neglect of the government and its discrimination in favour of the Jewish sector with respect to development projects of all kinds' (Lustick, 1980: 183). Village services, health and education all show the same pattern. The ineligibility of Muslims for military service again underlines their essentially second-class status, because 'the possession of veteran status is a prerequisite to a wide variety of jobs and public assistance programmes' (Lustick, 1980: 94).

The pattern of discrimination naturally extends to Jerusalem. As Israel Shahak (1986: 1, emphases in original) has written, 'only Jews have a right to permanent residence in Jerusalem as a *natural* right . . . the state of Israel does not recognise the right of an Arab or another non-Jew to live in Jerusalem *even if he was born there*'. Towards the end of 'Judaising' Jerusalem the state has also introduced a series of 'laws' designed to remove property from the hands of its Muslim or Christian owners and hand it over to Jewish settlers, 'including those who are known for their most aggressive and racist attitudes towards Arabs'. The government's decision to bar non-Jews from living in the Jewish quarter, 'which is much larger than the old Jewish Quarter following requisitions and evacuations' (Shahak, 1986: 2), was backed by a Supreme Court judge when a Palestinian resident appealed against his eviction. On the other hand, Jews are encouraged to settle in Muslim districts. Such discriminatory measures are opposed by Israeli 'moderates'; but, as Abdelwahab M. Elmessiri (1977: 169) has observed, 'the Jewish citizen in the Zionist state, whether he is for or against racism, benefits from institutional *de jure* discrimination'.

Despite all evidence to the contrary, apologists for the state of Israel continue to insist on the ethical nature of Zionism. Harold Fisch refers to its 'uncompromisingly ethical dimension' and puts the question: 'Can one dare to suggest that with regard to the Jewish–Arab struggle there is a marked difference in the conduct of the struggle on both sides? At the risk of seeming illiberal one must affirm that there is such a difference. The simple truth is that Israelis normally refrain from attacking civilians; Arabs normally do not' (Fisch, 1978: 143).

Even before the invasions of Lebanon and the *intifada* these claims were patently absurd. Through force the state of Israel was created and through force it has been maintained. Now even Yasser Arafat has been forced to cry 'uncle' (Chomsky, 1994: 229) and run up a 'typewritten white flag' of surrender, as the author of *From Beirut to Jerusalem*, Thomas Friedman, wrote with obvious satisfaction in the *New York Times* on 10 September 1993. Israel has extracted the grand prize of recognition from Arafat without having to give it in return (the recognition of the PLO as a negotiating partner in no way equates to the recognition of a state) and without having to make any commitments about settlements, Jerusalem, the rights of the 1948 generation of refugees or those who came after or indeed the long-term future at all.

But surely this is the way of the world: Israel has 'won' and is entitled to enjoy the fruits of victory; why should it be different from any other country – and if it were different could it still survive? Furthermore, surely, what makes history tick is not moral power but *actual* power (and ultimately firepower). The victorious powers in 1939–45 might have had right on their side; but it was not this that defeated the Nazis. The North American Indians, the aboriginal population of Australia (the list is endless) undoubtedly had right on their side, but not the might, and eventually went under. In the Middle East all agreements negotiated over the region over the last century have ultimately been based on the same logic of power. Thus the outcome in Palestine was inevitable: nothing the Palestinians could have done, agreeing with Western governments or opposing them, could have prevented these governments from doing precisely what they wanted to do. And setting up Israel in Palestine was what they wanted to do. Here Israel emerges as the fortuitous beneficiary of their ambitions, beginning with the British: Theodor Herzl simply wandered into their machinations and made himself useful.

But power is obviously a double-edged weapon. The strategic balance between Israel and the Arab states has already changed significantly. One day the Middle East state system as it is now constituted might no longer exist. The Islamic movements are working to change not just governments but systems across the Arab world. They have made striking gains. In many respects they have filled the gap created by the collapse of secular Pan–Arab nationalism in the 1960s. They are feared and vilified in the West largely *because* they represent the aspirations of many Arabs to be free of external domination.

Conclusions

Palestinian concessions leading up to the recognition of the Jewish state have given Israel the opportunity to make a real peace with the Palestinians; but it can only be based on a full withdrawal from the territories seized in 1967 and a political accommodation over Jerusalem. This is what the Palestinians themselves say they want, and both the Arab and the broader Islamic worlds would follow their lead; but, from everything the Government of Israel is saying (and allowing), it is clear that full withdrawal (military and settler) from the occupied territories is not on the cards. By using the Declaration of Principles to exploit Palestinian weakness even further Israel is losing an opportunity of historic magnitude. No process based on the consolidation rather than the weakening of the Israeli presence in the occupied territories (including East Jerusalem) can be called a 'peace' process. The present process is withering on the vine because Israel is using the Declaration of Principles as a screen behind which the seizure of land and the building of settlements in the West Bank is continuing as before.

Yet the Israeli leadership shows no signs of understanding that the moment lost might never be regained. In the nineteenth century the ability to conquer and hold vast territories convinced the 'Anglo-Saxon race' – not to speak of the French or the Russians – of their moral superiority over those they ruled. The approach of 'the West' and Israel in the twentieth century is suggestive of the same assumptions. There is the same sense of outrage when the Arabs struggle against their preordained fate: the 'Mohammedan fanatics' who troubled the imperialist powers more than a century ago have become the 'Islamic fundamentalists' of today. And as for the Palestinians, Western power (largely and latterly American) has made it possible to ignore their cries for justice. They are now being driven even further towards the atomised fate suffered by native societies in the nineteenth century: there is still talk among the 'extremists' of 'transferring' the Palestinians, but, even if this is no longer possible, the scope of development, the building of settlements and the redefinition of 'Greater Jerusalem' to place large parts of the West Bank within its municipal boundaries are calculated to demoralise the Palestinians so that, sooner or later, they will drift away and become human detritus.

But the Palestinians are a sophisticated and resourceful people, and 'Palestine' is unlikely to go away as an Arab cause. Indeed, the fate of the Palestinians is somewhat emblematic of the broader Arab fate: to be rendered powerless by unrepresentative governments, themselves rendered powerless by their dependency on external forces. The asymmetry between American and Israeli power on one hand and the weakness of the Arab state system on the other now threatens the sense among Arabs of who and what they are. The rapid growth of a nativist movement centring on religious belief is a sign of their refusal to accept this imposed fate.

The implications for Israel have been drawn out by Roberta Strauss Feuerlicht and others. What Israel has gained temporally, through power, Judaism has lost metaphysically and ethically. The crimes of the state (and considering a long and terrible record they can be described in no other way) have in their turn bred hate and a long sequence of bloody reprisals. The shock of what Israel did in Lebanon led Feuerlicht and others to point to the need for Jews to affirm their own identity independently of Israel. As she has written: 'The Israelis are surviving but not as Jews' (Feuerlicht, 1984: 250).

The ethical solution to the problems arising from the creation of Israel is present in United Nations resolutions acknowledging Israel's right to exist but setting out territorial limitations and the rights of the Palestinians as well. The 1993 Declaration of Principles represented another stage in the historical attempt to bury them – but when the Palestinians begin to emerge from this especially bleak period of their history, with whom will Israel then deal and what will there be left to talk about? Not the refugees, not Israel's return to the borders set by the United Nations in 1947, not the return to the 1967 borders, not the settlements in the West Bank, not Jerusalem and not a Palestinian state. As long as these questions are off the agenda, peace – real peace and not the imposed peace of 1993 – will be off the agenda too.

The nuclearisation of the Middle East underlines the dangers surrounding the success or failure of these negotiations. Although Israel routinely asserts that it will not be the first country to introduce nuclear weapons into the region, it is common knowledge that it has some two hundred nuclear warheads stored across the country. After the first disastrous week (as it certainly was for Israel) of the 1973 war, the government began preparing to deploy them; and there is obviously a terrible risk that they will be used at some time in the future. Israel's nuclear power is the cause of great alarm in the region, and was the reason for the reticence of Arab governments to make a fresh commitment to the Nuclear Non-Proliferation Treaty (NTP) when it came up for renewal in 1995. Instead of working towards a nuclear-free Middle East, the United States Government makes a lot of noise about Iran's nuclear *potential*, while quietly working to enhance Israel's nuclear capacity. As recently as 1995 the Clinton Administration approved the delivery of nine super-computers to Israeli universities: their purpose is to simulate the launching and detonation of nuclear weapons without the need for an actual test. There can be no doubt that the Arabs will be compelled to match Israel's nuclear power. 'Don't expect any country which is really fearing another country not to resort to all means of self-defence', the Deputy Secretary General of the Arab League, Mr Adnan Omran, said recently. 'If they have a nuclear bomb you have to have a nuclear bomb whether secretly or not.'

The air attack that destroyed the Osirak nuclear installation in Iraq in the 1980s is a clear signal of what Israel will do if another Arab country (or Iran) develops a nuclear weapons programme. As the Arab states must develop their own nuclear deterrent, a nuclear crisis seems inevitable some time in the future. The paradox, as the British correspondent David Hirst has written, is that 'an Israel unwilling to make true peace because of its nuclear and conventional edge may one day find its very existence threatened'. According to Adnan Omran: 'Remember [that] nuclear war will eliminate Israel from the map but it will not eliminate the Arab nation from the map.' This is the 'Samson option', the roof of the temple being pulled in over Israel and its enemies, the ultimate nightmare that cannot be discarded as long as Israel is strengthening its nuclear weapons capacity and forcing Arab governments to begin their own programmes. Only through a genuine reconciliation between Israel and the Arabs can these dangers be averted; only through reconciliation between Israel and the Palestinians can there be this broader settlement; and only through Israel removing itself entirely from the Palestinian territories seized in 1967, taking the refugee problem seriously and finding a formula for Jerusalem that meets Palestinian aspirations as well as Israeli can there be a durable Israeli–Palestinian settlement. Unfortunately, buoyed up by its military superiority and the continuing support of the United States, Israel is still seizing land, still settling, still consolidating its hold over Jerusalem and still driving real peace further into the distance. When Theodor Herzl founded the World Zionist Organisation in the late nineteenth century, he predicted that a Jewish state would be established in Palestine within fifty years. He was right, but will it still be there after the next fifty? The historic choices are now in the hands of the Israeli people and their government.

References

Aburish, Said K. (1994). *The Rise, Corruption and Coming Fall of the House of Sa'ud*. London: Bloomsbury.

Aruri, Naseer (ed.) (1984). *Occupation: Israel Over Palestine*. London: Zed Books.

Bruzonsky, Mark (1994). 'The Israeli Game Plan'. *New Dawn*, 26: 7–8.

Chomsky, Noam (1994). *World Orders Old and New*. New York: Columbia University Press.

Dodd C. H. and Sales M. E. (1970). *Israel and the Arab World*. London: Routledge & Kegan Paul.

Elmessiri, Abdelwahab M. (1977). *The Land of Promise: A Critique of Political Zionism*. New Brunswick, N.J.: North American.

Eveland, Wilbur Crane (1980). *Ropes of Sand. America's Failure in the Middle East*. London and New York: Norton.

Feuerlicht, Roberta Strauss (1984). *The Fate of the Jews*. London: Quartet Books.

Fisch, Harold (1978). *The Zionist Revolution. A New Perspective*. New York: St Martin's Press.

Handoussa, Heba (1990). 'Fifteen Years of US Aid to Egypt – A Critical Review'. In Ibrahim M. Oweiss (ed.), *The Political Economy of Contemporary Egypt*. Washington: Centre for Contemporary Arab Studies, Georgetown University.

Hudson, Michael C. (1977). *Arab Politics. The Search for Legitimacy*. New Haven: Yale University Press.

Ibrahim, Youssef (1994). 'Support for Arafat is Replaced by Enmity'. *New York Times News Service*, 2 December.

Ingrams, Doreen (1972). *Palestine Papers 1917–22. Seeds of Conflict*. London: John Murray.

Kazziha, Walid (1975). *Revolutionary Transformation in the Arab World*. London: Charles Knight & Company.

Lustick, Ian (1980). *Arabs in the Jewish State*. Austin: University of Texas Press.

Mansfield, Peter (1971). *The British in Egypt*. London: Weidenfeld & Nicolson.

Morris, Benny (1989). *The Birth of the Palestinian Refugee Problem 1947–1949*. Cambridge: Cambridge University Press.

National Lawyers Guild Middle East Delegation (1978). *Treatment of Palestinians in Israeli-Occupied West Bank and Gaza*. New York: National Lawyers Guild.

Peres, Shimon, with Arye, Naor (1993). *The New Middle East*. Dorset, Mass.: Longmead and Brisbane: Element.

Quandt, William B., Jabber, Fuad and Mosely, Lesch Ann (1973). *The Politics of Palestinian Nationalism*. Berkeley: University of California Press.

Roy, Delwin A. (1990). 'Egyptian Debt – Forgive or Forget?'. In Ibrahim M. Oweiss (ed.), *The Political Economy of Contemporary Egypt*. Washington DC: Centre for Contemporary Arab Studies, Georgetown University.

Said, Edward W. (1993). *Culture and Imperialism*. London: Chatto & Windus.

—— (1994). *The Politics of Dispossession. The Struggle for Palestinian Self-Determination 1969–1993*. London: Chatto & Windus.

Salt, Jeremy (1994–5). 'War by Other Means'. *Arena*, 14, 24–7.

Seale, Patrick (1988). *Asad of Syria. The Struggle for the Middle East*. Berkeley: University of California Press.

Shahak, Israel (1986). *Discrimination Based on the Law*. Israeli League for Human and Civil Rights: Jerusalem, 10.

Van Dam, Nikalaos (1981). *The Struggle for Power in Syria*. London: Croom Helm.

Woolfson, Marion (1980). *Prophets in Babylon: Jews in the Arab World*. London: Faber & Faber.

– 13 –

Religious Fundamentalism – A Threat to the State of Israel?[1]

Daryl Champion

When the Iranian Revolution erupted in 1978–9, it appeared as if a dormant curse had been unleashed upon an unsuspecting Western world. Haunting images of wild-eyed and beturbaned mullahs, black-chardored women, and fist-waving, slogan-chanting masses of Muslims flooded Western television and cinema screens and adorned the pages of newspapers, magazines and books. Everywhere, it seemed, this religious phenomenon from a medieval past was threatening vital Western interests.

Adding to the inherent virulence of this mass movement that was presented as sweeping the Islamic world was the proven menace of terrorism. And nowhere would a lethal fusion of Muslim ideologies and terrorist tactics have the potential to affect long-term regional stability more than in the then thirty-one-year-old Arab–Israeli conflict, a conflict that had already witnessed more than its share of tragedy. Palestinian acts of terror against civilian populations internationally had become established in the wake of the 1967 June War. The continuing social upheaval in Lebanon had also taken on a renewed religious overtone, with the appearance in force of such groups as the Shi'ite Hezballah. However, while the eyes of the Western world and the attention of its media were turned toward this rising tide of Islam in, arguably, the world's most volatile region, another religious fundamentalism was also on the rise.

This 'other' fundamentalism had quietly begun to press its agenda in April 1968 when sixty Israeli Jews established themselves in the West Bank Palestinian town of Hebron, captured by Israel in 1967: events had occurred that were 'destined to change the course of Israel's fortunes' (Rubinstein, 1984: 99). More than a quarter of a century later, this 'new' fundamentalism elicited international outrage on 25 February 1994 when twenty-nine Palestinian worshippers were shot dead in the Ibrahimi mosque in Hebron.[2] Dr Baruch Goldstein, the religiously-inspired Jewish settler who perpetrated 'the Hebron massacre', also died, and those who closely follow Middle Eastern affairs were largely appalled when Goldstein's colleagues and sympathisers exalted him as a hero and saint and praised his deed. The world was shocked again, perhaps even more so, when on 4 November 1995 the gun of another Jewish extremist, the 25-year-old law student, Yigal Amir, was turned fatally not against Arabs, but against the Israeli Prime Minister, Yitzhak Rabin.

Shock – as Ian Lustick pointed out in 1988 with specific reference to American reaction to the Jonathon Pollard spy case[3] – is attributable to ignorance of the resurgence of an extreme, right-wing Jewish nationalist religiosity (Lustick, 1988: ix). Even though this 'fundamentalism' received a relatively high profile in the immediate aftermath of the Hebron massacre, and an even higher profile with the assassination of Rabin, seldom has its threat to regional peace and Israel's stability been highlighted in specific and unambiguous terms in open public debate in the Western world. Yet the threat is not a new one; for many years informed observers of Middle Eastern affairs have been warning of the rise of a modern Jewish fundamentalism – an extremist religiosity that predated the Iranian revolution by around ten years, and that has 'developed into a major political and cultural force' in Israel (Lustick, 1988: ix). Now, even more than when Lustick wrote his detailed study of Jewish fundamentalism, 'it is the Jewish fundamentalist movement that has emerged as the greatest obstacle to meaningful negotiations toward a comprehensive Arab–Israeli peace settlement' (Lustick, 1988: 3).[4] Lustick has not been alone: 'Even more than Islamic fundamentalism, Jewish religious extremism has been a major barrier to a resolution of the situation in the occupied territories' (Palumbo, 1992: 11).

These Jewish religious nationalists have long held a policy of no-compromise on the re-establishment of biblical *Eretz Yisrael* – usually translated as 'Greater Israel' in today's political language – a policy that not only demands Israeli absorption of currently occupied Arab territories but, in many cases, also the annexation and settlement of western Jordan, large tracts of Lebanon and Syria, and the Sinai. Some of the most extreme advocate a Greater Israel stretching from the Nile Delta to the head of the Euphrates in southern Turkey. The settlement of further Arab lands could not, of course, be accomplished without a war of conquest; a war of conquest is precisely what a significant few in Israel advocate.

Besides regional war, religious Zionism – the ideology of the Jewish religious nationalists – threatens Israel's security domestically with

internal disharmony and instability; domestic strife should only be
expected when religious extremism seeks to impose itself on a society
that has its roots in secularism. Internal tension, however, is considerably more complex than a simple secular–religious divide, with
ethnic and class divisions contributing to the bigger picture. Israel can
be seen as living with inherent dichotomies, exacerbated by religious
nationalism and by a *de facto* alliance between extremist religious and
secular nationalists.

Related to domestic instability is the possibility that the influence
of extreme religious Zionism will continue to grow until the nature
of Israeli society is transformed. Such a society may not greatly differ
from neighbouring nations. The 'struggle against [Jewish] religious
extremism' could well be, as Yehoshafat Harkabi believed, 'ultimately
a matter of national cultural and religious survival' (Harkabi, 1988:
198–9).[5] It would certainly spell the end of the original Zionist ideal
of a secular, liberal-democratic state that was Jewish more by cultural
identity than by religion. Such a development would be likely to affect
continued United States and Western material and diplomatic support.
In a similar vein, what occurs in Israel is also likely to have far-reaching
implications for Judaism and world Jewry.

This chapter first provides a brief history of the contemporary
Jewish fundamentalist movement in Israel, together with a sketch of
its orientation. The growing political clout of the movement – which
is not homogeneous – is clarified, and put in the wider perspective
of Israeli politics. This exercise establishes that the threats that will be
discussed are not idle ones. The question of what constitutes 'fundamentalism' is broached when the links between religious and secular
Israeli 'fundamentalists' are examined. The piece focuses on the
internal dynamics of Israeli socio-politics, since the assassination of
Rabin confirms that the principal threat to Israel posed by 'religious
fundamentalism' is not one of war between states, but an internal
threat that challenges the cohesion of the Jewish state. With Israel's
widely-recognised status as a military mini-superpower, with the
usually unhesitating support of the United States and, more recently,
with open diplomatic and military relations with Turkey and Jordan,
it is clear that no other regional state poses a serious military threat
to Israel. Likewise, the security problems presented by groups such
as Hamas and Hezballah do not threaten the existence of the Jewish
state; in fact, the targeting of civilians by such groups is more likely
to increase the solidarity of Israelis. It is, instead, the actions of Jewish
extremists that will drive dissent from within, will further polarise
Israeli society, and will break down the cohesion of that society. Thus,

the ultimate threat to Israel – that is, to its existence – is not an external one, religious or otherwise, but an internal and Jewish one.

Of course, as with the analysis of most aspects of Middle East politics, any perception of 'threats to the state of Israel' is subject to rapidly moving events in a volatile environment that may see any scenario dramatically altered virtually overnight. Soothsayers and political scientists alike have more often than not been confounded by startling developments that allow for little more than a new round of dissection-in-hindsight, and a fresh wave of predictions. Therefore it is not the intention of this chapter to convince readers that Israel *will* suffer any of the identified threats, but to point out that they are possibilities, and that conditions for their manifestation have been created from within Israel itself, and to highlight an aspect of the Israeli–Palestinian dilemma that, to date, has received far too little attention.

Secularism Versus the Religious: Genesis of Jewish Religious Nationalism

Early Judaism recognised no formal distinction between institutions of religion and of state; Judaism, in its basic principle, is still more than an attitude to life: it is a way of life that is lived through the Torah and *halachah* (summarised in translation as 'religious law'). 'Render to Caesar the things that are Caesar's, and to God the things that are God's' – that familiar statement attributed to Jesus has, paradoxically, often been regarded as a religious sanctioning of the ideology of modern Western secularism and the separation of Church and State. There was, originally, no such basis for secular living in Judaism. Modern Israel, however, is in a uniquely ambivalent position. Born out of the secular European ideology of political Zionism, the state created by Jews for Jews has prided itself on its, still young, tradition of secular democracy.

One of Israel's most venerated religious figures is the Ashkenazi (European Jew, as opposed to Sephardi – or 'Oriental' – Jew) rabbi, Abraham Isaac Kuk (1865–1935), who is credited with reconciling religious Jews to secular Jewish nationalism. Rabbi Kuk, who was the inaugural chief rabbi of modern Palestine, was a man who believed in the combination of, and a balance between, the 'religious' and the 'secular'. Rabbi Kuk supported a Jewish return to Zion; most religious Jews regarded Palestine as a spiritual centre, and saw no need to create a political state.[6] This remained the case until the Nazi persecution of European Jews. But, even today, ultra-Orthodox Jews reject the state of Israel. Although very religious, these 'neo-traditionalist' *haredi* Jews have traditionally adopted a stance that is the polar opposite of those religious Jews who are also nationalists: unlike their brethren, who adhere to messianic, religious Zionism, *haredim* believe that 'the mutinous and atheistic State of Israel', far from heralding and hastening the arrival of the Messiah, is an obstacle to his coming; they even hope and pray that Israel 'will vanish' (Friedman, 1990: 131, 135; Sprinzak (1991: 17) refers to 'ultra-orthodox anti-Zionist extremists'). It was, therefore, no small gain for Zionism to achieve at least a partial religious sanction. It was Rabbi Kuk who paved the way for religious Jews to join secular Zionists in re-forging the ancient biblical kingdom of Israel; his son, Tzvi Yehudah, was to carry this reconciliation into a more radical phase.

Rabbi Tzvi Yehudah Kuk (1891–1982) preached a 'romantic interpretation' of (religious) Zionism (Lustick, 1988: 34; Palumbo, 1992: 15) that bore ancient Jewish apocalyptic imagery into the latter half of the twentieth century. The three salient features of this imagery were the return of the Jews from the diaspora to a recreated biblical Israel in its entirety, the rebuilding of the Temple, and the coming of the Messiah. All three features of the Kukist redemptive vision, together with apocalyptic wars of cosmic proportions, are believed by religious Zionists to be an inviolable part of the long-heralded and awaited salvation of the Jewish people.[7] The entire process entails the incorporation into modern Israel of all Israeli-occupied Arab land and the replacement of the current, Western-style secular democracy of Israel by traditional religious government. This includes the reconstitution of the ancient Sanhedrin, the Jewish supreme religious–political council. The rebuilding of the Temple naturally calls for the demolition of Muslim holy buildings occupying the Temple Mount. Additionally, a significant component of the metaphysical scenario is the Second World War Jewish Holocaust, often regarded as the harbinger of the redemptive process.[8] Religious Zionism's goal is to ensure that the redemptive enterprise in its totality proceeds apace.

Rabbi Tzvi Yehudah's vision of an Israel on the path to redemption developed in the school of thought he spawned as *rosh yeshivah* of the central Israeli Yeshivat ha-Rav. In the mid-1960s, disciples of Rabbi Tzvi Yehudah formed an élite core group centred on his beliefs. This group, *Gahelet* ('Embers'), evolved into Gush Emunim ('Block of the Faithful') in the aftermath of the 1973 October War. Gush Emunim (usually abbreviated to 'Gush') is a Jewish religious Zionist movement that, in Lustick's words, forms 'the organized focus of Jewish fundamentalism'. It is 'an umbrella organization' that, with the slogan 'The

Land of Israel, for the People of Israel, According to the Torah . . . of Israel', provides 'the clearest and strongest expression of fundamentalist tendencies in Israeli society'. It operates with 'a wide variety of organizations, political parties, prominent individuals, vigilante groups, institutes, and personal networks', and, 'by any measure, it has been the most successful extraparliamentary movement to arise in Israel since the state's establishment in 1948' (Lustick, 1988: 8; see also Sprinzak, 1991: 6, 107–9, 124–5). Rabbi Tzvi Yehudah's earliest followers included future Gush leader, Rabbi Moshe Levinger, future Tehiya[9] Member of the Knesset (MK), Rabbi Eliezar Waldman, and future National Religious Party (NRP)[10] MK, Rabbi Haim Druckman.

'Chosen people' and 'promised land' are central themes to the Jewish religious Zionist movement. These themes constitute a cornerstone for the policies of religious extremists who advocate the mass deportation ('transfer') of all Arabs from the occupied territories, if not from Israel proper. It is noteworthy that secular Zionism has an even longer history of the concept of 'transfer' (Shahak, 1989; Sprinzak, 1991: 28–30, 297–8; Masalha, 1992).[11] This notion of 'chosen people' – according to another Israeli scholar, Gideon Aran – allows Gush to condemn both ultra-Orthodox and liberal-Orthodox Jews, and to reconcile their interpretation of Judaism and messianism with secular Zionism. *Segulah*, 'the indelible and undeniable property characterizing the people of Israel who are unconditionally holy and in whose hearts hides a sacred spark', explains Aran, is deemed by 'mystic-messianic Gush Emunim' to be more important than living – even strictly – according to Torah and *halachah*. This means that secular Zionists, struggling for the sake of Israel, can be regarded as more holy than a religiously observant Jew who does not accept Gush's concept of *segulah*. It also means that Gush's 'elevated position allows them to treat the standards of the here and now with contempt and to behave with arrogance toward the rest of humanity, which has not yet been illuminated' (Aran, 1990: 170–4; see also Rubinstein, 1984: 122–3).

The importance of *segulah* in Gush ideology can be traced to the movement's grandfather, Rabbi Kuk the elder, who espoused a novel theory of comparative Jewish and Gentile (non-Jew) spirituality (see Chomsky, 1989: 214). Rabbi Tzvi Yehudah has stated:

> God has determined, once and forever, that we are a holy people, a reality of holy souls, holy bodies, part of the souls of the entirety of Israel which is entirely holy. There is a reality of a holy land, a strip of land which God chose – 'because God chose Zion.' This is a land 'whose fruit is holy'. . . . Thus have things been determined: This is a holy land and this is a holy people (Z. Y. Kuk, 1967a, quoted in Liebman, 1990: 82–3).

Within the broader Jewish religious Zionist movement, however, there is no unanimity on how messianic objectives should be reached. Gush provides Lustick with a prime example of radicals and moderates, relatively speaking, within the organisation. He describes 'a key division' between 'vanguardists', the more extreme members who would, for example, destroy the Dome of the Rock and the al-Aqsa Mosque to rebuild the temple, and 'consensus builders', who believe in a 'little by little' approach (Lustick, 1987: 130–4). Whether vanguardists or consensus builders, Gush activists believe in the integrity of a Jewish *Eretz Yisrael*. Three weeks before the 1967 June War, in his Israeli Independence Day sermon, Gush's father-figure stated:

> Nineteen years ago, on the very night that the decision of the United Nations to create the State of Israel was handed down . . . I sat alone – quiet and depressed. . . . I was not able to accept . . . that terrible news, that indeed 'my land they have divided' had occurred! Yes, where is our Hebron – have we forgotten it?! And where is our . . . Jericho, where – will we forget them?! And all of Transjordan – it is all ours, every single clod of earth, each little bit, every part of the land is part of the land of God – is it in our power to surrender even one millimeter of it?! (Z. Y. Kuk, 1967b, quoted in Lustick, 1988: 36.)

Rabbi Moshe Levinger – successor to the Gush leadership after Rabbi Tzvi Yehudah's death – said in 1988: 'Samaria and Judaea [the West Bank] belonged to the Jewish people even before 1967. We've known that they belonged to us all throughout history. We know that some day we will receive the East Bank of the Jordan as well. It's God's will' (Levinger, 1988, quoted in Palumbo, 1992: 170).

On the point of *Eretz Yisrael*, there is a link between religious Zionist fundamentalism and secular Zionism. Lustick writes: 'the beliefs and political behavior of secular ultra-nationalist Jews, drawn from activist elements of the Labor Zionist and Revisionist (right-wing Zionist) movements, require that they also be included within contemporary Jewish fundamentalism' (Lustick, 1988: 8). Furthermore, he adds:

> For . . . fundamentalist activists who are not religious, the Land of Israel, combined with the Bible and historicist notions of the 'destiny of the Jewish people', plays a role functionally equivalent to that of God for religious fundamentalists. . . . For all Israeli Jewish fundamentalists . . . an irreducible attachment to the Land of Israel, in its entirety, is at the core of their world view (Lustick, 1987: 126–7).

At this point, where both the religious and the secular are candidates for the title 'fundamentalist', the question of what is a fundamentalist is pertinent. There is no firm agreement on a definition; indeed, it has become a popular word, and is often employed recklessly, usually with little understanding. However, a general consensus does appear to favour the active pursuit of dogmatic or extreme policies. Extreme policies, in the Israeli context, would constitute those such as 'transfer', the annexation of occupied Arab territories, the conquest of further Arab land, denying Israeli Arabs equal citizenship rights, reforming Israel to make it a strict religious society based on Torah and *halachah*, and the rebuilding of the Temple after the demolition of the al-Aqsa Mosque and the Dome of the Rock: not all of these policies are strictly the exclusive domain of religious Jews. On defining fundamentalism, Lustick (1988: 6) has written:

> Individuals, organizations, or movements may be regarded as fundamentalist to the extent that they (1) base their activities on uncompromisable injunctions; (2) consider their behavior to be guided by direct contact with the source of transcendental authority; and (3) are actively engaged in political attempts to bring about rapid and comprehensive change.

Also searching for a satisfactory definition, Yehoshafat Harkabi (1988: 147–8) has written:

> The designation 'nationalist religious extremists' is of course very general, and includes various groups who are at loggerheads with one another. When I call them 'extremists' I am not assessing them according to a religious standard, but from the perspective of the policy they believe that Israel should adopt . . . Theirs is religious extremism in political terms.

And Menachem Friedman (1990: 127) has added his voice to the debate:

> We use the term to define a religious outlook shared by a group of believers who base their belief on an ideal religious–political reality that has existed in the past or is expected to emerge in the future. Such realities are described in great detail in the religious literature. And the fundamentalist believer is obliged to use whatever religious and political means are necessary to actualize these realities in the here and now.

Although the scholars appear to agree on the role of political activism in their definitions of fundamentalism, the fact that Friedman (1990) defines the ultra-Orthodox *haredim* as 'zealots' and 'conservative fundamentalists', while Lustick excludes them from his definition because of what he perceives as their non-political ideology, is illustrative of the differences that remain. Reflecting this lack of firm consensus, Rabbi Zev Falk, a professor of law at the Hebrew University of Jerusalem, declined to discuss 'religious fundamentalism' during a seminar that concentrated on the ultra-extreme Kach party in the wake of the Hebron massacre, saying there is 'no objective definition of "fundamentalism"' (Falk, 1994, unpublished).

Reinforcing the notion that the label 'fundamentalist' should not necessarily be confined to the religious, the Israeli political scientist, Ehud Sprinzak (1991: 15, 18), has revealed that 'hard-core members' of the Israeli radical right belong to 'both religious and secular' camps; has referred to 'secular neofundamentalism, which approves of Gush Emunim's theology from a non-orthodox angle'; and has pointed out that 'secular Zionists are legitimate partners in the process of redemption'. He also writes that: 'Most of the top leaders of the Tehiya, Moledet, and Tzomet, who have been playing a crucial role in spreading the new radicalism, are secular Jews who espouse the cause of the Greater Eretz Yisrael for reasons not obviously related to fundamentalist doctrines. So do the radical leaders of Likud' (Sprinzak, 1991: 20).

Sprinzak's incisive work draws distinctions between the various elements that, collectively, make up what he designates 'Israel's radical right'. However, these elements cut across Israeli society, and considering the natural alliance between what may be described as nationalist fundamentalism and religious fundamentalism, the term 'fundamentalism' in this essay is applied to both religious and secular extremists.[12] In this application, the adherence to an extreme nationalist ideology may be regarded as a substitute for religious ideology.

A unity of purpose – a 'symbiotic relationship' (Lustick, 1988: 8) – has tended to unite major segments of the Israeli religious and secular fundamentalist camps, a fact running beneath the surface in mainstream Israeli political culture, but highlighted from time to time. Not surprisingly, the religious fundamentalists have found their greatest support, ideologically and materially, in the Likud and some associated right-wing parties. In the Likud-dominated Knesset from 1977 to 1992, Gush was well represented in the government through its influence in the NRP. According to Lustick (1988: 9), Gush provided ideological paupers in Likud with a 'systematic and evocative symbol system . . . an aura of Jewish authenticity and Zionist idealism' and a vital, enthusiastic human resource for settlement of the occupied territories. In return, Gush gained political legitimacy, social credibility and tremendous governmental financial and infrastructural resources.

Daryl Champion

Settlement, land acquisition, religious affairs and education were areas particularly given over to Gush. The scale and the success of this 'symbiotic relationship' – in which 'the lines between Likud's secular nationalism and the messianic religion of the radicalized NRP became blurred' (Hader, 1992: 601) – can be glimpsed in the following passage:

> From 1977 until the end of 1984 two Likud governments poured more than $1 billion into Jewish settlement in the West Bank and Gaza Strip. ... The number of Jewish settlers in predominantly Arab areas of the West Bank increased from a few thousand to over 38,000. Sweeping land requisitions and zoning restrictions were implemented to provide a land reserve for future settlements. Virtually open access to cabinet ministers was afforded to Gush Emunim leaders. Generous employment opportunities in governmental and quasi-governmental agencies responsible for religion and social life, infrastructural development, security, and other spheres of life in the settlements were provided to Gush activists. Thus, fundamentalists gained the economic and administrative resources to recruit new followers and sustain a wide range of intensive political and practical efforts in support of their programme to transform the shape and direction of Israeli society (Lustick, 1988: 40–1).

Despite the more natural alignment of right-wing, secular Zionism with religious nationalist extremism, Labor Zionism, also, has a tradition of *de facto* co-operation with religious Zionism (Lustick, 1988: 31ff.). The religious influence on the Israeli education system was, in fact, first forged with Mapai acquiescence during Israel's early days;[13] and 'veteran and even leading figures of the Labour movement' have been vocal in their support for the Jewish integrity of 'the entire land of Israel' (Beilin, 1992: 160–1). Labor-religious co-operation was confirmed soon after the 1992 Israeli elections: the Labor Party, headed by another former army chief of staff, the late Yitzhak Rabin, in alliance with the ultra-Orthodox Shas Party (and the left-wing Meretz Party), announced it would 'thicken' (expand) existing settlements and commit itself to 'security settlements' (Kidron, 1992b: 5–7). Additionally, during Rabin's first term as prime minister 1974–7, his Labor government did nothing to restrain Gush's illegal settlement activities and, twenty years later, 'Gush Emunim leaders enjoy[ed] Rabin's friendship.' (Shahak, 1994a: 16).

The re-election of a Likud-led government in May 1996 heralds a return to an overtly strident settlement policy without recourse to Labor's public relations terminology. For example, the new right-wing Israeli Prime Minister, Binyamin Netanyahu, has openly indicated his support for the expansion of existing Jewish settlements and the creation of new ones. On his United States visit in July 1996, Netanyahu 'rebuffed American efforts to secure from him a promise not to construct new settlements in the West Bank, as opposed to expanding existing settlements', and he 'cited Israeli Government statistics showing that in the last four years under the Labor Party, the population of settlers on the West Bank and Gaza had grown from 96,000 to 145,000, which he called "natural growth." He then said, "I assume that no one here is expecting us to do less"' (Erlanger, 1996). This is an attitude the settler movement has greeted enthusiastically, with the Council of Jewish Communities in Judea, Samaria and Gaza planning to increase the number of Jewish settlers in the territories to 500,000 by the year 2000 (see *AgmoNet*, 1996; Islamic Association for Palestine, 1996; *Ha'aretz*, reported in *Friday Journal*, 1996b; Brown, 1996).[14]

Israeli Society: 'Hawkish', a 'Dovish Trend', or Polarising?

Substantial support for fundamentalist political parties in Israel is a fact: although commentators made much over the religious parties' loss of two Knesset seats in the 1992 elections, the total number of seats occupied by the fundamentalist bloc – albeit fragmented – rose from twenty-five to twenty-seven. The sixteen religious seats were taken by the NRP, Shas and the Orthodox Torah Bloc.[15] Eleven seats were won by the extreme, ultra-nationalist Tzomet and Moledet parties.[16]

While religious parties clearly increased their mandate to twenty-three seats in the 1996 elections,[17] the situation with respect to the secular nationalist bloc has become less clear, if more compact, with the alliance between Likud, Tzomet and Gesher.[18] Tzomet's influence cannot help but have the effect of pushing Likud further to the nationalist right,[19] and since Shas, the NRP and United Torah Judaism are part of Likud's coalition government, Likud can be seen to be the main umbrella party for the religious and secular right of Israeli politics.[20] The exception is Moledet, which suffered a crisis when two of its three MKs left the party toward the end of the thirteenth Knesset's term to form their own factions. Moledet recovered and regained two Knesset seats in 1996, but remains outside the Likud-dominated nationalist–religious bloc because, even for this bloc, Moledet's policies are too blatantly extreme.[21] However, the 66-seat majority of the Likud coalition government will be effectively bolstered to 68 in the 120-seat Knesset, since it will almost certainly enjoy the *de facto* support of Moledet.

The ultra-extremist fringes of the nationalist–religious right, even though unrepresented directly in the Knesset, are represented indirectly through the NRP and Moledet. Together, these two parties won the support of 312,206 voters – a total of 10.1 per cent of eligible votes, up from 7.4 per cent in 1992 (see Israel Foreign Ministry Information Division, 1996a; Smooha and Peretz, 1993: 450, table 1).[22] Coincidentally, the collective nationalist–religious right, which gained seats in 1996, won the same percentage of eligible votes as in 1992, at 46.9 per cent. However, this apparent maintaining of the status quo does not take into account the fact that 50.4 per cent of voting Israelis favoured Likud's nationalistic Binyamin Netanyahu over Labor's Shimon Peres (49.5 per cent). It also does not take into account the emergence of the HaDerech HaShlishit party, with four seats: although formed by MKs who broke ranks with Labor and who profess a median path between Labor and Likud, key policies in the party's platform are not ones that would displease the nationalist right.[23] When HaDerech HaShlishit's 3.1 per cent of the vote is added to the tally garnered by the nationalist–religious bloc, the result is more like a 50 per cent split between parties representing a distinct leaning to the right, and those representing the centre and left.

However, Yisrael Ba'aliya, a new party representing the interests of Soviet/Russian immigrants in Israel, was widely tipped to join the coalition of whichever bloc won the mandate to form a government; its principal interest is settlement, housing and employment for new immigrants, and the party may be described as ideologically neutral. The party is a partner in the Likud coalition government, but it cannot be included as part of the nationalist–religious bloc. By the same token, its seven MKs, representing 5.7 per cent of the vote, cannot be included in the centre–left bloc. Thus, using the results of the 1996 elections as a basis for analysis, Israeli society can be interpreted as leaning to the nationalist–religious right by a factor of around 50 per cent, while the centre–left enjoys a favour-factor of around 41.3 per cent (see Israel Foreign Ministry Information Division, 1996a). Sprinzak (1991: 311) supports this conclusion: 'the rhetoric of "Greater Eretz Yisrael" which [Likud] propagates together with the National Religious Party and the radical right is shared by more than 50 percent of the voting public'.

Moreover, two parties in the centre–left bloc that won seats in the fourteenth Knesset are Israeli-Arab: Hadash and the United Arab List. Arab parties, traditionally shunned by both Labor and Likud, have been marginalised from the processes of power in the Jewish state.[24] Thus, even though Hadash contains some Jewish members, and even though these two parties occupy nine seats in the Knesset – representing 7.1 per cent of the vote – the Israeli political left is divided in a way that has been irreconcilable; this was highlighted once again after the 1992 elections, when Labor brought Shas into its coalition to secure a majority government in the Knesset.[25] On the other hand, in 1996 the nationalist–religious right, although highly factionalised, has proved that it can cobble together a working coalition without appeal to parties outside its own bloc.

Since the Knesset's character echoes the nature of Israeli society as a result of proportional, democratic elections, various scholars have interpreted support for extremist politics as indicative of a disturbing trend: 'What has happened lately is that the centre has shifted much closer to these formerly marginal [extremist] elements' (Harkabi, 1988: 163); 'the movement it [Gush] represents can no longer be considered an extremist fringe group in Israeli society or politics' (Lustick, 1988: 14); 'It is wrong to assume that the mass murder in Hebron stemmed only from the opinions of a small group of extremists on the fringe of the Israeli political spectrum' (Shahak, 1994a: 16). The carefully studied analysis of Sprinzak (1991: 14) perhaps provides the clearest expression of the anatomy of the Israeli right: the radical right should not be seen as an isolated extremist faction that stands in diametrical opposition to both Israeli democracy and the moderate right, but rather as a very influential school that has been pushing the entire Israeli right toward greater ultranationalism, greater extralegalism, greater militarism, greater ethnocentrism, and greater religiosity. The radical right is neither separated historically nor detached politically from the larger Israeli right. It is instead the right pole of the Israeli nationalist continuum, whose left pole is the moderate right. It is a political and ideological camp of true believers whose values and ideas are sometimes shared by large numbers of Israelis who are usually not considered radical (see also Sprinzak, 1991: 13, 15).[26]

After the 1992 elections, Sammy Smooha and Don Peretz (1993) tacitly agreed with Leon Hader (1992) in arguing that these elections were 'critical' because, they thought, they marked the end of the Likud era – Hader's 'Second Israeli Republic' – and the beginning of a new, more pragmatic and 'dovish' Labor era – Hader's 'Third Republic'. Their arguments that Israeli society was changing were well presented and compelling: the politically restless Sephardi population, the influx of Russian immigrants, and the peace process – among other factors – did indicate a period of transition. But even then, there was preponderant evidence that suggested that the transition would not be smooth. While Smooha and Peretz admitted that, if anything, the total Israeli vote in 1992 still tended to favour the 'hawks', they questioned the significance of the figures, arguing they belied the underlying depth of attitudinal change.[27]

Gideon Doron (1996: 6–7), however, has cast doubt on whether this interpretation of the direction Israeli politics and society was taking was ever justified: he has written that '[Rabin] could not command a majority within his own party or among the public', and has referred to 'the [extensive] scope and intensity of opposition they [Rabin's activities] generated in Israel'.[28] In any case, the 1996 elections have proved that the Likud era is not at an end, and that the 'dovish trend' outlined by Hader, Smooha and Peretz has stalled at less than 50 per cent of the population. The ultimate questions that Hader, Smooha and Peretz failed to raise were: 'What will happen to the nationalist and religious extremists – a significant minority – as the posited moderating trend in Israeli society continues? What will be their reaction to the "dovish" policies that they so stridently oppose?' It was apparent, then, that Gush and its allies and sympathisers were unlikely simply to fade away: indeed they did not, and one reaction to perceived 'dovish' policies was the slaying of Yitzhak Rabin.

The 1996 Israeli elections have emphasised that various blends of right-wing policies – both secular and religious – enjoy a considerable and resurgent endorsement in Israel. The assassination of Rabin and the make-up of the fourteenth Knesset testify to the advancement of an ideological split – a polarisation of society – that was discernible in its early stages many years ago. The September 1993 Washington Declaration of Principles marked an intensification of this process, as is evidenced by a period that has been tragically dramatised by the Hebron massacre, Palestinian suicide bombers and the Rabin assassination. This polarisation is now beginning to reach a significant enough level to cause major civil disturbances over issues on which the two broad wings of Israeli society feel strongly. Such a development, like the fundamentalist movement itself, would not be new: Amnon Rubinstein was concerned by the prospect of social polarisation and by 'two contrasting phenomena' more than a decade ago, referring in 1984 to 'a silent truce' between 'the secular majority' and 'a determined fundamentalist group' (Rubinstein, 1984: xi, 121). Twelve years later, Gideon Doron (1996: 6) has written of 'the inherent contradiction and permanent tension that exists between politics and religion within the "Jewish Democracy"', and of 'an ideologically divided polity'. The impetus of a now well-established Israeli peace movement when set against the 1996 Likud bloc victory only serves to emphasise the potential for a damaging schism.

A polarisation of Israeli society was, in fact, dramatically illustrated by the 1996 vote for the country's prime minister: Netanyahu defeated Peres by a mere 29,457 votes, a margin of only 0.9 per cent.[29] This result highlighted the statements of many observers in the aftermath of Rabin's death; for example, *Jerusalem Report* editor, David Horovitz, commented that the Israeli population was split 'fifty–fifty' over the peace process, and that Rabin's assassination had *not* bridged a divided society (Horovitz, 1995). Immediately after the elections, similar comments were made. Horovitz (1996) once again emphasised that '[Israel] is a very divided country'; Israel's ambassador to Australia, Shmuel Moyal (1996), spoke of 'division' and 'rift' in Israeli society; and former Israeli prime minister, Yitzhak Shamir (in the *Australian Jewish News*, 1996), has been quoted as referring to 'deep divisions among Israelis'.[30] An aide to the Israeli prime minister-elect, in an official post-election statement, emphasised that:

> in the last several years, one of the most difficult phenomena we have witnessed has been the deepening of a rift within Israeli society and the increasing polarization between different public sectors. Therefore, Netanyahu views bringing about reconciliation as a priority of the first order in order to bridge gaps and to achieve a feeling of unity in Israel (Naveh, 1996).

The fact that Israeli society is deeply divided cannot be disputed. The narrow 1996 Netanyahu victory represents the entrenchment of socio-political polarisation, and the formation of a nationalist–religious coalition government has provided space for Gush and allied groups to relaunch settlement and other projects with renewed gusto.

Gush Emunim Projects and the Threat to Israel

Considering Gush's history and its establishment in Israeli political and social life, any initiative advocated by the religious nationalist movement must be treated seriously. The intensely motivating factor of apocalyptic belief creates a propensity for daring and potentially dangerous ideas and projects, as well as the determination to carry them out; as indicated, it already commands significant political and infrastructural resources that could be used to put them into effect. Even without official, government-sanctioned implementation, many Gush projects could cause dramatic upheaval, both internationally and domestically.

The much-dreamed-of rebuilding of the Temple is one such project. This is an event integral to the religious fundamentalists' vision of a pious Israel preparing the way for the coming of the Messiah. To those of Gush referred to by Gideon Aran as 'kabbalistic mystic-messianic' (Aran, 1990: 162), and especially to those Lustick dubs vanguardists, the sooner the Muslim sanctuaries occupying the site are demolished and the temple reconstructed, the better. Since these sanctuaries are sacred to Islam, there has been much speculation about what an Arab–Muslim response would be should the vanguardists carry out their plans.

Such an event would almost certainly propel Israel into another war. In both his works on Israeli fundamentalism, Lustick has quoted the same piece by Doron Rosenblum describing the consummation of the destruction of the Dome and al-Aqsa; furthermore, it is 'only a matter of time' (Rosenblum, 1985, quoted in Lustick, 1987: 136; 1988: 172–3). War involving such passions would be catastrophic; Israel could only emerge devastated, even if victorious. It is unclear how widespread such a war would be in the late 1990s, but Sprinzak (1991: 3) has referred to a Harvard University simulated war-game that concluded that a third world war might have been sparked had the Dome been destroyed by zealots in the early 1980s.[31] A conflict over the Dome could still give Israel reason to use its nuclear weapons: there is a stratum of Israeli society that is even prepared to resort to the pre-emptive use of such weapons in response to a conventional threat (see Kison, 1976, quoted in Hirst, 1984: 455–6; Shahak, 1994a).[32]

Short of war, the Temple Mount issue still has the potential to visit disaster upon Israeli society. The Temple Mount massacre of 8 October 1990 – when at least nineteen Palestinians were killed and 150 wounded, and many more killed and injured in ensuing demonstrations – testifies to the dangers of some activities of Jewish fundamentalist groups such as the Temple Mount Faithful, who provoked Palestinians by marching on the Mount to lay a 'foundation stone' for the 'third temple'. This relatively minor event can be seen as a harbinger for a tragic drama that could slowly, or quickly, drag the whole of Israel into bloody chaos.

Lustick also draws his readers' attention to the fact that some members of élite Israeli army units are also infused with messianic zeal, and are known to be uttering prayers for the rebuilding of the temple 'speedily in our own days' (Lustick, 1988: 173). They would, of course, have the wherewithal to realise their own prayers should they be determined to do so. The discovery of a Jewish terrorist underground in April 1984, when a well-advanced plan to destroy the Dome of the Rock was uncovered, confirmed the potential role of Israeli military personnel in such messianic undertakings. The plan involved '[m]ore than twenty skilled Israeli reservists' and 'huge quantities' of stolen army explosives (Sprinzak, 1991: 3). Sprinzak (1991: 4) also points to the fact that this Gush terrorist underground included 'highly educated and responsible men, some of them high-ranking army officers'. Israel Shahak (1994c) expresses concern at how the ranks of the Israeli army officer corps have been bolstered by 'a wave of entrants' from youth infused with national–religious ideology and, indeed, at the very structure of the army, which accommodates religious students – *Hesder Yeshivot* soldiers – in their own separate, semi-autonomous units, with their own rabbi. Most *Hesder* unit rabbis are associated with the Gush; many of these religious soldiers remain in the army after their draft period has concluded.

The presence of *Hesder* soldiers in the army is in addition to many radical settlers who have enlisted, and in addition to special settler and settler-dominated military formations in the occupied territories, especially in the West Bank. Shahak's fears (see also Shahak, 1994b) appear to be well founded: a West Bank religious settler has claimed – prior to the Hebron massacre – that he and fellow settlers have access to Israel Defence Forces (IDF) armouries, 'if necessary' (interview in Peled, 1994). It is also relevant to note that a sergeant from the élite Golani Brigade was arrested one week after the slaying of Rabin, indicted on charges of stealing weapons from his military base and giving them to Rabin's assassin, Yigal Amir and his brother, Hagai. Yigal Amir also served in the Golani Brigade; the weapons had been stolen over the course of a year, originally for attacks against Palestinians (see Segal, 1995b). A Golani Brigade battalion commander in November 1995 told the Israeli newspaper *Yediot Aharonot* that the 'disappearance of Army munitions is hardly unusual' (see Pinkas, 1995). The Lieutenant-Colonel also said: 'The unit is in the field most of the time; it's no problem to lay a hand on weapons. Maybe they [the Amir brothers] told [the sergeant who supplied the Amirs with weapons and explosives] "We'll shoot up the Arabs a little bit." And that's okay, that's something you should expect' (see Pinkas, 1995).

The most extreme Gush elements also sanction numerous other radical attitudes and policies, including the 'purification' of – the deportation of all non-Jews from – Jerusalem (Waldenberg, 1976, quoted in Rubinstein, 1984: 117; see also Harkabi, 1988: 152); the declaration of Christianity as idolatry – together with a decree to burn copies of the New Testament (Harkabi, 1988: 161–2); and the mass expulsion of Arabs from *Eretz Yisrael*. Even the mass extermination of all Arabs – 180–200 million people – whom some ultra-extreme rabbis have identified as being descended from the ancient Amalekites, has been consecrated (Harkabi, 1988: 153, 187). This genocidal edict is taken from a contemporary application of Deuteronomy 25: 17–19, in conjunction with other passages such as Deuteronomy 20: 10–18, in the Hebrew Bible (see also: 1 Samuel 15). Shahak (1994c) points out that 'Amalek' is now a term being applied to all potentially threatening Gentiles by Jewish religious educators in Israel. He quotes from a book by Dr Dov Ehrlich, published by the autonomous Department of Religious Education in the Israeli government's education ministry, for use in children's religious education:

> Amalekites can be now found all over, but especially within the borders of the Greater Land of Israel which the Lord gave to the Jews. The Amalekites are fated to hate us forever, so we are justly commanded to hate them twice as strongly. The Bible commanded us to exterminate the Amalekites. Just as we obeyed the command by exterminating the ancient Amalek, we now must do the same to the modern Amalek (Ehrlich, 1993, quoted in Shahak, 1994c: 18. For a hint of the religiously-inspired crisis in the Israeli education system, see Yariv, 1994).

Rubinstein (1984: 115–16) also discusses the 'eternal hatred' that some rabbis preach exists between Jews and the 'descendants of Esau', and how 'military rabbinical chaplains have scandalized the public by asserting that under Halachic law, Arab civilians may be killed in . . . wars of religious obligation' (see also Rubinstein, 1982). The 'Amalekite' issue – no doubt a novelty in the Western world – has been a subject of controversial public discussion in Israel (I. Shahak, pers. comm., 22 September 1994).

The task facing any Israeli government with respect to returning occupied Arab land to 'Amalekites' in the interests of a peace settlement can be appreciated. There are now around 120,000 Jewish settlers in the West Bank alone: settlement of the occupied territories has, of course, been one Gush project that has been actively – and relatively successfully – pursued over the last two decades.[33] The '*de facto* annexation process', promoted by successive Israeli governments since 1974, also had the goal during the Likud era of creating a fundamentalist-like nationalism and commitment to Greater Israel among ordinary Jewish settlers (Lustick, 1988: 156–60). Despite the apparent willingness of many of these non-ideological settlers to leave the territories and live within Israel proper, the withdrawal from occupied territories, especially from religiously significant portions of biblical *Eretz Yisrael*, stands as the most tangible potential for civil violence in Israel. Considering the strong settler–army bonds, especially in the West Bank, the possibility of outright defiance of the state in support of settlers by some units of the Israeli army must be acknowledged, especially since some extremist rabbis have already called on soldiers to refuse orders to eject settlers from Hebron (Margalit, 1994).[34] While Dan Margalit (1994: 22) fears a 'paralysed' Israeli army and government, Shahak (1994c: 19) even raises the suggestion of a military coup attempt. However, Sprinzak (1996), in response to the suggestion that '40 percent of the [Israeli] military belongs to the religious right', firmly rejected questions over the IDF's loyalty to the government.

Expressions of religious Zionism seeking the integrity of the promised land – for example, by Rabbi Shlomo Avineri – leave little room for doubt about the eventual results if the fundamentalists' established inroads into the Knesset and Israeli society are widened: 'We must live in this land even at the price of war. Moreover, even if there is peace, we must instigate wars of liberation in order to conquer it' (Avineri, 1982, quoted in Harkabi, 1988: 165). Similar attitudes have been publicly expressed by Rabbis Levinger and Waldman: for example, 'It is impossible to complete the Redemption by any means other than war' (Waldman, 1983, quoted in Lustick, 1987: 124. See also Palumbo, 1992: 170).[35]

The peace process is unlikely to affect such extreme religious nationalists other than to harden their attitudes: Yitzhak Rabin, despite an impressive military record and his firm stance as a 'security hawk', was openly regarded as a traitor by many religious Zionists for his willingness to surrender territory belonging to the Promised Land of the Jews. Sprinzak (1991: 19) and Doron (1996: 7) explain the process by which an Israeli leader may, by religious reasoning, be pronounced illegitimate, treasonous, and a fair target for execution by any believing Jew. In the investigations following his assassination, Israel's internal security service, Shin Bet, revealed its officials 'had received dozens of reports about possible assassination plans' targeting Rabin (Segal, 1995a).[36] Rabin's peace-making partner and his successor to the prime ministership, Shimon Peres, was forced to curtail his 1996 election day campaigning owing to threats made against him by Jewish extremists (O'Sullivan, 1996).

Whatever influence radical religious Zionists have brought to bear on the Israeli socio-political landscape to date, that influence stands to grow significantly if differences with the *haredim* can be bridged.[37] Even though religious Zionism and ultra-Orthodoxy have traditionally been opposed in their acceptance, and their interpretations, of the state of Israel, the possibility of an eventual alliance does exist. *Haredim* are, after all, co-religionists who are equally passionate and zealous in their wish to see religious observance permeate Israeli society. There are already examples, in fact, which demonstrate the potentiality for *haredi*–religious Zionist–nationalist *rapprochement*. One such example occurred during the lead-up to the 1996 elections, when a leading figure of the ultra-Orthodox Lubavitcher community in Melbourne, Australia, travelled to Israel to campaign among the country's *haredim* on behalf of the Netanyahu–Likud bloc: 'My role as the Lubavitcher Rebbe's representative was to try to ensure a right-wing government in Israel' (Gutnick, quoted in Lipski, 1996).

In so far as various strands of ultra-Orthodoxy participate in Israeli politics and society, they are capable of applying pressure, sometimes violently, to instigate a greater institutionalisation of religiosity.[38] Their differences with religious Zionists are rooted mainly in the timing of, and conditions for, the Messiah's arrival; but, this could be changing, as *haredim* have also claimed to feel part of a messianic dawning (Lustick, 1988: 167). The respect and obedience that *haredi* rabbis command from their followers would make likely a virtual overnight, *en masse* defection of *haredim* to the ranks of the religious Zionists, 'should key rabbis within the Haredi subcultures decide that wars or struggles over the Land of Israel or the Temple Mount do herald the approaching climax of the redemption process' (Lustick, 1988: 167). It is significant that a town devoted to ultra-Orthodox settlers has been built in the West Bank. Prominent ultra-Orthodox and Gush polit- icians have also officially co-operated, to the point of running in national elections as members of the same party. Shas members have also been among vocal proponents of nationalism and anti-Arabism (Lustick, 1988: 167). On what appears to be a paradox, Charles Lieb- man (1990: 81, note 3) writes: 'Among the *haredi* "doves", one hears the argument that Israeli sovereignty over Judea and Samaria is pointless from a Jewish point of view since Israel dares not act as it is enjoined to act by religious law; that is, to expel the non-Jews or at least destroy their places of worship'.

An ascendancy of a radical, ultra-Orthodox–Gush Judaism in Israel would have the potential profoundly to affect the Jewish diaspora and the Jewish faith itself. For example, ultra-Orthodoxy, which is antag- onistic to all forms of Judaism it regards as deviant, could withdraw its blessings from other branches of the faith.[39] This would unsettle relations between Israel and diaspora Jewry, and could have negative repercussions for the United States–Israel 'special relationship'. Thus, *haredim* radicalisation, if it were to occur, could have significant impli- cations for Israel's foreign relations, with friend and foe alike.

However, the further radicalisation of Israel, whether due to *haredim* or to religious Zionists, or to an alliance of all extremists, including the secular, would have ramifications not confined to Israel's foreign relations: domestically, such an eventuality could have tragic consequences for Israel, regardless of whether or not elements of the army were involved in acts of mutiny, as has been suggested by Margalit, Shahak and others. A vision of Israel divided internally along secular and religious lines, and between 'moderate' and 'extremist', is now one entertained and feared by many Israelis, including, before his assassination in November 1990, the ultra-extreme rabbi, Meir Kahane. Three times during his interview with Raphael Mergui and Philippe Simonnot, Kahane emphasised his fear of an Israeli civil war (see Mergui and Simonnot, 1987: 32, 34, 56).

Indeed, an act of civil war was committed on 10 February 1983, an act that was widely lamented in Israel as heralding the creation of an irreconcilable split in Israeli society: after a volatile pro- and anti-Lebanon war demonstration outside the Knesset, a grenade was thrown at a group of *Shalom Akhshav* (Peace Now) demonstrators by Israeli pro-war radicals. Emil Grunzweig, a 33-year-old Jew, was killed and ten others were wounded. Earlier the same day, harsh verbal clashes took place that not only reflected pro- and anti-war feelings, but also revealed deep ethnic and class divides, between the largely better-off Ashkenazim and the less-well-off Sephardim. Some of the insults hurled on that occasion would have seen a non-Jew in court almost anywhere in the world, on racial vilification or anti-Semitism charges: 'Ashkenazis . . . they should have left you in Auschwitz' (*Jewish Week*, 1983, quoted in Hirst, 1984: 442).

In the aftermath of those events, the then Israeli President, Yitzhak Navon, also publicly voiced the fear that the seeds of civil war had been sown (see Hirst, 1984: 443).[40] More than a decade later, these fears have received a new and more urgent emphasis with the November 1995 assassination of Prime Minister Rabin by a fellow Jew. One of the principal figures in charge of Israel's internal security at the time of the Rabin assassination, Shin Bet director Karmi Gillon, was appointed to his position in part because of his alleged awareness of the increasing threat posed by Jewish extremists: Gillon – who resigned after Rabin's murder – identified Kach and like-minded groups in a 1990 master's thesis in political science as 'a threat to Israeli democracy and as potentially able to provoke civil war' (Parks, 1995).

After Rabin's slaying, an Israeli documentary on religious Zionist figures made reference to speculation and discussion in Israeli society of the possibility of civil war (Levanon, 1995).[41] Sprinzak (1991: 312) has written: 'The specter of civil war haunts Israel . . . Given the deep ideological and political stakes involved, a civil war or major violent conflict cannot be ruled out.' According to Sprinzak (1991: 312), such a conflict would be most likely to occur if 'territorial compromise is imposed by a Labor-led government representing no more than 55 or 60 per cent of Israeli voters. Under such a scenario, Israel would be divided along major ideological lines, the right against the left with all the festering wounds of seventy years of Zionist history opened up.'

Sprinzak's remedy against civil violence is a national unity government – the formula widely called for by many prominent Israelis during and after the 1996 elections – the formula rejected by Prime Minister Netanyahu. However, whether such a government is formed or not, Sprinzak (1991: 312) goes on to write that 'both a civil war and a sophisticated armed revolt against the IDF are highly unlikely. . . . Instead, small-scale armed resistance and insurrectionary operations are probable.' Sprinzak (1996) reaffirmed this view that 'civil war is out of the question' – but his definition of civil war here is 'a major war in which 50 percent of the population is involved'. Clearly, there is emerging a consensus that relatively major destabilising civil violence is more than a remote possibility in a country that has hitherto been regarded as uniquely cohesive and a bastion of civilisation, democracy and the rule of law.

Another danger to Israel is the threat to its democracy posed by the undemocratic nature of religious Zionism. Meir Kahane spoke for many of Israel's religious nationalists when he said:

> Zionism and Western democracy are at odds. And according to Zionism, this country must be a Jewish state . . . you can't have Zionism and democracy at the same time . . . there's no question of setting up democracy in Israel, because democracy means equal rights for all, irrespective of racial or religious origins (Kahane, quoted in Mergui and Simonnot, 1987: 30–1).

The threat to Israel's political system is all the more dangerous because the state's democracy has always, in fact, been 'imperfect' (Sprinzak, 1991: 292). Even so, the peril is not so much an immediate one as one that is further down the track. Writing not of those who, like Kahane, reject Western-style democracy outright, but of those who profess allegiance to Israel's democracy, Sprinzak (1991: 295) states that 'the radical right's narrow interpretation of democracy is corroding Israel's political culture over time', and that the 'growth of the radical right and its popularity is a serious indication of the decline of Israeli democracy'. In this respect it is not insignificant that Kahane's funeral was 'attended by as many as 20,000 Israeli mourners' (Sprinzak, 1991: 250); and for those who might be tempted to think that Kahane's attitudes and influence died with him, Sprinzak (1991: 250) has the following to say: 'A short time after his assassination it was already clear that Kahane was much more successful in instilling

"Kahanism" in Israeli political culture, than in securing the future of Kach.'

Doron (1996: 9) likewise expresses concern over the nature of 'Jewish democracy': over the fact there is no formal distinction between the state, politics and religion; that the 'support of the pivotal religious voters is dear to any ruling government', leading politicians to 'muddle through from one crisis to another [rather] than establish religiously neutral ground for their polity'; and that it is for these reasons that 'Israel still does not have a constitution'. It is possible that the 'corrosion' of Israel's political culture outlined by Sprinzak – or, perhaps, its slow 'Lebanisation' – is only reinforced by 'the prevailing blindness . . . inherent in the perception of those Israelis who prefer to postpone as long as possible the need to resolve the contradiction between the religious and the political source of sovereignty' (Doron, 1996: 9). More tangibly, Doron suggests, both Labor and Likud must share blame for a loss of control over 'fringe groups' that has permitted them to 'redirect their aggression inward, toward the system itself' (Doron, 1996: 9).

Views such as those inspired by Kahane, together with the polarising of society – acknowledged publicly by such prominent figures as Netanyahu, Shamir, Moyal, Doron, Horovitz and many others – and the breaking down of domestic cohesion could spell the end of the original Zionist vision, and the end of Israel as it has existed since its creation in 1948. The spectre of now-materialised events such as the Temple Mount and Hebron massacres and the assassination of Rabin led Harkabi, in 1988, to write: 'The explicit assertion that a certain period is the beginning of the Redemption arouses a hope that can only be destructive. Paradoxically, no idea poses a greater menace to the survival of the State of Israel', and, 'An obsession with Messianism is liable to end in a national collapse' (Harkabi, 1988: 170, 173). Harkabi could hardly have taken heart when, two years later, Aran wrote that [Jewish] religion was 'usurping' nationalism, and that 'the messianization of Israel has been progressively gathering momentum' (Aran, 1990: 161, 165). This trend, if it continues, has the potential to precipitate social fragmentation, domestic volatility and political instability: all features characteristic of – to varying degrees – Lebanon and Syria.

Herein also lies a greater danger to Judaism as a whole. Aran dissects and isolates a threat posed to Judaism in the 'paradox rationality' of Gush. It concerns Gush's attribution of a mystical nature – of an 'inner' and 'outer essence' – to a 'holy trinity' of Torah, The Land and The Nation. The Land and The Nation, although appearing secular, are, according to Gush philosophy, essentially religious entities (Aran,

1990: 171). Here, again, is the principal Gush point of departure from the *haredim*, who perceive nothing particularly religious or mystical about the secular and profane nature of contemporary Israel and Jewry. Aran (1990: 171) writes, precisely, that this Gush rationality: 'contains a grave contradiction, which is injected into the traditional religion and threatens to explode it from within: from the moment the profane, which had threatened religion from the outside, is declared the realization of the sacred, the theology becomes exposed to an inner tension that it may not be able to contain'.

The threat to Judaism and to the diaspora is also bound to extreme interpretations of 'promised land' and 'chosen people'. The former, writes Liebman, 'provides the basis for territorial ultra-nationalism and [the latter] for ethnic ultra-nationalism' (Liebman, 1990: 83), and both provide 'a foundation for the grossest form of chauvinism' (Liebman, 1990: 93). However, Liebman also believes the extreme views associated with *segulah* and holy land are a result of 'misinterpretations' and 'misunderstandings' on the part of the disciples of the two Kuks (Liebman, 1990: 92–4).

Harkabi, on the other hand, admitted that an extreme, Kahane-like interpretation of Judaism is valid, albeit only one among many legitimate interpretations. He wrote that, 'The struggle is for the soul of the Jewish religion, our inner life and our image in the outside world. Furthermore, the fight is for our survival as a sovereign state, and perhaps even as a people' (Harkabi, 1988: 199). He believed it to be the rabbis' job to counter the religious extremists, who base their case on Bible, Talmud and great Jewish sages, and that, unless tackled from within Judaism, the extremists will undermine the religiosity and standing of Jews and the Jewish faith everywhere (Harkabi, 1988: 191–6).

It appears that Harkabi's hope was not in vain, for even some prominent Gush rabbis – concerned about the implications rampant extremism has for Judaism – have raised their voices to urge moderation (Rubinstein, 1984: 118). Similarly, Professor Falk believes that the 'phenomenon' represented by Kach 'has to be confronted' by Judaism in order to bring a 'return to balance' and 'adjustment to modernity' (Falk, 1994, unpublished).

Conclusion

When the former Israeli Deputy Foreign Minister, Dr Yossi Beilin, stated that, 'Islamic extremism is the enemy of all of us' (Beilin, 1993: SBS-TV), the informed listener could be forgiven for thinking that

Dr Beilin had forgotten something; that a complete picture was more complicated than such a generalisation. But, of course, Beilin was not addressing informed listeners: he was speaking to politicians, journalists and other establishment figures in Canberra during his 1993 Australian visit. It would have been among Beilin's charges to further 'Israel's campaign of the past several years to sell the idea that Islamic fundamentalism is the common enemy' (Neff, 1994: 10). This was exactly the situation emphasised in no uncertain terms just over a year later on Australian television by Beilin's immediate superior, Shimon Peres – then Foreign Minister – who promoted Israel's value as an island of civilisation and democracy amidst a chaotic sea of seething Muslim fundamentalism in the Arab world and Iran (Peres, 1994: NWS-9 TV). The Prime Minister, the late Yitzhak Rabin, also played his part: on 23 April 1994 he declared his intention to seek, with Boris Yeltsin, mutually beneficial policies to counter Muslim fundamentalism – 'the common enemy of Israel and Russia alike' (Rabin, quoted in Baram, 1994: 5). It would also be in Israel's interests to play down its own religious fundamentalism and potential for internal instability.

With the dramatically altered global geopolitical situation since the demise of the Soviet Union and the 1991 Gulf War, Israel has found itself in the position of needing to re-justify the approximately US$3 billion in aid it receives every year from the United States;[42] valuable diplomatic support from various other nations may also be promoted by playing on fears of sprawling Muslim neighbours. Thus, it is understandable why Israeli diplomats occasionally neglect to mention crucial aspects of Arab–Israeli–Muslim politics. Beilin was, however, more specific in his book, where, for example, he discussed the unique challenge presented to Israeli 'governing institutions' by a Gush terrorist underground, and how 'phenomena' such as Gush rendered Israeli society 'more fragile' (Beilin, 1992: 169–71).

While the threat of terrorist strikes against civilians within the 1967 Green Line is a harrowing reality, it is also little wonder that, considering the above, Israel tends to amplify the risk posed to its security by relatively weak organisations such as Hamas, and is prone 'to demonise the grand Islamic plot, orchestrated by Iran and spearheaded by Hamas' (Baram, 1994: 5). In fact, Israeli actions apparently aimed at weakening Hamas, such as the December 1992 mass deportations, have only served to radicalise Hamas' (replacement) leadership (see *Middle East International*, 29 April 1994, editorial; Abu-Amr, 1993: 14). There is also no doubt that the broader, politically conservative Palestinian Islamic movement was fostered by Israel's occupation authorities – at least until the outbreak of the *intifada* in December 1987 – in order to counter the PLO and fragment the Palestinian national movement (see, for example, Abu-Amr, 1993: 7–8; Usher, 1993). And despite genuine fear and outrage over acts of terrorism such as the suicide bombings of February and March 1996, which claimed sixty-three Israeli lives, the way Israel is making use of Hamas and other similar groups in international diplomatic campaigns bears resemblance to past efforts to radicalise the PLO deliberately (see Chomsky, 1989: 174).

In many ways, Hamas and Gush are strikingly similar: politically, both have displayed a predilection for compromising with their secular brethren in the pursuit of their goals and, universalist Islam as opposed to Jewish exclusivism aside, even many of their goals, and methods, are similar.[43] Both act more as an umbrella for a number of factions than as a single, coherent organisation, and the more temperate wings of both have shown signs of moderating their respective stances in the interests of longer-term political pragmatism.[44] On the other hand, the extremist wings of both appear to be entrenching themselves in hard-line positions; in the case of Gush, the 1996 Netanyahu electoral victory has spurred the movement into a renewed, triumphal drive to realise apocalyptic goals. By the same token, the 1996 election result has averted for the time being a major confrontation with the State over issues of Jewish religious nationalism. Just on the single, per-ennially thorny question of settlements, '[e]ven moderate critics of the settlers maintain that they have created a huge time bomb for Israel, whose safe defusing is becoming harder each day the occupation con-tinues' (Sprinzak, 1991: 15). Far from attempting any 'defusing' of this 'time bomb', the resources of the Israeli State under a Netanyahu government are likely to be utilised overtly, once again, in fostering nationalist–religious projects that will enjoy the general support of the Gush and other extremists.

There may indeed have been a 'dovish trend' in Israel, but the indications are that this trend was frozen at the 1996 elections at between 40 and 50 per cent of the population. Evidence suggests the other 50 to 60 per cent of the Israeli population is reacting negatively in response to the insecurities imposed by what has been perceived as a peace process that has been moving too rapidly. Within this 50 to 60 per cent of the Israeli population is an extremist but significant minority – between 20 and 25 per cent of the population – that, from inside Israeli society, may be capable of inflicting far more damage on the Jewish state than any foreseeable external threat.

While there is no doubt that the indiscriminate targeting of civilians in Israel on the part of the radical wing of Hamas presents security problems – and significantly contributed to the steeling of Israeli atti-tudes and the 1996 Netanyahu victory – such attacks do not represent a threat to the state of Israel in any ultimate sense. An end to the peace process as it has been conducted to date – likely under an Israeli nationalist–religious government – re-opens the way to regional instability and will provide breathing space for extremist elements to flourish within Israeli society. The consequences of these developments will have been generated from within the society; perhaps the most probable consequence, considering the widely-acknowledged polarised nature of contemporary Israeli society, is a further breaking-down of national cohesion and civil conflict.

Alternative Israeli destinies have presented themselves, and a resolution of the two is required if Israel is to prosper or even to survive as a coherent, sovereign nation-state. The 1996 Likud electoral victory represents the effective postponement of a coming to grips with the inherent contradictions of Israeli socio-politics; the longer the inevitable confrontation and effective resolution of these contractions are delayed, the more disturbing the confrontation will be when it does occur.

Notes

1. The author would like to thank the Politics Department of Flinders University, South Australia, for granting him the use of its facilities from July to September 1994 for the preparation of this chapter.
2. This deed, committed on a Friday in Ramadan, appears to have been calculated to display maximum contempt for the victims and their faith.
3. Jonathon J. Pollard, an American Jew and a civilian US Navy intelligence analyst with a top-secret security clearance, was arrested in November 1985 for spying for Israel.
4. Lustick is a professor of political science specialising in the Middle East; he is a Jewish American with a lifelong involvement, 'as a participant, leader, and resource person, in Jewish and Zionist organizations' (Lustick, 1980: xi).
5. The late Yehoshafat Harkabi was a professor of political science who taught in Israel. He was chief of Israeli military intelligence from 1955 to 1959.
6. There is a strong critique of Zionism among world Jewry that is not limited to any particular branch of the faith. Much Jewish

criticism of Zionism is based on what is perceived as having become Jewish spiritual tradition. Michael Selzer (1970: xi–xxii), for example, gives a concise explanation of this critique.

7. These wars have been linked to the biblical imagery of Gog and Magog of Ezekiel 38–39, imagery that bears a strong resemblance to the far older, epic mythology of ancient Canaan and Babylonia. Lustick (1987: 128–9) outlines the apocalyptic visions of Menachem Kasher, views rich with Messiahs, redemption and cosmic battles. Kasher's interpretation is noted for linking the Nazi persecution to modern Jewish apocalyptic thought.

8. See note 7 above. Rabbi Kuk the elder believed that the Balfour Declaration of 1917 heralded a new era for the Jews; it should be remembered, though, that he died in 1935.

9. 'Zionist Revival Movement' or 'Renaissance'. An ultra-nationalist political party formed in 1979, now dormant, whose policies included Israeli sovereignty over the occupied territories, extensive settlement programmes, and the uniting of the religious and non-religious segments of Israeli society.

10. The NRP, or Mafdal (Hebrew acronym), was formed in 1956, and advocates strict, formalised observance of the Jewish religion and tradition in Israeli life, based on Torah and *halachah*. The party is firmly linked with Gush Emunim.

11. Although Jewish religious fundamentalists may also include demographic and strategic, in addition to religious, reasons for 'transfer', radical secular Zionists promote the former arguments almost exclusively, but equally vehemently. For example, former Israeli army chief of staff and Tzomet leader, Raphael Eitan, is on record as dividing Palestinians into 'good' and 'bad', and has said of them: 'the bad ones should be killed, the good deported' (Eitan, quoted in Kidron, 1992a: 4). Eitan, appointed Agriculture Minister in the 1996 Netanyahu cabinet, has not moderated his stance; his views on the conduct of the peace process are reflected in comments made to Israeli journalists when, in July 1996 it was revealed that the new Likud bloc Foreign Minister, David Levy, had met with Palestinian National Authority President, Yasser Arafat. He is reported to have said that 'Arafat does not merit a meeting at a level higher than border guard' (*Friday Journal*, 1996c). Tzomet now forms part of the core of the new Israeli government after entering into an alliance with Likud in February 1996.

12. 'Fundamentalism' is a term best used sparingly at any time, but a consistent definition logically should not exclude those who are not particularly religious. Despite the argument in favour of

applying the term to secular extremists, this piece nevertheless focuses on the religious, particularly the Gush. Nevertheless, the role of secularists in the ongoing 'ascendance' (to borrow Sprinzak's description of the fortunes of the 'radical right' in Israel) of religiously-oriented extremism in Israel cannot, and should not, be played down.

13. Mapai (Israel Workers' Party) was the principal organised expression of socialist Zionism until its merger with other parties in 1968 to form the Israel Labor Party.

14. As a result of these attitudes and plans, property prices in West Bank Jewish settlements are reported to have increased by up to 50 per cent since Netanyahu's election victory (*Yediot Aharonot*, reported in *Friday Journal*, 1996a).

15. Shas ('Sephardic Torah Guardians'), is a Sephardi ultra-Orthodox breakaway party from Agudat Israel, formed in 1984; it won six seats in 1992. The Orthodox Torah Bloc is, as its name suggests, an Orthodox religious party (four seats in 1992). The NRP took six seats in 1992. The total number of Knesset seats occupied by religious parties at the beginning of the Likud era in 1977 numbered sixteen; thus, in one respect, they maintained a certain status quo in 1992, which allowed them to achieve their 1996 gains to a level of representation well above their eighteen seats of the 1988 elections.

16. Moledet ('Homeland') is a nationalist party formed in 1988; its major goal is the expulsion of Palestinians living in the West Bank and Gaza. Moledet won three seats (up from two) in 1992. Tzomet was originally formed in 1984; soon thereafter the party merged with Tehiya, only to split from that alliance in 1987. Tzomet's eight 1992 seats represented a dramatic gain over its two seats in the previous Knesset.

17. Shas, after winning ten seats in the 1996 elections, is now the third largest party in the fourteenth Knesset, behind Labor (34 seats) and the Likud bloc (32 seats). The NRP is equal fourth with Meretz with nine seats. United Torah Judaism – a new party created early in 1996 as a result of an alliance between Agudat Israel and Degel HaTorah – won four seats.

18. Gesher – a party founded and led by David Levy after his split from Likud in 1995 – formally joined the month-old Likud–Tzomet alliance on 2 March 1996.

19. This trend has been initially underlined, and ironically so, not by Tzomet's influence but by pressure from Gesher's David Levy – widely regarded as a moderate of the right – to have the internationally acknowledged nationalist ideologue, Ariel Sharon,

included in the Netanyahu cabinet. Sharon's reputation as a 'hardliner' is such that his appointment to the cabinet had the potential to disturb relations between the Clinton and Netanyahu administrations (Freedland, 1996). Sharon was made minister of a new portfolio especially created for him, that of national infrastructure, 'expected to be the third largest after defence and education, with an estimated \$2 billion budget' (Freedland, 1996).

20. An alternative interpretation to what may appear to be the consolidation of the nationalist–religious right is that Likud, rather than becoming an 'umbrella' party for this bloc, has actually been weakened through its Tzomet–Gesher alliance, and that the 1996 gains of the religious parties were made at the expense of Likud as voters were liberated from the major parties by the new electoral system, which, for the first time, allowed direct voting for a prime ministerial candidate. Under the new system, the successful prime minister-elect has the opportunity to form the new government even though his party may have won fewer Knesset seats than a rival party. However, even though Likud's power as a single party may have waned somewhat, it is, in fact, acting as an umbrella for the nationalist–religious right, and the 1996 election results did represent a triumph for this bloc.

21. Moledet supporters include former followers of Meir Kahane's Kach party, permanently disqualified from the Israeli electoral process before the 1988 elections because of its racist ideology. Baruch Goldstein was a follower of Kahane and a supporter of Kach. A counsellor at the Israeli embassy in Canberra, Opher Aviran (1996), has described Moledet as a 'fascist party'. Sprinzak (1991: 9–13, 293) argues that 'fascist' is not a term that can be applied to Israel's radical right; the closest group to fascism, in his reckoning, is Kach – a 'quasi-fascist movement' (Sprinzak, 1991: 233–4).

22. Voter turnout for the 1996 elections was 79.3 per cent; invalid votes for the Knesset amounted to approximately 2.17 per cent out of a total of 3,119,195 votes cast (see Israel Foreign Ministry Information Division, 1996a).

23. Formed in June 1994 and a member of the 1996 Likud coalition government, HaDerech HaShlishit ('The Third Way') is opposed to the establishment of an independent Palestinian state. The party's platform also includes policies such as: 'Israel is entitled to retain territories captured in a war of defense'; 'Settlements will not be removed'; and 'The development of settlements and an intensive effort to populate the entire eastern "backbone" of Israel (from the Golan Heights to Eilat)'. Reference is also made in the

party's platform to 'the land of Israel', a term favoured by religious Zionists and denoting biblical *Eretz Yisrael* (see Israel Foreign Ministry Information Division, 1996b).

24. History has demonstrated in the government of national unity of the late 1980s that Labor has more in common with Likud, and indeed with other religious and nationalist parties, than with the non-Jewish left.

25. During 1995, however, the Rabin government was forced to rely on support from the five MKs of Hadash and the Arab Democratic Party. Support was also received from two MKs who had split from Tzomet. A Rabin minority government was precipitated by the departure of Shas from the Labor coalition. Gideon Doron (1996: 9) outlines the crisis of Jewish legitimacy that Rabin faced – and, indeed, that any Israeli government would face – through reliance on Arab MKs.

26. Gush's role in the radicalisation of Israeli society was summed up in novel expression by the Israeli newspaper columnist, Doron Rosenblum, when he wrote that Gush has frequently managed to metamorphose 'the criminal to the crazy, the crazy to the odd, the odd to the mistaken, the mistaken to the good, the good to the excellent, the excellent to the accomplished reality, and the accomplished reality to the consensus view' (Rosenblum, 1985, quoted in Lustick, 1988: 180).

27. The authors claimed that 'probably less than half of Likud and Tzomet voters [half in 1992 = 408,796] were ideologically committed and prepared to pay a high price for a Greater Israel' (see Smooha and Peretz, 1993: 445–56; 462, note 27; 461–2). A reasonable assumption is that very close to 100 per cent of those who voted for the NRP, Moledet, Tehiya, and the small but radical religious Zionist parties of Geulat Israel and of Torah and Land might be committed to hardline religious-nationalism; adding their combined 240,448 votes to the 408,000-odd harder-line Likud and Tzomet voters reveals a total of approximately 648,000 Israelis – which does not include the Orthodox/*haredim* blóc – who would have been 'ideologically committed', and 'prepared to pay a high price', to see extreme nationalist policies carried out. This figure represents around 24.5 per cent of the 2,616,841 Israelis who voted in 1992. Sprinzak (1991: 16) estimates that 'extreme attitudes regarding the indivisibility of the Land of Israel, bitter hostility toward Arabs and special expressions implying never-ending war against the PLO, and a constant siege mentality along with enthusiastic utterances about religious redemption . . . are shared by about 20 to 25 percent of the Jewish citizens of

Israel'. Hader (1992: 610, note 34) also pointed to a 1990 poll that depicted Israeli society divided roughly into three camps: 30 per cent of Israeli Jews considered themselves 'doves', 30 per cent were 'security hawks' and 40 per cent were 'ideological hawks'.

28. Doron is a professor of political science at Tel Aviv University, and was a political strategist for Rabin's 1992 election campaign. For examples of the kind of popular feeling of opposition to the policies of the former Labor government and its leaders to which Doron is referring, see Dan and Eisenberg (1996), and Stock (1996).

29. Invalid votes in the election for prime minister, 'mostly blank slips', stood at around 4.76 per cent – more than double the proportion of invalid votes cast for the Knesset. Voter participation in the prime ministerial election was slightly higher than in that for the Knesset (see Israel Foreign Ministry Information Division, 1996a).

30. The point that both Moyal and Shamir were making was that such 'divisions' and 'rifts' might be 'healed' somewhat through a Likud–Labor government of national unity.

31. A more conservative result, according to this simulation, would have been 'a new phase in the Middle-East conflict, a crisis broader, deeper, and longer-lasting than anything in the past' (Sprinzak, 1991: 3).

32. There is now no doubt that Israel possesses a small nuclear arsenal, and the means and the will to use it (see Hersh, 1991; Aronson, 1992; Black and Morris, 1992: 437–42). Black and Morris (1992: 442–3) leave unresolved the suggestion that Israel may also possess chemical and biological weapons.

33. The Gaza Strip contains around 5,000 settlers, and the Golan Heights at least 15,000. East Jerusalem, which, along with surrounding environs, was unofficially annexed by Israel immediately after its capture in the June War on 28 June 1967, is now home to around 120,000 Jewish Israelis.

34. Rabbi Haim Druckman was filmed on video issuing such an edict (footage shown on 'Dateline', 1995).

35. Sprinzak puts into perspective the thinking of the secular and religious 'radical right' with regard to Israel's military prowess (see, for example, Sprinzak, 1991: 19).

36. Gideon Doron's comments should also be borne in mind: that Rabin and his policies did not elicit opposition only from the nationalist–religious extremist fringe.

37. The fact there is a gap to be bridged underlines the still-factionalised nature of the nationalist–religious bloc that has

formed the government of the fourteenth Knesset. Not only are there differences between the secular parties (Likud–Tzomet–Gesher, HaDerech HaShlishit and Yisrael Ba'aliya) and the religious parties (Shas, NRP and United Torah Judaism), but there are also major differences between the three religious parties, especially between the NRP on the one hand, and Shas and United Torah Judaism on the other. Even within United Torah Judaism there is tension between the Agudat Israel and Degel HaTorah factions.

38. For example, in July 1996 ultra-Orthodox Israelis clashed violently with police over the issue of Sabbath closures of Jerusalem's Bar Ilan Road.

39. Concern over this aspect of Jewish relations – as well as over the polarisation not only of Israeli society, but of world Jewry – was expressed soon after the 1996 elections by Sydney's Rabbi Brian Fox: 'The [election] results will cause a major split between Israel and the Diaspora. There will be a Likud Israel and Labor Diaspora. Israel will move to the right religiously and of concern is that the rights, access and sense of security of Progressive and secular Jews will be largely ignored' (Fox, quoted in Labi, 1996). Jewish community leaders in the United States are also 'wary' of 'Orthodox moves to disenfranchise Reform and Conservative Jews living in Israel' (Goodstein, 1996). (See also Kleinfield, 1996.)

40. Israeli ethnic and class divisions owe much to the young state's early immigration policies, which failed adequately to accommodate Sephardim: a fact, according to Labor's former Deputy Foreign Minister, Yossi Beilin (1992: 39), that has 'left a mark on Israeli society that survives to this day' (see also, for example, Beilin, 1992: 97–8, 149–50, 182; Beyer, 1992; Smooha and Peretz, 1993: 452–4).

41. Shortly before Rabin's assassination, former Tehiya MK, Geula Cohen (1995) publicly announced that 'the civil war has begun; this is the moment before the first fatality . . . it does not matter who is the first victim, a soldier or a settler'. The electronic Middle Eastern commentary service that distributed this extract from the Israeli daily *Ma'ariv* ridiculed the notion of a potential Israeli civil war.

42. Chomsky (1983: 10) has suggested the real figure of United States aid to Israel *c.* 1978–83 could have been up to '60 per cent higher than the publicly available figure'. The *Washington Report on Middle East Affairs* (1993: 114) published a table listing 1993 United States grants, interest, loan guarantees and compound interest on

previous grants given to, or paid on behalf of, Israel, totalling US$11.321 billion. Smooha and Peretz cite Israel's 'heavy dependence' on US (and other Western nations') economic, military and political aid as one reason for a pragmatic trend in Israeli domestic politics that resulted in Likud's 1992 election defeat (Smooha and Peretz, 1993: 460–1). Hader (1992) agrees. Although Netanyahu is reported to be concerned about Israel's dependence on the United States, his July 1996 meeting with President Clinton and other US establishment figures appears only to have reaffirmed US support for Israel at contemporary levels (see, for example: Israel Line, 1996; Kutler, 1996; Lippman, 1996).

43. Shahak (1995) directly compares 'Israel's extreme right' with Hamas, and concludes that there is no difference between the crimes and acts of indiscriminate terrorism of either (in relation to this debate, see also Milton-Edwards, 1995).

44. With respect to moderating influences within Hamas see, for example, Usher (1994) and Suleiman-Amayreh (1994).

References

Abu-Amr, Ziad (1993). 'Hamas: a historical and political background'. *Journal of Palestine Studies*, 22 (4): 5–19.

AgmoNet (1996). 'Settlement Expansion in the Works'. *AgmoNet* electronic journal, Tel Aviv (http://www.agmonet.co.il/), 15 July.

Aran, Gideon (1990). 'Redemption as a Catastrophe: The Gospel of Gush Emunim'. In E. Sivan and M. Friedman (eds), *Religious Radicalism and Politics in the Middle East*. Albany and Jerusalem: State University of New York in association with the Harry S. Truman Research Institute for the Advancement of Peace, the Hebrew University.

Aronson, Geoffrey (1992). 'Hidden agenda: US–Israeli relations and the nuclear question'. *Middle East Journal*, 46 (4): 617–30.

Australian Jewish News (1996). 'Netanyahu begins coalition talks' (7 June).

Avineri, Shlomo (1982). 'The People and its Land'. *Artzi* (Jerusalem). Quoted in Harkabi, Y. (1988). *Israel's Fateful Decisions*, trans. L. Schramm, p. 165. London: I. B. Tauris.

Aviran, Opher (1996). *Israel: Post-Election Peace. Is it Still Possible?* Public address presented at the National Jewish Centre, Canberra, 15 June.

Baram, Haim (1994). 'What to do about Hamas'. *Middle East International*, 474: 5–6.

Beilin, Yossi (1992). *Israel: A Concise Political History*. London: Weidenfeld & Nicolson.

—— (1993). Reported on 'World News'. SBS Television, 27 April.

Beyer, Lisa (1992). 'The same tribe?' *Time*, 20 April: 65.

Black, Ian and Morris, Benny (1992). *Israel's Secret Wars: A History of Israel's Intelligence Services*. London: Futura.

Brown, Derek (1996). 'Right wing puts pressure on Netanyahu'. *Guardian Weekly*, 21 July.

Chomsky, Noam (1983). *The Fateful Triangle: The United States, Israel and The Palestinians*. Boston: South End Press.

—— (1989). *Necessary Illusions: Thought Control in Democratic Societies*. London: Pluto Press.

Cohen, Geula (1995). Extract from the Israeli daily *Ma'ariv*. '"Civil war" in Israel?' Distributed electronically by *Mid-East Realities* ('Lie of the Week' commentary series), 29 August.

Dan, Uri and Eisenberg, Dennis (1996). 'Spoken like a proud Jew!' *Jerusalem Post* (Internet Edition, 18 July: http://www.jpost.co.il/).

'Dateline' (1995). Video footage of Rabbi Haim Druckman issuing edict to IDF soldiers to disobey orders. SBS Television, 11 November.

Doron, Gideon (1996). 'Israel and the Rabin Assassination'. *Current History*, 95 (597), (January): 6–9.

Ehrlich, Dov (1993). *Adey Ad* (Heb. *Forever and Ever*). Quoted in Shahak, I. (1994c). 'Is Israel heading for civil war?'. *Middle East International*, 477: 18.

Erlanger, Steven (1996). 'Netanyahu airs differences with Clinton on peace issues'. *New York Times*, 10 July.

Falk, Zev (1994). 'The Problems of Jewish Orthodoxy in the Modern World'. Seminar paper presented at the University of Sydney, 28 February.

Freedland, Jonathon (1996). 'Sharon casts cloud over Netanyahu'. *Guardian Weekly*, 14 July.

Friday Journal (1996a). Reporting from the Israeli daily *Yediot Aharonot* on property prices in Jewish settlements. Distributed by IAP's *AlAkhbar* 'Muslim World Daily News Briefs', 12 July.

—— (1996b). Reporting from the Israeli daily *Ha'aretz* on the renewed Jewish settlement drive. Distributed electronically in the IAP's *AlAkhbar* 'Muslim World Daily News Briefs', 15 July.

—— (1996c). Report from Beit Hanoun, Israel, on Netanyahu ministers protesting at Foreign Minister Levy's meeting with Arafat. Distributed electronically in the IAP's *AlAkhbar* 'Muslim World Daily News Briefs', 24 July.

Friedman, Menachem (1990). 'Jewish Zealots: Conservative versus Innovative'. In E. Sivan and M. Friedman (eds), *Religious Radicalism and Politics in the Middle East*. Albany and Jerusalem: State University of New York in association with the Harry S. Truman Research Institute for the Advancement of Peace, The Hebrew University.

Goodstein, Laurie (1996). 'Netanyahu wows his closest friends'. *Guardian Weekly* (*Washington Post* section), 21 July.

Hader, Leon T. (1992). 'The 1992 electoral earthquake and the fall of the "Second Israeli Republic"'. *Middle East Journal*, 46 (4): 594–616.

Harkabi, Yehoshafat (1988). *Israel's Fateful Decisions*, trans. L. Schramm. London: I. B. Tauris.

Hersh, Seymour M. (1991). *The Samson Option: Israel, America and the Bomb*. London: Faber & Faber.

Hirst, David (1984). *The Gun and the Olive Branch: The Roots of Violence in the Middle East*. London: Faber & Faber.

Horovitz, David (1995). Interview on 'Dateline'. SBS Television, 11 November.

—— (1996). Interview on 'International Report'. Radio Australia, 30 May.

Islamic Association for Palestine (1996). 'New settlement expansion in O.T.' *AlAkhbar* electronic news service, 15 July.

Israel Foreign Ministry Information Division (1996a). 'The Israeli elections: Final results'. IFMID election information provided electronically (http://www.israel-mfa.gov.il & gopher://israel-info.gov.il).

—— (1996b). 'The Third Way – Platform April 1996'. IFMID election information provided electronically (http://www.israel-mfa.gov.il & gopher://israel-info.gov.il).

Israel Line (1996). 'Israel will move towards economic independence in coming years'; 'Netanyahu addresses joint session of Congress'. Electronic information service of the Consulate of Israel, New York, 10 July.

Jewish Week (18 February 1983). Quoted in Hirst, D. (1984). *The Gun and the Olive Branch: The Roots of Violence in the Middle East*, p. 442. London: Faber & Faber.

Kidron, Peretz (1992a). 'Rabin's balancing act threatens his commitment to peace'. *Middle East International*, 429: 3–4.

—— (1992b). 'Partial settlement freeze'. *Middle East International*, 431: 5–7.

Kison, Ephraim (1976). *Jerusalem Post*, 25 April. Quoted in Hirst, D. (1984). *The Gun and the Olive Branch: The Roots of Violence in the Middle East*, pp. 455–6. London: Faber & Faber.

Kleinfield, N. R. (1996). 'Curiosity and doubt await premier on trip to New York'. *New York Times*, 11 July.

Kuk, Tzvi Yehudah (1967a). 'Israeli Independence Day Sermon'. From 'The Sanctity of the Holy People in the Holy Land'. In Y. Tirosh (ed.), *Religious Zionism: An Anthology*, p. 144. Jerusalem: World Zionist Organization, 1978. Quoted in Liebman, C. S. (1990). 'The Jewish Religion and Contemporary Israeli Nationalism'. In E. Sivan and M. Friedman (eds), *Religious Radicalism and Politics in the Middle East*, pp. 82–3. Albany and Jerusalem: State University of New York in association with the Harry S. Truman Research Institute for the Advancement of Peace, The Hebrew University.

—— (1967b). 'Israeli Independence Day Sermon'. In 'This is the state of which the prophets dreamed'. *Nekuda*, 86 (26 April 1985): 6–7. Quoted in Lustick, I. (1988). *For the Land and the Lord: Jewish Fundamentalism in Israel*, p. 36. New York: Council on Foreign Relations.

Kutler, Hillel (1996). 'Striking a chord with Congress'. *Jerusalem Post*, 14 July (Internet Edition, 18 July: http://www.jpost.co.il/).

Labi, Sharon (1996). 'Liberal Judaism "the real victim of Israel's elections"'. *Australian Jewish News* (Sydney edn), 14 June.

Levanon, Yeud (1995). *119 Bullets + Three*. Home Productions Ltd. On 'The Cutting Edge'. SBS Television, 4 June 1996.

Levinger, Moshe (1988). From *US News and World Report*, 4 April. Quoted in Palumbo, M. (1992). *Imperial Israel: The History of the Occupation of the West Bank and Gaza*, p. 170. London: Bloomsbury.

Liebman, Charles S. (1990). 'The Jewish Religion and Contemporary Israeli Nationalism'. In E. Sivan and M. Friedman (eds), *Religious Radicalism and Politics in the Middle East*. Albany and Jerusalem: State University of New York in association with the Harry S. Truman Research Institute for the Advancement of Peace, The Hebrew University.

Lippman, Thomas W. (1996). 'Netanyahu affirms his hard-line image: Clinton assures support despite differences'. *Washington Post*, 10 July.

Lipski, Sam (1996). 'Gutnick's "sweetest victory of them all"'. *Australian Jewish News*, 14 June.

Lustick, Ian S. (1980). *Arabs in the Jewish State: Israel's Control of a National Minority*. Austin: University of Texas Press.

—— (1987). 'Israel's Dangerous Fundamentalists'. *Foreign Policy*, 68: 118–39.

—— (1988). *For the Land and the Lord: Jewish Fundamentalism in Israel*. New York: Council on Foreign Relations.

Margalit, Dan (1994). 'Cancer in the heart of Hebron'. *Ha'aretz*, 1 April. In *Middle East International*, 473: 21–2.

Masalha, Nur (1992). *Expulsion of the Palestinians: The Concept of Transfer in Zionist Political Thought, 1882–1948*. Washington, DC: Institute for Palestine Studies.

Mergui, Raphael and Simonnot, Philippe (1987). *Israel's Ayatollahs: Meir Kahane and the Far Right in Israel*. London: Saqi Books.

Middle East International (1994). Editorial. 'Hamas raises the stakes'. 474 (29 April): 2.

Milton-Edwards, Beverly (1995). 'The factors behind Hamas' suicide bombings'. *Middle East International*, 507: 18–19.

Moyal, Shmuel (1996). Interview on ABC-PNN Radio, 6 June.

Naveh, Danny (1996). Post-election statement on behalf of Binyamin Netanyahu. Reported in *Ha'aretz*: extracts distributed by Israel Line, electronic information service of the Consulate of Israel, New York, 31 May.

Neff, Donald (1994). '"Extremism" the new enemy'. *Middle East International*, 476: 10–11.

The New English Bible (1970). Oxford: Oxford University Press and Cambridge University Press.

O'Sullivan, Arieh (1996). 'Threats on Peres subdue Polling Day politicking'. *Jerusalem Post*, 30 May (Internet Edition, 1996 Election Feature: http://www.jpost.co.il/).

Palumbo, Michael (1992). *Imperial Israel: The History of the Occupation of the West Bank and Gaza*. London: Bloomsbury.

Parks, Michael (1995). 'Chief K fights Israel's new foes'. *Sydney Morning Herald* (syndicated from *Los Angeles Times*), 8 April.

Peled, Micha X. (1994). *A Season Inside God's Bunker*. On 'The Cutting Edge'. SBS Television, 3 May 1994.

Peres, Shimon (1994). Feature Interview. On 'Nightline'. NWS-9 Television, 25 August.

Pinkas, Alon and news agencies (1995). 'Excerpt about Hagai Amir and Dror Adani'. *JPOL Digest* 578, 18 November (Jerusalem Post Internet News Section: http://www.jpost.co.il/).

Rosenblum, Doron (1985). 'The Temple Mount will be blown up'. *Koteret Rashit*, 131: 20–1. Quoted in I. Lustick (1988). *For the Land and the Lord: Jewish Fundamentalism in Israel*, p. 180. New York: Council on Foreign Relations.

Rubinstein, Amnon (1982). 'Rabbis give the nod to Arab genocide'. *Ha'aretz*, 7 April. Translated by I. Shahak and reproduced in *Al-Fajr*, 21–27 May.

—— (1984). *The Zionist Dream Revisited: From Herzl to Gush Emunim and Back*. New York: Schocken Books.

Segal, Naomi (1995a). 'Police widen probe into whether assassin acted alone'. *Jewish Telegraphic Agency*, Jerusalem. Posted on *Jewish Bulletin of Northern California Online* (http://www.jewish.com:80/bk960223/pagehome.htm), 17 November.

—— (1995b). 'Yigal Amir indicted for murder of Rabin; brother, friend charged'. *Jewish Telegraphic Agency*, Jerusalem. Posted on *Jewish Bulletin of Northern California Online* (http://www.jewish.com:80/bk960223/pagehome.htm), 8 December.

Selzer, Michael (ed.) (1970). *Zionism Reconsidered: The Rejection of Jewish Normalcy*. London: Macmillan.

Shahak, Israel (1989). 'A history of the concept of "transfer" in Zionism'. *Journal of Palestine Studies*, 18 (3): 22–37.

—— (1994a). 'The ideology behind the Hebron massacre'. *Middle East International*, 471: 16–17.

—— (1994b). 'Baruch Goldstein and the Israeli army'. *Middle East International*, 474: 16–17.

—— (1994c). 'Is Israel heading for civil war?' *Middle East International*, 477: 17–19.

—— (1995). 'Is Israel's extreme right any worse than Hamas?' *Middle East International*, 509: 19–20.

Smooha, Sammy and Peretz, Don (1993). 'Israel's 1992 Knesset elections: Are they critical?'. *Middle East Journal*, 47 (3): 444–63.

Sprinzak, Ehud (1991). *The Ascendance of Israel's Radical Right*. New York: Oxford University Press.

—— (1996). 'The entire nation was shocked' (edited transcript of interview conducted by Claudia Burke). *Current History*, 95 (597), (January): 8.

Stock, Eric (1996). 'Why Likud won'. *Australian Jewish News* (Sydney edn), 7 June ('Why we won!' in Melbourne edn).

Suleiman-Amayreh, Khalid M. (1994). 'Hamas debates its next move'. *Middle East International*, 476: 17–18.

Usher, Graham (1993). 'The rise of political Islam in the occupied territories'. *Middle East International*, 453: 19–20.

—— (1994). 'Hamas seeks a place at the table'. *Middle East International*, 475: 17–19.

Waldenberg, Eliezer (1976). From *Ha'aretz*, 9 May. Quoted in Rubinstein, A. (1984). *The Zionist Dream Revisited: From Herzl to Gush Emunim and Back*, p. 117. New York: Schocken Books.

Waldman, Eliezar (1983). 'Struggle on the road to peace'. *Artzi* (Jerusalem). Quoted in Lustick, I. (1987). 'Israel's Dangerous Fundamentalists'. *Foreign Policy*, 68: 124.

Washington Report on Middle East Affairs (1993). 'Cost of US grants to Israel in Fiscal Year 1993'. July/August: 114.

Yariv, Zira (1994). 'Little Monsters'. *Yediot Aharonot*, 18 March. In *Middle East International*, 472: 22.

Index

Index

Index

Jerusalem, 273, 276, 284–95 *passim*, 313, 328n33
jihad, 78, 79, 81–2
Jordan, 60, 83, 135, 143, 268, 272

Kafi, 'Ali, 73
Kahane, Meir, 317, 318–9, 320
Kartal, Remzi, 231
Kazakhstan, 175, 177, 178, 180, 188–91, 199–200, 213
Kebir, Rabah, 81
Kennedy, John F., 261
khobzists, 65
Khomeini, Ayatollah, 210, 265
Kirghizstan, 176, 178, 180, 190–1, 192, 199–200
Kurdistan Front, 234, 251–2n23
Kurds,
Iraq, 33, 34, 38, 60, 205, 234, 238, 239
Turkey, 20, 21, 38, 225–57
Kuwait, 60, 201–5 *passim*, 220, 266, 281

Labor Party (Israeli), 269, 286, 306, 308, 309, 317–8, 319, 325n13, 325n17
Lebanon, 26–7, 60, 87–104, 266
civil war and, 21, 35, 36
Israel and, 263, 271, 280, 284, 289, 293, 298
Levinger, Rabbi Moshe, 302, 315
Likud Party, 268, 286, 305–10 *passim*, 314, 316, 319, 323

Madani, 'Abbas, 73
Madani, Husayn Ahmad, 48–9
Madrid Conference, 267
Maronite Christians, 89, 90, 91, 277
Meretz Party, 306, 325n17
millet system, 25, 33
Moledet Party, 305, 306, 307–8, 326n21
Morocco, 60, 68, 81, 83, 272
Mubarak, Hosni, 66, 68, 72, 73, 208, 270
Muslim Brotherhood (Muslim Brothers), 67–8, 74, 77, 81–2, 118, 271
see also fundamentalism (Islamic)

Nasser, Gamel, 62–3, 64, 77, 79, 109, 141
nationalism, 27, 105
Central Asia and, 175–6, 178 188–94
ethnic, 37–8, 266, 227, 230, 264
state formation and, 27, 105, 153–73 *passim*, 277, 279, 320
National Pact, Lebanese 89–91, 98
National Religious Party (NRP), 302, 307–8, 325n17

NATO (North Atlantic Treaty Organisation), 200, 210
Netanyahu, Binyamin, 306–7, 308, 311, 322, 325–6n19, 330n42
Newroz, 232, 237, 238, 239, 240, 241
New Wafd, 67, 75

Öcalan, Abdullah ('Apo'), 227, 228–9, 230, 231–2, 237–42 *passim*, 245
Oman, 205
Operation Accountability, 271–2, 274n2
Orthodox Torah Bloc, 307
Ottomans, 25, 32, 61, 88, 209, 225, 278
Özal, Turgut, 229–30, 236–7
ÖZDEP (Free Democracy Party), 243

Pakistan, 81, 186, 199–200, 220
Peace Now (Shalom Akhshav), 317
Peres, Shimon, 286, 308, 311, 315, 321
peshmerga, 238
Pir, Kemal, 227
PKK (Partiya Karkerên Kurdistan), 225–57 *passim*
ceasefire and, 240–2
civilian killings and, 227, 249n5
Gulf War and, 249n4
'total war' and, 242–6
PLO (Palestine Liberation Organisation), 32, 205, 275–6, 286–7
Israel and, 226, 259–96 *passim*, 321–2
Pollard, Jonathan, 263, 298, 323n3
praetorian state, 246–8
PSK (Partiya Sosyalist a Kurdistan), 226–7
PSKT (Partiya Sosyalist a Kurdistana Tirkiyê), *see* PSK

Qatar, 203, 205
Qur'an, 50, 106–8, 153, 161, 210

Rabin, Yitzhak, 259, 269, 273, 286, 298, 306, 310–21 *passim*
Rafsanjani, Hashemi, 200, 207, 217, 220, 266
rape, 32, 35
Reagan, Ronald, 260, 263
Romania, 262
Russia/CIS,
Central Asia and, 163, 183–4, 187, 188–91
Iran and, 209, 213
see also Soviet Union/USSR

Sadat, Anwar, 65–7, 77, 79, 80, 262, 284
safe havens, 36–7

Index